The Layman's Guide to the New Testament

The
Layman's Guide
to the
New Testament

WILLIAM M. RAMSAY

John Knox Press
ATLANTA

Library of Congress Cataloging in Publication Data

Ramsay, William M.
    The layman's guide to the New Testament.

    Bibliography: p.
    Includes index.
    1. Bible. N.T.—Introductions. I. Title.
BS2330.2.R38   225.6'1   79-87742
ISBN 0-8042-0322-9 (pbk.)

© copyright John Knox Press 1981
10 9 8 7 6 5 4 3 2
Printed in the United States of America
John Knox Press
Atlanta, Georgia 30365

To my sons,
Mack and John.

Foreword

I have written this book with two groups of readers particularly in mind.

1) My students are probably like those in most colleges and universities which offer courses with titles such as "Survey of New Testament Literature." They include an interesting mixture, with a few Jews, an occasional Buddhist or Muslim, and some who profess no religion of any kind. But most are Christians in their late teens, conservative theologically, often devout, but having little background in critical study of the Bible.

2) I have been privileged over the years to be associated with a large number of Sunday School teachers, church officers, members of adult classes, and other interested lay people. Capable, motivated, but with limited time for study and relatively untrained, they have loved the Bible but have recognized their need for readily available help for understanding what the Bible means.

I hope, too, that many ministers, Directors of Christian Education, and graduate students will find this volume a useful reference tool, a resource for teaching, and a readable review of each New Testament book in the light of current scholarship. But it is particularly for the first two groups that I have written.

With these people in mind I have had four goals.

1) This New Testament GUIDE is intended really to be an introduction. It does not assume a great deal of prior knowledge of New Testament criticism on the part of the reader. Technical terms which are useful are explained. A real effort has been made to write in understandable and readable language. Views of some scholars which may be upsetting to beginners have been introduced gently.

2) The approach is intended to be genuinely ecumenical. My own point of view seems to me to be generally in the middle of the mainstream of present-day biblical scholarship. But this volume is written with respect for the scholarship and integrity of those in the very conservative camp as well as those of the opposite extreme. At most points where I have taken a position on a controversial issue, I have at least footnoted to the work of scholars on the other side.

3) I hope I have allowed the challenge of the New Testament itself to come through. For nineteen centuries readers have found the New Testament to be fascinating literature. No volume which is lifeless and dull, therefore, can be a completely valid introduction. Too often I have read works on the New Testament which have somehow managed to conceal why it is that people have been ready to live and even die for the New Testament's truths. I have not preached in this GUIDE. I have tried to be "objective." But I hope that I have helped my readers to

stand imaginatively with the first-century readers of the New Testament and to hear with them its call to decision.

4) Finally, I have wanted to build on ideas which have been developed in New Testament scholarship since some of the older introductions were written.

Insofar as I have succeeded, part of the thanks must go to my wife, DeVere Maxwell Ramsay, for her suggestions and for help in many ways; to my brother, Professor Charles M. Ramsay, Ph.D., of the Department of Bible at Austin College, Sherman, Texas, who has made comments on the entire manuscript; and to my former colleague at King, Dr. Massey Mott Heltzel, for many helpful criticisms. Special thanks are due Mrs. Ann Peake and her staff in the King College library, to the extension department of the library at Union Theological Seminary in Virginia, and to Miss Anita Ryan, the King College student who efficiently typed the manuscript. A word of acknowledgement is due, too, to the *Presbyterian Outlook* and its former editor, Dr. Aubrey N. Brown, Jr. While there are probably not a dozen paragraphs in this volume that are actually copied from my weekly page in that journal, its readers may discover that I have sometimes made use of ideas first written for them.

William M. Ramsay
Bristol, Tennessee

Contents

I Some Principles of Biblical Interpretation

—Regardless of his or her religious views, any student of literature will agree that the Bible has been the most influential book in the history of the Western hemisphere.

—Any student of world religions will list the Bible among the great classics of religious literature.

—Traditionally, Christians have agreed in going much further, speaking of their holy book as the inspired word of God, the message on which they base their claim to salvation.

The problem which makes our present study necessary, however, is the difficulty of understanding what the Bible says. Christians in the United States are split into more than three hundred different denominations, in part because they cannot agree on what this book means. In religious wars Christians have slaughtered each other because of different interpretations of the Bible. More recently people have been known to begin reading the Bible, full of high expectations for finding inspiration and guidance, only to give up the study after a few pages because they found themselves confused, even bored.

Dogmatic partisans of particular religious or social ideologies, from the Ku Klux Klan to Hitler's Nazis to radicals of the Left, have twisted the Bible to support their own prejudices. In cynical despair others have joked that "you can prove anything by the Bible," and have given up trying to understand it.

Those who take the trouble really to study it, however, find the Bible no harder to understand than many other works of ancient literature. Even little children find many of its stories immediately intelligible. Analyses of vocabulary and sentence structure have shown many passages to be comprehensible when read by the average fourth-grade boy or girl. More difficult passages become clearer as they are analyzed and set in historical context.

This chapter, therefore, will present certain principles of interpretation which students of the Bible have found helpful as they have sought to understand the New Testament. It may be true that in a sense "you can prove anything by the Bible." But you cannot prove just anything if you follow the principles which will be proposed here.

First, however, we will look at some ways which have been used in the past with perhaps only limited success.

Some Alternative Approaches

Naive literalists have sometimes suggested that the Bible really needs no interpretation. Let the believer simply read in faith, ready to obey, and the Holy Spirit of God will himself make clear the meaning of the Scripture.

As will be noted at the end of this chapter, most Christians will agree that nothing is more important in receiving a divine message from Scripture than a heart open to receive such truth. It is quite another matter, however, to go from the recognition of the proper role of faith in religion to the assumption that study and interpretation of the Bible are not necessary.

"Believe, obey, and don't ask all those questions," the naive literalist proposes.

"But exactly what am I to believe and obey?" one may reply. As soon as that is asked, the question of interpretation is inevitably confronted.

Since the New Testament was originally written in Greek, and since any translation involves interpretation, one might argue that the naive literalist, to be perfectly consistent, ought only to quote it in the original language.

To the religious believer, the attitude of the heart *is* important to understanding. But men of equally good will have differed and do differ as to the meaning of the New Testament. It is not simply lack of "faith," but also failure to study carefully, using sound principles of interpretation, which is the cause of much misunderstanding.

Authoritarian interpreters of various kinds have undertaken to settle all controversies in an apparently simple way. Let the "expert" or the officially appointed interpreter explain the true meaning of the Scripture.

Clearly there is some wisdom in this approach. If there are recognized authorities in the interpretation of Shakespeare's plays or Robert Browning's poetry, there should be experts in interpreting biblical literature. One would be foolish to ignore the help which can come from scholars who have given their lives to its study.

This approach, however, also presents problems. For one thing, the authorities do not all agree, and the student must then pick which authority to believe. Leaders of the Counter-Reformation church burned at the stake Protestant reformers who translated and taught the Bible. It was not that these Roman Catholics did not want the biblical message to be heard. It was that they feared that the translations and interpretations produced by "unauthorized" teachers might do more harm than good. To the Pope alone, the Roman Catholic church subsequently said, had been given the gift of infallibility in faith and morals, and that only when he spoke *ex cathedra*, officially defining a doctrine, settling an issue. Protestants in turn were ready to kill Roman Catholics in religious wars to defend the official interpretations of Protestant churches.

As a matter of fact, however, biblical scholars, both Catholic and Protestant, expert and less expert, find that they must use sound principles of biblical interpretation such as will be described in this chapter. It is interesting to note how large a consensus on matters of interpretation is emerging across denominational lines among those who use reasonable principles in understanding the Bible. Publications jointly produced by Catholic and Protestant scholars show the strength of agreement among students today.

The allegorists of the early church undertook to explain the Bible by means of symbolism which they professed to find in it. Clement of Alexandria, for example, proposed to solve problems of interpretation in this manner. There are three meanings in Scripture, Clement wrote: the literal, the moral, and the spiritual or mystic. Aware of the errors in naive literalism, Clement believed he could help his readers to discover the deeper, hidden meanings. For example, Luke 7:36–50 tells the story of how a woman anointed Jesus' feet with ointment as an act of devotion. Clement writes that "the feet anointed with fragrant ointment mean divine instruction travelling with renown to the ends of the earth. . . . Besides it shows the Lord's passion, if you understand it mystically thus: the oil . . . is the Lord Himself. . . . But the ointment, which is adulterated oil, is the traitor Judas."[1] The scarlet cord used to identify the house of Rahab so that it would be spared from destruction when the Hebrews attacked Jericho (Joshua 2:18) really means, according to Clement, the red blood of Jesus. The medieval church repeatedly spoke of the two swords the disciples possessed (Luke 22:38) as referring to the temporal and the spiritual powers, state and church.

The Reformers and more responsible Roman Catholic interpreters came to denounce allegory as distortion of Scripture, a device for reading into it any idea which happened to appeal to the teacher.

The rationalists of the seventeenth and eighteenth centuries, by contrast, attempted to interpret Scripture in the light of reason alone. In the Bible, they said, we find reflections of many ideas characteristic of the times in which Scripture was written. The New Testament speaks of people being possessed by demons. We now know—they said—that this is a superstitious way of describing insanity. But in the Bible we also find much that is quite reasonable, much that is eternal truth. These rational teachings contain the message of the Bible for us. Interpretation of the Scripture, Spinoza wrote, "requires only the aid of natural reason."

Thomas Jefferson, following the rationalist approach, produced a version of the New Testament in which all that he regarded as contrary to reason was omitted. Thus the miracles of Jesus and the story of his resurrection were left out. But the Golden Rule and the Sermon on the Mount, which Jefferson regarded as quite reasonable, remained.

One difficulty with this system of interpretation was that it left progressively less and less in the Bible as views changed about what might be demonstrated by reason. Reason does have a proper place in the understanding of Scripture, but if one expunges from the Bible all that cannot be rationally proved, very little may be left indeed.

"The History of Religions" school of interpreters and their allies in the nineteenth century attempted to understand biblical religion developmentally and in relation to other religions. Anthropologists may trace the evolution of pagan religion from primitive animism through polytheism to more sophisticated forms. Just so, these scholars argued, one may use the tools of science to trace the development of the Bible. It is essential for understanding a passage that it be set in its original historical context. But some of these scholars placed such emphasis on scientific techniques of historical research that they even argued that a professor of Bible should never be a Christian, since religious convictions might interfere with detached, rational, impartial judgment.

One of the contributions of the late Karl Barth was to remind the world that, important as it is to understand any passage in the light of its historical setting, the Bible professes to be a word from God to the reader, has been regarded as containing a message for the church in every age, and demands a response of faith if it is to be comprehended on its own terms. Detached scholarship *alone* can never disclose spiritual truth. The Bible, according to Barth, must be read as a kind of personal letter, with the reader's name and address on it.

Finally, *Rudolf Bultmann* and his followers have said that the key to understanding the New Testament is what Bultmann called *demythologization*. Bultmann's approach has been at the same time so influential and so controversial that it merits extended comment here. The New Testament, this twentieth-century German scholar recognized, presupposes a first-century view of the universe. Its writers assumed that we live on a flat earth with a heaven above to which Jesus after his resurrection could "ascend." We now know that the earth is round. Which way would be "up" for an ascension from our round earth? For twentieth-century man to understand the New Testament, Bultmann argues, he must strip away the first-century trappings of a prescientific world-view, take stories out of their "mythological" pattern, and present the biblical call to decision in terms comprehensible to modern man. "According to mythological thinking, God has his domicile in heaven. What is the meaning of this statement? The meaning is quite clear. In a crude manner it expresses the idea that God is beyond the world, that He is transcendent. The thinking which is not yet capable of forming the abstract idea of transcendence expresses its intention in the category of space."[2] The story of Jesus' ascension is not to be ignored. It is to be understood as a graphic way of saying that Jesus, as one "above" us, makes absolute demands which we must obey.

To critics who accused him of watering down the New Testament to fit modern tastes, Bultmann replied that his was the opposite intention. "To demythologize is to reject not Scripture or the Christian message as a whole, but the world-view of Scripture, which is the world-view of a past epoch. . . . To demythologize is to deny that the message of Scripture and of the Church is bound to an ancient world-view which is obsolete.''[3] It is to present the challenge of the existential (present, immediate, life-and-death) demand of the New Testament unconcealed by an outmoded science.

Many scholars who are ready to agree with Bultmann in rejecting the idea that heaven can be located in space still feel that when Bultmann "de-mythologizes" the miracles and the bodily resurrection of Jesus, he has gone too far toward making the modern scientific world-view more authoritative than Scripture.

"Post-Bultmannians," those who acknowledged their debt to him in subsequent writings, have tended to be somewhat less skeptical than he about the historical credibility of the Gospels.[4]

Some Basic Principles of Interpretation

Many other emphases in interpreting the New Testament could be described. The list given will illustrate the diversity of approaches used by scholarly—and often very devout—thinkers. Thus far this chapter has emphasized differences in perspective. Actually, there has been far more agreement than disagreement. Catholic and Protestant, conservative and liberal, ancient and modern scholars—almost all would agree on the value of certain basic principles of biblical interpretation which underlie the writing of the present volume.

Use of the principles now to be stated leaves room for many differences of opinion on many points. But a broad consensus exists today among biblical scholars that principles such as the following are helpful in understanding the New Testament.

It has proved useful to many to think of interpretation of the New Testament as the careful effort to answer three broad questions. These may be applied to whole books or to relatively short passages. The three questions are:
1) What does this passage *say*?
2) What does this passage *mean*?
3) What does this passage mean *to me* personally?

What Does This Passage Say?

Obviously, a first step in understanding the Bible is to read it carefully. Yet, however obvious it seems, the need for firsthand encounter with the text must be stated emphatically. The author of this GUIDE has found students who seemed more ready to read books *about* the New Testament than to read the New Testament itself. Studying neither this GUIDE nor any other commentary on the New Testament can be a substitute for the careful and repeated reading of the Bible itself.

The question "What does this passage say?" implies another principle: ideally the New Testament must be read in the original Greek. Any translation is already an interpretation, the translator's understanding, in modern language, of what the original Greek text meant. Since the days of the Reformation, great stress has been laid on studying the Bible in its original languages.

Students who cannot read Greek may make use of two admittedly fallible substitutes. They may make use of commentaries written by scholars who are competent in the language of the New Testament. They may also make use of a variety of translations, especially those such as the Revised Standard Version and the New English Bible, produced by scholars recognized as especially competent in Greek.

Fully to get at what a passage says requires one other step. We must try to reconstruct what the original writer actually wrote before the passage was copied and recopied over the centuries. We do not now possess a single "autograph" of any book of the New Testament, that is, the actual piece of parchment on which Paul, Mark, or any other New Testament author wrote. We have only copies of copies, the earliest coming from decades after the original writings.

At first this seems a very serious problem. There are more than two hundred thousand variations in ancient Greek manuscripts of the New Testament. Nearly one word out of every eight appears in a different form—perhaps a different tense of a verb, a different case ending, or even a different word altogether—in some Greek manuscript. Such a fact ought to cause the student to avoid commitment to too literal an interpretation of any particular text.

Yet it is agreed by all New Testament students that the variations in the manuscripts, while affecting the precise understanding of many verses, do not constitute a threat to our understanding of the main ideas of the New Testament. No doctrine is dependent upon a disputed reading.

Moreover, language scholars called "textual critics" have developed scientific techniques for determining what was the most likely original of any given text. This study, sometimes called "lower criticism," is of a kind which can be carried on effectively only by a small group of highly trained linguists. But it has been done with such care that, while many questions remain, one can read contemporary editions of the Greek text of the New Testament with assurance that they do not distort the meaning of the original manuscripts. This GUIDE will not deal with problems of textual criticism; it will assume that we have a reasonably accurate text.

What Does the Passage Mean?

This second question is the question of interpretation more narrowly defined. It is for the purpose of helping the student to find answers to it that this GUIDE is written.

The question involves many subquestions and requires the student to undertake many activities which may throw light on the meaning of the passage. Here are some suggestions:

1) Relate any passage to its context in Scripture, to what comes before it and

to what comes after it. One of the easiest ways to distort a text is to take it in isolation from its setting in Scripture. For example, in Matthew 5:38 Jesus quotes from the Old Testament: "An eye for an eye and a tooth for a tooth." Taken by itself, that verse endorses getting even with one's enemies. But read in context, it is found that Jesus' meaning is something quite different, for he quotes this law in order to say that it is inadequate. The very next verse continues, "But I say to you, Do not resist one who is evil. But if any one strikes you on the right cheek, turn to him the other also."

In this connection it is wise to look at whole passages before trying to determine the meaning of individual parts. The wise interpreter will, if possible, read a whole chapter, even a whole book, before settling on the meaning of a given verse. It is helpful to outline a book or a passage in order to get a grasp on its main ideas. In the light of those ideas, one may more adequately analyze and relate details.

2) Look for repeated words and ideas. Often these will give a clue to what the author meant, helping us to avoid reading different meanings into his material. For example, if the reader wants to get at the meaning of Paul's Letter to the Philippians, let him note how often words such as "joy" and "rejoice" occur. (See Phil. 1:4, 18, 19, 25; 2:2, 28, 29; 3:1; 4:1, 4, and 10.) One can scarcely go wrong in concluding that Paul, in spite of repeated references to his being in prison, is writing a letter of joy.

3) Look for the light which can be shed on a passage or book by setting it in its historical context. To ask "What does a book mean?" involves asking "What did it mean when it was written, to the one who wrote it and to those who first read it?"

This process, known as "higher criticism," involves asking about a biblical book or passage such related questions as the following:
—Who wrote it?
—When was it written?
—To whom was it written?
—Why was it written?
—What was the situation of the writer and of the readers?
—What would the book mean in that particular situation?

Commentaries, Bible encyclopedias, and many other books are designed to help answer such questions. This GUIDE is particularly concerned with these matters.

Here are three of a multitude of possible illustrations which show how a knowledge of history can help us understand the New Testament. The stories of Jesus' frequent conflicts with the Pharisees over the Sabbath law, conflicts which helped lead to his crucifixion, make more sense when we know who the Pharisees were and why they believed the Sabbath to be so important. The stories in Acts concerning conflict within the early church over the status of uncircumcised Gentile converts can be understood much more readily when we know something about the Jewish emphasis on circumcision and the relationship of Jews to Gentiles in the first century. And the book of Revelation, full of strange figures which have inspired wild speculations in many ages including our own, is much more comprehensible when we understand it as relating to the persecution of the church by the Roman government.

4) Compare one passage with another on the same subject. For example, looking at the account of Jesus' crucifixion in each of the four Gospels helps us to a more complete picture of events. Cross-references in most Bibles will help one find comparable passages.

5) Try imaginatively to reconstruct the emotional impact of the passage by asking, on the basis of the historical information you have gleaned, how the writer must have felt as he penned these words and how his first readers must have felt as they read them. When, at a time in which his readers may have been threatened with being burned at the stake, the author of First Peter wrote, "Do not be surprised at the fiery ordeal which comes upon you . . . But rejoice in so far as you share Christ's sufferings" (1 Peter 4:12–13), he was not giving cold, logical advice. To miss the emotional impact is to miss the point of the passage.

This leads directly to the last question.

What Does This Passage Mean to Me Personally?

Every book of the New Testament is written to demand a response.

It is easy for the student of the Bible to fall into one of two opposite errors. He may rush too quickly into responding to what he thinks the Bible means without going through the discipline of study which this chapter has described. Thus the student may dismiss the whole biblical message as superstition without ever really having understood it. Or he may adopt some belief or practice which the biblical writer never intended.

On the other hand, it is a mistake to regard the Bible simply as a piece of ancient literature, to study it as one might an antique, and never get around to making a decision about the challenges its pages are written to present.

To guide the student in making decisions about his own religious convictions and practices lies beyond the scope of this GUIDE. This volume is designed to give help in dealing with the second of our questions, "What does the Bible mean?" The personal appropriation of the Bible's message is a matter of decision which must be left to the reader.

Many other books deal helpfully with how one can grow in personal application of the biblical message. Suggestions such as the following have been found beneficial:

—As you read the New Testament, ask what things in your own life or in our world are like those of the people for whom this work was written.

—Ask what change you might make in your life if you did what this passage proposes.

—Read the passage with a newspaper in one hand, asking what the New Testament is saying, through you, to the world described in that paper.

—Pick out verses or ideas which especially appeal to you. Why do you like them?

—See what meaning, if any, you can find for your life in the verses or ideas that do *not* especially appeal to you.

—Consider what the passage suggests you ought to pray about.

It must be repeated that, as important as considerations of this kind certainly are, they lie beyond the purpose of this particular GUIDE.

Yet a recent approach to interpretation called "the new hermeneutic" has emphasized that language is used because it accomplishes results. Scholars of this school warn us that we have not grasped the message of the New Testament until we have been *grasped by* it, until God's Word has begun to accomplish a change in our lives.

This approach reminds us that no interpretation of the Bible can be done without in some way involving theological assumptions and presuppositions, however unconscious the student may be of having them. The Bible is written to change our minds and hearts. And one has not understood the Bible if he has not recognized that its writers are issuing a challenge. Far apart as they are in many things, interpreters of Scripture as diverse as Rudolf Bultmann and Billy Graham agree on one thing: from start to finish, the New Testament is a call to decision.[5]

II The Historical Setting of the Gospels

To understand fully the story of Jesus' life, it is helpful to be aware of two facts of history:

1) Jesus lived and taught among the tensions of a people only forty years away from suicidal political revolution.

2) At least by the standards of twentieth-century secularistic society, many of the people among whom Jesus taught seem almost fanatically religious.

How this political and religious situation came about and how recognition of it sheds light on the Gospels' story is the subject of this chapter.

The Political Situation

To understand the story, you must date it, Luke tells us, and it is to be dated by its political setting. "In the fifteenth year of the reign of Tiberius Caesar, Pontius Pilate being governor of Judea, and Herod being tetrarch of Galilee, and his brother Philip tetrarch of the region of Ituraea and Trachonitis, and Lysanias tetrarch of Abilene, in the high-priesthood of Annas and Caiaphas, the word of God came" (Luke 3:1–2). Matthew also dates his story politically. "Now when Jesus was born . . . in the days of Herod the king . . . "(Matt. 2:1).

In this respect, of course, the Bible is quite different from most other religious literature. The Bhagavad-Gita of the Hindus is a timeless work, the origins of its story lost in antiquity. The Tao Te Ching of the Taoists gives scarcely a hint of the events contemporary with its origin.

By contrast, Roman soldiers march through the pages of the New Testament. Guerrilla bands pillage the hills around Jerusalem. Passive resisters gaze toward heaven hoping for a cosmic deliverer from Roman oppressors. Quislings have sold out to Israel's new masters. Heroic legalists try to preserve Judaism against the encroachments of "modern" Greco-Roman civilization. And almost every page of the Gospels reflects one or more of these historical factors.

Here are some especially relevant elements of the situation.

Greco-Roman Culture Threatened Judaism

Students are often surprised to discover the high degree of civilization and sophistication which was characteristic of the world of the first century A.D. Schooled in the idea of progress, some students automatically relate the word "ancient" to such words as "primitive" and "backward."Actually, it was the

Dark Ages, centuries later, which saw the Mediterranean world reduced to near savagery.

A. C. Bouquet, in *Everyday Life in New Testament Times,* reminds us of such facts about the Greco-Roman world as the following: Almost all stylish women wore lipstick. Dyed hair (especially red or blonde) and permanent waves were in fashion, sometimes even for men. One famous glamour girl kept a herd of three thousand asses to provide milk for her daily milk bath, to give her a lovely complexion all over. One student wrote home, "Don't fidget about my mathematics, for I'm working hard." Another, with his mind on girls instead of books, wrote, "Brunettes for me. I always did like blackberries." Country folks loved to go to fairs, where they would see sideshows featuring marionettes, acrobats, rope-walkers, jugglers, and fortune-tellers. Beach resorts were crowded each summer. Astronomers not only knew that the earth was round, but had calculated the distance around it as being twenty-four thousand miles and the distance to the sun as ninety-two million miles.[1]

In themselves, of course, none of these manifestations of a "modern," "secular" culture was significant. But they remind us of a crisis brought about by the intrusion of a new way of life which did threaten Judaism's adherence to a pattern of living, almost every detail of which was supposed to be guided by what Jews regarded as the very Law of God.

The crisis had come about in this way.

In the year 334 B.C. Alexander the Great, king of the Greek city state of Macedon, began to conquer the world. Alexander fought not only for his own glory, but also for a kind of missionary purpose. As a youth he had been tutored by the philosopher Aristotle. No philosopher himself, Alexander nevertheless sought to spread the enlightenment of the Greeks to the barbarian world. Both as a conqueror and as a missionary he was remarkably successful. When, more than three centuries later, Paul set out as a different kind of missionary to conquer the world for Christianity, he could be understood in every country he visited when he spoke Greek. Greek had become the language of people throughout the empire. The New Testament could be written in Greek and be read by literate people anywhere.

With Greek language and philosophy went a non-Jewish way of life. Following Alexander's death his empire was divided, and Palestine was soon under the dominion of Syria. To their Syrian overlords Jews seemed a stubborn people in their continuing refusal to adopt the ways of Greek civilization. Finally, in 168 B.C., Antiochus IV, who called himself "Epiphanes"("God Manifest"), undertook to stamp out Judaism once and for all. Since pork was unclean according to Hebrew law, he sacrificed hogs on the altar at Jerusalem. Circumcision, Sabbath observance, and the keeping of Hebrew festivals were forbidden.

First and Second Maccabees, books of the Apocrypha which appear in Roman Catholic Bibles but are omitted in most Protestant and Jewish Bibles, describe the

Hebrew resistance. Ninety-year-old Eleazar climbed bravely up to the torture wheel rather than eat pork. Seven brothers were fried alive rather than submit. (Stories of such martyrdoms still inspired Jews in Jesus' day.)

Passive resistance, however, failed. A thousand Jews were slaughtered when they refused to do battle on the Sabbath. A group of brothers called the Maccabees (the "Mallet-Headed") gathered a guerrilla band in the hills and began more active resistance. They won against the odds, and Judea was set free. Judas Maccabeus became king.

Unfortunately, the Maccabees and the Hasmonean dynasty they established proved stronger militarily than religiously. Hellenization (spread of Greek culture) continued, and the dynasty grew corrupt. When, in 63 B.C., brothers became rivals to the throne, Pompey of Rome moved in to "re-establish order." Judea became a captive satellite state of the expanding Roman Empire.

In Jesus' Day Rome Ruled Palestine Through Cruel Dictatorship

At the time of the birth of Jesus, Herod the Great, who sat on the throne in Jerusalem, claimed the title "King of the Jews." He owed his throne and his title, however, to his Roman masters.

Matthew is much concerned to set Jesus, whom he pictures the Wise Men as calling by Herod's title, "King of the Jews," in relation to this King Herod.

Herod seems to have been a man of considerable ability. He succeeded in murdering the entire family of certain rival claimants to his throne, some forty-five people. He was able so effectively to curry favor with changing factions in Rome that he had Roman support throughout his thirty-three year reign. He instituted a remarkable building program, including the construction of a magnificent theater, an amphitheater, and the Hebrews' third (and last) Temple, the one in which Jesus was to worship. A strong law-and-order man, he reduced crime and brought stability. Many found it to their advantage to support Herod.

Thousands of Herod's more devout subjects, however, hated him. Herod himself was only nominally a Jew, descended from the Idumeans, a race converted to Judaism by conquest. He introduced Roman sports, dress, and temples in Jerusalem. Above all, his oppressive taxes were regarded as robbery to pay off his foreign masters, the Romans.

Terrified by the slightest hint of threat to his throne, he murdered even his wife and two of his own sons on charges of plotting rebellion. Punning on two similar words, the emperor Augustus is said to have quipped, "I would rather be Herod's *hog* than Herod's *son.*" Even during his final illness he gave orders for the execution of forty protest demonstrators and another of his own children. His known cruelty is reflected in the story in Matthew's Gospel that Herod ordered all boy babies in Bethlehem to be killed because one of them was reported to be a claimant to Herod's own title, "King of the Jews."

Shortly after an eclipse of the sun in the year 4 B.C., riddled with what was probably venereal disease, the old dictator died. According to Matthew 2, it was during the last days of the reign of this king Herod that Jesus Christ, the "King of the Jews," was born.

Jesus Lived in a Land on the Verge of Suicidal Revolt

Palestinian stability died with Herod.

His will decreed that his kingdom should be divided among three of his sons. The emperor soon deposed Archelaus, the ruler of Judea and Samaria (the southern half of Palestine), because of Archelaus' misrule. Guerrilla bands, perhaps inspired by the memory of the Maccabean revolt, began to form.

In A.D. 6, probably stirred up in part by a major taxation comparable to the one Luke relates to the birth of Jesus, armed rebels seized the Roman arsenal at Sepphoris, a town in Galilee (northern Palestine) only a few miles from Jesus' home in Nazareth. In punishment the Romans crucified 2,000 Jews. It is not unlikely that the adolescent Jesus walked a road lined with crosses on which hung the bodies of these nationalists.

Perhaps some two hundred thousand Jews died in uprisings against and punishments by the Roman authorities during the century leading up to the revolt of A.D. 66–70.

Secular history has not been much kinder to Pontius Pilate than has the Bible. In A.D. 26 he was appointed Roman procurator (governor) in Judea. He alienated his subjects at the very beginning by causing the Roman soldiers to carry the ensigns, symbols of Rome, into Jerusalem as they arrived. These winged figures were regarded by the Jews as being "graven images," prohibited by the Commandments. Valuing "progress" more than Judaism, Pilate again infuriated the people by taking money from the Temple treasury to pay for an aqueduct to bring water to Jerusalem. When Pilate slaughtered a band of pilgrims under the mistaken impression that they were a revolutionary mob, the Roman emperor finally acceded to the demands of a Jewish protest delegation and dismissed Pontius Pilate.

Insecure in his authority, Pilate had earlier yielded, John 19:12 tells us, to the cry of the mob demanding Jesus' crucifixion: "If you release this man, you are not Caesar's friend; every one who makes himself a king sets himself against Caesar."

Tourists who visit the Roman forum today still see the Arch of Titus commemorating the final victory of the Romans over the Jews. In A.D. 66, the rebellion in Palestine reached a pitiful, futile climax. Repeated riots brought hundreds of deaths. Finally, in A.D. 70, after a long siege, Jerusalem fell. Carvings on Titus' arch show captives and the seven-branched candlestick of Herod's Temple being paraded in triumph through the streets of Rome. What Mark 13:2 pictures

Jesus as prophesying came almost literally to pass. Of the Temple at Jerusalem, scarcely one stone was left upon another.

Even then, not all hope of Messianic deliverance was exhausted. In A.D. 132, one Simon ben Kosibah was hailed as the "Son of the Star," the Messiah. His pitiful revolt resulted in the stamping out of the Jews' last hope of rescue by violence.

Matthew's story of the star at Jesus' birth may reflect the association of star and expectation of the Messiah-King (Num. 24:17). Clearly the inscription placed on the cross over Jesus' head indicates that he was executed as one whom Roman authorities feared as presenting the threat of revolution: "The King of the Jews" (Mark 15:26).

The Religious Situation

The Gospel events took place in a time of tensions that were not only political but also religious.

One cannot fully understand the New Testament without realizing that religion played a far larger part in the lives of most first-century Jews than is the case with most twentieth-century Western people. Perhaps one would need to travel to India today to observe a culture so dominated by religious concern. There were, of course, many who were relatively indifferent to Judaism's tradition. But, far more than is the case for most of our contemporaries, religion was of enormous importance for thousands of Jews in New Testament times.

Knowing the following factors in the religious situation of the day is especially helpful in understanding the New Testament.

Judaism Preserved the Old Testament Faith

In part, at least, Jesus must be understood as a devout Jew living among devout Jews. Of course, as we shall see, Jesus so differed from Judaism that during his ministry he was in constant conflict with Jewish leaders. Nevertheless, we must emphasize that Jesus was a Jew. Jesus worshiped in the Jewish synagogue and taught from the Jewish scripture. The first Christians were Jews. The church emerged at first as a sect within Judaism. Not only in such books as Matthew and Hebrews, which emphasize this idea, but throughout the New Testament Jesus is proclaimed as the fulfillment of the Old Testament expectation.

To understand the New Testament adequately, therefore, one must study the Old. That study lies beyond the scope of this volume. Here, very briefly, are only a few of many Old Testament ideas presupposed in the New Testament.

1) The God of the Gospels is the *same God* the Hebrews worshiped: one, sovereign, righteous, just, and loving. Jesus *did* announce that with his coming, God was about to do something new. Jesus did *not* announce a new God. He did

not even profess primarily to be giving new information about the character of that God. He was proclaiming the God of Abraham, of Isaac, of Jacob, and of the prophets.

2) Israel's God was one who *revealed himself in mighty acts.* Here the biblical God must be distinguished from the gods both of Greek philosophy and of the Oriental religions. Thinkers and holy men and women related themselves to these pagan deities through the discovery of universal concepts or through mystic experiences available to all who would rightly open themselves to them. But the God of the Jewish scriptures was revealed primarily through what he did. This is not to deny, of course, the importance of the understanding of these historical events in the minds of those inspired prophets and teachers who wrote the books of Jewish scripture. But one must emphasize the distinctive part that actions attributed to God played in Jewish faith.

Thus the Old Testament centers around one story to which many stories contribute. According to that story, God had called Abraham to be the ancestor of a chosen people. God had miraculously rescued his descendants, a group of bricklaying slaves, from bondage in Egypt. He had conquered Palestine for them, established their kingdom, disciplined them with exile when they sinned, and, in the days of Cyrus of Persia, restored them to their homeland. Hebrews saw these events of history as miracles, wonders, signs of the activity of God.

It was a new activity, more than a new concept, of this same God which the Gospel writers claimed to be describing.

3) These acts of God were understood as being for the establishment and preservation of *a unique, chosen, holy people.* They were expressions of God's loving concern for Israel. Even the judgment of God could be understood as part of the guidance and protection of the Elect. Sometimes the concept of the Chosen People led to an almost fanatical attempt to preserve the race uncontaminated by any foreign influence. Ezra, as the Jews sought to rebuild the chosen nation after the Babylonian captivity, forced all Jews who had married Gentiles to divorce them. Sometimes the concept of the Chosen People emphasized the unique mission of the Jews to the world. Isaiah 49:6 pictures God as saying to the Elect:

> I will give you as a light to the nations,
> that my salvation may reach to the end of the earth.

Christians were to come to think of Christ and of the church in relation to Isaiah's vision.

4) Judaism was distinctively *a covenant religion.* Archaeologists have unearthed copies of ancient Mideastern treaties by which a powerful emperor might take under his rule and protection a small, weak, neighboring nation. Perhaps such covenants formed a model for the Hebrews' understanding of their relationship with God. In any event, they held that following God's rescue of them from Egypt, God had condescended to enter into a covenant with them. He would

be their Lord and protector. They, as the prophets were to interpret it, were in a sense "married" to the Lord. They had agreed to respond to God's deliverance and continuing preservation of them by being faithful exclusively to this one God. God had saved and would save them. They in turn agreed to respond in attitudes of the heart, in cultic worship, and in ethical living. Their prescribed response to the grace of God was codified in law.

The New Testament was to speak of Christ as having instituted a "new covenant."

5) In this covenant God *demanded righteousness in social relationships.* Amos, the first of the Hebrew prophets whose words are preserved for us as a book of the Old Testament, had pictured God as ready to judge Israel

> because they sell the righteous for silver,
> > and the needy for a pair of shoes.   (Amos 2:6)
>
> I hate, I despise your feasts,
> > and I take no delight in your solemn assemblies. . . .
>
> But let justice roll down like waters,
> > and righteousness like an everflowing stream.   (Amos 5:21–24)

Prophets denounced even kings themselves if they failed to show concern for the poor or used their power simply for their own advantage. Perhaps no other religion has ever tied together so closely love of God and active concern for one's fellow man.

Jesus was popularly identified by his contemporaries as being another prophet, perhaps in part because of his insistence that the coming of the kingdom of God he was announcing demanded godly relationships between people.

6) The Jews nurtured and expressed this faith through *cultic practices.* Perhaps few first-century Jews would have drawn a sharp distinction between ethical practices such as honesty and charity and "cultic" practices such as circumcision and Sabbath observance. Both were equally part of the Law of God. The modern distinction between the two, however, may be helpful for contemporary students. God, the Hebrews were sure, not only demanded concern for one's neighbor; he commanded participation in certain ceremonies, in worship, and in practices designed to mark the Jew as distinct from the rest of humankind.

Jesus, like any other Jewish boy, was circumcised in infancy, bearing on his body the indelible mark of his being part of the covenant people.

Particularly in the Gospel According to John, we find Jesus participating in the Jewish festivals conducted annually at the Temple in Jerusalem. Most important among these for the New Testament was the Passover. It involved the yearly celebration of God's redemption of his people from Egypt and the establishment of the covenant. Participants shared a meal which included a sacrificed lamb. The Gospels record Jesus' eating a meal at this Passover season with his disciples the night before his death, and the Passover imagery helped the New Testament writers to interpret the meaning of Jesus' death as a redeeming, covenant sacrifice.

Perhaps most difficult of all to preserve against the encroachments of Greco-Roman culture, Jews observed the Sabbath, keeping free from all work the period from sundown Friday evening until sundown Saturday evening. Controversy with those who most rigidly adhered to the Sabbath law was a factor leading to Jesus' death.

In Jesus' Day Competing Groups of Jews Represented Differing Views

Thus far, first-century Judaism has been presented as though its people were all of one mind. This was far from the case. Controversies within the Jewish community are repeatedly reflected within the Gospels' stories.

Josephus, the Jewish writer whose histories written late in the first century shed a flood of light on New Testament times in Palestine, speaks of "four philosophies" influential among Jews of his day.

1) *The Pharisees* are so prominent in the story that the word "Pharisee" occurs in the Gospels more than eighty times. Though only some six thousand out of perhaps a million and a half Palestinian Jews were Pharisees, their influence with the people and their opposition to Jesus made them of great importance to the Gospel writers.

Though nobody knows exactly how the Pharisees originated, it is known that the sect had been in existence for a century and a half by Jesus' day. The name "Pharisees" apparently means "the Separated Ones," given them presumably because they sought to be different from other people by being more holy. The Pharisees represented devoutly determined resistance to the threat of Greco-Roman culture. Pharisees saw their worldly neighbors compromising their faith and practice at point after point. Ancient puritans, they resolved to compromise nothing. To preserve the Law, they fenced it about with tradition, so that by keeping the strictest traditional interpretations of the Law they would be certain not to break even the slightest detail.

Their heroes and heroines were those who, according to their tradition, had most courageously resisted even the slightest surrender to pagan pressures. The book of Tobit described how an old Hebrew in captivity lost his sight in his concern to keep ceremonial laws such as those governing the burial of the dead. As a reward, his fortune was restored, his son was given a beautiful wife, and his eyes were healed, all by the miraculous intervention of an angel. The book of Judith described how, even in the camp of an enemy, this lovely widow refused to eat food which was not kosher, always carrying with her her own kosher food and wine. She was able to beguile the invading general with her charms, murder him on his bed, and rescue her people. God, the Pharisees were sure, would protect and deliver those who thus obeyed his Law.

Much as they added their traditional interpretations to the Law, so these devout people developed doctrines which went beyond the direct words of the Jewish scripture. They argued for belief in the resurrection and a life after death. They believed in angels and demons. They believed in predestination and foreordination by God, who plans all that will come to pass.

One who knows the Pharisees only through the New Testament is likely to get an inaccurate view of these good people. Jesus' attacks on them need not be applied to all the Pharisees. They were looked upon as, and probably were in fact, the best Jews of their day. The word "Pharisee" has come to mean "hypocrite", but their original intent was to be uncompromising guardians of God's Law.

2) *The Sadducees* were the party of compromise. If the Pharisees chose to protect every word of the Law by adding traditional interpretations, the Sadducees accepted as authoritative as little as seemed possible for good Jews. Thus they regarded as binding on them not the whole of the Old Testament, but only the Torah, the books of the Law, the first five books of the Bible. They rejected belief in angels and demons. And as to a future life, they rejected that belief, seeming to have been successful in finding rewards of a different kind here on earth.

Most dictators learned long ago that it is easier to dominate a religion than to stamp it out. The Romans chose this shrewder strategy. The Jews continued to have their high priest in their Temple, but the high priest had to be appointed in cooperation with the Roman authorities. He could continue in office only so long as he pleased his Roman lords. Often his stay in office was short indeed.

There were rewards for those who served Rome. The Sadducees came to be the priestly class, the leaders in the *Sanhedrin* (the Jewish supreme court of seventy members), and the wealthiest of the Jews. Sophisticated, more Greek than Hebrew, affluent in a poverty-striken land, and cooperating with their conquerors, the Sadducees tended to be despised by many of their countrymen.

Matthew 16:1–12 describes Jesus' condemnation of the Pharisees and Sadducees. Matthew 22:23–33 describes their attempt to ridicule Jesus' belief in a future life.

3) *The Essenes* are best known to us through the most remarkable discovery of buried treasure in modern times.

In 1947, a teen-aged Arab goatherd who was chasing a runaway found himself in a cave on a mountain overlooking the Dead Sea. There he stumbled upon an earthen jar. It contained the first of the famous Dead Sea Scrolls, part of the library of a curious Jewish sect not unlike the later Roman Catholic monks.

The Pharisees tried to live everyday lives as middle-class Jews in the world, but in accordance with God's Law. The Essenes, however, turned their backs on the sinful world. To the wilderness they went, away from the corruption of the cities. There they set up their own communes, rather like medieval monasteries. Most of these communes were for men only, though a few included families. An applicant for admission went through a year's probation. When admitted, he deeded over all his property to the community, went through a ceremony not unlike baptism, swore to live a strict and righteous life, and began to share in the common meals.

The Essenes regarded themselves as the army of the Sons of Light. Whenever the awaited age of the Messiah should come, they would stand ready to fight the forces of evil and darkness.

The Essenes are never mentioned in the New Testament. But their sharing, baptized, kingdom fellowship was so much like the early Christian church that some have proposed that many early Christians, even Jesus himself, might have been members of this sect. Most scholars now reject the suggestion that Jesus was ever an Essene, but we shall see that there are real similarities between the Essenes and John the Baptist.

4) Finally, there were *the Zealots*, a kind of Palestinian Liberation Organization, secretly plotting violent revolution to be carried out when the Messiah came to lead them. We have already noted their heroic but futile raids.

Luke 6:15 tells us that one of Jesus' disciples was "Simon who was called the Zealot." Fear that Jesus, who was being hailed as Messiah, might stimulate a Zealot uprising was a factor in the execution of Jesus by the nervous Romans.

Three Religious Emphases of First-Century Judaism Particularly Influenced Jesus' Life and Its Interpretation

Most Jews, of course, did not belong to any of these four parties. The common people, "the people of the land," had little time or means, perhaps, for participation in such movements.

Still, there were synagogues for worship and study in every Jewish town, more and more of them with synagogue schools for teaching the youth. Religious zeal seems to have been widespread, at least by twentieth-century standards. And the movements we have examined exemplified attitudes and concerns not confined to their members.

Three of these religious emphases characteristic of the first century have such bearing on the Gospel accounts that we must take note of them.

1) *Legalism* was highly developed. Only six thousand Jews wore the broad tassels of the Pharisees' band. But Josephus tells us that the common people looked up to these Pharisees as examples of what all should be. The Law, the Torah, was the very word of God.

Strict observance of the Sabbath symbolized obedience to all the Law. Pharisaic tradition spelled out precisely what Sabbath observance required. For example, when the question arose as to whether, on the Sabbath, one might put a bowl over an annoying gnat in order to rid oneself ot it, it was ruled that doing so would be a form of hunting, strictly illegal on the holy day. One must not wear a new robe on the Sabbath, because there might still be a needle left in it. It would be a sin to carry even that much of a burden on Saturday. Some rules suggested evasions. It was a sin, of course, to tie a knot in a rope on the Sabbath. But one might tie a knot in a sash, since getting dressed was necessary for decency. Hence, if a well rope broke on Saturday, it was permitted to mend it with the temporary use of a sash. When Jesus set human need above such Sabbath rules, some Pharisees began to plot his death.

2) *Expectation of the Messiah* seems to have been widespread and to have taken a variety of forms.

Though the Pharisees did not attempt armed resistance to Rome, they were no less dedicated to liberation than were the Zealots. It was simply that their methods were different. If all Israel would but keep two Sabbaths perfectly, they promised, the Messiah, the promised king, would come with deliverance.

The Dead Sea Scrolls seem to imply that the Essene communes awaited not just one, but two Messiahs, one kingly and one priestly. The Essenes would be the Lord's army in that coming day.

The Zealots were all too ready to follow any attractive military leader in the hope that he was the one promised to lead them in the slaughter of the Romans.

Perhaps it was because he rejected all these ideas of Messiahship that Jesus strictly forbade his disciples to tell people that he was the Messiah. But the belief that Jesus had brought at last the fulfillment of their hopes and dreams undoubtedly drew the crowds who became his first followers.

3) Closely related to the expectation of the Messiah was the intense *expectation of the final days of this world*.

> And the horns of the sun shall be broken and he shall be turned into darkness;
> And the moon shall not give her light, and be turned wholly into blood.[2]

So prophesied the author of "The Assumption of Moses," a work popular among first-century Jews, as he wrote of the coming cataclysm.

> The heavens shall thunder loud . . .
> and the gates of Hell shall be opened.[3]

The Dead Sea Scrolls thus described the last day.

> Ye mighty kings who dwell on the earth, ye shall have to behold Mine Elect One, how he sits on the throne of glory and judges
> Azâzêl, and all his associates, and all his hosts in the name of the Lord of Spirits.[4]

A typical apocalypse, falsely attributed to Enoch, described the cosmic judgment of Satan and the nations in these terms.

"Eschatology," teaching about the last things, the doctrine of the end of the world, had produced its own kind of literature from which the passages just quoted are taken. Called "apocalyptic" literature, this distinctive kind of writing flourished among a people desperate for deliverance.

Several characteristics of apocalyptic literature of the period must be listed:

—It professed to be giving secret information about the coming future.

—It was in a style full of symbols which only insiders might understand.

—It viewed this world from the perspective of heaven, as though the author were watching events on earth from the point of view of some heavenly being.

—It divided history into periods.

—It predicted the blackest troubles as coming in the period just before the climax of the story.

—At that climax there would be a cosmic battle between the forces of evil and the forces of good, with God's legions triumphing.

—It envisioned a great judgment day, the vindication of the righteous, and the conquest of evil.

—It hinted or flatly stated that all these cataclysmic events were to happen very soon.

In many of these apocalypses there was the promise of a Messiah.

It was with ears at least partly trained by this kind of preaching that Jesus' first hearers heard him announce what Mark reports as a summary of his first preaching: ''The time is fulfilled, and the kingdom of God is at hand; repent, and believe in the gospel''(Mark 1:15).

III The Writing of the Gospels

In the beginning was the event.

Jesus lived; Jesus taught; Jesus died. At Easter something so amazing occurred that it caused the disciples to spend the rest of their lives telling the world that Jesus also rose from the dead. The Gospel stories were born in historical events.

It is true that the nineteenth-century German scholar Bruno Bauer seriously proposed that Jesus never actually existed. Recognizing apparent difficulties and inconsistencies in the Gospel accounts, he argued that the Gospels were simply religious fiction. The effect of his proposal was to demonstrate its impossibility. Today it would be difficult to find even one competent historian who would doubt that Jesus really lived. Mark, the first written Gospel, was penned only about thirty-five years after Jesus' death. The other records of Jesus' life are too early, too many, too diverse, and yet in too much basic agreement not to have their source in some nucleus of actual fact. And it is far easier to suppose that the religious movement which spread so rapidly over the Roman Empire was the creation of a powerful personality than that the personality was the fictional creation of the movement.

In being centered so directly on historical events and the person in the midst of them, Christianity is unique among religions. Devout Muslims respect the memory of Muhammed, surely a historical individual of remarkable gifts. Muslims, however, would be the first to affirm that their religion centers on Allah's message, not on the person of Muhammed the messenger. Whether or not Arjuna ever lived is a question which has no bearing on the truth of the Hindus' Bhagavad-Gita. Christianity, however, begins with the story of a real man. Rudolf Bultmann, who devoted much of his study to the comparison of the Gospel stories with other literature in similar form, writes that the Gospels are unique, therefore, in the religious literature of the world. This particular kind of literature cannot be paralleled even in style and form to any other anywhere.

In the beginning was the event. But for our knowledge of this crucial event, or series of events, we are dependent upon written sources. The only written sources which really help us are those within the New Testament. There are two brief references to Jesus in the writings of the Jewish historian Josephus, but many scholars regard the longer of these as being an insertion by a Christian copyist. The writings of Jewish rabbis who mention Jesus come from a later period and seem to be simply reflections of Jewish-Christian controversy. Roman historians did not hear of Jesus until the Christian movement had spread over the empire.

We can learn some things about Jesus' life, as we shall see, from books of the New Testament other than the Gospels, but the details are disappointingly few. It is the Gospels, the first four books of the New Testament, which tell us almost everything we know about the earthly life of Christ.

Fortunately, one Gospel writer gives us a brief account of how and why he wrote:

> Inasmuch as many have undertaken to compile a narrative of the things which have been accomplished among us, just as they were delivered to us by those who from the beginning were eyewitnesses and ministers of the word, it seemed good to me also, having followed all things closely for some time past, to write an orderly account for you, most excellent Theophilus, that you may know the truth concerning the things of which you have been informed.   (Luke 1:1–4)

To some this account of the writing of a Gospel must seem disappointing. The Koran, the Muslims believe, was dictated by an angel. The Book of Mormon was handed down from heaven, according to the Church of Jesus Christ of Latter-Day Saints. Pious Christian paintings have shown angels dictating to biblical writers. But the claim Luke makes is simply that he did a careful job of research. Many Christians are ready to affirm, however, that they trust a claim of research such as Luke's more than any boast of a "miraculous" origin. This chapter will consider what can be deduced about how Luke went about this task.

Taking Luke's account of how his Gospel was written as typical of the others as well, we shall use it as a basis for considering the origins of the Gospels.

Oral Traditions About Jesus

Even though Mark probably wrote his account of Jesus' life about A.D. 65, only some thirty-five years after Jesus' death, and though we have letters written by Paul from perhaps as early as about A.D. 50, there still remains what has been called a "dark tunnel" of twenty years between Jesus' death, about A.D. 30, and our oldest Christian writings. What kind of sources did the Gospel writers use? How did they penetrate that tunnel?

From the Beginning the First Preachers Told About Jesus' Life

Luke says that his story came in part from those who from the beginning were "ministers of the word."

Acts gives us an account of what these first preachers said. Admittedly, Acts was written fifty or more years after the life of Jesus. There is reason to believe, however, that by comparing the summaries of sermons in Acts with passages in which Paul reports what seem to be accounts of the Gospel as he first heard it, the content of the first preaching can be reconstructed.

The Greek word used for the content of the first preaching is *kerygma*. It means "proclamation." It was used for the announcement of victory. It implies the joyful proclaiming of good news. A *keryx* was a herald, and the first preachers thought of themselves as heralds reporting a triumph.

In his highly influential book *The Apostolic Preaching and Its Developments*, the late C. H. Dodd points to the following summary in Acts as very probably typical of the earliest sermons:[1]

> You know the word which he sent to Israel, preaching good news of peace by Jesus Christ (he is Lord of all), the word which was proclaimed throughout all Judea, beginning from Galilee after the baptism which John preached: how God anointed Jesus of Nazareth with the Holy Spirit and with power; how he went about doing good and healing all that were oppressed by the devil, for God was with him. And we are witnesses to all that he did both in the country of the Jews and in Jerusalem. They put him to death by hanging him on a tree; but God raised him on the third day and made him manifest; not to all the people but to us who were chosen by God as witnesses, who ate and drank with him after he rose from the dead. And he commanded us to preach to the people, and to testify that he is the one ordained by God to be judge of the living and the dead. To him all the prophets bear witness that every one who believes in him receives forgiveness of sins through his name. (Acts 10:36–43)

Other summaries of sermons in Acts and in Paul's letters are similar.

If this was indeed the kind of thing which the first preachers regularly said, then we may summarize the part of the typical sermon which described the earthly life of Jesus as including the following elements:

1) It began with an account of John the Baptizer and his baptism of Jesus. This baptism was associated with an anointing of Jesus by the Holy Spirit.

2) Some account was given of Jesus' deeds. Emphasis was laid on his power, the goodness of his actions, his healing, and his exorcisms of evil spirits, in conflict with the devil.

3) Some account of Jesus' preaching or teaching was also given.

4) Mention was made of chosen witnesses (the disciples).

5) The story moved from Galilee to Judea and Jerusalem.

6) The one event of Jesus' life specifically described here—and in all other summaries of early sermons—was his death. Of that death, details begin to be noted, even in this brief summary: the role of his enemies and the manner of his execution.

7) His resurrection was announced, with specific mention of Jesus' appearance to his disciples and his commission to them to spread the Good News.

The striking thing about these seven points is that they would serve equally well as a short summary of Mark or, indeed, of any one of the four Gospels.

Luke says that he based his Gospel in part on what he had heard the first preachers say. Similarly, early and consistent tradition affirms that Mark based his Gospel on what he had heard in preaching, the sermons of Jesus' disciple Peter.

What is proposed, then, is that the *kerygma*, this form of preaching which seems to have been much the same throughout the early church, included an account of the life of Jesus. No doubt different stories and sayings of Jesus were told by different preachers in different sermons. But the basic, common *kerygma* provided the framework, the outline, when Gospel writers set down their stories of Jesus' life. And the stories and sayings of Jesus, the sermon illustrations used by these "ministers of the word," made up the body of each Gospel.

The Gospels Contain Stories and Sayings Handed Down by These First Preachers

Scholars called "form critics" have argued cogently that the individual stories gathered together on the framework of each Gospel show signs of having been told and retold separately before they were written down as we now have them.

This view fits well with the fact that the stories do not appear in our Gospels in the same order. For example, the parable of the Sower occurs early in Mark's Gospel (chapter 4), a bit later in Luke's Gospel (chapter 8), and not until the middle of Matthew's account (chapter 13). Mark tells of the healing of the man with the withered hand near the beginning of his story of Jesus' life (chapter 3), while Luke puts it in chapter 6 and Matthew not until chapter 12. The Lord's Prayer is given as part of the Sermon on the Mount in Matthew 6. In Luke 11 it is part of private instruction given later by Jesus to his disciples. The simplest explanation is that these stories and sayings were not the invention of the writers, but part of the oral traditions of the church handed down by the many early preachers. Each writer has used a familiar story at the place in his Gospel where it would best illustrate the point he was making.

One form critic has compared the separate stories of Jesus, handed down by word of mouth, to separate pearls which the Gospel writers have strung together, each in different order to present his distinctive insights into the truth.

Form critics have attempted to analyze these stories on the basis of the forms or patterns in which they seem repeatedly to occur. Such critics have not always agreed in their analyses, but three such patterns or forms will be noted here.

The most obvious form is that of the *parable*. The traditional definition serves well: "A parable is an earthly story with a heavenly meaning." Jesus told so many parables that, perhaps with a touch of Oriental hyperbole, Mark 4:34 says that Jesus never spoke in public without using a parable. Familiar examples of parables are Luke 15:3–7 (the Lost Sheep), Luke 10:29–37 (the Good Samaritan), and Mark 4:3–9 (the Sower and the Soils). One can readily see how these little stories could be remembered easily and handed down orally.

A second form has been called the *pronouncement story*. It consists of a saying of Jesus embedded in an account of some incident of his life, so that the two would be remembered together. For example, Mark 2:23–28 tells how Jesus' disciples, walking through a grain field on the Sabbath, plucked and ate bits of wheat. When the Pharisees accused them of desecrating the Sabbath by threshing grain on the holy day, Jesus replied, "The sabbath was made for man, not man for the sabbath." Story and saying would be remembered together. Mark 2:15–17 gives another illustration. Jesus' enemies attack him for associating with the outcasts of society. He replies, "Those who are well have no need of a physician, but those who are sick." Incidentally, it should be noted that many, many of Jesus' sayings are in this style of witty couplets or balanced phrases which would be easy to remember and pass on orally.

The third form is the *miracle story*. In a typical miracle story, (1) a need is noted; (2) Jesus' help is sought; (3) there is an expression of faith; (4) a memorable miracle is performed, and (5) the story ends with a notation about the response of those who saw the miracle. The response may be one of faith, astonishment, or even anger. Matthew 9:1–8 contains all five of these elements in its account of the healing of a paralytic.

Some scholars have attempted to determine the age of a story by analysis of its form. Not all agree, however, that this attempt has been entirely successful.[2]

There are hints which enable scholars to make guesses concerning which strands of the tradition are earlier or later. For example, it seems evident that Jesus told a story about a lost sheep and a shepherd who goes out to find it. Luke 15:1–7 sets this story in the context of Jesus' replying to Pharisees who attacked him for associating with sinners. The meaning, in this setting, is clearly a defense of Jesus' association with outcasts. In Matthew 18:10–22 the story is immediately followed by instruction concerning special care to be taken to win back delinquent church members. Many have argued that the setting in Luke is the original one. By placing it in a different context, Matthew's Gospel has applied the same story—quite helpfully—to the later situation of church discipline. Lastly, John 10:11 does not repeat the by now familiar parable but richly develops its meaning in relation to Christ and all the faithful: "I am the good shepherd. The good shepherd lays down his life for the sheep."

As different situations arose in the life of the church, different sayings and stories were recalled and new meanings were found in them. We have emphasized the place of preaching in the development of the oral tradition. Worship, instruction, and other concerns of the church doubtless also helped preserve the stories of Jesus. Our point here is simply that the stories circulated orally, were easy to remember, and are older than the written Gospels in which we now find them.

Gospel Writers Selected and Arranged This Material
for Their Special Purposes

To return to Luke's account of how he wrote his Gospel, Luke tells us that by the time he writes, "many have undertaken to compile a narrative of the things which have been accomplished among us." He was familiar, therefore, with many stories of Jesus' life. Some of these he evidently considered of inferior quality. He selected from among the many stories in circulation those which fit his particular purpose and which suited his standards of credibility.

It is John's Gospel which spells out this concern for selection most clearly, in words which would apply in many ways to the other Gospels also.

> Now Jesus did many other signs in the presence of the disciples, which are not written in this book; but these are written that you may believe that Jesus is the Christ, the Son of God, and that believing you may have life in his name.   (John 20:30–31)

With Oriental hyperbole John says that Jesus did so many things that the world could not contain the books it would take to record them all (John 21:25)! He has carefully selected those stories and sayings which he feels will win the reader to faith in Jesus as the Christ, the Son of God, and lead that reader to new life.

In short, as we have seen, the Gospels must be understood against the background of the *kerygma*. They grew out of gospel sermons. They are not simply cold, objective biographies. They are evangelistic tracts. Their contents were selected for evangelistic purposes. This is most obvious in John, the latest of the Gospels. But though less explicit, it is also the case with the others, even the earliest, Mark. Lest we miss the point that he is trying to win us to believe, Mark introduces his story as "The beginning of the gospel of Jesus Christ, the Son of God" (Mark 1:1). Every Gospel is written to give us not simply the writer's record of what Jesus said and did, but also his understanding of who Jesus really was and what he can mean to the reader. Each Gospel is a call to the decision of faith.

This is why there is so much that the Gospels do *not* bother to tell us about Jesus. What was his childhood like? We have only one story about Jesus between his infancy and age thirty (Luke 2:41–51). What did he look like? What is really the historical order of events described in such different sequence in our four Gospels? In what sense did Jesus think of himself as Messiah? Such questions are not answered for us, in part at least because they were not the theological concern of our Gospel writers.

It is true that other pious authors soon undertook to fill in the gaps in the Gospel stories. Here are a few stories about Jesus which are relatively unfamiliar to most modern Christians.

—Jesus' parents sent the boy Jesus to school. He knew so much more than the teacher, so confused the poor man, that the teacher soon begged Mary and Joseph not to send Jesus back again.

—The child Jesus made a pigeon of clay, clapped his hands, and the bird miraculously flew away.

—A playmate accidentally bumped into Jesus, knocking down the Son of God. Jesus cursed him for this blasphemy, and the boy dropped dead. After the child's parents complained to Joseph, Jesus graciously resurrected the boy.[3]

These and many other equally incredible stories are preserved for us in apocryphal gospels, accounts of Jesus' life beloved by many early Christians but eventually rejected by the church as false. Noting them points us to a second criterion of selection used by the Gospel writers. Luke tells us that, aware of other accounts of Jesus' life, he wrote his so that his reader would now know what was the truth.

Much recent scholarship has so emphasized the theological purpose of the Gospel writers that it has neglected their evident concern for reporting the facts. We have seen that they do not report all the facts. And we have seen that they do not report just facts, but also their interpretations of the meaning of those facts. But the Gospel writers were not, they tell us, producing fiction to support theology. Had they been doing so, they might well have included stories such as those just described. Each Gospel writer, like Luke, wants his reader to know the truth, the truth as he has learned it from many sources. Luke claims to have talked with "eyewitnesses." Assuming that he is also the author of Acts, we may well believe that he had opportunity to meet eyewitnesses in the journeys he describes there. A credible tradition says that Mark is reporting what he learned from Peter, who was very much an eyewitness of the events described. At the very least, our Gospels are based on oral and written sources developed within the lifetime of the first preachers. And while most scholars deny that our Gospels of Matthew and John in the form in which we now have them are actually from the pens of these Apostles, the names of these Gospels suggest at least that in some way they rest upon a tradition that goes back to two of the original Twelve.[4]

Our Gospel writers, then, have selected stories told by the early church and have strung these "pearls" together, each in his own fashion, on a thread also spun from the first sermons, to win readers to faith through confronting them with the truth.

The Written Records

When Luke tells us that "many have undertaken to compile a narrative," he implies that he is familiar not only with oral sources such as we have been describing, but also with written accounts of the life of Jesus. While there are differences of opinion, most scholars believe that we can describe two of the written sources Luke used.

Mark Is Our Oldest Gospel and Was One Source for Matthew and Luke

Several reputable scholars still support the tradition that Matthew was the first of our four Gospels to be written.[5] The great majority, however, believe that Matthew and Luke already knew Mark's Gospel and made use of it when they wrote.

The chief reason for this view is that so much of Mark seems to have been copied by the other Gospel writers, though adapted by them to fit their language, style, and purposes. Of the eighty-eight paragraphs which make up Mark, only three are not found in either Matthew or Luke. Matthew reproduces approximately ninety percent of the subject matter of Mark. More than half of the contents of Mark can also be found in Luke.

Moreover, where Matthew or Luke varies from Mark in wording or in outline, the other will be found more likely to agree with Mark. Almost never do Matthew and Luke agree with each other but differ from Mark.

Since Mark's Gospel is a primary source for both Matthew and Luke, its origins are of great importance for New Testament study. Our best source of information is the *Ecclesiastical History* of Eusebius, written around A.D. 330, but quoting from earlier accounts. According to Eusebius, here is what happened.

Emperor Nero undertook to stamp out the church in Rome. Among those martyred was Peter, leader among Jesus' twelve disciples and of the Roman congregation. After the death of Peter, according to Eusebius, "Mark, the disciple and interpreter of Peter, himself handed down to us in writing the substance of Peter's preaching."[6]

Similarly, Eusebius quotes the early church leader Papias as having written about A.D. 140:

> The elder used to say this also: Mark became the interpreter of Peter and he wrote down accurately, but not in order, as much as he remembered of the sayings and doings of Christ. For he was not a hearer or a follower of the Lord, but afterwards, as I said, of Peter, who adapted his teachings to the needs of the moment and did not make an ordered exposition of the sayings of the Lord.[7]

Mark appears repeatedly in the New Testament as a young leader in the church from its earliest days, acquainted with Peter, Barnabas, and Paul (Acts 12:12, 25; 15:39; 2 Tim. 4:11). Though it is challenged, there seems to be no compelling reason to doubt the report of Eusebius, Papias, and Irenaeus that he is the author of our Gospel. If so, we may infer that Mark is giving us the stories of Jesus which he had heard directly from the firsthand accounts of Peter. This fits nicely with the fact that next to Jesus himself, by far the most prominent character in Mark is the Apostle Peter. Mark's Gospel, in a sense, may be Peter's own story of Jesus. At the least, it gives us the story as it was told in Rome soon after Peter's martyrdom.[8]

Matthew and Luke Also Had a Written Collection of Jesus' Teachings: "Q"

There are also more than two hundred verses in both Matthew and Luke which cannot have been copied from Mark because they do not occur in that Gospel. These two hundred or more verses are so nearly alike in the two Gospels that most scholars believe that they must come from one common written source. Almost all of them report sayings attributed to Jesus. A reader wishing to confirm the idea that the two Gospels appear to be using the same source may compare such passages as the following:

Matthew	Luke
5:39–44	6:27–31
6:9–18	11:2–4
8:19–22	9:57–60
13:31–33	13:18–21

At times one of the writers seems fuller in his report, at times the other. Therefore, it seems more likely not that one is copying from the other, but that each is copying from some now lost manuscript.

Of course it cannot be absolutely proved that such a document ever existed.[9] However, there is such widespread agreement concerning such an early collection of Jesus' teachings that it has been commonly given the name "Q" (from the German word *Quelle* meaning "source"). The document must have been older even than our Gospels of Matthew and Luke, perhaps as old as Mark itself (c. A.D. 65). Could a copy be found today, of course millions of dollars could not buy it!

Using These and Other Sources, Our Writers Composed Their Gospels

We are now ready to describe what seems the likely origin of the Gospels as we have them.

Mark was written about A.D. 65, following the death of Peter, by Peter's younger disciple and interpreter. Mark is based on the stories told by Peter himself in his preaching and teaching.

Matthew was composed between A.D. 80 and 90 by a writer who put together Mark's account of Jesus' deeds with the collection of Jesus' teachings now commonly designated as "Q." To these two sources he added the material peculiar to his Gospel, which scholars designate as "M."

For centuries this Gospel has borne the name of one of Jesus' twelve Apostles. Eusebius tells us that as early as A.D. 140 Bishop Papias wrote:

> So then Matthew recorded the oracles in the Hebrew tongue, and each interpreted them to the best of his ability.[10]

Two reasons make it highly unlikely, however, that the Gospel as we have it is the work of a Palestinian Jew such as Matthew, an actual Apostle and eyewitness of the events described. First, an eyewitness would not have copied so extensively from Mark's admittedly secondhand report. Second, a Palestinian Jew would probably not have quoted from the Greek translation of the Old Testament (called the Septuagint). A Palestinian disciple would have quoted from the original Hebrew. Yet, where the Greek version of the Old Testament differs from the Hebrew, this writer almost always bases what he says on the Greek Septuagint's version. He quotes from the Septuagint so often that it seems clear that he is himself a Greek-speaking Jew, one of the hundreds of thousands of such "Hellenists" living outside Palestine, not one who followed Jesus in Galilee.

How, then, did the name of Matthew get attached to our Gospel? Though it can be only an attractive conjecture, it has been suggested that the Apostle Matthew was in fact the author of "Q." "Q" was the *logia*, or collection of sayings, attributed to Matthew by Papias. The editor who joined Mark's account of Jesus' deeds to "Q," Matthew's account of Jesus' teachings, attributed his work to Matthew as the source of most of what in his Gospel was different from Mark's.

If this theory is true, it means that Matthew does contain many firsthand recollections of the teachings of Jesus. It must be said, however, that this is only one theory and, again, is only attractive conjecture.

In much the same way, but with somewhat different emphases, *Luke* produced his Gospel, also probably in the early eighties. He too added to Mark and "Q" distinctive material which scholars designate by the letter "L."

As early as A.D. 175, we find references to this Gospel as the work of Luke, the companion of Paul. While this identification has been disputed, it still seems the simplest explanation. The argument for it runs as follows: Luke 1:1–4 contains a brief preface to the Gospel addressed to one Theophilus. Acts 1:1 is apparently addressed to the same person and refers to an earlier book, almost certainly the Gospel. The two books, then, are by the same author. Acts, in turn, from chapter 16:10 on, has frequent stories told in the first person ("God had called *us*," "*we* made a direct voyage," etc. [Acts 16:10—11]). The author appears to be claiming to have been a companion of Paul during much of the latter part of Paul's life. Coupled with this is the fact that in Colossians 4:14 Paul speaks of his companion "Luke the beloved physician" and 2 Timothy 4:11 speaks of the faithfulness of someone named Luke. Luke appears in Paul's letters, but only at places where Acts might suggest that the author was present. He is not so prominent that a Gospel would have been attributed to him had he not written it. Therefore, it is argued, the tradition that Luke is the author seems valid.

This view has been strongly attacked by many scholars, who point to apparent differences between the life of Paul as one might reconstruct it from Paul's letters and the account of Paul's life in Acts. However, the view that Paul's companion Luke is the author is still widely held.[11]

Ancient and consistent tradition attributes the Gospel According to *John* to one of the most prominent of Jesus' twelve Apostles. The church historian Eusebius quotes an earlier source as reporting:

> Last of all, John, perceiving that the external facts had been made plain in the gospel, being urged by friends, and inspired by the Spirit, composed a spiritual gospel.[12]

John, however, is quite different from the other three Gospels. The question of its date and authorship are very complex. There are strong reasons for questioning the traditional view. Because of the problems involved, and because the Fourth Gospel is in many ways the climax of the New Testament, this Gu i ie will delay discussion of John until chapter 13.

The First Three Gospels, the "Synoptics," May Easily Be Compared

In content, in origin, and in structure, the first three Gospels are much alike. Because, as we shall see, they may be easily compared by being placed in parallel columns, they are often grouped together. Their common title, the "Synoptics," means that they "see together" the life of Christ.

We have seen that they are mutually related in origin. Adopting B.H. Streeter's "four document hypothesis,"[13] one may chart their relationships in this way:

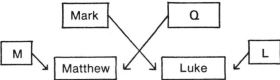

Matthew combines Mark and "Q" with his particular material, "M." Luke combines Mark and "Q" with his particular material, "L." Each arranged the order of this material for his own purposes. But the result is still quite similar. (Most Bibles, in the margins or in footnotes, will have cross-references to help the reader compare how the different Gospels tell the same stories.)

Any book called a *harmony* of the Gospels will place the Synoptics' accounts side by side for easy comparison. For example, the three Gospels tell the story of how Jesus healed Peter's mother-in-law. Here are the accounts:

Matthew 8:14–17	Mark 1:29–34	Luke 4:38–41
And	And *immediately* he left the synagogue,	And he arose and left the synagogue,
when Jesus entered Peter's house,	and entered the house of Simon and Andrew, with James and John.	and entered Simon's house.
he saw his mother-in-law lying sick with a fever;	Now Simon's mother-in-law lay sick with a fever, and *immediately* they told him of her. And he came and	Now Simon's mother-in-law was ill with a *high* fever, and they besought him for her. And he stood over her and
he touched her hand,	took her by the hand and lifted her up,	
and the fever left her.	and the fever left her. . . .	rebuked the fever, and it left her. . . .
That evening they brought to him many who were	That evening, at sundown, they brought to him all who were sick or	Now when the sun was setting, all those who had any that were sick with various diseases brought them to him;
possessed with demons;	possessed with demons. And the whole city was gathered together about the door.	
and he	And he healed many who were sick with various diseases,	and he laid his hands on every one of them and healed them.
cast out the spirits with a word. . . .	and cast out many demons;	And demons also came out of many, crying, "You are the Son of God!" But he rebuked them,
	and he would not permit the demons to speak. because they knew him.	and would not allow them to speak, because they knew that he was the Christ.

*This was to fulfil what
was spoken by the prophet
Isaiah,* "He took our infirmities and bore our diseases."

Certain words have been italicized so that typical differences of emphasis may be noted, even in so short a story.

Matthew, writing to Jewish readers to present Jesus as the promised Messiah, quotes from the Jewish scriptures, as he so often does, a passage which he sees Jesus as fulfilling.

Mark, typically picturing Jesus as a man of action, twice uses a favorite word, "immediately." Often, as here, he gives vivid details which to some have suggested that he is reflecting Peter's eyewitness account.

Luke, a physician, seems here (and perhaps elsewhere) to take an interest in details of healing.

John, typically different from the Synoptics, does not tell this story.

The Synoptics, of course, differ in more ways that those here noted. They not only differ in emphasis and in the order in which they tell the stories, but they also seem at times to be in conflict in their reports of certain facts. Some of these differences will be noted in the next chapters.

Here, however, our purpose is to call attention to the essential agreement among the Synoptics as a basis for our study of the life and teachings of Jesus.

Finally, the Church Selected Our Four Gospels and the Other New Testament Books, Recognizing Them as an Authoritative "Canon"

The four Gospels contained in our New Testament were not the only ones written by early Christians. We have seen (page 29) how pious imagination provided stories of the boyhood of Jesus, with tales of his confounding his teachers and resurrecting dead playmates. Nor are the epistles which are found in our New Testament the only letters revered by early Christians. The Epistle of Clement (written about A .I. 96) seems to have been regarded as authoritative by many churches. Our book of Acts had its rivals, too. The Acts of John, for example, described the sufferings and triumphs of that Apostle. It reported that one night he had to sleep in a bed so infested with bedbugs that John at last informed their leader that he was an Apostle and needed exclusive use of the bed. Obediently the insects filed out, only to return as the Apostle left the next morning.

Not only did other books compete for acceptance by the church, but several books now found in our New Testament are not included in early lists. Second Peter, Hebrews, James, and Revelation were among those whose authority was disputed or only slowly accepted.

Gradually, however, the twenty-seven books which form our New Testament were recognized as the New Testament "canon" (from the word for "measuring rod" or "ruler"), the church's rule for faith and practice. The Synod of Carthage (A.D. 397) made official what had already been widely accepted in the church.

The acceptance of these books—and only these books—as the New Testament canon seems to have been based on such beliefs as the following:

1) These books were regarded, rightly or wrongly, as the works of Apostles and famous leaders of the early church. Though few now would attribute Hebrews to the Apostle Paul, the belief that he wrote it undoubtedly helped establish it in the minds of church members as authoritative. Other books were accepted as they were attributed to other great men of the early church.

2) These books were regarded as inspired by the Holy Spirit. We have noted that they were the work of human authors and that our Gospels were the product of a kind of historical research. This, however, does not mean at all that the church did not find the Holy Spirit active in the entire process of the writing of its sacred books. God, they were sure, had guided the writers to give the church the Good News through these human agents. The inspiration of these books was borne in upon them as they read these little volumes and in them were confronted with the figure of Jesus and the call to the decision of faith. Readers still have this experience today.

3) These books stood closest to the crucial events of the life, death, and resurrection of Jesus. It was, the church believed, in Jesus Christ that God had revealed himself. No more books could or need be added to the canon, they believed, since that revelation was complete in the mighty act of God these books described. Only at the return of Christ could something really new be added. The canon was complete because it pointed to Christ, who was complete.

It is, therefore, to the Gospels' story of his life and teachings that we turn in the next chapter.

IV The Gospel According to Matthew

E. J. Goodspeed writes:

> The Gospel of Matthew is the most successful book ever written. It has had the largest circulation, exerted the greatest influence, and done the most good.[1]

Though it was probably not the first Gospel to be written, from the earliest collections of the books that now make up our New Testament, Matthew seems always to have been placed first. Perhaps it was because the first Christians loved it most. It is with Matthew that we shall begin our study of the life and teachings of Christ.

Outline and Emphases

Did Matthew think of Jesus as a kind of "new Moses"? So some scholars have argued. The baby Moses was hidden from Pharaoh; Jesus was hidden from Herod. Moses came out of Egypt; so did Jesus. Moses wandered in the wilderness; Jesus was tempted in the desert. From Mount Sinai, Moses delivered the Law; from another mountain Jesus delivered the Sermon on the Mount. Tradition attributed the first five books of the Old Testament, the Torah, the books of the Law, to Moses. Matthew groups Jesus' teachings into five major collections or discourses, the new "law" of the Christians. And when, after his resurrection, Jesus gives the Great Commission, in Matthew he does so from a Sinai-like mountain. That commission, as reported by Matthew, is not to preach the gospel to all nations, telling them good news. It is for "teaching them to observe all that I have commanded you," the new law (Matt. 28:20).

It may be going too far to say that Matthew collected Jesus' teachings into five discourses because there were five books of Moses. Perhaps his organization was simply for convenient, ready reference as his book was used by teachers instructing new converts. If the convert was not now to live by the old Jewish Law, how was he to live? As he pleased? By the time Matthew wrote, probably some Christians had misunderstood Paul as saying that. Matthew answers: By no means! "You have heard that it was said to the men of old . . . but I say to you." Matthew quotes Jesus repeatedly in the first body of teachings (Matt. 5). The old law was replaced by Jesus' commands.

Probably from the first century to the twentieth, students have memorized the outline of Matthew by counting off the five discourses on the fingers of one hand. (Jewish teachers were fond of numerical helps to the memory.) Between each of the following discourses, Matthew incorporated stories of Jesus' life, taken mostly from Mark:

1) How are citizens of the kingdom to live? The Sermon on the Mount provided clear guidance, set in relationship to Jewish law, tradition, and practice (Matt. 5—7).

2) How are traveling preacher-disciples to conduct themselves on their evangelistic journeys? Jesus' words as he sent out the Twelve supplied the answers (Matt. 10).

3) What were those parables Jesus told? Matthew gathered seven and put them together for ready reference (Matt. 13).

4) How shall Christians conduct themselves toward each other and as they face persecution? Jesus' words about humility and sacrifice, as he journeyed toward Jerusalem and his own martyrdom, provided the answer (Matt. 18—20).

5) How will it all end? Matthew collected Jesus' eschatological sayings, predictions of the future and the end of the world, as a final discourse (Matt. 24—25).

Note how Matthew even marks each of these discourses with the phrase "When Jesus had finished these sayings"(Matt. 7:28; 11:1; 13:53; 19:1; and 26:1).

Add the stories of Jesus' birth and infancy at the beginning and of his death and resurrection at the end, fill in between the discourses with miracle stories and stories of Jesus' growing conflicts with his enemies, and the student in the first century or the twentieth finds in Matthew an easily remembered manual for Christian faith and practice.

But it was not simply as in some sense a "new Moses" that Matthew interpreted Jesus. Rather, he saw Jesus as the fulfillment of *all* the Old Testament. Leaf through the first few chapters of Matthew in any modern translation which sets off Old Testament quotations as though they were poetry, and one will see how time after time Matthew quotes from the Jewish scriptures. Fifteen times he uses the word "fulfil," often in some phrase such as "All this took place to fulfil what the Lord had spoken by the prophet." So convinced was Matthew that the whole of the Old Testament was fulfilled in Christ that he could see every detail of Jesus' life as somehow foreshadowed there and could speak of passages in the Old Testament as related to Jesus in ways which would be more acceptable to his Jewish-Christian readers in the first century than to more "scientific" interpreters in the twentieth.

For example, Matthew sees the infant Jesus' return from Egypt as fulfilling the words originally spoken of all Israel's deliverance from the land of Pharaoh. "Out of Egypt have I called my son"(Matt. 2:15; Hos. 11:1). Seeing Jesus as in some sense a "new Moses," he could interpret the story of the Exodus—in ways modern scholars might call "figuratively"—as referring also to Jesus. Similarly, the prophecy in Isaiah 7:14 of a child to be named Immanuel as a sign of deliverance in Isaiah's day could be interpreted as referring to the newly born Immanuel—Deliverer, Jesus.

It is most especially as the prophesied king whose coming ushers in the prophesied kingdom that Matthew presents Jesus. Almost every saying and story of the Gospel can be understood as in some sense related to that theme.

Jesus' ancestry is traced through the kings of Judah. The birth stories set Jesus "who has been born king of the Jews" in contrast to King Herod. John the Baptizer announces that the kingdom is coming, baptizes Jesus, who then must battle through with Satan the meaning of the heavenly voice which has addressed Jesus with a royal title. Jesus' first preaching is summarized, "Repent, for the kingdom of heaven is at hand." Matthew 5–7 gives the new "law" of the kingdom. Kingly words of authority are followed by deeds of authority (Matt. 8–9), astonishing the crowds. Conflicts arise as the kingdom is proclaimed by Jesus and his disciples. Matthew 13 reports seven parables of the kingdom. At the "Great Confession," Peter and the disciples hail Jesus with titles reserved for the Messianic king. Still speaking of the kingdom, Jesus goes to Jerusalem. There, as he is crucified, there is placed above his head that same title, "The King of the Jews" (Matt. 27:37). He dies, wearing a crown, but a crown of thorns. Soon, however, the risen Christ in Matthew announces "All [kingly] authority in heaven and on earth has been given to me. Go, therefore and make disciples of all nations," teaching them to obey the king's commands.

No literary masterpiece such as the books of the New Testament can be described in a simple outline without threat of serious distortion. Matthew is a complex weaving together of themes and counter-themes. We have already given one outline, focusing on one emphasis of Matthew. But the following outline, centered on what seems even more a major theme of the book, the promised king and his kingdom, will provide the framework around which this chapter will survey the Gospel.

Subject Matter	Chapters in Matthew	Theme
Birth and Infancy	1—2	The King Is Born
Baptism and Temptation	3—4	The King Prepares
The Sermon on the Mount	5—7	The Kingdom Is Proclaimed
Miracle Stories, the Disciples, Opposition	8—15	Conflicting Responses to the King
The Great Confession	16—17	The King Is Recognized
Teachings on the Way to Jerusalem	18—20	The Cost of the King's Company
The Last Week and Easter	21—28	The King Is Crowned

With this overview we turn now to a part-by-part study of the Gospel.

Birth and Infancy—The King Is Born—Matthew 1—2

"Where is he who has been born king of the Jews?" the mysterious magi inquire (Matt. 2:2). Matthew answers first of all, in effect, "Squarely in the middle of the royal Davidic line of true Judean kings."

The Gentile Luke traces Jesus' ancestry from Adam, father of all men. But to Matthew, Jesus is the son of King David of Israel and the son of Abraham, the father of the Chosen People (Matt. 1:1).

It is through David and Solomon and the other kings that Jesus' ancestry is traced. The whole picture is so perfect to Matthew that he must describe it with the use of sevens, the perfect, sacred number beloved of Jewish teachers. The whole ancestry from Abraham to Jesus is grouped in three pairs of sevens. It did not matter to Matthew that one must count some ancestor twice or there are only forty-one names on the list and that comparison with 1 Chronicles 3:11–12 suggests that some names have been dropped. Matthew is using a Jewish teacher's way of subtly telling his readers that Jesus is the perfect prince of the royal line.

Luke tells the story from Mary's point of view, but Matthew concentrates on Joseph. (We will defer discussion of the meaning of the virgin birth until our comments on Luke in the next chapter.)

As we meet Mary and Joseph, they are engaged but not yet married. "Betrothal," or engagement, however, was a formal and very binding affair in Judea, with a public exchange of vows and the giving of a ring. Such betrothals often lasted a full year before the actual wedding. Couples were normally betrothed in their teens, brides in their early teens. There is no biblical basis for the tradition that Joseph was an old man.

Shocked at the discovery that his bride-to-be is pregnant, Joseph is ready to break the engagement. But an angel reassures him. Jesus is to be the fulfiller of prophecy. His name Jesus means "Savior"; the title Emmanuel means "God with us." Joseph, reassured that a miracle is taking place, goes ahead with the marriage.

Who are the "Wise Men" who come seeking the true-born "king of the Jews" in the court of the puppet pretender? For Matthew they seem to represent the foreigners of the Gentile world who at the beginning of the story give a foretaste of the end. Matthew's is the most Jewish of the Gospels, repeatedly, in every way it can, presenting Jesus as the promised Jewish Messiah. Yet it is Matthew who at the end of the Gospel specifically speaks of "all nations" as destined to come under the rule of this king. As a hint of that end even from the beginning, he tells of the worshipers from the East.

Their number is not given. Pious legend once set their number at twelve, later at three. Perhaps Matthew thinks of them as magi, Persian priests and astrologers, worshipers of the god of light, who wore round felt hats and long white robes. (The English word "magician" comes from "magi.") Modern astronomers have associated the star with the conjunction of Saturn, said to have been associated in the ancient world with the Jews, and Jupiter, symbol of kingship. This conjunction took place in 7 B.C., appeared, disappeared, and reappeared, as seems to have been the case with the Christmas star (Matt. 2:7–10).

Such speculation, however, may be a modern effort to read Matthew's story asking questions about history and science of an account in which the author intends rather to express theological truth. Matthew's only interest is that these Gentiles learn from Micah's prophecy (Matt. 2:5–6), journey with heavenly guidance to the ancestral home of the great King David, and there bring tribute to the newborn "king of the Jews." Having fulfilled their prophetic task, they disappear into the night.

However, that other king, Herod, remains. So fearful for his throne, as we have seen, that he would murder even members of his own family, Herod is pictured as slaughtering every male infant in the village of Bethlehem. Even here, Matthew is sure, Herod is unwittingly fulfilling Scripture (Matt. 2:17–18). But Jesus, like Moses before him, escapes the cruel king, and after crossing the nearby border into Egypt, outside Herod's power, makes his exodus from Egypt some time later. Even then the family takes up residence, not back at Bethlehem, but nearly a hundred miles to the north in Nazareth.

From the beginning, Matthew is saying, there is conflict over King Jesus and the kingdom of God.

Baptism and Temptation—The King Prepares—Matthew 3—4

Some fascinating possibilities are opened up by the fact that the traditional location of Jesus' baptism is almost within sight of the cave in which were found the first Dead Sea Scrolls.

As news of the buried treasures of the Qumran commune spread west, a few scholars created a sensation by proposing that Jesus must once have been a member of an Essene community. That suggestion has been largely abandoned. But if John the Baptizer had been associated with these holy ascetics, a number of questions may be answered. Why was he there in the wilderness, quoting Isaiah, denouncing the sins of the city, baptizing, and preparing for the coming of the Messiah? At least the discovery of the Essene library lets us know that John was not the only Jew in that wilderness or the only one with concerns of this kind. Here are some parallels between John and the Qumran people:

—Both had left the city for the rough, wild-West-like wilderness in the region of the Dead Sea.

—Both led ascetic lives. John is pictured as wearing skins and eating grasshoppers. The Essenes renounced conventional family life and luxury.

—Both renounced the sins of society. John preached against the Pharisees and Sadducees so vehemently that Matthew pictures him as calling them sons of snakes!

—Both practiced a purification by water, some kind of ceremony related to forgiveness of sins.

—Both looked for the imminent coming of the Messiah and his kingdom.

—And the verse of Isaiah which Matthew uses to introduce his account of John the Baptizer is one repeatedly quoted in the Dead Sea Scriptures:

> The voice of one crying in the wilderness:
> Prepare the way of the Lord . . .   (Matthew 3:3)

Matthew summarizes John's message in one sentence, "Repent, for the kingdom of heaven is at hand" (Matt. 3:1).

Whatever else that coming kingdom meant to John, it was to be a time of cosmic judgment. "Every tree therefore that does not bear good fruit is cut down and thrown into the fire" (Matt. 3:10).

The crowds flocked to hear this wilderness preacher with the odd clothes and the threatening message. There seems reason to believe that popular Jewish thought of the time had regarded the era of the prophets as over. No more prophets would come until the kingdom should dawn at the Messianic age. But now here was a prophet indeed, in the very pattern of the ancient Elijah, announcing the kingdom. A century and more after Jesus, there were traces of a John the Baptizer cult, still followers of the desert preacher.

Yet as Matthew describes him, John regarded his mission as only one of preparation. "I baptize . . . with water . . ., but he who is coming after me is mightier than I." He pictured that coming one also in terms of cosmic judgment. "His winnowing fork is in his hand" (Matt. 3:11–12).

At this point one must separate John from the Essenes. They had retreated from the world, as do monks to a monastery. John drew the world to him and sought to prepare the masses for what was coming. And while the Essenes dreamed of that which should come, Matthew tells us that John recognized the One, already come in Jesus.

Eager always to present Jesus in an exalted way, Matthew adds to Mark's account the report that John proposes that he should be baptized by Jesus, not the other way around. But Jesus identifies himself with John's movement. "Let it be so now" (Matt. 3:15). John baptizes him.

The significance of the baptism for Jesus, however, comes not in something John does, but in something the Spirit of God does. Jesus, Matthew tells us, hears a "voice." There is no indication that the crowd heard the voice. Apparently we are to understand this as an inner experience. "This is my beloved Son, with whom I am well pleased" (Matt. 3:17).

Footnotes in many Bibles cross-reference the two phrases of this "voice" to two passages of the Old Testament. "This is my son" may be derived from Psalm 2. That psalm appears to have been a coronation song for a Hebrew king, given the exalted title "Son of God." After the Hebrew monarchy perished, it was regarded as a prophecy of the coming of the great Messiah king.

But the phrase "my beloved Son, with whom I am well pleased" has a completely contrasting origin. It seems to echo Isaiah 42:1, the first passage of the songs of the "Servant of the Lord." That servant is given as "a light to the nations" (Isa. 42:6). But the salvation which the servant brings comes through vicarious suffering.

> He was despised and rejected by men;
>   a man of sorrows, and acquainted with grief;
> . . . .
> Surely he has borne our griefs
>   and carried our sorrows;
> . . . .
> But he was wounded for our transgressions,
>   he was bruised for our iniquities;
> upon him was the chastisement that made us whole,
>   and with his stripes we are healed.   (Isaiah 53:3–5)

If the "voice" was recalling these passages, what we are to understand is this: at the time of his baptism, two ideas are borne in upon Jesus' soul. Of how he has lived and how he has thought of himself previously, Matthew gives us only one hint: Matthew 13:55 implies that Jesus' neighbors in Nazareth thought of him as living quite an ordinary life. But now Jesus feels a double and apparently conflicting call:

1) He is to be the promised king, the Messiah, so exalted that he could be called "Son of God," to whom the psalmist could picture God as promising, "I will make . . . the ends of the earth your possession. You shall break them with a rod of iron . . ." (Ps. 2:8–9).
2) He is to be the Suffering Servant who will be a "light to the nations" by giving his life vicariously for the world.

Careful search of rabbinic literature has yet to discover any Jewish writer of the time who put these two ideas together. The conquering Messiah was one thing. The Suffering Servant was regarded as something else, probably persecuted Israel itself.

Now, however, Jesus at the same time feels himself called to be the Savior of the world and yet to save it by suffering and dying for it.

Mark describes Jesus' reaction as being that the Spirit "drove" him into the wilderness. Matthew tells us that for forty days he did not even eat. Alone in the desert he must battle through the meaning of the apparent revelation that has come. What can it mean that he is to be King and Servant at the same time?

Television cameras, of course, cannot record spiritual struggles. Matthew, in pictorial terms, describes Satan as though he stood visibly before Jesus, addressed him audibly, and took him physically to various places. The meaning behind his graphic language, however, is that of Jesus' wrestling with the implications of the "voice" which has come to him. The temptations are divided into three, Jewish writers having a love for that number. The first two are prefaced by the phrase translated "If you are the Son of God." The "if," however, might validly be translated "since": "Since you are the promised king. . . ." The temptations offer three alternative paths to Messiahship.

1) Jesus could be a bread king, an economic Messiah. He replies that food is not what really matters (Matt. 4:3–4).

2) Jesus could be a wonder-working sensation. He could do a public dive off the pinnacle of the Temple and so impress the crowds that his recognition factor and popularity ratings would make him invincible (Matt. 4:5–7). Significantly, in the Synoptics the miracles ascribed to Jesus seem always to be intended to help people, never to make a display of his power.

3) He could become the conqueror the Zealots dreamed of, vanquishing the kingdoms of the world by the devil's own methods. The one who taught "Love your enemies" could never choose that (Matt. 4:8–11).

Each of these routes to Messiahship Jesus rejects with a verse of Scripture. Somehow he is to be the Messiah by being the Servant of God. Already, Matthew is suggesting, there are hints of the coming cross.

The Sermon on the Mount—The Kingdom Is Proclaimed —Matthew 5—7

"From that time Jesus began to preach, saying, 'Repent, for the kingdom of heaven is at hand'" (Matt. 4:17). In that one sentence Matthew summarizes Jesus' whole message.

It can hardly be questioned that the announcement of the kingdom of God was the heart of Jesus' preaching. The first verse of the Sermon on the Mount promises it (compare Matt. 5:3, 10, and 19). Virtually every parable begins "The kingdom of heaven is like . . ." (see Matt. 13). Such verses as Matthew 7:21; 8:11; 11:11; 16:19; 18:1 and 23:13 confirm its centrality throughout the Gospel. When Jesus sends out his disciples to preach, it is with the same message, originally announced by John the Baptist, "The kingdom of heaven is at hand" (Matt. 10:7).

That this summarizes Jesus' proclamation is clear. What is not so clear is what Jesus meant by it. Here are some divergent but widely held views.

1) The late Albert Schweitzer shocked the world of Christian scholarship with an interpretation commonly called *thoroughgoing eschatology*.[2] According to Schweitzer, when Jesus said that the kingdom was at hand, he meant that the end of the world was just about to occur. Many texts seem to support that view. When Jesus sends out his disciples to preach, he tells them, "You will not have gone through all the towns of Israel, before the Son of man comes" (Matt.

10:23). Following the Great Confession by Peter (see pages 50–52), Jesus announces, "Truly, I say to you, there are some standing here who will not taste death before they see the Son of man coming in his kingdom" (Matt. 16:28). His last discourse deals with the end of the world and includes the statement "Truly, I say to you, this generation will not pass away till all these things take place" (Matt. 24:34; see also pages 56–57). According to Schweitzer, Jesus became convinced that if he became the Suffering Servant prophesied in Isaiah, giving his life, God at Jesus' death would send the kingdom. When, on the cross, he realized that the end of the world did not seem to be coming, he cried in disillusionment, "My God, my God, why hast thou forsaken me?" (Matt. 27:46). While some Christians have been horrified at the suggestion that Jesus could have proclaimed a mistaken time-table about the kingdom, others have replied that disappointment was part of the suffering the Savior "tempted in all things like as we" had to endure.

2) The nineteenth-century *liberal view*, against which Schweitzer was reacting, proposed that Jesus thought of the kingdom as beginning first with his followers but gradually growing to include the whole world. The kingdom is compared to seeds the sower sows (Matt. 13:3), a grain of mustard seed which grows into a tree (Matt. 13:31), and the yeast which will leaven a whole lump of dough (Matt. 13:33). Liberals liked to quote from Luke 17:20–21, "The kingdom of God is not coming with signs to be observed . . . for behold, the kingdom of God is in the midst of you" (or within you). The kingdom, they said, was simply the response by more and more people to the rule of God in their hearts, an inner, growing fellowship.[3]

3) British scholar C. H. Dodd proposed a view often called *realized eschatology*.[4] According to Dodd, the kingdom actually did come with Jesus. Jesus, Dodd noted, defends himself to his enemies with these words, "But if it is by the finger of God that I cast out demons, then the kingdom of God has come upon you" (Luke 11:20). "The kingdom of God is in the midst of you" (Luke 17:21), wherever Jesus is. The first Christians went out to preach not just a future hope, but something which had already begun. The era of death was ended with Christ's resurrection. The new age had begun. The kingdom might look small as a grain of mustard seed now, but in the end its importance would be manifest to all.

4) More traditionally, many have understood the kingdom to mean *the church*.[5] With Jesus' death and resurrection the world did not come to an end, but the Christian church as such did begin. While Matthew is the only Gospel which pictures Jesus as using the actual word "church" (and it is only in two places in Matthew), all the Gospels describe Jesus as calling a company of disciples and establishing a fellowship with them at the Last Supper. The rest of the New Testament says relatively little about "the kingdom," but the word "church" is used more than a hundred times. Upon that church, its members believed, God poured out the Holy Spirit, inaugurating a new age.

Perhaps most Christian thinkers are inclined to synthesize elements from all of these views. That the calendar is divided into B.C. and A.D. bears witness to the fact that a new age did dawn with the coming of Jesus. At the same time, most Christians still look forward to a future coming. Jesus, it must be noted, stated that neither he nor anyone else could predict exactly when the end would take place (Matt. 24:36).

Our records, then, are not entirely clear about any schedule for the coming of the kingdom, implying that the kingdom is somehow both present and future. What is made quite clear, however, is how men and women are to respond to the announcement of the kingdom, how citizens of the kingdom are to live. Two paragraphs after Matthew has summarized Jesus' preaching as "Repent, for the kingdom of heaven is at hand," he begins three chapters of collected sayings of Jesus about the life-style of citizens of that kingdom. Matthew 5, 6, and 7 are commonly called the Sermon on the Mount. They compose probably the best-loved summary of what Jesus had to say.

A look at the cross-references in most Bibles will show that sayings which Matthew has grouped together in these chapters are reported by Luke as having been given at various times during Jesus' career. Luke 6 does report a "Sermon on the Plain," but it is much shorter than Matthew's three chapters, and such familiar parts of the Sermon on the Mount as the Lord's Prayer are related by Luke to quite different contexts. We have seen that chronological order was not as important to the Gospel writers as theological order or patterns helpful for teaching. Matthew apparently has grouped these sayings together and put them right at the beginning of his account of Jesus' teaching to let his readers know from the start what he regards as the main things Jesus had to say about the new "laws" of the dawning kingdom.

Whether they were put together by Matthew or originally delivered as one address, these sayings do follow each other in a logical order. Matthew 5—7 can be outlined in various ways, such as this:

—Introduction: All the joy of the kingdom of heaven is now at hand for those who are willing humbly to accept God's gift (5:1–16).

—With the coming of the kingdom, the *traditional laws* will no longer do. They are only halfway measures. Your King now commands complete purity, utterly unselfish love (5:17–48).

—The traditional *ceremonial practices* will not help either. God's kingdom is a matter not of the external signs of piety, but of the whole heart (6:1–18).

—The old *worldly concerns* must be forgotten, too. Food and clothes do not matter. You must concentrate on just one thing, God's rule, and leave everything else to God (6:18–34).

—Conclusion: In the final examination, the judgment, only those whose whole lives are pointed toward serving God in love of their fellowman can meet the tests of the Kingdom (Matt. 7).

Matthew, the good teacher, begins with three times three sayings in the easily remembered "beatitude" form. Since the word translated "blessed" could well be translated "happy," some have called these Jesus' rules for happiness. Others, however, have said that they should be read more nearly as exclamations: Oh, the happiness of the poor in spirit, for theirs is the kingdom of heaven!" A. M. Hunter begins each beatitude with "Congratulations!"

The emphasis in the beatitudes is on humility and openness to God and to one's fellows. "Poor in spirit" seems to mean "conscious of spiritual need," though some suggest it implies also identification with the poor and needy of the world. William Barclay identifies the happy mourner of verse 4 as one "whose heart is broken for the world's suffering and for his own sin, for out of his sorrow he will find the joy of God!"[6] The meek are those with power, but power under control. Mercy, purity, peacefulness, and a willingness even to undergo persecution are characteristics of citizens of the kingdom (Matt. 5:3–12). Such people are the kind who can carry out God's mission to the world, can be its "salt" and its "light."

The second half of the chapter focuses on the relationship of the kingdom's "law" to the Law of Jewish tradition. On the one hand, the old Law is not abolished. But it is transcended. The demands of the kingdom are even more radical than those of the Jewish scriptures (Matt. 5:17–20).

Twice, three specific examples of these radical demands are now given (Matt. 5:17–48): "You have heard that it was said, . . . but I say. . . ."Specific areas of application are to the old laws against murder, adultery, putting away a wife without divorce proceedings, false swearing, exacting more than just retribution, and hating anyone other than one's enemy. In each case Jesus' point is that the demands of the kingdom go so much further than the old Law that they make the old obsolete. Not only murder, but anger is now prohibited. Not only adulterous action, but lustful thoughts are forbidden. Not simply careless putting away of one's wife, but divorce itself is condemned. Not simply false swearing, but all swearing is forbidden, unnecessary because of the honesty of the citizens of the kingdom. Not simply justice in retribution, but *no* retribution coupled with active concern for those who wrong us, is Jesus' command. And the commandment to love can no longer be limited to loving one's neighbor. Even enemies are to be loved. Such commands as these about loving even one's enemies constitute the heart of Jesus' ethical teaching.

Having dealt with the old laws, Jesus now deals with the old ways of showing one's religion. Almsgiving, prayer, and fasting were three pious practices which distinguished the most devout Jews. Jesus seems really to be making fun of those who make a display of such rituals. He laughs at the Pharisee who blows a trumpet to attract a crowd before dropping a coin in a beggar's cup. Such people are hypocrites, actors. What matters is not public practice, but one's secret, inner concern (Matt. 6:1–18).

That concern must be an undivided loyalty to the kingdom. In the crisis of the kingdom's advent, there is no longer any time for concern for material things. No second master can be tolerated. There is no room left for worldly cares, nor any need for them. Only one thing matters: the kingdom of God and his righteousness (Matt. 6:19–34).

The coming of that kingdom means the coming of the judgment. But the standards by which we will be judged may be surprising. We ourselves will be judged by how judgmental we have been of other people. We will be judged by a Father's mercy; therefore we should treat others as we wish them to treat us. The standards are too narrow for most people. But those who can meet the tests of the kingdom can stand fast, no matter what storms may come (Matt. 7).

The beatitudes (Matt. 5:3–12), the Lord's Prayer (Matt. 6:9–13), and the Golden Rule (Matt. 7:12) have always been among the best-loved passages of the New Testament. The words about loving one's enemies (Matt. 5:44) and turning the other cheek (Matt. 5:39) have inspired not only Christians such as Martin Luther King, but also non-Christians such as the great nonviolent leader of Hindus, Mahatma Gandhi.

Miracle Stories, the Disciples, Opposition—Conflicting Responses to the King—Matthew 8—15

Curiously, Matthew 7 concludes, what startled the crowd most was not what Jesus said, but the way he said it. They "were astonished at his teaching, for he taught them as one who had authority, and not as their scribes." The typical Jewish rabbi claimed no authority for himself. He delighted rather in handing down what his teacher had said that *his* teacher had said. In utter contrast, a repeated refrain of the Sermon on the Mount had been, "You have heard that it *was* said . . . But *I* say . . . ." As we shall see, scholars debate in what sense, if any, Jesus claimed to be the Messiah. But evidently one could not hear such teachings as those collected in the Sermon on the Mount and doubt that the teacher regarded himself as somehow uniquely related to God's kingdom. The crowd had reason to be "astonished."

Repeatedly, therefore, the Gospel comments on the reactions of people to Jesus. Some interpreters have said that what we know about Jesus is not so much any historical facts as the impression he made on people, the effect he had on the lives both of enemies and of followers. By describing the reactions of others, the Gospel writers subtly challenge the reader to decide how he or she also will respond.

Having for three chapters described Jesus' *words* of authority, Matthew now describes his authoritative *deeds*. Matthew 8 and 9 are largely a collection of miracle stories with comments on the contrasting responses these actions of Jesus begin to elicit.

In direct violation of the Law, Jesus touches a leper (Matt. 8:1–4). Jesus does not contract leprosy. The leper *becomes clean!*

Jesus heals the servant of a Roman army officer who recognizes authority when he encounters it. This Gentile's response is contrasted with that of many of God's own people (Matt. 8:5–13). The Roman has shown *faith.*

Jesus' healing of Peter's mother-in-law leads to a gathering of a crowd of people around Jesus (Matt. 8:14–17). They *bring needs.*

No partial response to his authoritative call will do. "Leave the dead to bury their own dead." "Follow me," Jesus commands (Matt. 8:18–22). He demands the response of *commitment.*

Though people may hesitate, the winds and the sea *obey* him, and many men *marvel* (Matt. 8:23–27).

But the reactions can be negative. After he healed the demoniacs but caused a stampede among the hogs (Matt. 8:28–34), some people *begged him to leave.*

That negative reaction now begins to harden into opposition. Scribes are shocked when Jesus claims authority to forgive sins (Matt. 9:1–8). Jesus' willingness to fraternize with social and moral outcasts offends the Pharisees (Matt. 9:9–13). Even John's disciples are puzzled (Matt. 9:14–17). Yet, in spite of Jesus' deliberate effort to avoid the spread of stories about his healing (Matt. 9:27–31), "the report . . . went through all that district" (Matt. 9:18–26). By the end of chapter 9, though the crowds still wonder what to make of such a man, the Pharisees are ready to *attack Jesus as being in league with the prince of demons* (Matt. 9:32–34).

To summarize, Matthew repeatedly notes one or more of three kinds of response. Most people are simply amazed; they do not know what to think. A few are roused to hatred and begin to attack. But there are also a few who respond in faith and are healed, or even, like Matthew himself in Matthew 9:9, answer Jesus' call and become his disciples.

Matthew 10 is devoted to these disciples.

They are presented as an odd mixture, these twelve laborers in the kingdom "harvest" (Matt. 9:37–38).

Peter is always listed first, is mentioned far more often than any of the others, seems to be identified as the leader in such passages as John 21:15–19 and Matthew 16:13–20, and clearly is the spokesman of the earliest church in Acts 2. A rather consistent picture emerges of his character: talkative, impulsive, unstable, capable of cowardice but also of repentance. In view of the fact that the Gospel stories derive so largely from Peter through Mark, it is especially significant that the portrait we have of him is so honest, so far from flattering.

Andrew, his brother, seems less vocal, though it is noted that it was Andrew who first brought Peter to Jesus. John 1:35–42 identifies him as having been a disciple of John the Baptizer.

James and John were also fishermen. Mark 1:20 speaks of their being associated with their father and with "hired servants," which may imply a relatively prosperous, established fishing business. John is traditionally identified as the "disciple whom Jesus loved," referred to repeatedly in the Fourth Gospel and as the author of that Gospel. Such passages as Mark 5:37, 9:2, and 14:33 imply that these two brothers, along with Peter, constituted the inner circle of the Twelve. Their mother hoped that they would receive the highest places in the kingdom (Matt. 20:20–28). What James actually received was the first martyrdom among the disciples (Acts 12:2).

Of the rest little is said. Philip has a Greek name and is pictured in John 12:20–22 as instrumental in bringing certain Greeks to Jesus. Bartholomew is usually supposed to be the same as the Nathanael mentioned in John 1:47 as "an Israelite in whom is no guile," praise he so readily accepts that it may be intended to indicate that he is a Pharisee. Thomas is known as the doubter for his failure to believe in the first reports of the resurrection (John 20:24–29). Matthew is identified as a tax collector. Thus he was a social outcast, hated for collaborating with Rome. In complete contrast, Luke 6:15 calls the second Simon a Zealot, one of the militant opponents of the Romans. Of Thaddaeus and the other James we have no information even for conjecture. Last on the list, of course, is the traitor Judas. Later pious tradition told stories of the martyrdom of all but Judas.

Jesus sends them out with the same message John the Baptizer and Jesus had proclaimed earlier: "The kingdom of heaven is at hand" (Matt. 10:7). Chapter 10 now gives instructions to the disciples. They are to move rapidly. They are to expect but not to fear persecution. They are to heal as well as preach. Many scholars suggest that these sayings were remembered particularly and perhaps adapted for use by Early Christian evangelists after the resurrection.

Chapters 11 and 12 pick up again the story of the varied reactions to Jesus: the *questioning* of John, the *unrepentance* of the cities, the *faith* of those who will accept his invitation. By 12:14 the *opposition* has reached such intensity, brought to a crisis related to the healing on the Sabbath of a man with a withered hand, that the Pharisees enter into the first *plot to kill* Jesus.

The longest parable of Matthew 13 is a kind of explanatory analysis of these varied responses. The various kinds of people are compared to various kinds of soil, responding differently to the "seed" of the gospel.

More and more frequently now we are told that Jesus must withdraw from determined opposition. Herod's execution of John the Baptizer causes one withdrawal (Matt. 14:13). Even his popularity with the people after feeding multitudes twice necessitates withdrawals (Matt. 14:21–22; 15:38–39). An attack by the Pharisees and scribes over Jesus' failure to keep their traditions precedes another (Matt. 15:21). He is now forced to go to the borders of Galilee and even beyond (Mat. 15:21; 16:13). The last withdrawal takes Jesus all the way to Caes area Philippi.

The Great Confession—The King Is Recognized—Matthew 16—17

The Great Confession at Caesarea Philippi is the turning point in all three Synoptics. For the first time the "Messianic secret" is openly discussed. Instead of withdrawing from his enemies, Jesus henceforth moves toward the center of his opposition. In Matthew he now speaks of the founding of the church. For the first time he clearly announces his intention of dying on a cross. And he now summons his disciples to go with him to Jerusalem and to die. These are developments which merit careful study.

We have seen that Jesus has repeatedly been forced to withdraw from bitter opposition. By the time of the event described in Matthew 16:13-28, Jesus had retreated all the way to Caesarea Philippi, perhaps the farthest from Jerusalem he ever traveled. (The retreat described in 15:21 may have been about the same distance.) Here he was out of the reach of Herod Antipas, the Herod who had recently killed John the Baptizer. This distant location is itself significant.

Not only has Jesus withdrawn from enemies; he has retreated from crowds of followers attracted by bread and miracles. Far from claiming to be Messiah, he has repeatedly and sternly forbidden those whom he has healed to tell others about him (see Matt. 8:4; 9:30; Mark 1:25, 34; 3:12, etc.). The message with which he sent the disciples was that of the coming of the kingdom, not the coming of the promised Messiah. When John the Baptizer sent messengers to confront Jesus with the question "Are you he who is to come?" Jesus replied enigmatically. "Go and tell John what you hear and see: the blind receive their sight and the lame walk, lepers are cleansed and the deaf hear, and the dead are raised up, and the poor have good news preached to them. And blessed is he who takes no offense at me" (Matt. 11:4-6). Demons recognize him, and the crowd wonders. But Jesus refuses any title.

As early as 1901, the German scholar Wilhelm Wrede proposed an explanation for this "Messianic secret." The early church, he suggested, had faced a problem. The first preachers were proclaiming that Jesus was the promised Messiah. (In Greek the word is "Christ.") But those who had heard Jesus preach could object that Jesus never made any such claim. Mark, Wrede argued, therefore invented the "Messianic secret" idea. Jesus knew that he was Messiah— Mark claimed—and the demons repeatedly recognized him. But Jesus chose to keep his identity secret. Actually, Wrede believed, Jesus did not think of himself as the Messiah at all. His message concerned God and the kingdom, not himself.

While New Testament scholars since Wrede have had to deal with his question, by no means all have agreed with his solution to the mystery. If Jesus did not at least implicitly claim Messiahship, why was he crucified? To many it has seemed more likely that Jesus rejected such titles as "Messiah," "King," and "Son of God," not because he did not in some sense believe them properly his, but because his understanding of the nature of his Messiahship was so completely in contrast to the popular expectation. Jesus saw his role as being not that of a conqueror of Rome, but of the Suffering Servant who would give his life for humankind.[7] Only once did Jesus publicly claim the title Messiah. But that was at the moment when the claim was sure to bring about his death. In Mark 14:61-62, as Jesus is on trial for his life, he is challenged by the high priest: "Are you the Christ?" This time he replies without any equivocation, "I am."

The Synoptic writers hesitate to try to read Jesus' mind or to enter into or speculate about his self-consciousness. Some insight as to what Jesus thought of himself may be found in the story of Peter's Great Confession.

Now a fugitive in the mountains, with only his closest followers accompanying him, Jesus himself raises the question concerning his identity. "Who do men say that I am?"

The answers give us insight into the popular perception of Jesus. People generally regarded him as another in the distinguished line of prophets, another Elijah, Jeremiah, or John the Baptizer.

"But who do you say that I am?" Simon Peter replied, "You are the Christ." (Matt. 16:15):

With that confession, all kinds of new things suddenly begin to happen. In Matthew, Jesus accepts the title, blessing Peter for voicing it. With Peter's confession Jesus announces the founding of the church. Jesus announces that he is going to Jerusalem to die and he calls his disciples to accompany him, eventually to lose their own lives for his sake.

The meaning of Jesus' words to Peter have been the subject of bitter Protestant-Catholic controversy. To traditional Roman Catholics, the meaning has seemed simple. Jesus says, "You are Peter." (The word Peter means "rock.") "On this rock I will build my church" (Matt. 16:18). To Peter, Christ has given the keys of the kingdom. These keys Peter in turn has passed down to his successors, the bishops of Rome, the Popes.

Protestants have placed the emphasis on the confession, not on the man. If Peter becomes the foundation of the church, they have argued, it is simply that he is the first to voice this confession of faith in Jesus as the Christ. The power of the keys is given to the other Apostles too, in Matthew 18:18, to all the church of believers. Many passages in the New Testament show Peter as a leader in the church, Protestant thinkers have admitted, but none attributes the infallible authority of a Pope to Peter, much less to his successors.

The issue is not yet resolved.

In any event, no sooner has Jesus accepted the title Messiah and spoken of the church than he announces that he is going to Jerusalem to die. The disciples are shocked and protest vehemently. Instead of withdrawing his announcement, Jesus simply challenges them to come with him and to lose their lives too.

Just one week later, Jesus and three disciples are said to have experienced the only mystic vision of its kind recorded in the Gospels, the transfiguration. The disciples see Jesus with shining face, talking with the long dead Moses and Elijah (Matt. 17:1–8).

Yet once again Jesus announces his impending death (Matt. 17:22–23). And now the geographic notation become more pointed (Matt. 17:22, 24; 19:1; 20:17, 29; 21:1). He is on his way to Jerusalem and the cross.

Teachings on the Way to Jerusalem
—The Cost of the King's Company—Matthew 18—20

Three times Jesus is pictured as announcing that he is going to Jerusalem to die: Matthew 16:21; 17:22–23; and 20:18–19. Over the sayings which Matthew has collected to form chapters 18—20 falls the shadow of the cross. All are set in the context of the final journey to Jerusalem. While it may not be quite clear why every one of these sayings is recorded at this point, almost all can be seen as related to the concept of humility and loving sacrifice.

The disciples have recognized who Jesus is. Jesus has accepted the title "Messiah" or "Christ." But now he must help them understand the Servant's concept of salvation through sacrificial suffering.

It is not the ambitious, but those who have childlike humility who will be greatest in the kingdom, Jesus explains to these future leaders in Matthew 18:1–6.

Undivided loyalty is demanded (Matt. 18:7–9).

All souls, however insignificant or unworthy they may seem, are important in the kingdom. Therefore, citizens of the kingdom are to treat their brothers with the utmost loving patience. God has forgiven us. We must forgive others (Matt. 18:10–35).

Even the demands of sex may have to be denied in favor of the absolute demands of the kingdom (Matt. 19:10–12). Childlike humility is the key (Matt. 19:13–15). That kingdom may demand that one give away everything else simply to follow Christ (Matt. 19:16–22). The rewards of the kingdom are real, but they are for those who are willing to sacrifice, to be "last" rather than seeking to get ahead (Matt. 19:23–30).

God alone will decide who is to receive the various rewards of the kingdom (Matt. 20:1–16). Jesus himself will receive a cross, he reminds his followers (Matt. 20:17–19). When the mother of James and John, ambitious for her sons, asks that they be given the top places in the kingdom which they feel must surely now be about to be established, Jesus, the Servant-Messiah, explains, "Whoever would be great among you must be your servant, and whoever would be first among you must be your slave; even as the Son of man came not to be served but to serve, and to give his life as a ransom for many" (Matt. 20:26–28).

It is not the ambitious disciples, but two blind beggars whose eyes are opened (Matt. 20:34).

With these teachings the company has arrived at Jerusalem, the city where Jesus will die.

The Last Week and Easter
—The King Is Crowned—Matthew 21—28

The Gospels' story of Jesus' life is really the story of his death. More than one-fourth to nearly one-half of each of the Gospels is devoted to just one week, the last. What has been said of Mark would apply equally well to the other three: each Gospel is a passion narrative with a long introduction.

As we have seen, Matthew has used many literary devices to point us to what is coming. Now, as his story arrives at the account of Jesus' last week, the pace of the narration slows. The time sequence becomes clear as never before in the Gospel. We can trace Jesus' movements geographically and by the days of the week. From the night of his arrest, we can almost trace events hour by hour. The details are so full and vivid that many have suggested that an account of this last week must have been written before any of our present Gospels were set down.

Though scholars who challenge this chronology can be found, the traditional day-by-day sequence, celebrated by Christians in Holy Week ceremonies, seems well enough attested in Mark to be used as a framework for our study here.

Palm Sunday was the day of what has been called Jesus' "triumphal entry" (Matt. 21:1-11). The title is misleading. The little parade into Jerusalem was more in the nature of a nonviolent demonstration in the modern sense than anything military or "triumphant." On the surface, at least, nothing happened except that a group of Galilean pilgrims to the Passover feast shouted slogans while Jesus rode silently among them on a donkey.

However, more was involved. Matthew is literally correct when he writes that "This took place to fulfil what was spoken by the prophet" (Matt. 21:4). Zechariah 9:9 had foretold one who would be a king but who would come humbly riding on a donkey. A conquering king might enter a city riding in a war chariot. Zechariah had spoken of a king who would enter humbly, a king of peace. It may be that Jesus was deliberately acting out Zechariah's prophecy, publicly claiming, without saying a word, to be this kind of king. Some have spoken of this as an "acted parable,"[8] the first of three symbolic actions of Jesus during this last week. (The other two were the cleansing of the Temple and the Last Supper.)

Two facts support the view that Jesus may have been deliberately acting out his claim to this unique kind of Messiahship. First, there are indications that the entry was deliberately, perhaps even secretly arranged in advance, even with a kind of password for securing the donkey (Matt. 21:1-3). More important, while Jesus had previously forbidden any public claim that he was Messiah, on this day he seems to have accepted without protest the crowd's acclamation of him as "Son of David" (the great king).

Monday was the day of the cleansing of the Temple. Matthew makes it appear that this second "acted parable" took place on Palm Sunday, but Mark's Gospel, on which most of Matthew's report seems to be based, makes it clear that the casting out of the money-changers took place the following day.

At the time of the Passover, thousands of pilgrims from all over the Mediterranean world swarmed into Jerusalem. Obviously, a Jew who sailed from Ephesus or Corinth could not easily bring with him on the boat a lamb or even a pigeon for sacrifice (see Lev. 12:8). For the convenience of the pilgrims, such animals were sold in the Temple courtyard. Moreover, it was required that the sacrifices be bought with special coins. Those who swapped this Temple currency for the foreign money brought by the worshipers from many lands were allowed to make a sizable profit. The Passover had been commercialized; the Temple had become a market for profiteers.

Jesus was horrified. " 'My house shall be called a house of prayer,' " he quoted, "but you make it a den of robbers" (Matt. 21:13). For one moment, at least, he turned over tables and drove out these salesmen of piety-for-a-price.

For Jesus' enemies, this was the last straw. Mark 11:18 tells us that it was in reaction to this episode that the chief priests and scribes began the final plot which, four days later, resulted in Jesus' death.

Tuesday is often called "The Day of Conflict." Though they were ready now to kill him, Jesus' enemies were aware that he still had enormous support among a populace never far from riot and revolution. They therefore resolved to discredit him publicly by asking him questions which would have the effect of exposing the ignorance of the country carpenter. Matthew describes four such questions:

1) "By what authority are you doing these things, and who gave you this authority?" the religious authorities (the chief priests) demanded (Matt. 21:23). Jesus had received no official training as a rabbi. He had not been appointed a priest. Who was he to say what should and should not go on in the Temple and to claim to be a teacher in Israel?

Jesus' answer was to return the challenge with a question of his own: What authority did John the Baptizer have? He demanded that they answer. Unwilling to attack the revered memory of John, and aware that to admit that John—and by implication, Jesus—could have authority apart from official channels, the priests retired in confessed confusion.

Matthew here reports three parables which interpret the whole tragedy of the rejection of Christ by the Chosen People. Jesus' enemies were all the more frustrated (Matt. 21:45–46).

2) The Pharisees now took their turn. "Is it lawful to pay taxes to Caesar?" (Matt. 22:17). The question was designed to place Jesus in a hopeless position either way he answered. If he said "No," he could be prosecuted for advocating resistance to the Roman government. If he said "Yes," he would lose his popularity with the nationalistic crowd. Though on the surface Jesus' answer could be regarded as a clever evasion of a trick question, Christian interpreters see profound meaning in it. Jesus asked his hearers to note Caesar's picture and inscription on a Roman coin. Then he replied, "Render . . . to Caesar the things that are Caesar's, and to God the things that are God's" (Matt. 22:21). Civic responsibility goes hand in hand with true religion. We read that the frustrated Pharisees "marveled" and simply "went away."

3) It was the Sadducees' turn (Matt. 22:23–33). We have seen that this party rejected belief in a future life. Determined now to succeed where their opponents had failed, they came to Jesus with another trick question. Evidently they were aware that Jesus had expressed belief in a life beyond death. What, they asked him, will be the future state of a woman who on earth had seven husbands? Surely, it was implied, when she met all seven again in heaven, it would be a kind of hell!

Jesus gave a double reply. He said that there is no marriage in heaven, but more important, there is a future life. The basis on which he defended this faith was from that part of the Bible which the Sadducees themselves accepted as authority. God in Exodus 3:6 had identified himself in this way: "I am the God of Abraham, the God of Isaac, and the God of Jacob." "He is not God of the dead, but of the living." That is to say, God is a God who has a loving concern for living individuals. He will not simply let his people die.

Far from destroying his influence with the people, the Sadducees' question had brought Jesus new acclaim as a teacher (Matt. 22:33).

4) Finally, the Pharisees made a last attempt. This time, however, the question was a legitimate, if enormously difficult, one. Of all the many sayings of the Jewish scriptures, which is the greatest law? Jesus' answer this time was straightforward, and its report serves Matthew as a kind of summary of this aspect of Jesus' teaching: "You shall love the Lord your God with all your heart, and with all your soul, and with all your mind. This is the great and first commandment. And a second is like it. You shall love your neighbor as yourself. On these two commandments depend all the law and the prophets" (Matt. 22:37–40).

The questioning ends with a quotation by Jesus from Psalm 110, the passage from the Old Testament quoted more than any other in the New. As understood here and elsewhere, it pointed to the Messiah as greater even than David himself (Matt. 22:41–46).

Having put his enemies temporarily to flight, Jesus, in complete contrast to his pattern of withdrawal earlier in his ministry, now gives a lengthy and public denunciation of the scribes and Pharisees. The entire twenty-third chapter of Matthew is devoted to an attack in which he brands them as hypocrites, blind fools, whitewashed tombs, snakes, and children of hell! By the end of this day, leaders of all influential factions must have been ready to cooperate in destroying him.

The last of Matthew's five great collections of Jesus' teachings is in some ways the most puzzling. Matthew 24—25 contains Jesus' "Little Apocalypse," his teachings on eschatology, the doctrine of the last things, the end of the world.

We have already noted that there is great difference of opinion concerning how the sayings of Jesus about the end time are to be interpreted. On the one hand it might seem quite simple. "Truly, I say to you, this generation will not pass away till all these things take place" (Matt. 24:34). As it stands, such a verse seems to make clear that Jesus expected the end of the world within his lifetime.

Cosmic signs and catastrophes seem to be prophesied as preliminaries to the final cataclysmic event. The faithful are to stand fast, however, in the assurance of imminent deliverance.

More careful study, however, suggests that one must be cautious about accepting too certain a schedule. For one thing, it is to be noted that Jesus' discourse is in reply to two questions. The disciples ask: (1) When will the Temple be destroyed? and (2) When will the end of the world be? (Matt. 24:1–3). We have seen that Matthew put together sayings of Jesus on similar subjects even though they were spoken at different times. It is possible that some of the sayings of Jesus in Matthew 24 may be thought of as referring to the destruction of the Temple, which did occur in A.D. 70, within the lifetime of many of his hearers, rather than to the end of the world.

There are hints that Jesus expected a future for this world long enough that "this gospel of the kingdom will be preached throughout the whole world, . . . to all nations; and then the end will come" (Matt. 24:14).

And finally, it may be noted that Jesus flatly states that neither he nor anyone else knows either the day or the hour (Matt. 24:36). We are to be always ready, for no one knows when the end will be (Matt. 24:44; 25:13).

Rather, what we have in Matthew 24 is a discourse in the standard apocalyptic form which was beloved by Jews of the first century. That pattern has been described on pages 21–22. Almost all the characteristics of such literature described there appear in Matthew 24. In a sense Jesus is simply pictured as using a standard literary device. What is significant is the meaning he imparts to this pattern, the particular use to which he puts it. That characteristic, uniquely Jesus-like addition is found in the parable with which the discourse ends (Matt. 25:31–46).

In that parable one finds the standard imagery of conventional Jewish apocalyptic literature. There is the throne, the judgment, the division of the saved from the lost, and their sentencing to heaven or hell. Up until this point we have been on familiar ground.

But now a new standard of judgment is introduced. "As you did it to one of the least of these my brethren, you did it to me" (Matt. 25:40). The way one treats the poor, the sick, the prisoner, the least worthy, will in the end turn out to be the way one has treated the Judge! No other apocalypse before had proposed quite that!

According to Matthew, that was the last—and some would say the greatest—parable Jesus ever told.

Wednesday is conventionally referred to as the day of rest in Bethany. Jesus seems to have stayed in this suburb of Jerusalem with friends, walking the two or three miles into the city each morning.

Only two events are recorded. A woman enters the house where Jesus was staying and pours expensive ointment on his head. Jesus now accepts the gesture of worship without protest and interprets it as a prelude to his death (Matt. 26:6–13).

And on the same day, Judas makes his bargain to betray his Lord for thirty pieces of silver (Matt. 26:3–5, 14–16).

It is not entirely clear either what Judas did or why he did it. Since we read that the next night he led a band of police to the garden of Gethsemane, it seems likely that what he did for Jesus' enemies was to show them Jesus in a remote place. There they could arrest him without fear of the rebellious crowd and have him safely in the hands of Roman authorities by morning.

The only motivation given is money. It seems incredible, however, that one expecting to receive a high place in a kingdom about to be established at any moment should exchange an anticipated throne for thirty coins. Some have proposed that Judas was simply impatient. Jesus had been three days in what should have been his capital city. He had done nothing but talk. Judas hoped to force Jesus now to act, to begin the revolution Judas understood him to have been promising. Others have supposed that Judas had become completely disillusioned. The promised kingdom had not and would not come. He would make the best bargain he could. Thirty pieces of silver was better than nothing.

Maundy Thursday is the name traditionally given to the night of the Last Supper (Matt. 26:17–35).

The Passover, still faithfully celebrated today in the homes of millions of religious Jews, is a feast in which each family commemorates the rescue of the Hebrew people from Egypt in the days of Moses. Exodus 13:1–16 describes its institution. Each part of the meal was significant. The lamb was a sacrifice to God. The herbs were to be bitter, as a reminder of the sufferings of slavery. The bread was unleavened, for there had been no time for yeast to make dough rise on the night the Hebrews escaped. A son had died, the Exodus story said, in every home where the blood of the lamb was not sprinkled on the doorposts. The rescued people had been led by Moses to Mount Sinai, where they had entered into a covenant with God.

In conventionally Jewish fashion, Jesus ate the Passover with his disciples. But now he made this traditional ceremony a third "acted parable." As he broke the bread and passed it to his disciples, he announced, "This is my body." The cup, too, was given new meaning. "This is my blood of the covenant, which is poured out for many for the forgiveness of sins" (Matt. 26:26–29). A new covenant was being announced, with a new people. This covenant was to center on a new sacrifice, Jesus' own sacrifice, to be accomplished the next day. Variously called the Lord's Supper, the Communion service, or the Mass, the reenactment in different forms of this meal has been the heart of Christian liturgy from that time on.

Some years ago a resolution was proposed in the Knesset, the Israeli Parliament, that the condemnation of Jesus of Nazareth be declared invalid. The one who made the motion did not mean to determine one way or another as to whether Jesus was guilty of the charges on which he was executed. He simply noted that there appeared to be such irregularities in the judicial procedures that the trial should be declared illegal. The Knesset rejected the proposal on the grounds that they could scarcely reverse an action of a Jewish Sanhedrin of more than 1,900 years ago, its court records long ago lost. The resolution did have the merit, however, of noting that the report of the trial, at least as we have it, suggests a kind of legal lynching.

Seized in secret, Jesus is tried at midnight, evidently by enemies concerned to push through a verdict of guilty. No convincing witnesses, however, could be found to accuse Jesus of any major crime. But now the high priest places Jesus on the witness stand. He has heard a rumor, at least, that Jesus claims to be the Messiah. Perhaps there is an opportunity here. "Tell us if you are the Christ." (Matt. 26:63). Though Matthew elaborates Jesus' answer, Mark 14:62 quotes Jesus as giving the completely unambiguous reply, "I am." That declaration on the part of such a man was enough. It was blasphemy. To the Jews blasphemy was a capital offense. The trial was no longer needed. The torture could begin.

Outside, the other disciples had run away, and Simon Peter was denying that he had ever heard of Jesus (Matt. 26:69–75).

On *Good Friday* the Romans crucified Jesus.

Jewish readers have sometimes found what has seemed an anti-Semitic bias on the part of certain New Testament writers, including Matthew. Whether that bias is really present or not, anti-Semitism has surely been one of the besetting sins of Christians down through the centuries. So-called Christians have branded Jews as "Christ-killers" and have harassed and persecuted them in horrible ways throughout subsequent history. Such actions, however, really have not the slightest justification in the Gospels. Whatever their private prejudices may have been, the biblical writers are agreed in presenting the crucifixion as the sin of all humankind, not of any one particular race. The spiritual is wisely addressed to all people when it asks rhetorically, "Were you there when they crucified my Lord?" The implied answer, of course, is "Yes," whatever the racial or religious background of the one who answers. This, surely, is the fundamental meaning of the New Testament's teaching about responsibility for Jesus' death.

But even if one deals with the historical facts more narrowly, the responsibility rests equally on Romans and other Gentiles as well as on Jews. Apparently Jewish courts were not allowed to carry out sentences requiring capital punishment. Therefore Jesus was taken to the Roman procurator (governor), Pilate. Jesus gave this lackey of the Roman emperor the only response he deserved: "he gave him no answer" (Matt. 27:14). Seeking to curry favor with the people, Pilate offered to release to the gathering crowd one political prisoner, apparently hoping they would choose the innocent Jesus. Stirred up by their leaders, however, the mob demanded Barabbas, probably a Zealot. Unable to find any crime in

Jesus, but unwilling to stand against the crowd, Pilate attempted to abdicate responsibility by washing his hands of the whole affair (Matt. 27:24). It was a futile gesture.

Now at last the King was crowned, but with thorns (Matt. 27:27–31).

Crucifixion was death by slow torture through exposure. Regarded as too cruel for use on Roman citizens, it was a death for criminal slaves. In spite of familiar pictures to the contrary, it seems usually to have been the case that the condemned prisoner carried not the entire cross, but only the crosspiece to the place of execution. The upright section of the cross would already have been planted in the ground. It was the custom that the charges on the basis of which a criminal was executed were placed over his head. The inscription over Jesus' head read: "This is Jesus the King of the Jews". (Matt. 27:37).

The story of the death is told with an economy of words, suggesting rather than spelling out the details of the torture. Brief mention is made of the carrying of the cross, the refusal of a pain-killing drug, the ridicule from the crowd and even from the others being executed, and the continuing thirst.

The climax of suffering is indicated in one horrible cry, often called the "cry of dereliction" It was so firmly rooted in Christian tradition that it was remembered even in its original form in the Aramaic, the Hebrew dialect Jesus spoke. "Eli, Eli, lama sabachthani?" "My God, my God, why hast thou forsaken me?" Some scholars, recognizing that these words are a quotation from Psalm 22, have interpreted them as implying that Jesus was quoting a Psalm which ends with assurance of victory. There is no hint, however, in the Synoptics that the "happy ending" of the Psalm was in Jesus' mind. Rather it is the cry of the utmost spiritual torment. Even God seemed to have abandoned Jesus now.

One might imagine that the Christian church would have tried to cover up the fact that its founder died in an agony of defeat. The ancient world still thrilled to Plato's story of the death of Socrates: calm, content, unconcerned in the face of death. Yet far from concealing the story of Jesus' death in misery, the New Testament writers made it the very center of their accounts. The spiritual torment was for them even more important than the physical torment.The disappointment, loneliness, and sense of failure which overcame Jesus are made as clear as his bodily suffering. Socrates died in the complacency of self-assured reason; Jesus died in the agony of self-sacrificial love. Even the pagan executioners were moved. "Truly this was the Son of God!" (Matt. 27:54).

On *Easter* the good news began to be spread: Jesus is risen!

As will be noted in the next chapter, our accounts of the events of Easter and the days immediately following it are difficult to put together. No description of the actual resurrection is given. The order and even the location of the appearances of the risen Christ are reported differently in the different accounts. The early records agree completely, however, on one great fact: he rose. For the first Christians that was the only fact that mattered.

Explanations which are alternatives to the Christian belief that Jesus really rose have been less than satisfying. Matthew seems to have been familiar with an attempt to brand the story of the resurrection as a hoax perpetrated by the disciples, who stole the body of Jesus in the night (Matt. 28:11–15). Efforts have been made from time to time to reassert this idea. But men do not go out and "turn the world upside down" inspired by a self-perpetrated hoax. Others have suggested that the disciples were the victims of visions, hallucinations brought on by wishful thinking and expectations encouraged by words of Jesus. Actually, however, there is every indication that the awareness of the resurrection came as a complete surprise to the utterly discouraged followers of Jesus.

Something happened which changed Peter. Once a coward who before a serving-maid denied even having known Jesus, now he was ready to announce Jesus' Messiahship before the very court which had recently condemned Jesus to death. Something happened which turned the scattered, frightened disciples into the nucleus of a dynamic, rapidly-spreading chruch.

Matthew's account of what had happened is this: On Sunday morning two women went to the tomb, found it empty, and were told by an angel that Jesus was risen. The reassembled followers now met in Galillee. There Jesus appeared to them, again like Moses on a mountain. Now he spoke with full kingly power. "All authority in heaven and on earth has been given to me. Go therefore and make disciples of all nations baptizing them in the name of the Father and of the Son and of the Holy Spirit, teaching them to observe all that I have commanded you; and lo, I am with you always, to the close of the age" (Matt. 28:18–20).

The only "proofs" the New Testament was to offer of the resurrection were these: the testimony of these and other witnesses, the life of the spreading church, and the continuing experience of that promised presence.

With this proclamation of Jesus' final "Great Commission," Matthew calls his reader to his or her own decision of response.

V Mark and Luke

Four Gospels, the early church felt, were too good to lose. When it collected its sacred books, the church put Matthew first, perhaps because it loved Matthew most. But it did not abandon the other three. Even though ninety percent of Mark was reproduced in Matthew or Luke, they preserved it, and Luke was equally treasured.

Discussion of the Fourth Gospel, John, the climax of the New Testament, will be delayed until the last chapter of this GUIDE. But this chapter will focus on the distinctive contributions of the Second and Third Gospels, Mark and Luke.

Much twentieth-century scholarship has attempted to get behind our Gospels to their sources. The goal has been to try to determine what was said about Jesus before our Gospels were written down. More recent scholarship, however, has also been interested in what it has called *redaction criticism*. This is the study of how the Gospel writers put together their material, how they edited it. What their sources were, we will never know for sure. What we can work with is their finished products.[1]

In this chapter, therefore, we will look at some of the major themes around which Mark and Luke have organized their reports of stories and sayings of Jesus. The chapter will not go through either Gospel in detail, nor will each be outlined. Their basic frameowrk is the same as Matthew's. Since most of the content of Mark is reproduced in Matthew, it will not be discussed again here. Rather, we will look at the special emphases which distinguish the second and third of the Synoptics.

The Gospel According to Mark

Studying Mark was once regarded as rather a waste of time. Early nineteenth-century biblical scholars thought of it as simply a cut-down version of Matthew.

A century later, Mark was the most studied book in the Bible. Two ideas concerning Mark seemed to make it our most important source of information about Jesus. First, it was regarded as our oldest source, closest to the events it described, probably based on Peter's preaching, and thus historically most trustworthy. And second, it was regarded as having the least theological "bias," presenting Jesus "objectively" as the man he really was, not "distorting" the story by reading into it speculation about his divine nature.

The first idea, though challenged today by many reputable scholars, is still widely held.[2] The tradition that the Gospel is the work of Mark, a companion of Peter, who wrote it shortly after Peter's death, is ancient. Detective-like efforts to get behind Mark's writing to oral or written sources have not produced unanimous agreement. Many scholars, it is true, feel that the story of Jesus' death, the "passion narrative," is so full of vivid and apparently accurate details that it must have been written much sooner than Peter's death (A.D. 64 or 65). Others have suggested that the "Little Apocalypse" (Jesus' teachings about the end of the world) in Mark 13 may have been a written source. Some have noticed a curious duplication of stories in Mark 6:30—7:23 and Mark 8:1–21. There, in the same sequence, are two feedings of multitudes, two crossings of the lake, two disputes with the Pharisees, and two discourses related to food. Perhaps, it is argued, Mark found two accounts of the same events. They had become so different in being told and retold that he did not recognize their basic identity. At best, however, reconstruction of Mark's sources can now be only more or less convincing speculation. There are good reasons to believe that the Gospel According to Mark is our oldest written Gospel, that it does come from the church at Rome, and that it may indeed have been written quite soon after Peter's death. That it seems to anticipate the fall of Jerusalem (which occurred in A.D. 70) and that it pauses to explain certain Jewish customs or terms to Gentile readers are facts which fit in nicely with the traditional account of the Gospel's origin. Thus, for our knowledge of the life of Jesus, Mark's Gospel as we have it is itself our first, basic source of information.

But that Mark is free of theological "bias" has been shown to be completely false. For all the many human touches in its story of Jesus, Mark lives up to the promise of its opening phrase. Here is "the beginning of the gospel of Jesus Christ, the Son of God." Mark, too, is preaching a kind of sermon, is giving a theological interpretation concerning who he believes Jesus is: "Christ" and "Son of God." He understands Jesus' death as a "ransom" which will bring the salvation of many (Mark 10:45). He is sure Jesus is the "Son of man" who will come at the end to judge the world.

Though Greek scholars speak of Mark's relatively rough style, his little booklet is a work of inspired genius. Mark originated a completely new literary form, the gospel, quite unparalleled in Greco-Roman or Hebrew literature. He filled his seemingly simple account of the events in the life of one man with highly complex theological concepts. Virtually every line of the book bears witness to Mark's faith in Jesus as the Christ (the anointed one or Messiah) and Son of God. And almost every line at least subtly calls upon the readers, themselves facing persecution, to remain faithful, even though they, like their Master, may be on the way toward martyrdom.

This chapter will trace three related themes around which Mark wove his stories.

A Call to Faithfulness in the Midst of Persecution

Set Mark's writing in its context, Rome at the time of Nero's horrid persecution of Christians, and its words about the cross come alive with new meaning. The Roman historian Tacitus tells in gruesome detail the situation Mark's readers faced. It had been rumored that Nero himself had started the fire which in A.D. 64 had destroyed much of Rome. Tacitus writes:

> To dispel the report Nero made a scapegoat of others, and inflicted the most exquisite tortures upon a class hated for their abominations, whom the populace called Christians. The Christus from whom the name had its origin had been executed during the reign of Tiberius by the procurator Pontius Pilate. The mischievous superstition was thus checked for the moment, but was reviving again, not only in Judea, the original seat of the evil, but even in the capital, where all that is anywhere hideous or loathsome finds its center and flourishes. Accordingly some were first put on trial; they pleaded guilty, and upon the information gathered from them a large number were convicted, not so much on the charge of arson as because of their hatred of humanity. Wanton cruelty marked their execution. Covered with skins of wild beasts they were torn in pieces by dogs, and thus perished; many were crucified, or burned alive, and even set on fire to serve as an illumination by night, after daylight had expired. Nero had offered his own gardens for the spectacle, and exhibited races, mingling with the crowd in the garb of a charioteer, or himself driving. Hence, even for criminals who deserved extreme and exemplary punishment, there arose a feeling of compassion; for it was not, it seemed, for the common weal, but to glut the cruelty of one man, that they were being destroyed.[3]

In all probability, among the many who died in that persecution were Peter and Paul.

It was in that situation that Mark wrote to Christians facing the possibility of being crucified, burned alive, or even "set on fire to serve as an illumination." To them he wrote that Jesus had said on the way to his own death, "If any man would come after me, let him deny himself and take up his cross and follow me. For whoever would save his life will lose it; and whoever loses his life for my sake and the gospel's will save it" (Mark 8:34–35).

Thus, Mark's story of Jesus' life was written almost as much as a story of Jesus' death, a death in which Jesus' followers were all too likely to share.

Here we recall Kahler's famous saying that the Gospel is "a passion narrative with an extended introduction." Nearly half of Mark is devoted to Jesus' journey to Jerusalem and the last week of his life. But even of the rest of the book, Marxsen has written that Mark was composed "backward." That is, even the first chapters of Mark are written with repeated hints of the cross that is coming at the end.

Norman Perrin proposes that there is a kind of three-way parallelism in Mark.[4] The Gospel begins with John the Baptizer, who came preaching and was "delivered up" to his martyrdom. Jesus came preaching and was "delivered up" to be crucified. But also the disciples, Jesus' followers, are sent out to preach, and they are warned explicitly that "they will deliver you up to councils; and you will be beaten in synagogues; and you will stand before governors and kings for my sake" (13:9).

Mark 1 begins with John the Baptizer, who was tu be killed by Herod. As early as the second chapter, Mark pictures Jesus as warning the disciples about himself that "The days will come, when the bridegroom is taken away from them" (2:20). By the next chapter (3:6) Jesus' enemies are already plotting to kill him. And in the next chapter a parable warns that Satan will attack all who sow the word (4:15) "Teacher, do you not care if we perish?" his frightened disciples cry in the storm (4:38). They are saved by his authoritative voice.

After Peter's Great Confession (Mark 8), Jesus is pictured as clearly announcing two things: he is going to die, and his disciples will have to die for him. Three times Jesus specifically foretells his coming death (8:31; 9:31; and 10:33). Each such saying is followed by a demand that the disciples sacrifice too. "Whoever is ashamed of me and of my words in this adulterous and sinful generation, of him will the Son of man also be ashamed" (8:38). "If any one would be first, he must be last of all and servant of all" (9:35). "Whoever would be first among you must be slave of all. For the Son of man also came not to be served but to serve, and to give his life as a ransom for many" (10:44–45).

Over and over, Mark tells his readers who were then facing the very kind of persecution about which he says Jesus warned, the disciples failed to understand. Indeed, some have said that Mark's Gospel is the story of three conflicts: Jesus' conflict with Satan and his demons, Jesus' conflict with the Pharisees, and Jesus' conflict with his disciples!

"Do you not yet perceive or understand? Are your hearts hardened?" he demands of them. "Do you not remember? . . . Do you not yet understand?" (8:17–21). When Peter, who has just made the Great Confession, tries to separate salvation from martyrdom, Jesus calls him Satan! (8:32–33). He repeats his announcement of the cross, but they did not understand the saying" (9:32). There are repeated promises to those who do sacrifice for Christ. "Whoever loses his life for my sake and the gospel's will save it." (8:35). "Truly, I say to you, there is no one who has left house or brothers or sisters or mother or father or children or lands, for my sake and for the gospel, who will not receive a hundredfold now in this time, houses and brothers and sisters and mothers and children and lands, with persecutions, and in the age to come eternal life." (10:29–30).

Yet still they do not understand. Before and after his section concentrating on this instruction of the disciples, Mark sets a story of a blind man who receives his sight. (8:22–26; 10:46–52). The disciples, however, are still blind until the resurrection. When Jesus is arrested, Mark tells us — with such candor that his account surely must be historical, not just the invention of a disciple later — the disciples "all forsook him and fled." (14:50).

However historical all this may indeed be, there are several hints which make it clear that Mark is not simply writing *about* disciples of the year A.D. 30. He is also writing *to* later disciples. The warnings and the promises are addressed to "any man" (8:34). "Whoever" would be first must be a servant (10:44).

The address to future disciples is most clearly stated in Mark's "Little Apocalypse" (Mark 13). We have noted in our discussion of the parallel passage in Matthew (see pages 56–57) how difficult it is to understand this discourse. But one message is clear. Jesus is pictured as predicting to his disciples that they will be persecuted. "And when they bring you to trial and deliver you up, do not be anxious . . . And brother will deliver up brother to death, and the father his child, and children will rise against parents and have them put to death; and you will be hated by all for my name's sake. But he who endures to the end will be saved" (13:11–13).

And lest any think that these words referred only to those disciples actually present when Jesus spoke them, Mark reports a final note at the end of the discourse. "What I say to *you* I say to *all*: Watch" (13:37, italics added).

To early Christians facing the possibility of literal crucifixion, Mark writes of Jesus' own leadership in facing death. There is symbolism as well as history in his moving notation: "And they were on the road, going up to Jerusalem, and Jesus was walking ahead of them" (10:32).

Apocalyptic Battle with the Forces of Satan

As Mark saw it, the struggle which cost Jesus his life and in which Christians were challenged to risk theirs was not simply a this-worldly conflict with human opposition. It was really a battle with Satan and his legion of demons, a cosmic spiritual conflict with a hellish host.

Some ages have found it easier to think in such terms than has our own. The Old Testament speaks of Satan, Belial, and the obscure Leviathan. Mark also speaks of Be-el'zebul (3:22). Revelation which develops most fully the idea of cosmic conflict, adds the names of Abaddon and Apollyon. By the seventeenth century, when Urbain Grandier was burned after one of history's last great trials for sorcery, he could name Ashtoreth, Essas, Celsus, Acaos, and Cedon, the fallen thrones, and Alexh, Zabulon, Nephtalius, Cham, Nriel, and Achas, the distressed Principalities. Indeed, one medieval computation estimated the number of demons at 1,758,064,176, or rather more devils than there were people at that time. More conservative sixteenth-century reports, one notes with a certain relief, limited the number to only around 7,500,000. The rise of modern science and the era of the "Age of Reason" in the seventeenth and eighteenth centuries directed men's attention toward more natualistic interpretations of their experience. The latter part of the twentieth century has seen a curious revival of interest in satanism and the occult.

While a modern psychiatrist might explain the phenomenon in different terms, there evidently were in the first century all too common kinds of afflictions popularly diagnosed as demon- possession. The Jewish historian Josephus tells us that he personally witnessed the exorcism of one demon. The evil spirit was drawn out through the patient's nose, the exorcist using a ring that was said to be a relic of King Solomon, who had died a thousand years earlier. Jews boasted that the emperor of Rome himself had once turned to a rabbi to exorcise a demon from his royal daughter. Evidently certain Pharisees were believed to be skilled in curing demoniacs (Math. 12:27).

Over and over, Mark pictures Jesus as casting these evil spirits out of the people whom they have possessed. One indication of factual basis for Mark's repeated stories of such cures is his report of Jesus' enemies' opposition to these exorcisms. At no point do they accuse him of not really effecting the cures. They never suggest, for example, that the healings are faked. They are so manifestly fact that Jesus' enemies have to try to explain them away as being the product of Satanic rather than divine power! (See Mark 3:22).

Mark is interested in all Jesus' miracles of healing, but it is especially his casting out of demons that Mark emphasizes. Matthew begins his account of Jesus' ministry with the Sermon on the Mount. But Mark begins with the story of Jesus' victory over an "unclean spirit" (1:21-28). Mark's next story ends with the comment that Jesus "cast out many demons" (1:34). Two chapters later another summary of Jesus' activities emphasizes exorcism (3:11-12). Jesus' enemies attack him, charging not that he does not really exorcise evil spirits, but that his evident power to do so must come from Be-el'zebul (3:20-30). Jesus, however, continues his war with the demons (5:1-11; 7:24-29; 9:14-29).

Just as Jesus' followers are called to follow him in facing suffering and death, so they are called to join in his struggle against the hosts of Satan. When the Twelve are appointed, they are specifically given two duties: preaching and exorcism (3:14). When they are sent out on their first mission, they find that they do indeed have this authority (6:7-13). The story of a subsequent failure, however, warns of the difficulty the disciples were to find in this task (9:14-29).

What Mark is telling his readers is not simply that Jesus and the Apostles were able to effect startling cures of a bizarre emotional disturbance. Mark sees these exorcisms as dramatic hints that Jesus and his followers are engaged in a cosmic contest. Though Jesus keeps his identity "secret" from men, the demons know him immediately and scream their protests as he invades their territory (Mark 1:24). In Jesus the Spirit of God is waging war with Satan. It is, Mark tells his readers, an apocalyptic struggle.

Right at the beginning, at Jesus' baptism, the Spirit of God had descended upon him. "The Spirit immediately drove him out into the wilderness. . . . And he was . . . tempted by Satan" (1:9-13). Jesus himself interprets his exorcisms as a sign that Satan's house is being entered and plundered and that Satan himself is being bound (3:20-30). Jesus' struggle, in which Mark's readers are challenged to participate, is a spiritual fight to the death, not simply against human opposition, but with an unseen, hellish host. Another New Testament writer was to voice the same idea: "For we are not contending against flesh and blood, but against the principalities, against the powers, against the world rulers of this present darkness, against the spiritual hosts of wickedness in the heavenly places" (Eph. 6:12).

Probably it is this eschatological context, this interpretation of Jesus' ministry in terms of the final struggle with Satan, that gives us the key for understanding Mark's enigmatic title for Jesus, *the Son of man*. Ask Mark who Jesus is, and repeatedly this title seems to be his answer. Yet no one is quite sure what "Son of man" means. Thirteen times the title occurs in Mark: 2:10, 28; 8:31, 38; 9:9, 12, 31; 10:33; 13:26, 32; 14:21, 41, 62. Strangely, the phrase appears only on the lips of Jesus. According to Mark, "Son of man" seems to be Jesus' favorite title for himself, but nobody else ever uses it about him. What adds to the mystery is that it is raely used in the letters of Paul or the other Epistles, nor is it frequent in John. Many scholars have suggested that it appears that Jesus did use it himself, but that, except for the Synoptics with their report of Jesus' own practice, the other New Testament writers tended to avoid it because they, too, were not quite sure what it meant.

A popular misunderstanding has set it over against another title frequently used of Jesus, "Son of God." Jesus, later creeds affirmed, had two "natures": divine and human. The title "Son of man" has been used to affirm Jesus' humanity, "Son of God" his divinity. In the New Testament, however, the two titles are never contrasted in this way.

Some interpreters have argued forcefully that the title does particularly relate to Jesus' involvement in human suffering and death. "And he began to teach them that the Son of man must suffer many things, and be rejected by the elders and the chief priests and the scribes, and be killed" (8:31; cf. 9:9, 31; 10:33- 34; 10:45; 14:21, 41). It is proposed that from Ezekiel, itself an eschatological book, Jesus selected a title focusing on his identification with suffering humanity. Some scholars translate the title simply as "the Man."[6]

By contrast, others have noted that Jesus repeatedly uses the title in relationship to the coming eschatological judgment. It is used most strikingly in this way when such use is sure to bring Jesus' conviction for blasphemy. And you will see the Son of man sitting at the right hand of Power, and coming with the clouds of heaven" (14:62; cf. 8:38; 13:26). This is the way "Son of man" is used in the Old Testament apocalyptic book Daniel.

> I saw in the night visions,
>> and behold, with the clouds of heaven
>> there came one like a son of man,
>> and he came to the Ancient of Days
>> and was presented before him.
> And to him was given dominion
>> and glory and kingdom,
> that all peoples, nations, and languages
>> should serve him;
> his dominion is an everlasting dominion,
>> which shall not pass away,
> and his kingdom one
>> that shall not be destroyed.   (Daniel 7:13-14)

The book of Enoch, a "pseudepigraphic" book, a "false writing" which did not get recognized as worthy of inclusion in the Old Testament, similarly depicts the Son of man as a cosmic judge of nations and of demons.

Noting that Jesus speaks of the Son of man in the third person, some have suggested that Jesus did not claim to be the Son of man but rather looked forward to that figure's coming at the end of the age. To take that view, however, one must throw out those sayings, already noted, in which Jesus speaks of the coming sufferings of the Son of Man. There are also sayings in which Jesus seems to claim already to possess the authority of the future judge (2:27-28).

The understanding of the title which seems to the present writer to fit best with its varied uses is this: Jesus *did* avoid the title "Christ," which to most Palestinian Jews would have connotations of kingship in revolt against Rome. He *did* deliberately choose an enigmatic and ambiguous title. But as he used it, it was full of eschatological implications. On the one hand it suggested an invader of the demons' domain, whom the evil spirits recognized as having come to destroy them (1:24). As Son of man, Jesus invades even death itself (8:31; 9:9; 10:45, etc.). But in winning that victory, he prepares for his coming as the Son of man, the cosmic judge (14:26, for example). It would seem that Mark, at least, understood the title in this way.

This whole theme of Jesus as the leader in the battle of heaven against hell reaches its climax in Mark's Little Apocalypse" in chapter 13. Here, as we have seen, Mark's readers are warned of persecution. But the events there described go far beyond Christians being human torches for Nero's garden party. "But in those days, after that tribulation, the sun will be darkened, and the moon will not give its light, and the stars will be falling from heaven, and the powers in the heavens will be shaken. And then they will see the Son of man coming in clouds with great power and glory" (13:24-26).

Mark's readers face almost certain death. But they have nothing to fear. Jesus is the Son of man. As Son of man he has invaded Satan's domain, even ransomed victory from death itself. That Son of man will come again. And when he does, "then he will send out the angels, and gather his elect from the four winds, from the ends of the earth to the ends of heaven" (13:27).

The Memory of the Human Jesus

> And they were bringing children to him, that he might touch them; and the disciples rebuked them. But when Jesus saw it he was indignant, and said to them, "Let the children come to me, do not hinder them; for to such belongs the kingdom of God. Truly, I say to you, whoever does not receive the kingdom of God like a child shall not enter it." And he took them in his arms and blessed them, laying his hands upon them.
>
> (Mark 10:13-16)

To Mark, we have seen, Jesus is a martyr leading martyrs to the cross. He is an eschatological conqueror of demons and a cosmic judge. But he is also a human being who takes little children in his arms and blesses them!

Mark's account of Jesus' life is shaped in part by the desperate situation in which his readers found themselves. It is no simple biography of a man, but a work with apocalyptic overtones picturing Jesus as a conquering Judge. But we must now note that Mark's Gospel is also filled with vivid scenes and human touches which many scholars see as genuine reflections of the life of Jesus of Nazareth as a man on earth. The story of Jesus with children in his arms has no parallel in merely apocalyptic literature. Mark is presenting a picture of a man.

Repeatedly the other Gospel writers, as they quote from Mark, seem to feel it necessary to add phrases or omit ideas in order to point up for readers the divinity of Jesus. Where Mark reports Peter's Great Confession as simply "You are the Christ" (8:29), Matthew has it, "You are the Christ, the Son of the living God" (Matt. 16:16). To Mark, Jesus is "the carpenter" (6:3). Matthew alters this to make Jesus "the carpenter's son" (Matt. 13:55). In Mark the Spirit *drove* Jesus into the wilderness (1:12). Matthew reports rather that the Spirit simply *led* (Matt. 4:1). In Mark, Jesus "sighs" (7:34; 8:12), feels compassion for hungry people (6:34), is sometimes surprised (6:6), and can become angry (3:5; 8:33; 10:14). He can become so tired that he needs to rest (6:31-32). All three Synoptics tell the story of the rich young ruler. But it is only Mark whose account still contains the words "And Jesus looking upon him loved him" (10:21; cf. Matt. 19:16–30; Luke 18:18–30.)

Some thirty times Mark uses the word "immediately," usually referring to some action of Jesus or to some response to him. Perhaps this is only an idiosyncrasy of Mark's style. Perhaps it reflects the character of Peter, Mark's teacher. But perhaps there is in it memory of Jesus' own personality, his sense of urgency.

Mark does not hesitate to report what seem to be human limitations upon Jesus' knowledge. The other Gospels carefully omit the story of the Syrophoenician woman, through whom Jesus seems to have had to learn that the gospel is not limited to Jews (7:24-30). Mark can report that Jesus needed a second effort to cure the blind man at Bethsaida (8:22-26). And the way in which Matthew 13:58 revises Mark 6:5 shows the trend of later writers. Matthew says that in Jesus' home town "he did not do many mighty works there, because of their unbelief." Mark, however, had written flatly, "And he *could* do no mighty work there" (italics added). Sometimes, Mark seems to suggest, Jesus had to experience even failure.

We have already noted, similarly, the honesty with which the Gospels, perhaps especially Mark, report the far from heroic behavior of the disciples, whom later legend was to canonize as "saints."

It is the contention of this GUIDE that Mark does represent a vivid, historical memory of what scholars have called "the Jesus of history." The story has been written to meet the needs of a later period. It has been given profound theological interpretation. But it has not been invented by pious imagination. Mark wrote, as we have seen that Luke claims to have written, on the basis of reports about an actual person and real events, that his readers might know the truth (cf. Luke 1:1–4).

A Note About the Ending of Mark

In the oldest Greek manuscripts, this Gospel ends with Mark 16:8, "And they went out and fled from the tomb; for trembling and astonishment had come upon them; and they said nothing to any one, for they were afraid."

Some scholars, noting this manuscript evidence, have argued that that is where Mark did actually end his story. He has given repeatedly Jesus' promise that he will return at the *eschaton*, the end of the world (8:38; 13:26; 14:62). Mark ends his story precisely where his readers are, looking forward hopefully to that coming judgment day.[9]

Most scholars, however, believe that the ending of Mark has been lost. While none of the various endings added in ancient manuscripts are from Mark's original, their existence bears witness to the fact that early Christian copyists sensed that the ending was missing. Long before Mark wrote, the story of Easter was an essential part of the first preaching (see, for example, 1 Cor. 15:1–8). Mark 14:28 and 16:7 seem to suggest that Mark is preparing the reader for an account of a resurrection appearnce in Galilee. Language scholars report that hardly any other sentence in any known Greek manuscript ends, as does Mark's Gospel, with the Greek preposition *gar* ("for"). It is evident, therefore, they say, that the manuscript is broken off in mid-sentence. The remarkable thing is not that the end of the scroll has been lost, but that copies of so much of it have been preserved for more than nineteen centuries. We can be grateful that we have as much of his Gospel as we do.

The Gospel According to Luke

Greek scholars have called Luke the literary masterpiece of the New Testament.

Traditionally commentators have spoken of Luke as the Gospel to the Gentiles, noting that it is probably the only book in the New Testament whose author was not a Jew.

More recently, interpreters have focused on Luke's picture of Christ as the great liberator, champion of the poor (and some have claimed forerunner of the movement for women's liberation).

The emphasis on liberation is made clear in the way in which Luke begins his account of Jesus' ministry. Matthew followed his account of Jesus' baptism with the Sermon on the Mount, Jesus' teaching of a new law. Mark told instead of an exorcism. Luke, however, places first a story of Jesus' announcing that he has come to bring release to captives and good news to the poor.

While it is an expansion of Mark 6:1-6, this dramatic story is found only in Luke 4:16-30. Though it is the first sermon Luke records, verse 23 indicates that Luke does not think of it as chronologically the first sermon Jesus ever preached. Apparently Luke puts it first because he sees it as expressive of the purpose of Jesus' whole ministry.

Jesus has returned to Nazareth, the town in which he grew up. At the synagogue on the Sabbath, he is given the opportunity to read the scripture and to speak, not an unusual privilege in a synagogue for a Jewish male. What he reads, however, and the interpretation he gives it, produce a riot!

The passage read is from the second half of the prophecy of Isaiah and is similar to the "Servant Poems" we have discussed on pages 16 and 42–44. These had always been understood as referring to the mission of the nation Israel itself. But Jesus announces, "Today this scripture has been fulfilled in your hearing." Apparently he is claiming that it is in his own ministry that these words are to come true.

Here then, is Jesus' understanding of what he had come for, according to Luke:

> The Spirit of the Lord is upon me,
> because he has anointed me to preach good news to the poor.
> He has sent me to proclaim release to the captives
> and recovering of sight to the blind,
> to set at liberty those who are oppressed,
> to proclaim the acceptable year of the Lord.
>
> (Luke 4:18–19, quoted from Isaiah 61:1–2)

Jesus had come for "the poor," "the captives," "the blind," "the oppressed." When he went on to suggest that God's people had failed in this mission which he now was assuming, the angry mob attempted to lynch him!

By placing the story at the beginning of his account of Jesus' ministry and by telling it in such detail, Luke has signaled his reader that it is important. It is a kind of brief introductory summary of Luke's version of the whole Gospel. We will confine our study of what is unique in Luke primarily to examining certain themes suggested by these verses.

The Gospel for All Peoples

Luke's is a Gospel written to a Gentile, by a Gentile, and for Gentiles. To him Jesus is one who has brought a revolution which has broken down the old barriers of race.[10]

Whoever is meant by the "most excellent Theophilus" to whom the Gospel is addressed in Luke 1:3, that person has a Greek, not a Jewish, name. Tradition says that the author was Luke, a man with a Greek name, one who enters the story in Acts as a companion of Paul when in Acts 16 (the beginning of the "we" passages) Paul crosses from Asia into Europe. Primarily because of the difficulty of reconciling Acts' account of Paul's life with that which Paul himself gives in Galatians, many have rejected this tradition. But most of those who do not ascribe the book to a companion of Paul agree that the Gospel appears to be the work of a Gentile. Over and over it emphasizes that Jesus came not for one race, but for all.

When the child Jesus was brought to the Temple for ceremonies traditional at the birth of Jewish boys, Luke tells us, old Simeon took the baby in his arms and sang that he would be "a light for revelation to the Gentiles" (2:32; cf. Isa. 42:6–7).

Matthew had traced Jesus' ancestry through Abraham and the Hebrew kings (Matt. 1:1–17). Luke, however, has a different genealogical table, leaving out most of the Hebrew kings, but going back to Adam, the father of all races (3:23–38).

Matthew tells us that when Jesus sent out the disciples he charged them, "Go nowhere among the Gentiles" (Matt. 10:5). Luke tells the same story but carefully omits those limiting words (9:1–6).

It is Luke alone who tells the story of the Good Samaritan, the man of the wrong race and religion who is held up as a model in preference to certain respectably pious leaders among the traditional people of God (10:29–37).

Other Gospel writers report Jesus' enigmatic saying, "Some are last who will be first, and some are first who will be last" (13:30; cf. Matt. 19:30 and Mark 10:31). But it is clear from the context in which Luke sets it that Luke understands this as having a racial meaning. The Gentiles, formerly last, are now to have a high place in the kingdom of God.

Jesus as the Bringer of Economic "Revolution"

Mary's Magnificat (1:46–55) has been called "the most revolutionary song ever sung"!

Matthew's account of Jesus' birth, as we have seen, prepares us for the coming of the promised Jewish king, a new Moses. Luke's account promises instead a kind of revolution, one especially for the cause of the poor and oppressed. Unique to Luke is a psalm attributed to Mary, Jesus' mother, as she looks forward to the birth of her child. She sings of God that now:

> He has shown strength with his arm,
> he has scattered the proud in the imagination of their hearts,
> he has put down the mighty from their thrones,
> and exalted those of low degree;
> he has filled the hungry with good things,
> and the rich he has sent empty away. (Luke 1:51–53)

Luke's story of Jesus' birth goes on to report that the news is announced not, as in Matthew, to rich magi from the East, but to "certain poor shepherds" in Judean fields.

As we have seen, Luke pictures Jesus announcing his mission as being to "preach good news to the poor" and "release to the captives," and "to set at liberty those who are oppressed"(4:18). At least three parables develop the theme of concern for those in need. Luke 10:29–37 extols the Good Samaritan as a true "neighbor" because he does not even let lines of race or religion prevent him from helping the man in need. Luke 12:13–21 pictures "gentle Jesus" as bluntly calling a rich man "fool" for trusting in his wealth when judgment is at hand. And in Luke 16:19–31, Jesus pictures rich Dives and poor Lazarus as swapping places in the life to come. Dives had been unconcerned for the poor. Jesus is willing to use standard apocalyptic symbolism and picture the rich but selfish Dives as damned for eternity, "in anguish in this flame."

Luke's version of the Beatitudes spells out his revolutionary concern unambiguously. Matthew 5:3–12 interprets the Beatitudes spiritually. "Blessed are the poor *in spirit.*" "Blessed are those who hunger and thirst *for righteousness*" (italics added). But Luke 6:20–23 reports these sayings in unadorned economic terms. "Blessed are you poor. . . . Blessed are you that hunger now, for you shall be satisfied. Blessed are you that weep now, for you shall laugh." An economic reversal is promised.

And to add emphasis to the promise of a world turned upside down at the coming *eschaton* (the end), Luke's report adds a series of warnings. "But woe to you that are rich, for you have received your consolation. Woe to you that are full now, for you shall hunger. Woe to you that laugh now, for you shall mourn and weep"(6:24–25). However justified Matthew may have been in interpreting the

Beatitudes in terms of the spirit which receives blessedness, many scholars believe that Luke's version may be closer to the actual words of Jesus.

It is Luke, also, who tells us the story of one man who got Jesus' message. Zacchaeus is pictured as wealthy, dishonest, and one of the hated tax collectors. But when he meets Jesus, his repentance manifests itself both in a new honesty in his business and in a new concern for the poor (19:1–10).[11]

Forerunner of a Kind of "Women's Liberation"

Long before the modern movement for asserting the rights of women, students had noted a third group for whom Luke shows a special conern. We have seen his concern to voice the good news that no one is to be excluded from the kingdom because of race or economic class. But Luke also pictures Jesus as ignoring the ancient boundaries which lower the status of half the world because of their sex.

Matthew's account of Jesus' birth centers on Joseph. But Luke's is the story of two women. One is Elizabeth, Mary's cousin and the mother of John the Baptist. The other is the story of Mary, the mother of Christ. It is to a woman that the angel Gabriel comes. It is a woman who blesses Mary as the mother-to-be of the Lord (1:41–45). A woman, Anna, recognizes in the baby at the Temple the future Savior (2:36–38). It was women, Luke alone tells us, who provided the financial support for Jesus' ministry (8:1–3). And in Luke's account of the resurrection, it is a whole group of women who first hear the news that Jesus is risen (24:10).

In all four Gospels Jesus is pictured as ministering to women. Luke adds to the others the story of Jesus' raising from the dead the son of a widow of Nain (7:11–17).

But what may have been for Luke the most shocking story of this kind is one which he alone reports. Jesus is in the home of Mary and Martha. He actually teaches Mary as though she were intellectually the equal of a man, to the distress of Martha, who would have preferred to have her sister join her in the more traditional "woman's work" in the kitchen (10:38–42). In much of the Gentile world, women were regarded as a man's property. To Aristotle, for example, they were but a little above the rank of slaves. Jews had perhaps the highest regard for women of any people in the first century. And yet even among them there were disputes as to whether women should be taught. "I would rather teach my daughter obscenities than to teach her the law," one sexist rabbi is quoted as saying. But Luke's Gospel is one in which women have a place quite equal to that of men.[12]

The Matter of Miracles

Among the "oppressed" for whom Luke says Jesus came were the sick and the blind.

Early in this century, W. K. Hobart proposed that this Gospel's detailed accounts of healings and use of technical medical terms showed that the author really must have been the one whom Paul calls "the beloved physician" (Col. 4:14). Further study called this view into serious question, suggesting that the vocabulary would be equally suitable for a lawyer or for many other educated Greeks. Nevertheless, there is in Luke sufficient emphasis on healing that the following comments on miracles are appropriate at this point.

The Buddhist scriptures contain a lovely story of a miracle alleged to have been performed by Gautama Siddhartha. An evil man attempted to seduce a beautiful young virgin, beginning by praising the beauty of her eyes. "Then take them!" she protested, and plucked her eyes out. Her sacrifice to preserve her chastity so shamed the lecher that he was converted. And the Buddha, upon hearing the story, miraculously restored the virtuous maiden's sight.

Now it must be said that most twentieth-century Americans, upon hearing this tale, dismiss it as pious legend from a superstitious land and age. But the question inevitably arises concerning the miracles reported in the New Testament: Are they to be rejected in the same way? Most ancient religions have claimed miracles which would be disputed today. It has been wisely remarked that in the first century, Christianity could not have been believed without miracles, but that today it is hard to believe precisely because of those same miracles.

Students of the Bible have given many answers to the problem of miracles, most of which are variations upon one or another of the following four.

1) Some flatly reject the miracle stories.

The eighteenth-century philosopher David Hume, for example, argued that miracles would be a violation of the laws of nature created by nature's God, a contradiction. More important, one ought not to believe a report of an alleged miracle unless it is more difficult to believe that the report was in error than that the miracle took place. A story from centuries ago, written perhaps by one who does not even claim to have been an eyewitness, told among superstitious people in a pre-scientific era, can hardly be accepted in modern times, Hume alleged.[13] Following a similar line of reasoning, Thomas Jefferson produced an edition of the New Testament from which all miracles had been excluded.

2) A second approach accepts such stories as spiritually but not literally true.

Many devout scholars assume it as a dogma not to be questioned in a scientific age that miracles, at least of a physical kind, simply do not and cannot happen. Yet they recognize that to cut out all the miracle stories would be to leave the Gospels in shreds. The task of the interpreter, therefore, is to find what meaning there may be for modern man in these ancient tales. The story of the cleansing of a leper, for example, may symbolize for us the sense of cleansing from sin which the believer may experience today. A disciple of Bultmann might "demythologize" the story of how Jesus gave sight to a blind man by speaking of the new insights the Good News brings to those who encounter the figure of Christ in the pages of the Gospel. The stories of Jesus' raising the dead suggests the transition from "inauthentic existence" to "authentic existence" described in existential philosophy.[14]

3) More conservative scholars have accepted some or all of the miracles but have sought to justify their views critically.[15]

Some of these scholars have accepted Hume's challenge that each report of a miracle must be judged on its own merits. Nevertheless, they have accepted many such stories as historically true. The understanding of the universe as a clocklike, cause-and-effect machine, assumed in Hume's day, has now been discarded, these scholars argue, by science itself. Discoveries such as those leading to Heisenberg's principle of indeterminacy are said to challenge the assumption that every event must be predictable. Modern psychosomatic medicine gives us at least partial insights into how healings may, in extraordinary circumstances, take place quite apart from the use of medicines or surgery. While New Testament reports of miracles need be accepted no less critically than those attributed to the Buddha, for example, they need not be rejected on the basis of a presupposition that only mechanically predictable events can happen. Where so remarkable a personality as Jesus was present, one may believe that remarkable, unexpected things did occur.

4) Finally, more conservative scholars, on theological grounds, have accepted it as a matter of faith that every biblical story reported as history must be believed as factually true.

God created the universe, they note. He therefore can alter its usual pattern of operation whenever he wishes. That Jesus, as God incarnate, God come as a man, could and did do the miracles reported in the Scripture, Fundamentalists hold to be infallible. To doubt these stories, they argue, would be to doubt both the deity of Jesus and the authority of God's Word. This would violate Christian theology as they understand it.

Whatever may be the correct view concerning miracles, it is important to note that Jesus did not want faith in his gospel to rest on belief in such wonders and signs. The Synoptics agree that when asked to prove himself by doing miracles, Jesus flatly refused (Matt. 16:1–4; Mark 8:11–13; Luke 11:29). The miracles he did were to help people, not to impress the credulous. Jesus demanded faith on the basis of moral, not physical, authority. Typically, the Christian today does not arrive at faith in Jesus because he has first believed the reports that Jesus did miracles. On the contrary, because he has first been grasped by the spiritual power of Jesus, he may, indeed, come to believe that Jesus did physical miracles too.

The Birth of Jesus

Of the many stories in the New Testament, few are more loved or more debated than that of Jesus' birth.

While some see belief that Jesus was born of a virgin as a fundamental of the

faith, others regard the story as typical of primitive religious myth. Millions celebrate it every Christmas in carol and pageant. Yet it must be admitted that as history the story abounds in problems.

One problem concerns the date. Luke carefully sets the story in the context of
a worldwide taxation during the time "when Quirinius was governor of Syria"
(2:1). Quirinius, however, does not seem to have become governor of Syria until
several years after the death of Herod (4 B.C.), in whose lifetime Matthew says
Jesus was born. And the first worldwide taxation of which we have any record did
not occur until A.D. 7. An uncertain solution which some have proposed to the
problem rests on the fact that Quirinius did hold a lesser office in Syria as early as
7 B.C., and that in 7 B.C. there was a decree for census and taxation in Egypt.
Perhaps, it is proposed, that census also included Palestine.

Much more serious is the problem which relates the story to the traditional
pattern of religious legends. Greek and Roman mythology abounded in stories of
children born to human mothers after intercourse with mythical gods. Tourists
may yet see on the walls of the temple at Luxor a carving in which an Egyptian
Pharaoh pictured his mother as encountering a god and then bearing him a son,
that Paraoh thus being both human and divine. Legends of miracles related to the
birth of Gautama are part of Buddhist tradition. Defenders of the historicity of the
biblical narratives have replied that their highly moral nature, their relative con-
temporaneousness with the events described, and their setting in real history set
the stories of Jesus' birth quite apart from myths such as those of Greek religions.

Another problem is the complete silence of the rest of the New Testament
concerning Jesus' birth. Not Mark, not John, not Paul, not any other New Testament writer ever mentions the virgin birth. Did they not believe it? Did they not
know of it? Did they simply not think it important for their purposes?

Finally, there is the problem of the apparent differences between the story as
Luke tells it and the story as we have it from Matthew. One has only to ask who
Jesus' grandfather was to discover an apparent discrepancy. Luke 3:23 tells us
that Jesus' earthly father Joseph was the son of Heli, but Matthew 1:16 says he
was the son of one Jacob. A traditional answer, that Luke is tracing Jesus' ancestry through Mary, ignores the difficulty that Luke seems clearly to say that he is
speaking of Joseph's ancestors. The two lists do not even agree concerning all the
ancestors of King David.

Reading the two stories, one seems to find completely different understand-
ings of how it happened that Jesus of Nazareth was born in David's home town of
Bethlehem. Luke tells us that the Holy Family makes a special trip from their
home in Nazareth to Bethlehem because of a census for tax purposes. The child is
laid in a manger because there is no room for these travelers in the local inn
(2:1–7). Matthew, however, says nothing of any previous residence in Nazareth.
In Matthew the family welcomes the Wise Men in a "house"(Matt. 2:11), with
no hint that it is not their own home. The reason Jesus grew up in Nazareth,

according to Matthew, is that the family had to flee Bethlehem in order to avoid persecution by Herod—a persecution apparently unknown to Luke.

At least a partial understanding of some of the differences between Matthew and Luke comes from a recognition of their different purposes and emphases. For example, Matthew has used a genealogical list which would trace Jesus' ancestry through all the kings of Israel and back to Abraham, the father of the Hebrews. This fits his concern to show Jesus as the fulfiller of the hope for the promised King of the Jews. The Gentile Luke, however, was quite content with a genealogical list which included no Jewish king except David, but which traced Jesus' ancestry back to Adam and to God, from whom all races have come (3:23–38). Matthew the Jew was concerned to set Jesus in opposition to the false king of the Jews, Herod. The Gentile Luke, writing to the "most excellent Theophilus," is more concerned to relate Jesus to the Roman Empire. For some Christians, however, problems still remain.

What makes such problems especially important to many is the emphasis placed on the virgin birth of Jesus by traditional theology. As they recite the Apostles' Creed, millions of Christians affirm faith in Jesus as "conceived by the Holy Ghost, born of the Virgin Mary." Originally, it seems, "born of the Virgin Mary" was included in the creed to emphasize Jesus' humanity. He was born of a woman, not handed down from heaven. "Conceived by the Holy Ghost" affirmed Jesus' deity. Fundamentalist theologians, however, have often interpreted doubt concerning the virgin birth to be doubt concerning the deity of Christ.

On the other hand, other devout Christian scholars have replied that the story of the virgin birth seems peripheral to New Testament Christianity. Only Matthew and Luke mention it, and having told their stories, they refer to it no more. The rest of the New Testament writers say nothing about it at all.

Some may find a partial reconciliation of conflicting views by thinking of the virgin birth in terms of two miracles. The *biological miracle* that Jesus was born without an earthly father to a virgin mother really does not seem to have been important to most New Testament writers. Christian historians may face honestly the difficulties noted above, though the present writer does not find these insurmountable.

The *theological miracle* of the uniqueness of Jesus as both God and man, the doctrine symbolized in the creed by "conceived by the Holy Ghost, born of the Virgin Mary," may indeed be regarded as essential to New Testament Christianity. Every part of the New Testament affirms both the humanity of Jesus and the uniqueness of his relationship to God. That faith, however, rests on grounds quite independent of historical analysis of the stories of Jesus' birth.

Finally, it is important to note the literary form of the birth stories. As Matthew has filled his account with quotations from the Jewish scriptures—music to his readers' ears—so Luke has filled his story with songs, ancient Christmas carols. The angel who appears to Jesus' uncle Zechariah bursts into song (1:13–17). Mary's Magnificat has been sung through the centuries (1:46–55). When speech is restored to Zechariah, he sings his prophecy (1:67–79). To the shepherds, angels announce Jesus' birth by singing a carol (2:14). And old Simeon's Nunc Dimittis, sung as he holds the infant Jesus in his arms, was to become part of the musical liturgy of the church through the ages (2:29–32). (Most modern translations of the New Testament will print these passages in such a way as to show the reader that they are poetry.) Luke has written not a newspaper account, but a kind of grand opera or oratorio on the birth of Jesus.

Historical analysis of the birth stories is helpful.[16] But the literary interpreter must also note that one has not fully grasped the good news Luke intended to convey until he has with joy sung Christmas carols.

The Resurrection

At least one miracle, the New Testament affirms, is essential. "If Christ has not been raised," Paul writes, "then our preaching is in vain and your faith is in vain"(1 Cor. 15:14). Every Gospel ends with the announcement of the good news of the resurrection. Every other book of the New Testament assumes or affirms it. Every line of the New Testament is written by a Christian committed to belief in the resurrection of Christ.

Again, it must be admitted, there are problems. It has sometimes been said that the Easter stories of the four Gospels agree on almost nothing except the one big fact that on the third day Jesus rose. (But on the truth of that fact each writer would stake his life!)

Who first saw the risen Christ? Matthew 28:9 indicates that two women did so. Luke 24 gives no hint that the women saw Jesus. Rather, in Luke, Jesus appears first to two disciples on the road to Emmaus and then to the Eleven. John 20 makes the first appearance to Mary Magdalene alone, not to the other women, and then describes an appearance to ten, not eleven, disciples. Paul, in 1 Corinthians 15:5, seems to specify that the first appearance was to Peter, then to the Twelve.

Where did the resurrection appearances occur? Matthew records the appearance to the disciples as on a mountain in Galilee. Mark 16:7 hints that the lost ending of Mark must have described an appearance there. Luke 24, however, sets all appearances in or near Jerusalem. John has Jesus appear in both places.

Such problems are probably not now completely solvable on the basis of historical research.[17] That such differing accounts had developed by the time the New Testament books were written shows that the accounts of Easter must have been told and retold very early indeed and in every diverse place to which the gospel first spread. Thus, the resurrection affirmation itself was no gradually developed legend. It was central to the Good News from the very beginning.

What the New Testament writers emphasize is that men and women in various places and ways began to experience the presence of the risen Christ. They give no account of the actual resurrection itself. They never tell what a television camera would have recorded had there been one outside the tomb on Easter morning. The repeated mention of the empty tomb does bear witness to the Gospel writers' certainty that there had occurred an actual, material event. But their emphasis is not on a physical phenomenon; it is on a spiritual triumph and its continuing significance in the lives of people.

The skeptic may argue that the New Testament writers offer no absolute *proof* of the resurrection. They do profess to offer strong *evidence*. They give the witness of those who encountered the risen Christ. They challenge each reader to learn in his own experience. They give also the experience of the community of believers, the church, in the mighty acts which they report Jesus continued to do in and through them by means of his living Spirit.

But the story of those acts and those witnesses is the subject of the next chapter.

VI   *The Acts of the Apostles*

"In the first book, O Theophilus, I have dealt with all that Jesus began to do and teach." So begins Luke in Acts 1:1. In this second book, the same author, writing to the same reader, picks up precisely where the first volume ended. Now, Luke implies, he will tell what the risen Christ *continued* to do, by means of his Holy Spirit, in and through the infant church.[1]

The Nature and Purpose of Acts

Acts as History

For nineteen centuries readers have found Acts' story fascinating. Suddenly filled with a new sense of power from on high, Acts tells us, the Apostles began to shout their message to the world. Heroically they braved persecution, performed miracles, won converts, and spread the infant church. So Acts tells the story. Serious question has been raised, however, as to whether Acts is true to the facts.

Nineteenth-century critics were almost unanimous in regarding Acts as worthless, at least as history. The book was regarded as a second-century collection of legends, slanted to try to forge a cover-up for the split between Peter and Paul which Galatians was thought to reveal. In Galatians 2:11, Paul writes of Peter, "I opposed him to his face, because he stood condemned." Acts had been written, they argued, to suppress the scandalous memory of the early rift about the place of Gentile converts in the church and to make the relationships among early leaders appear to have been all sweetness and light. Acts was believed to be full of edifying fiction and distortion produced more than a century after the events it professed to report. The crucial period between the events recounted in the Gospels and the clear picture of the early church found in Paul's letters was described as a kind of twenty-year "dark tunnel." Into it, it was said, Acts failed to shed any dependable light.

Curiously, it was the almost accidental discovery of a boundary marker in Turkey which caused the pendulum of critical evaluation of Acts' accuracy to swing toward the opposite extreme. British archaeologist Sir William M. Ramsay—no kin to the writer of this GUIDE—set out, about the turn of the century, to retrace the journeys of Paul. He began his expedition assuming the prevailing view that Acts was a collection of legends written in the middle or late second century. His discovery of a stone boundary sign showed him that Paul, in fleeing from Iconium to Lystra and Derbe, really would have crossed the border into Lycaonia, as stated in Acts 14:6. What made this minor detail significant was that the boundary of Lycaonia had been there only from A.D. 37 to A.D. 72, during which period Paul's alleged flight had taken place. A writer of a century later, relying simply on legend or imagination, could neither have known nor invented this little detail. Startled by his discovery, Ramsay began to unearth other archaeological evidence which seemed clearly to indicate that the author of Acts possessed accurate, detailed, and probably firsthand information.

By 1922, the pendulum had swung so far that J. W. Hunkin could write the following as propositions to which the great majority of scholars, at least in Great Britain, would agree:

(i.) That the Acts is a product not of the second century but of the first.

(ii.) That there is a very strong probability that the author of the "we sections" is the author both of Acts and of the third gospel: [The "we sections" are the passages in which the author states that "we" did certain things, apparently claiming to have been present at the time. See Acts 16:8–9, etc.]

(iii.) That he possesses a great deal of accurate information with regard to St. Paul's journeys, some of it being first-hand:

(iv.) That whatever be his sources for the early chapters of the Acts these "Scenes from Early Days" are well chosen and consistent, and give a picture of the march of events which is at any rate, on the whole, correct in outline.[2]

The second half of the twentieth century, however, has seen the pendulum of critical thought swing back in the direction of skepticism with regard to the historicity of Acts' stories. Three major lines of argument have convinced many that Acts is of limited value to the historian.

1) Acts, especially in its early chapters, includes stories of miracles. It reports that language barriers crumbled (2:6), the sick were healed (5:16), prisoners were miraculously released (12:6–11), and the dead were raised (9:36–42). Especially if he or she begins with the assumption that all miracle stories must be false, the critic is likely to be skeptical about the historicity of Acts.

2) Repeatedly Acts seems to be in conflict with the genuine letters of Paul. For example, it is said that "speaking with tongues" in Acts 2 is quite different from what Paul describes in 1 Corinthians 12—14; Galatians 1—2 gives a picture of Paul's actions following his conversion quite different from that in Acts 9, and the true story of the Jerusalem Council in Galatians 2 conflicts with that in Acts 15.

3) Finally, recent scholarship has emphasized that the author of Acts wrote as a theologian, not as a historian. There are dozens of events any modern historian

would have reported but about which Acts is completely silent. When, near the end of Acts, Paul at last arrives at Rome, the church has already been founded there. But the author gives us no hint as to how this occurred. Whatever happened to the Apostle John and to most of the other disciples? Acts quickly lets them drop from the story. From other sources we know that there was soon a flourishing church in North Africa. Acts gives us detailed accounts of the founding of some insignificant congregations in Turkey but tells us nothing of so prominent a church as that in Alexandria, Egypt. Rather, the author has picked stories or, it is alleged, even invented stories which would illustrate the particular theological themes he wanted to develop.[3]

In spite of these objections, however, many scholars have continued to argue—effectively, in the view of the present writer—that Acts may be regarded as a valuable source of historical information about the infant church. The arguments to the contrary, however, are so strong that we need here to review the case given in defense of the general historicity of Acts' account.

1) Consistent, repeated, and very early tradition attributes the book to Luke, a companion of Paul. This is more noteworthy since Luke was not otherwise especially distinguished in church history (see above, pages 32 and 33). Apocryphal books created by the imagination of later Christians were usually attributed to much more prominent early leaders.

2) The use of the first person at the beginning of Luke, again in Acts 1:1, and repeatedly from Acts 16 on (in the "we passages") can be explained most simply by supposing that the author of the whole two-volume work, known to Theophilus, is claiming to have been present at the times indicated. Every test of vocabulary and style seems to indicate that the "travel diary" is by the author who wrote the rest of the book.

3) The differences between Acts and certain of Paul's writings, especially Galatians, are real, and they certainly suggest that Acts is not infallible as history. Some of these differences may be explained partially, however, in ways to be noted in the discussion of Galatians in chapter 9. (Paul, too, is straining to make some theological points!) As a matter of fact, the detailed agreements between Acts and the letters of Paul are more striking than the differences. They are especially remarkable since the writer shows no sign of having before him copies of the letters themselves. Agreement on so many details, incidental in both Acts and the Epistles, seems inexplicable in a work of later pious imagination. The writer clearly had access to a great deal of accurate information.[4]

4) We have already noted that archaeologists such as Sir William M. Ramsay found Luke accurate on many details which would have been difficult for a second-century writer to know.[5]

5) Finally, there are indications that Luke had access to and made use of both written and oral sources. This, of course, is what the author claims in Luke 1:1–4.

Some of these sources show traces of going back to the earliest days of the church.[6]

It is perhaps possible that some Christian scholars, in their pious effort to be scrupulously honest and not to base their theology on a theory of biblical infallibility, have actually leaned over backward to be skeptical about the historical accuracy of their sacred book. The Jewish scholar Klausner, by contrast, writes of Acts:

> But even in the first part of the book, that is to say, in the first twelve chapters, there is so much information containing details and names, that it would have been difficult to obtain them by hearsay and to remember them so exactly unless the author had had a written source before him. Thus it is necessary to assume that also in the first chapters the author made use of written sources along with oral.[7]

Acts as Theology

If Luke's accuracy as a historian continues to be debated, his originality as a theologian is currently more and more admired. Whatever one's view concerning the historicity of Luke's stories, any careful reader will find that Acts is not meant to be a modern newspaper report or a research paper "objectively" describing the early church. Luke wants to persuade Theophilus. He has chosen to tell some stories and to ignore others because he has certain ideas he wishes to emphasize. He introduces these themes in the very beginning of Acts.

The disciples, Luke begins by telling us, were confused. Jesus had risen. And yet the world still went on. "Lord, will you at this time restore the kingdom to Israel?" they asked (1:6). Is the kingdom at last really "at hand"? Is the final judgment now about to come?

> He said to them, "It is not for you to know times or seasons which the Father has fixed by his own authority. But you shall receive power when the Holy Spirit has come upon you; and you shall be my witnesses in Jerusalem and in all Judea and Samaria and to the end of the earth."
>
> (Acts 1:7–8)

Into these verses, deliberately emphasized by their placement at the beginning, the author has packed much of the message he plans to develop. Here are three major theological emphases of Acts these verses introduce:

1) The Acts of the Apostles is really a book about the *powerful acts of the Holy Spirit.*

More than half a century after Good Friday and Easter, the end of the world still had not come. Jesus, Mark had reported, had promised that there were some who heard him teach who would live to see the kingdom of God come with power (Mark 9:1). Matthew 16:28 even quoted the saying as being that they would see the Son of man himself coming. Now decades had passed and that end had not come. In his Gospel, Luke did not quote Mark 9:1.

What *had* come, Luke was sure, was the Holy Spirit. "Will you at this time restore the kingdom?""It is not for you to know" about God's schedule, the risen Christ replies in Acts 1:7. "But you shall receive power when the Holy Spirit has come upon you." Acts 1 is the story of that promise. Acts 2 is the story of Pentecost, the fulfillment of the promise. The rest of Acts is the story of that Spirit's power.

In his Gospel, Luke had written of "the Holy Spirit" (translated "the Holy Ghost" in the King James Version) about as often as had the other two Synoptic writers put together. Now, in the twenty-eight chapters of Acts, he uses that phrase or its equivalent nearly fifty times.

Acts 2 describes in highly dramatic fashion the first outpouring of that Spirit. In the power of that ecstasy the disciples speak in tongues, begin their mission of witnessing, and win their first converts.

In subsequent chapters the power of the Spirit is directly related to the disciples' bold witness when on trial (4:8; 5:32), the writing of scripture (4:25; 28:25), the authority of the Apostles (5:3), the character of those to be selected for church office (6:3), the restoration of sight to the blind Saul (9:17), comfort (9:31), Jesus' own power (10:38), conversion (10:44), the character of the saintly Barnabas (11:24), the appointment of the first officially designated missionaries (13:2), Paul's authority (13:9), joy (13:52), common Christian experience across lines of race (15:8), divine guidance for the church (15:28) and for individuals (16:6), prophecy (19:6; 20:23; 21:11), and the work of elders (20:28). In short, Luke implies that *all* the good things the Apostles do or have are understood in Acts to be through the power of the Holy Spirit.

2) The Acts of the Apostles is a book about *the acts of the church*. More than fifty years after Easter, the kingdom of God had not come—not, at least, in the way it had been expected. What *had* come, however, was the Spirit-filled community, the church.

Jesus himself is never recorded as using the word "church" except in Matthew 16:18 and Matthew 18:17. Many regard these two verses as employing a term which was not used until after Jesus' earthly life. But not only is the word "church" used repeatedly in Acts, the idea of the ongoing Christian community is basic to the whole book.

Hans Conzelmann proposes that Luke saw all history as divided into three periods.[8] The first was the age of the Law and the prophets, ending with John the Baptist (Luke 16:16). The second, "the mid-point," was the period of Jesus' life described in Luke's Gospel. The third is the era of the Spirit and of the church which begins with Acts. It will continue until the return of Christ. The eschatological hope has not been abandoned. Luke still expects Jesus to return at the end of the age (1:11). But the community is not to "stand looking into heaven," concentrating on the future (1:11). It has a job to do and a fellowship in which to participate here and now. Some day the kingdom will come, but now there is the church.

In Acts 1 the risen Christ gives that church its commission. Later in that chapter the church replaces Judas, thus beginning to organize for its task. In Acts 2 it begins its witness, adding three thousand converts to its number. An ideal, sharing community is described in Acts 2:42–47. Acts 3—4 describes the community heroically and prayerfully facing persecution. Again Acts 4:32–37 describes a church in which the kingdom ideals of the Sermon on the Mount are now being realized. (For a similar summary picturing the ideal church, see Acts 5:12–16.) Again the church expands its organization (6:1–6), for the purpose of even better sharing. Through the whole book Luke continues the story of how this community dealt with problems and spread its gospel and its fellowship.

In his Gospel Luke had pictured Jesus as having to break down barriers between races and classes (see above, pages 73–78). Now he pictures the church as the community in which that ideal fellowship has been realized. "And all who believed were together and had all things in common; and they sold their possessions and goods and distributed them to all, as any had need" (2:44–45). Gentiles, too, are welcomed into that loving company. The story of the admission to the church of the Roman centurion Cornelius (ch. 10) is so important to Luke that he tells it all over again in the next chapter. From Acts 13 on, the book is the story of the spread of the church into Gentile lands and among Gentile peoples.

3) Finally, among its theological emphases to be noted here, the Acts of the Apostles is the missionary story of their *acts of witnessing to the "word" more and more widely to the world.*

We have noted that Christ's Great Commission as recorded in Acts 1:8 calls upon the church to be "witnesses in Jerusalem and in all Judea and Samaria and to the end of the earth." The whole book can be thought of as outlined around that theme verse.

The witness in Jerusalem is described in Acts 1—6:7. That section ends with the editorial summary "And the word of God increased; and the number of the disciples multiplied greatly in Jerusalem" (6:7).

The witness beyond Jerusalem is introduced in Acts 6:8 with the story of Stephen. His address (ch. 7) seems designed to protest restriction to a sacred temple, land, or race. And with his death, we are told, the church members "were all scattered throughout the region of Judea and Samaria." Thus Acts 6—12 can be thought of as telling how the second part of the Great Commission began to be fulfilled. A summary in Acts 9:31 reports, "So the church throughout all Judea and Galilee and Samaria had peace and was built up." A similar summary in Acts 12:24 ends the section.

The witness to the world has already been hinted at by the story of the conversion of the Gentile Cornelius (10—11:18) and the founding of the church at Antioch (11:19–30). But from Acts 13 on, the book concentrates almost exclusively on the worldwide witness of the church. The missionary activity of Luke's great hero, Paul, becomes the center of the whole story. Acts ends with Paul's arrival at Rome, the capital of the world.

A characteristic summary Acts uses at the end of the first section is "the word of God increased" (6:7; cf. 12:24; 19:20). Catching the significance of this phrase, the title of a recent study book calls Acts the story of *The Word in Action*.[9] Acts is the story of witnesses, but it is also the story of the spreading power of the "word" to which their witness was borne.

Luke the theologian writes as a witness to that "word."

The Purpose of Acts

Is Acts history or theology? It is certainly theology. Luke undoubtedly selects and to some extent shapes his stories to illustrate the gospel he is preaching to a church more than fifty years after some of the events he describes.

Yet we have seen that Acts contains accuracies most easily explained on the theory that Luke did have access to much historically valuable information. The present writer attaches more value to Acts as a work of history than do most who currently write on this subject.

Perhaps a figure to suggest how Luke has blended fact and faith may be suggested by an ancient legend, itself probably pure fiction. Tradition says that Luke was an artist. At least two medieval churches contain paintings of the Virgin Mary piously believed to have been painted by Luke. Luke really was a kind of artist—with words.

Luke has painted for us a word-portrait of the infant church. No good portrait is limited to the exactness of a photograph. An artist attempts to bring out the character of his subject, expanding a line here, deepening a shadow there. But he does not thereby seek to produce to fiction. He attempts rather to present the truth more profoundly than a photographer could. In this sense, at least, we may believe that the writer, more than fifty years after some of the events he seeks to describe (but not without information), has written in order that his readers may know the truth.

Scenes from the Earliest Days

For nineteen hundred years Christians have been inspired by the word-pictures of the earliest days of the church "painted" in Acts 1–12. Just what these controversial vignettes present will now be summarized.

The Ascension

Two centuries latter, pious pilgrims began to visit Jerusalem to see an empty tomb. Where was Jesus' body? Ascended into heaven, Acts 1 replies. But when

Christians began to recite, as part of the Apostles' Creed, "He ascended into heaven," they meant more than just a spatial relocation of Jesus' flesh and bones.

Every part of the New Testament affirms that Christ is risen from the dead. Repeatedly he is also spoken of as in heaven and at "the right hand of God" (Rom. 8:34; Heb. 1:3; 1 Peter 3:22; cf. Eph. 1:20; Col. 3:1). That Jesus now has the status symbolized by these words is basic to the New Testament faith.

Except in the disputed ending of Mark (16:19), however, it is only Luke who discribes Jesus' ascension—going "up" bodily into heaven—as an event seen by his disciples.

The story in Acts 1 is written in terms of a first-century cosmology in which heaven was thought of as "above" a flat earth. Subsequent recognition that the earth is round and that "up" is a relative term has not altered the significance of what the theologian Luke intends. His story implies at least three things:

1) Jesus, Luke is saying, was not raised from the dead simply to die again. Modern efforts (such as *The Passover Plot*)[10] proposing theories of a temporary resuscitation of Jesus' body miss the point of the biblical claim. Jesus, the church was sure, had permanently triumphed over death, had entered a new kind of life.

2) Jesus' ascension into heaven is, for Luke, a sign of his heavenly status, his conquest of all that opposed him in this world of human sin and limitation. Jesus is now "beside" God, exalted, in a position of equality with the Almighty himself.

3) The ascension of Jesus' body into heaven is for Luke a necessary preliminary for the coming of the Spirit. That Spirit, free from all physical, spatial limitations, becomes at Pentecost the moving force behind the witness of the Apostles all over the world.

The Election of Matthias

After the death of Judas there seemed to be the need for a new Apostle to lead in that witness. So far as we know from the New Testament, however, Matthias, the one selected, never did much leading.

Late legend said that the cannibals were about to eat him. He had gone as a missionary to the Ethiopians. Just in time, however, this thirteenth Apostle was rescued—by Andrew! An apocryphal gospel teaching a heresy usually called Gnosticism was falsely attributed to Matthias. The New Testament, however, never mentions his name again after his selection in Acts 1.

The choosing of an additional Apostle, however, is significant. Luke is saying that from the first, the church regarded organization for its task as important. As there had been twelve tribes of Israel, the ancient people of God, and twelve Apostles in the days of Jesus' earthly life, so the new community must have its twelve. But first, Luke tells us, the church had to wait for the Spirit to come before it could begin its witness.

Pentecost

Suddenly, Luke says, born in spiritual ecstasy, that witness began.

Almost every book of the New Testament speaks of the Holy Spirit. Belief in this powerful presence was clearly part of the Christian faith from the beginnings of the Christian witness. It is only Acts 2, however, which describes the coming of that Spirit as an identifiable event on a particular day, the Jewish feast day of Pentecost. With miraculous manifestations of fire and the sound of wind, Luke tells us, the confused disciples were suddenly transformed. Once they had timidly waited. Now, so moved that some onlookers thought that they were drunk, the disciples began to shout out the gospel to the world.

The Gentile Luke pictures Pentecost itself as already pointing to the fulfillment of Jesus' command to be witnesses "to the end of the earth." The setting is Jerusalem at the feast of Pentecost (so called because it came fifty days after Passover). From all over the world Jewish pilgrims, speaking every language, had come "home" to their holy city for the ceremonies. As the Spirit-baptized disciples began to "speak with tongues," some of these pilgrims, it is true, heard only what sounded to them like the babbling of drunkards. But, miraculously, others heard in these same voices the disciples' praise of God, transcending all barriers of language and nation.

Scholars have proposed various explanations of this puzzling story.

1) More conservative scholars have said that here at the beginning of the Christian mission a miracle occurred and the disciples were temporarily enabled to speak foreign languages they had never been taught.

2) C. S. Mann suggests the possibility that the disciples spoke classic Hebrew, the language of the Old Testament, rather than the locally popular Aramaic dialect, and thus to their surprise, the Jews from abroad understood.[11]

3) More liberal students have suggested that the "speaking with tongues" of the early church was always a pouring forth of unintelligible sound (such as is described in 1 Cor. 14:2) which "no one understands." Luke, writing at a later time and unfamiliar with the practice, reported an ideal crossing of language barriers which did not then literally take place. Rather, his story reflects how, by his day, the gospel had begun to cross barriers of race, nation, and tongue.

4) Still others have suggested that the miracle was more in the hearts and ears of the hearers then in the tongues of the speakers. To some the utterances did sound like drunken nonsense (Acts 2:13). But those more open to the Spirit were able to understand, each in his own way, the praise of God (Acts 2:11).

Whatever be the explanation of the historical facts, Luke hints at theological meanings in the phenomena he pictures. Jewish tradition said that when the Law was given to the Jews, seventy tongues of fire appeared on Mount Sinai—one for each of the other Nations of the world. Now these tongues of fire reappear. The separation of nations and languages at the tower of Babel has now been reversed

The Jewish scriptures had pictured isolated instances of the Spirit's coming upon individuals (Judg. 14:6; 1 Sam. 10:10; etc.). But Luke sees in the worldwide church the fulfillment of Joel's prophecy that the Spirit will be poured out upon "all flesh" (Acts 2:17). Jesus' own promise had come true (Acts 1:5–8).

The "speaking in tongues" brought a mixed reaction from the crowd, Luke tells us. But Peter's sermon, presumably in common Aramaic, is said to have won three thousand converts (2:41)!

The Preaching

In the twentieth century the sermons summarized in the book of Acts have gained new recognition as expressions of the *kerygma,* the gospel proclaimed by the early church. In his now classic *The Apostolic Preaching and Its Developments,* British scholar C. H. Dodd compared these sermons with passages in which Paul seems to be quoting tradition he himself had been taught (1 Thess. 1:9; 1 Cor. 1:23; 2:1–2; 15:1–7; Rom. 1:1–5; 10:8–9; Gal. 3:1). Running through both, Dodd found what appeared to be almost the same pattern. Dodd summarizes the sermons in Acts in the following propositions:

> First, the age of fulfillment has dawned. . . .
>
> Secondly, this has taken place through the ministry, death, and resurrection of Jesus, . . . with proof from the Scriptures that all took place through "the determinate counsel and foreknowledge of God. . . ."
>
> Thirdly, by virtue of the resurrection, Jesus has been exalted at the right hand of God, as Messianic head of the new Israel. . . .
>
> Fourthly, the Holy Spirit in the Church is the sign of Christ's present power and glory. . . .
>
> Fifthly, the Messianic Age will shortly reach its consummation in the return of Christ. . . .
>
> Finally, the *kerygma* always closes with an appeal for repentance, the offer of forgiveness and of the Holy Spirit, and the promise of "salvation."[12]

Several lines of investigation suggest that these sermons, thus summarized, do reflect the ideas characteristic of the earliest preachers.

1) Dodd showed how similar these are to the ideas Paul seems to have learned from his predecessors.

2) A word study of the use of the Greek verb *kerussein* (to preach) throughout the New Testament will show that its objects are nearly always the kinds of things described in Acts' sermons.

3) The language and style, though that of Luke's good Greek, are said to bear uncharacteristic echoes of Aramaic, a Palestinian dialect foreign to our Greek author. Some have argued that he must have used an Aramaic source for some of these sermons.

4) The eschatology (doctrine of the end) and Christology (doctrine concerning who Jesus is) implied in these passages are not those of Luke's emphases. They seem more characteristic of an earlier time.

This is not to say, of course, that Luke has given us stenographic reproductions of the actual sermons. He says quite explicitly that he is attempting only a summary (2:40). But for the reasons stated above, we can believe that Acts does give us insight into the kind of thing the early preachers really did say about Jesus.[13]

If, then, we ask what was the earliest Christology, what was the earliest understanding of who Jesus was, the answer we get from these earliest sermons is perhaps surprising. It does not appear that the first Christians could have recited the Nicene Creed, with its phrases about Jesus borrowed from Aristotelian metaphysics (such as that Jesus was "of one substance" with God the Father). On the other hand, there is no hint that, as some scholars once argued, Jesus was first thought of as a man, and only gradually came to be revered as God.

Rather, the sermons say such things about Jesus as the following.[14]

1) Jesus was described in terms of the *cosmic Judge of popular Jewish eschatological expectation*. Peter is pictured as quoting Joel's account of the final catastrophic events, now said to be at hand:

> . . . and wonders in the heaven above
> and signs on the earth beneath,
> . . . .
> the sun shall be turned into darkness
> and the moon into blood,
> before the day of the Lord comes.   (Acts 2:19–20; cf. Joel 2:30–31)

The day spoken of in a book of the Pseudepigrapha or "false writings," the Assumption of Moses, had arrived when

> . . . the horns of the sun shall be broken and he shall be
> turned into darkness;
> And the moon shall not give her light, and be turned wholly
> into blood.[15]

In that *eschaton*, that end, Jesus, Peter announces, "is the one ordained by God to be Judge of the living and the dead." (10:42).

This kind of understanding of Jesus is not a characteristic emphasis of the Greek Luke. Vivid descriptions of cosmic judgment were popular, however, among some first-century Jews. Later the book of Revelation was to develop this aspect of the primitive *kerygma*.

2) Jesus was seen as the *fulfillment of the Jewish scriptures*. "David says concerning him (2:25); "God foretold by the mouth of all the prophets, that his Christ should suffer" (3:18); "To him all the prophets bear witness" (10:43):

over and over the sermons affirmed that all the Old Testament had pointed to Jesus. We have seen how Matthew developed this idea in his Gospel. Hebrews explores this idea even more fully.

3) Yet Jesus was described also as *a man who had lived on earth.* "Jesus of Nazareth, a man attested to you by God with mighty works and wonders and signs which God did through him in your midst" is the subject of Peter's sermon in Acts 2. In Acts 10 Peter preaches of "how he went about doing good and healing all that were oppressed by the devil, for God was with him" (v. 38). One fact about Jesus' life which is mentioned in all the sermons is his death. We have seen that an outline of the sermon in Acts 10 would serve almost equally well as an outline of Mark, so firmly was this story built into the primitive *kerygma* (see above, pages 24–26).

4) Central was the announcement of *Jesus' resurrection* (2:24, 32; 3:15; 10:40; etc.). It is the resurrection which is particularly to be associated with the two great titles for Jesus which Peter is pictured as proclaiming at Pentecost: "Lord" and "Christ" (2:36). That the title "Lord" was used of Jesus even as early as the days of the Aramaic-speaking church seems clear from Paul's quotation of the formula *Maranatha* in its original Aramaic (1 Cor. 16:22). Probably it is to be understood as meaning originally that Jesus was the Messianic king promised in Psalm 110, the passage from the Old Testament most often quoted in the New. The frequency of the use of the title and of the quotation of that Psalm throughout the New Testament bears witness to its antiquity. The title "Christ" or "Messiah" also was soon so widely used of Jesus that it came to be almost a second proper name for him. But in the early days its original connotation of "the Anointed One" surely must have been felt. Hebrew kings were anointed for office. When the dynasty of David was dethroned, the hope still endured of the great anointed kind to come. Peter was announcing the fulfillment of that hope.

Is it possible to penetrate back to the very earliest Christian "creed" or confession stating what the very first Christian believed about Jesus? Tracing back the earliest formulas in Scripture and the liturgies for baptism and worship, one always arrives at an original formula. It is the one implied by the climax of what Luke presents as the first Christian sermon: "Jesus Christ is Lord" (cf. 2:36).

5) Finally, the first sermons spoke of Jesus as a *living and present power.* It is Jesus who has poured out the Holy Spirit upon the believers (2:33). In his name miracles are performed and forgiveness is granted (2:38; 3:16; etc.). He is the church's "Leader" and "Savior" (5:31).

Norman Perrin has argued forcefully that for Luke himself, Jesus is in a sense "the first Christian," the example and model for his followers. That, however, is not the emphasis of these sermons. In these early utterances Christ is not presented simply as the first of a group. He is uniquely the author of ecstasy, the object of devotion, and one who in his relationship to the believers occupies a place and assumes titles heretofore reserved for God himself. He is not simply the church's example and leader, but its Lord.

The Ideal Community

Was this first church a "commune"? Were the first Christians "communists"? We read such summaries as the following: "And all who believed were together and had all things in common; and they sold their possessions and goods and distributed them to all, as any had need" (2:44–45; cf. 4:32). In his Gospel Luke had pictured Jesus as preaching a kind of economic revolution in behalf of social justice. Now, he tells us, at least for "one brief, shining moment," Jesus' ideal was realized.

A closer reading, however, makes clear that such a verse as that quoted above is not to be taken as the whole picture. Luke does want to present the first church as an inspiring ideal. He wants to show the chruch as a sharing, praying, preaching, daring community. But Acts also records quite frankly selfishness, dissension, and dishonesty among the first church members. Ananias and Sapphira, we are told, sold a piece of property, brought half the proceeds to the Apostles, and claimed to be giving them the whole price. The sin for which they were condemned was not that of keeping back half the money. Whatever sharing there was, it evidently was strictly voluntary, not required of all church members. It was when they were caught in a lie that Ananias and his wife fell dead (5:1–11).

We are also told of an early dispute between the native Palestinian Jewish-Christians and their Greek-speaking brothers over the distribution of food to the poor (6:1–6). Again the church adds to its organizational structure, selecting what were later called "deacons"—all of whom have Greek names—to see that the Greek-speaking widows get their fair share. That dispute may have been the ancestor of subsequent disagreement resulting from the spread of the church beyond Palestine and the Jewish race, as at least one faction of the church aggressively spread the gospel through the Roman empire.

Though he pauses in this way to caution us not to imagine that the first Christians were really sinless, Luke continues to picture the church in ideal terms, a model for his own generation. These exemplary Christians witness heroically and with marvelous success. They share all they have. And in persecution they so pray that "the place in which they were gathered together was shaken" (4:31). Equally shaking to the reader is the account of what they prayed for. As Luke tells it, they did not pray to be spared; they prayed to have the courage to go on preaching even though they faced persecution (4:29).

Persecution

Face persecution they did!

There are so many stories of arrests, trials, and escapes, that Harnack supposed they must include duplicate reports of the same events. No doubt all were written to inspire a later generation of Christians still facing persecution, as well as to inform them. In any event, the first chapters of Acts abound in accounts of troubles with the authorities.

Acts 4 tells of an arrest and trial of Peter and John. This first time they are let off with a warning. Acts 5 tells of a second arrest, with the Apostles being set free by angels. Then, arrested again, they are freed through the intercession of the wise Rabbi Gamaliel. Acts 7 describes the first martyrdom, that of Stephen. Acts 12 reports the execution of James, the first of the Twelve to give his life for his Lord. And Acts 12 records a fourth arrest of Peter, who is again set free by an angel. Meanwhile, we are told, persecution has begun to scatter the first Christians.

It is ironic that for a few years Jews seem to have persecuted Christians. Christians have been persecuting Jews for sixteen centuries! Soon, of course, it was the Roman, not the Jewish, authorities who threatened the church.

In our study of the Gospels we noted certain reasons for the antagonism between Jesus and even the best Jews. Let the reader also recall that only by tenacious adherence to the Law, usually coupled with a love of the holy land and the Temple even by those living far away, did Judaism survive. Jews grew up on the story of the seven brothers who were skinned and fried rather than eat pork. Jews grew up daily scanning the skies for a deliverer from the hated Romans. Naturally they would not look kindly on the spread of a new teaching which seemed to undermine their faith. And authorities whose jobs depended upon pleasing the Romans were not going to be happy that the "rebellion" they thought they had crushed now seemed to be rising again. Twenty-eight times in one century the high priesthood changed hands, usually at the insistence of those who took orders from Rome. Fearful that their turn to lose power was at hand, the establishment moved to crush the new sect.

In the case of Stephen, one of those elected to administer food (Acts 6:1–6) but who seems also to have been a prominent preacher, antagonism finally led to violence. They lynched him.

Stephen

Presumably his trial began in orderly fashion. Following custom, Stephen would have been brought in wearing mourning clothes, a sign of the prisoner's penitence for sin. The seventy judges and their leader in the Sanhedrin, the Jewish court, would have sat in a semicircle. Two notaries would have kept a record, one to record evidence in Stephen's defense, one the evidence for the prosecution.

For centuries the long address attributed to Stephen in Acts 7 has puzzled the commentators. "Stephen's reply at first seems absurd and inept," wrote Calvin. "Many things in this speech have not very much pertinency to the matter which Stephen undertook," admitted Erasmus. One modern commentator suggests that Luke himself did not understand it. At the very least, it is so different from anything else in Luke's Acts that we may believe that here, surely, Luke is making use of some written source purporting to summarize what Stephen at some time actually said.

Perhaps a key to understanding Stephen lies in his reference to Jesus as the "Son of man" (7:56). This is almost the only place in the New Testament outside the Gospels in which this enigmatic phrase is used of Jesus, almost the only place where it appears except on the lips of Jesus himself. Apparently later Christian thinkers went on to titles which made more sense to them than did this one from Jewish apocalyptic literature. The apocalyptic book of Daniel had described the Son of man:

> And to him was given dominion
>   and glory and kingdom,
>   that all peoples, nations, and languages
>   should serve him.   (Daniel 7:14)

Perhaps this Christian with the Greek name who worked among people from other nations resident in Jerusalem (6:9) was the first to take seriously the idea that Jesus' kingdom must break out of Judaism, "that *all* peoples, nations, and languages should serve him."

The charges brought against Stephen involved his speaking against both the Temple and the Law. Puzzling as his long address in Acts 7 is, three themes emerge: God is above the holy land, the Chosen People, and the holy Temple. Repeatedly God has worked outside these limits of place and race.

Infuriated, Stephen's hearers became no longer a court of law, but a kind of lynch mob. Jewish Law called for an orderly procession to the place of execution, with opportunity given right up to the last minute for a reversal of the death penalty. But now they "rushed together upon him" (7:57). Praying, like Jesus, for the forgiveness of those who killed him, Stephen was stoned.

To be stoned, a criminal was thrown into a pit or a cell in which the witnesses against him could stand above him and drop big rocks upon him. If the missiles of the witnesses themselves failed to kill him, then the whole crowd might join in crushing him with their stones. Guarding the coats of Stephen's executioners was young Saul of Tarsus (7:58).

The Spread of the Church

In the persecution which followed, in which Saul/Paul later confessed he had indeed been a leader (Gal. 1:13), the church at last began to spread into Judea and Samaria and beyond.

Later, writers repeatedly affirmed that the Christian world mission was really at the command of the risen Christ (Acts 1:8; cf. Matt. 28:19; etc.). But Acts is probably right that the first Christians remained largely in Jerusalem until they were driven out.

It is probably no accident, however, that the radiating forth of the gospel begins in relation to Stephen. His, we have seen hinted, was the vision of a kingdom of the Son of man which would include "all peoples, nations, and languages"—even Samaritans.

"You are a Samaritan and have a demon," Jesus' enemies had snarled, according to John 8:48. "Samaritan" was the worst name they could think to call him. Desperate as they had been for funds and friends, the little group of Jews who set out to rebuild the Temple after the Babylonian captivity had rejected the offer of help from Samaritans, half-breed Israelites (Ezra 4:1–3). These Samaritans, in turn, had set up their own temple on Mount Gerizim (John 4:20). Stephen, however, had had little regard for temples (7:48). We are told that after Stephen's death, "Philip went down to a city of Samaria, and proclaimed to them the Christ" (8:5). Even these hated Samaritans received the Holy Spirit (8:17).

Chapters 8–11 continue to describe how the gospel radiated from Jerusalem, as foreshadowed in Acts 1:8. An Ethiopian eunuch, possibly a Jew by birth but prevented from full participation in Judaism by the law of Deuteronomy 23:1, was baptized.

The crucial departure from Judaism, however, is dramatized for us in the story of the baptism of Cornelius, a Roman. So important to Luke is the account of this Gentile's conversion and acceptance into the church that he devotes nearly two chapters to the story, in effect telling it twice (10:1–11:18). Peter himself is pictured as the leader in the matter, and he acts as the result of special revelation.

Critics have questioned the story in the light of Peter's subsequent refusal to eat with Gentiles (Gal. 2:12). Paul tells us on the basis of firsthand observation, however, that Peter did frequently eat with Gentiles, in violation of Jewish law. Luke has highlighted this particular instance as a dramatic way of telling his readers that the gospel did break out of all racial restrictions.

The critics are surely right, however, that the great leader in taking the gospel to the Gentiles and in working out the theology of that world mission was not Peter. It was that Saul of Tarsus who guarded the coats of Stephen's executioners and who helped lead the persecution which drove the Christians from Jerusalem. To Luke, Saul/Paul is so important that Acts 13–28—more than half of the book—is devoted to the life of this one man. To his story we must now turn.

Paul

He was "a man rather small in size, bald-headed, bow-legged, with meeting eyebrows, a large, red, and somewhat hooked nose," says the *Acts of Paul and Thecla*, a book of pious fiction popular in the second century. "Strongly-built, he was full of friendliness, for at times he looked like a man, at times like an angel."

As a description of Paul's physical appearance, the passage is too late to be of much value, though it is so unflattering as to suggest some possibility that it may owe something to memory, not just hero-worship. But the last clause is one Luke himself might have liked. At times Paul "looked like a man, at times like an angel."

He never succeeded in becoming a perfect saint, and indeed Paul would have been the first to admit it (Phil. 3:14). He did become, next to Jesus, the dominant figure of the New Testament. Of its twenty-seven books, thirteen bear Paul's name. Some of these, as we shall see, probably should be thought of rather as dedicated to his memory than as actually from his pen, yet even so, his influence on them is clear. Two more books, Luke and Acts, are traditionally attributed to a disciple of Paul. Thus, well over half the New Testament is related to this one Apostle.

Paul has, in fact, been called "the second founder" of the Christian faith.

Clearly he was Luke's hero. Acts 9 is the story of Paul's conversion. From Acts 13 on, the other Apostles almost fade out of the story. Nearly the first half of Acts consists of scenes from the early church. But the rest of Acts is devoted entirely to stories of Paul.

Early Life and Conversion

Paul was born, Luke tells us, a Jewish citizen of Tarsus, a prominent city in what is now Turkey. He bore the name of history's most famous man of his tribe, King Saul. But as a Roman citizen he also had a Roman name, Paul. Tarsus contained one of the great universities of the ancient world, and Luke pictures Paul as able to quote Stoic philosophers when presenting the gospel to Greek thinkers (17:28). Yet it was as a strict Pharisee in Jerusalem, taught by Rabbi Gamaliel, that Paul was trained, according to Acts 22:3. Some have interpreted Acts 7:58 and 26:10 as implying that Luke thought of Paul, though still young, as having already risen to be a member of the Jerusalem Sanhedrin, a kind of Jewish supreme court. More modestly, Paul simply wrote, "I advanced in Judaism beyond many of my own age among my people, so extremely zealous was I for the traditions of my fathers"(Gal. 1:14). Paul did admit that he had been "a Hebrew born of Hebrews" and "blameless" in his rigidly righteous adherence to the Jewish Law (Phil. 3:5–6).

As such, Luke tells us, this young man fairly snorted with murderous rage as the Christian movement grew (9:1). "Extremely zealous," to use his own phrase, he once "persecuted the church of God violently and tried to destroy it" (Gal. 1:13–14; cf. Phil. 3:6).

His conversion amazed his new brothers in Christ, both Luke and Paul tell us (Gal. 1:23–24; Acts 9:26). It has puzzled scholars ever since.

Its story is so important to Luke that he tells it three times (9:1–30; 22:1–21; 26:1–23). Some details vary in the retelling. In Acts 9:7 Paul's companions hear a voice but see no one; in Acts 22:9 his companions do see the great light but hear no voice. Perhaps mystic experiences do not lend themselves to the kind of factual reporting one expects on television's evening news. But the basic outline is the same. Paul was sent from Jerusalem to Damascus to lead in suppression of the church there. (Galatians 1:17 implies that Paul had already become a resident of Damascus.) On the road to that Syrian city he was struck blind by a vision. In Galatians 1:16 Paul simply says that God "was pleased to reveal his Son to me." Three days later the persecutor of the faithful had become a baptized, seeing Christian!

Determined to understand the story in modern terms, some have proposed that Paul was subject to some kind of epileptic seizures or trances. Acts does picture him as having repeated "visions"(9:3; 16:9; 22:17; 23:11), and in 2 Corinthians 12:1 Paul confirms this picture.. Was epilepsy or perhaps recurring (hysterical?) bad eyesight (related to the Damascus road blindness) the "thorn in the flesh" complained of in 2 Corinthians 12:7 (cf. Gal. 4:15; 6:11)? It must be noted that only a man of considerable mental and physical vigor could have done all that both Acts and Paul's letters indicate he did.

Other psychologically oriented students have noted that the "voice" is reported as saying to Paul at his conversion, "It hurts you to kick against the goads"(26:14). Does Luke mean to imply that Paul's conversion climaxed a long spiritual struggle comparable to that which Paul described later in Romans 7?

Actually, neither the historian nor the psychiatrist can fully explain such experiences. Paul's letters bear witness to his conversion but give us no details (see, for example, 1 Cor. 9:1; 15:8; and Gal. 1:15–16). What is certain is that he who once persecuted the church became its most influential writer, its most celebrated missionary, and the hero of the second half of Acts.

His temper was never fully converted. He still could call his enemies "dogs" (Phil. 3:2). Translators discretely gloss over it, but what he really says about his opponents who continue to advocate circumcision is that he wishes they would go castrate themselves (Gal. 5:12). Even Luke could picture Paul as cursing the high priest and calling him an ugly name (Acts 23:3). "At times he looked like a man."

But, to use one of Paul's favorite phrases, he was a man "in Christ."

The First Missionary Journey

One of the unsolved mysteries of biblical study is that while Acts pictures Paul as preaching in Jerusalem soon after his conversion, Paul himself, in Galatians, swears that instead he went to Arabia and did not go to Jerusalem for three years (Gal. 1:7–21). If in the years described in these verses Paul was already a missionary, what is usually called Paul's "first missionary journey" was really his second. Acts 9:30 does speak of a journey to Tarsus (cf. Gal. 1:21).

Nevertheless, what began at Antioch in Cilicia was a "first." Antioch, a seaport, was the third largest city in the Roman Empire. There, in this multiracial metropolis, an interracial church had already been established (11:20). Barnabas had secured Paul to help in the leadership of this unusual congregation. And there, Luke tells us, for the first time as far as we know, two men were formally commissioned to be missionaries (13:1–3). Jesus' Great Commission sending his disciples "to the uttermost parts of the earth" was at last beginning to be carried out fully.

Since Paul is pictured as setting out on journeys from Antioch three times, it is customary to speak of Paul's "three missionary journeys." These are found in Acts 13—14; 15:36—18:22; and 18:23—21:16. The route of each of these travels as recorded by Luke is readily traceable in any Bible atlas.

Paul's companion Barnabas was from Cyprus (4:36); it was to Cyprus that they went first. (Much later tradition said that Barnabas finally was martyred in Cyprus.) Though they crossed the island preaching, Acts saves its account of their message until its story of Paul's arrival on the mainland. In Cyprus he is pictured as making a favorable impression on the proconsul (13:6–12). At least one inscription has been found indicating that a few years later Cyprus was indeed governed by a proconsul and that his name was Paulus. There is, however, no record anywhere else of Sergius Paulus having actually become a Christian, though it is known that the church in Cyprus was quite strong two centuries later.

It is Paul's experience at Antioch in Pisidia—not to be confused with the Antioch in Cilicia, from which Paul's journey began—that Luke describes in detail (13:13–52). Apparently Luke means us to understand that this is typical of Paul's message and method everywhere and of the response which Paul received.

In Paul's day as in ours, there were Jews in every city. Josephus quotes the geographer Strabo as having written: "This people has already made its way into every city, and it is not easy to find any place in the habitable world which has not received this nation and in which it has not made its power felt."[16] To the synagogue Paul and Barnabas go. In accordance with custom, they are given the opportunity to speak. The sermon is typical not so much of Paul as of the early *kerygma* common to all. Acts 13:38–39, however, with its promise of a freedom the Law could not give, may be Luke's hint of a distinctive Pauline emphasis, one we will see developed at length in Paul's letters.

Equally typical is the response. Some become Christians; others run Paul and Barnabas out of town (13:48–50)!

Curiously, it is Gentiles who are converted in this Jewish synagogue. The explanation is this. For one brief period in its history, Judaism was itself a missionary religion (Matt. 23:15). Disillusioned, even repelled, by pagan religions, many non-Jews had been attracted to the worship of the biblical God. Some had actually become Jews, undergoing circumcision as a sign that they were "proselytes." Others, known as "God-fearers," worshiped at the synagogue without being circumcised or restricting their diet to kosher food. It was among these Gentile converts and near-converts to Judaism, Luke tells us, that Paul had his greatest success. The synagogue split. The Gentile group, with some Jews, became the nucleus of a church. But the leaders of the more conservative Jewish establishment brought political pressure to bear on Barnabas and Paul and forced them to leave town.

The Jewish-Gentile pattern was repeated in Iconium (14:1–7). But at Lystra, Luke describes Paul's first recorded head-on encounter with real paganism.

> Toues Macrinus also called Abascantus, and Batasis son of Bretasis having made in accordance with a vow at their own expense [a statue of] Hermes Most Great along with a sun-dial dedicated it to Zeus the sun-god.[17]

So reads an inscription dug up near the little Turkish village where the great city of Lystra used to be. Another inscription read, "Kakkan and Maramoas and Iman Licinius priests of Zeus."[18] Clearly, the two gods for whom Paul and Barnabas were mistaken were worshiped in Lystra. In fact, the good people of that province believed that Zeus and Hermes might arrive incognito at any time. They had been taught as children the story of how the two gods, disguised as mortals, had been hospitably received by a Lystra couple, Philemon and Baucis, who had been rewarded. Now Paul and Barnabas, having healed a lame man, are mistaken for these gods themselves. The speech attributed to Paul in Acts 14:15–17 is our oldest account of a Christian address to a pagan audience.

Again forced by a Jewish faction to flee for their lives, Paul and Barnabas retraced their steps and eventually returned to Antioch in Cilicia, the city from which their journey had begun.

Their report is significant. They had been opposed in Cyprus, evicted from Antioch in Pisidia, nearly stoned in Iconium, and actually stoned almost to death in Lystra. But what they are said to have reported is that God had "opened a door of faith" (14:27)!

The Jerusalem Council

The church, Luke tells us, was shaken by its own success. Were all those Gentiles really to be let into the church and, if so, on what basis? Luke's story of the council has also shaken modern critics.

The issue was both racial and religious. The Jews were God's Chosen People, not the Gentiles. If Gentiles were to be admitted, surely they must first become good Jews. The first Christians were law-abiding, orthodox, circumcised Jews, worshiping in the Temple. There is no indication that the Christian leaders in Jerusalem overtly sought to exclude all Gentiles. But they did see the process of becoming part of God's people as including the ceremony of circumcision. This had been the sign of the covenant, Genesis 21:4 affirmed, since the days of Abraham and Isaac.

Acts 15 describes a kind of formal Apostolic council to deal with the issue raised by the flood of Gentile converts. Apostles, elders, and others gather in solemn assembly. Peter makes a speech. James, Jesus' brother, whom later tradition called the first Bishop of Jerusalem, presides. A formal, written decree is adopted and circulated to the churches. It represents a victory for Paul, but there are certain compromises in that a few dietary restrictions are to be imposed on the new converts (15:28–29).

Critics have objected that nowhere in his epistles does Paul mention such a decree, though he is repeatedly involved in the issue. The author of Galatians, it is argued, would never have accepted the "compromise" on food. (Defenders of the Acts account have replied that pork chops are never served at conference dinners involving Christians and Jews today, though Christians do not thereby feel they are involved in "compromise.") The account in Galatians 2 of the same or a somewhat similar meeting represents a much less formal gathering with no written decree. Luke, it is charged, has idealized and enlarged the story to emphasize the importance of the decision for his Gentile readers.

Either way, Luke has dramatically presented an issue which certainly did arise. And he is clearly right that the church did come—not without dissension— to accept Gentiles apart from the Jewish Law.

The Second Missionary Journey

"Saint" Barnabas and "Saint" Paul did not always get along. Their partnership ended with a spat over "Saint" Mark (15:36–40). A nephew of Barnabas, John Mark—presumably the Mark to whom the Gospel is traditionally ascribed— had accompanied them at the beginning of the first missionary journey but had turned back. (No reason is named for his retreat, but the stonings and threats of stonings they faced might have discouraged some later Christians!) Paul refused to go again with Mark, and he and Barnabas went their separate ways. (2 Timothy 4:11 implies a later reconciliation.) Paul now set out with a companion named Silas.

Paul's original goal was to revisit the churches founded on his first trip in what is now Turkey (15:36). In response to what Luke is sure was divine guidance, however, Paul made a momentous decision: he crossed over into Europe (16:6–12). It is at the time of this decision, incidentally, that Luke seems to be claiming that he himself first entered the story (16:10).

Readers whose ancestors came from Europe may be disappointed to find that Paul's reception in Macedonia (northern Greece) was as stormy as it had been in Asia Minor. Again it was a "God-fearer," a Gentile who worshiped with the Jewish community, who was his first convert. Thus a traveling saleswoman, Lydia, was the first known Christian convert on European soil (16:14). Her home became headquarters for the church to which Paul was later to write the Philippian letter.

Soon, however, Paul was arrested at the instigation, Luke tells us, of the owners of a slave girl who was a fortune-teller. They were incensed because Paul, by exorcising her, had destroyed their livelihood. Delivered by an earthquake, a frightened jailer, and his own claim to the privileges of Roman citizenship, Paul was able to go on south through Greece.

A repeated theme is the prominent place of women in the churches established by Paul. Priscilla was to be a leader in the work (8:26; cf. 1 Cor. 16:19; Rom. 16:3). Lydia has been mentioned. "Leading women" are specifically noted among converts at Thessalonica (17:4). Women were again important at Beroea (17:12). At each of these places, also, it is the Gentiles from the fringes of the synagogues who form the nucleus of the infant church. In his Gospel, Luke had pictured Christ as having come to break down barriers of race and of sex. Now, he is saying, that process was under way.

By the time Paul arrives at Thessalonica for the usual pattern of preaching and the buildup to a riot, his fame has preceded him. "These men who have turned the world upside down have come here also," his enemies exclaim, "saying that there is another king, Jesus" (17:6–7). The revolution Jesus had announced had already upset the world!

Paul's brief stay at Athens does not fit into the preach-and-riot pattern—or any other. Luke uses it to present, with all his dramatic skill, the encounter of the Christian gospel and Greek philosophy. At the intellectual capital of the world, Paul is invited to present his new ideas to a group of Epicurean and Stoic philosophers. Unlike his hearers in a Jewish synagogue, these men have no knowledge of the Jewish scriptures. The announcement about Jesus is the same, but the long introduction from the Old Testament, characteristic of almost all other sermons in Acts, is missing here in Acts 17:22–31. In its place is an attack on superstitious, pagan religion, likely to please his Epicurean hearers, and actual quotations from Stoic philosophers concerning the kinship of humankind as children of an omnipresent God, an idea calculated to please Paul's Stoic hearers. Though some modern critics have questioned whether Paul would really make such use of pagan thought-forms, others have replied that Paul confesses himself ready to adapt and adjust to his audience in many ways (1 Cor. 9:19–23). A century later Justin Martyr was ready to argue that Socrates had been a Christian before Christ! Paul, of course, was not ready to go that far in relating his message to Greek philosophy, but Acts 17 bears witness to an early trend of Christian thought that was to lead in that direction.

Paul's longest stay on this journey was eighteen months at Corinth. To the church there he subsequently wrote letters which became part of the New Testament. The usual pattern again emerges, with the synagogue split and the Gentiles related to the synagogue forming the nucleus of the church. A minor detail is crucial for New Testament chronology. The proconsul called in as the inevitable riot is brewing is one Gallio. He is known to have been a half-brother of the Stoic philosopher-statesman Seneca. He occupied the position of proconsul only briefly, about the year A.D. 51. Apparently the legal charge brought before him against Paul was that he was trying to win people to a new religion. Jews were granted religious freedom in the Roman Empire, but proselyting was illegal. Gallio, however, chose to regard the whole matter as simply a squabble among Jewish sects.

Acts 18:22 pictures Paul as reporting in again at Jerusalem and Antioch at the end of the second journey.

The Third Missionary Journey

Naked to the waist, Artemis bared her multiple breasts in her images to show that she was goddess of sex and fertility. Her first stone idol, legend said, had fallen from heaven (19:35). Rich King Croesus had contributed columns fifty-five feet high to surround her temple of marble and gold. Hundreds of prostitutes there were the priestesses with whom intercourse constituted the worship of the goddess.

It was at Ephesus, the center of this worship of Artemis, that Paul spent two years, the major stay of his last missionary journey.

Acts 19 attributes so many miracles to Paul that the sick are pictured as being cured even by contact with his handkerchiefs! Exorcisms are especially mentioned.

Such stories have caused many to dismiss this chapter as "legendary." Two things, however, should be noted in its defense. Writing at this time from Ephesus back to Christians at Corinth, Paul himself, in an undisputedly authentic passage, could speak of things he and his readers had witnessed which they both regarded as "signs and wonders and mighty works" (2 Cor. 12:12). How one explains these may be debated. But that such things occurred appears to be presented as an irrefutable claim.

And we know that exorcism was practiced in the ancient world, by pagans and Jews as well as Christians. Jewish law did not forbid it. The only question was whether it was in the name of the true God or of evil powers. An early medieval text seems to indicate that Jewish exorcists sometimes used certain names, unaware that they included those traditionally attributed to the "three magi" of Matthew 2 (see above, pp. 40–41.)!

The inevitable riot occurred apparently in the twenty-four-thousand-spectator stadium later to be unearthed by archaeologist J. T. Wood in the nineteenth century. "Great is Artemis of the Ephesians!" chanted the hysterical mob, egged on by merchants of temple souvenirs who had began to see Paul as a threat to their business. As so often, Luke pictures the civil authorities as refusing to find Paul guilty of any crime.

Though Luke mentions Paul's returning to visit the churches he had founded in Greece, the emphasis is now placed on his solemn return journey to Jerusalem. It is reminiscent of Jesus' last trip to that same city. Repeatedly Paul is warned that as he goes there, he is going to his death (20:22–23; 21:11).

The Arrest and Trial of Paul

Of the twenty-eight chapters of Acts, the last eight center on his arrest at Jerusalem and the court proceedings which followed. Such emphasis on these legal affairs seems so out of proportion that Harnack proposed that Acts was written as a brief for Paul's trial in Rome, and that the "most excellent Theophilus" was Paul's judge. More likely, Luke in this form was presenting a model defense of Christian faith at a time when many later Christians were being threatened by many later judges.

Paul was arrested, Luke tells us, in yet another riot, this one growing out of the false charge that he had brought a Gentile into that part of the Temple restricted to Jews (21:28). Arrested, he was smuggled to Caesarea just in time to escape a lynch mob (ch. 23).

Antonius Felix, Paul's first judge, appears in a bad light both in Acts and in secular history (ch. 24). In A.D. 53 the Emperor Claudius had appointed him procurator of Judea, the same position Pilate had once held. Born into slavery, Felix and his brother Pallas had been set free, and Pallas had become a favorite of the emperor until he fell into disgrace in the year A.D. 55. Josephus says that Felix did suppress robbers and murderers, but "he himself was more hurtful than them all." It seems likely that he was involved in the murder of the high priest Jonathan. He married three times, one wife being Drusilla, sister of one of the infamous Herods. Tacitus tells us that Felix "revelled in cruelty and lust, and exercised the powers of a king with the outlook of a slave." He was eventually called to Rome to stand trial for misgovernment, and he was banished. He still had not received the bribe he had hoped to collect from Paul (24:26).

About the year A.D. 60, Festus was chosen by Nero to succeed Felix. He emerges in Acts and elsewhere as a more just and vigorous administrator. Had he lived, perhaps he might have been able to delay or prevent the suicidal revolution which brought the destruction of Jerusalem within a decade. But Festus died only two years after coming to Palestine.

Beginning in 509 B.C., Roman law, the *Lex Valeria*, had made it obligatory that citizens of Rome who appealed to the Roman rulers be given the privilege of trial before the high court. Though originally the law had applied only to Rome and its suburbs, six centuries later it evidently had been broadened to include citizens of Rome everywhere. Most inhabitants of the Roman Empire, of course, were subjects but not citizens. Having waited in prison for two years because of Felix's hope for a bribe, and resisting Festus' proposal to return him to authorities at Jerusalem who almost certainly would condemn him, Paul exercised his special right as a citizen.

"I appeal to Caesar!" he cried.

"You have appealed to Caesar; to Caesar you shall go!" (25:11–12).

Yet Luke gives us one more dramatic court scene. King Herod and the Princess Bernice would have worn robes of royal purple, with golden circlet crowns on their heads. Festus, as a Roman governor, would have worn a scarlet robe. The captains of the five cohorts of the Roman legion stationed at Caesarea would have stood behind him, and a phalanx of legionnaires must have formed the ceremonial guard. The occasion was the first state visit by the neighboring king upon the new Roman governor. Bernice was not the current Herod's wife, but his sister. Their relationship was the subject of public scandal. In this dramatic setting Luke presents for one last time Paul's testimony. Once more Paul is found guiltless. But his appeal to Caesar must stand. Paul will go to Caesar (26:32).

Acts 27 gives what is perhaps the most vivid and detailed account of a historic sea voyage in all ancient literature. The largest boats of the time were only about 140 by 36 feet. Two hundred and seventy-six people and the cargo must have been packed in! When he describes the shipwreck, Luke pictures the prisoner Paul as actually assuming command.

The Ending of Acts

The ending of Acts has puzzled commentators for decades. The story breaks off with Paul enduring two years of house arrest at Rome, still preaching (28:30–31). Inevitably the reader asks, "What happened then? Why does Luke not tell us more?"

Some have suggested that Luke stopped there because it was at that point in time that Acts was written.

Others have proposed that Luke intended to write a third volume, or even that he did write one which is now lost.

Most, however, believing the book to have been written in A.D. 85 or later, have assumed that Luke stopped here because the movement of the gospel from Jerusalem to Rome provided for this Gentile the climax of history. Nine chapters earlier he had alerted his readers that Rome was Paul's goal (19:21). Now, providentially but not at all in the way Paul had intended, Paul's goal is accomplished. He is preaching in the capital of the world.

Tradition says that Paul was not crucified, as a Jew or a slave might have been. He was given the "privilege" of a Roman citizen convicted of a crime. He was beheaded.

But his letters continued and multiplied his ministry. To them we now turn.

VII   Introducing
the Letters of Paul

—Paul was "the second founder of Christianity."

—Wilhelm Wrede

—"There has really never been a more monstrous imposition perpetrated than the imposition of the limitations of Paul's soul upon the soul of Jesus."

—George Bernard Shaw

—Paul was "the first Christian, the inventor of Christianity! Before him there were only a few Jewish sectaries."

—Friedrich Nietzsche

—"Christian theology is a series of footnotes to St. Paul."

—Sydney Ahlstrom[1]

—"Our beloved brother Paul wrote to you . . . letters. There are some things in them hard to understand."

—2 Peter 3:15–16

Understanding Paul's Letters

More than half the books of the New Testament are either by Paul or traditionally attributed to him. Obviously, to understand the Christians' book, one must understand Paul's letters. But Paul has been understood—or misunderstood—in a bewildering variety of ways, as the quotations above indicate. One modern commentator suggests that nobody ever understood Paul, from the first century on— until that commentator wrote his book!

Here are a few of the varying efforts to get at some key idea by which to unlock Paul's meaning.

Some Contrasting Interpretations of Paul in History

1) Paul "was a Greek, child of a Greek mother and a Greek father. He went up to Jerusalem . . . and . . . was seized with a passion to marry a daughter of the priest. For this reason he became a proselyte and was circumcised. Then, when he

failed to get the girl, he flew into a rage and wrote against circumcision and against Sabbath and Law.''[2] So a group of third-century Christian opponents of Paul's doctrines attempted to "explain" him, by smearing his reputation, in a book they falsely attributed to James. Ebionite heretics, conservative Jewish Christians still holding to the Mosaic Law, continued for years to attack Paul as a subverter of the "true Christianity" of Jesus the Jew.

2) In complete contrast, the second-century heretic Marcion taught that Paul was the only true Apostle precisely because Paul had attacked Judaism. A kind of anti-Semite, Marcion argued that the Jewish Creator God described in the Old Testament was a false deity of law, even vengeance; but "our Christ was commissioned by the good God to liberate all mankind."[3] Marcion rejected Matthew as too Jewish a book. But he regarded Paul's letters—after he had censored out of them what he disliked—as truly authoritative.

3) ''Paul is the most heretical of heretics,''[4] wrote Martin Luther, identifying with him as he faced being excommunicated as a heretic himself. In a battle with a sense of guilt which has fascinated modern psychiatry, Luther had attempted to find salvation through the most zealous legalism of medieval Christianity. He had watched his fellow monks. "They wore hair shirts; they fasted; they prayed; they tormented and wore out their bodies. . . . And yet the more they labored, the greater their terrors became."[5] He himself had tried to outdo them. It was in his study of Paul's letters to the Galatians and the Romans that Luther found release. Justification, getting right with God, came not by such ascetic practices nor by any other good works. Salvation, Paul seemed to be saying, was God's free, unearned gift, received by faith alone (Rom. 1:17). Luther interpreted Paul's struggle against Pharisaic legalism as he understood it. To Luther, the key to Paul's gospel could be expressed in these words: "The truth of the Gospel is this, that our righteousness comes by faith alone, without the works of the Law." On this "heresy" of Paul's protest against orthodox Jewish legalism, Luther took his stand against the orthodoxy of his day.

4) With Paul, Christianity left Judaism and took on aspects derived from Greek culture. So certain nineteenth-century thinkers decided. With the aid of Greek philosophical concepts, he universalized and rationalized what might otherwise have become simply a Jewish cult. Or, according to the so-called History of Religions School, Paul aided the process by which Jesus' teachings of love were fitted out in the trappings of the Greek mystery religions. In such religions as Mithraism and the Isis cult, one might be initiated into a kind of religious fraternity under a "Lord," a mediator-savior who linked man and God. Such a "lord" might die and rise again. The candidate might be "born again" by being sprinkled with the blood of a sacrificed bull, or even gain union with his "Lord" by drinking blood. Scholars influenced by this approach drew comparisons between such practices and Paul's ideas concerning baptism, the Lord's Supper, and the role of the "Lord" Jesus.

5) To Albert Schweitzer, Paul and such Greek religions "have in common their religious terminology, but, in respect of ideas, nothing."[6] Rather, "It is only the acceptance of the fact that the Apostle's doctrine is integrally, simply and exclusively eschatological"[7] which enables us to understand it. Jesus had proclaimed that the kingdom was at hand. Paul believed that Jesus, the eschatological Messiah, was soon to return to bring in that kingdom. In the meantime the believer might have the new life of one who is "in Christ." This mystic union, this " 'being-in-Christ' is the prime enigma of the Pauline teaching; once grasped it gives the clue to the whole."[8]

6) No great believer in eschatology, Adolf Harnack argued that Paul transformed the simple religion *of* Jesus into a religion *about* Jesus. Jesus had taught the Fatherhood of God and the brotherhood of all men. But with Paul, "The formation of a correct theory of and about Christ threatens to assume the position of chief importance, and to pervert the majesty and simplicity of the Gospel. . . . Paul became the author of the speculative idea that not only was God in Christ, but that Christ himself was possessed of a peculiar nature of a heavenly kind."[9] The center of Christianity became not love, but orthodox belief about Jesus as "Son of God."

7) Existential philosophy was the key by which the twentieth- century thinker Rudolf Bultmann sought to unlock Paul's meaning. Paul does not offer us metaphysical speculations about the nature of God, Bultmann affirms. Rather, he presents God always in relation to man and man in relation to God. Paul's theology, according to Bultmann, is really "anthropology."[10] When Paul talks about God, he is to be understood today as really talking about the possibilities of man. The "salvation" Paul proclaims can be interpreted in the light of the "authentic existence" which Bultmann's one-time collegue, existentialist philospher Martin Heidegger, described.

8) Finally, among many contemporary thinkers, one may note that to the "post-Bultmannian" Ernst Käsemann, Bultmann's approach seems too individualistic. History, apocalyptic, and Christology are as important to Paul as anthropology, and they cannot be reduced to statements about an individual Christian. Like Schweitzer, Käsemann sees apocalyptic as "the mother of Christian theology." And Paul writes not first of all about the individual Christian, but about Jesus Christ. For Paul, Käsemann says, Christ is the center of a historical process, "salvation history," as well as Savior of individual men and women.[11]

Perhaps 2 Peter 3:15–16 was right about Paul's letters! "There are some things in them hard to understand." This chapter has presented—in admittedly very brief and over simplified form—eight interpretations. There are many, many others. The reader is challenged now to study Paul for himself and to arrive at this own understanding of these letters.

But first it is important to note that the word "epistle" means simply "letter." These books of the Bible are in the form of everyday correspondence.

The Form of the Letters

Early in the third century A.D., a student named Thonis wrote home. Apparently he wanted his father to come and bring him money for his school fees.

> To my lord and father Arion from Thonis greeting. Before all else I make supplication for you every day, praying also before the ancestral gods of my present abode that I may find you and all our folk thriving. Look you, this is my fifth letter to you, and you have not written to me except only once, not even a word about your welfare, nor come to see me; though you promised me saying "I am coming," you have not come to find out whether the teacher is looking after me or not. He himself is inquiring about you almost every day, saying, "Is he not coming yet?" And I just say "Yes." Endeavour then to come to me quickly in order that he may teach me as he is eager to do. . . . I send my salutations to all our folk, each by name, together with those who love us. Salutations also to my teachers. Goodbye, my lord and father, and may you prosper, as I pray, for many years along with my brothers whom may the evil eye harm not. [Postscript] Remember our pigeons. [Addressed] To Arion my father from . . .[12]

Whether Thonis' father ever came with the money to pay the teacher to continue Thonis' education, we will never know. The point in reproducing the letter here is this: the form of that very ordinary letter from a student to his father is the form of nearly every one of the New Testament epistles of Paul.

Thonis' request for his father's help could be outlined like this:

1) the name of the sender and the receiver
2) a salutation
3) a prayer to the writer's god for the one to whom the letter is sent
4) the message
5) personal greetings to others
6) a concluding blessing
7) a postscript about something the writer had forgotten to say earlier

If the reader will look at First Thessalonians, usually regarded as the earliest of Paul's letters, he will find that it follows very much the same outline.

1) 1 Thessalonians 1:1 gives the names of the senders and tells us to whom the letter is written.
2) There follows, in the same verse, a salutation; "Grace to you and peace." ("Grace" is a word especially loved by Christians; "peace" is still a traditional Jewish greeting.)
3) Verses 2–3 contain the prayer for the recipients, though this prayer, of couse, is in the name of Christ, not Thonis' ancestral gods.
4) The message now follows.

5) 1 Thessalonians 5:26 conveys greetings to friends.
6) Paul started to conclude with 1 Thessalonians 4:1, thought of more he needed to say, and finally concluded with a blessing in 5:28.
7) There is no real postscript on this letter, but note that Second Thessalonians has one in 3:17–18.

That postscript in Paul's own hand implies that the rest of the letter was dictated to a secretary. Galatians 6:11 adds to the impression that this was Paul's habit. No doubt either Silvanus (Silas) or Timothy, both of whom are mentioned in the first verse of both First and Second Thessalonians, often served as Paul's secretary.

Paul wrote letters, therefore, in quite the ordinary form, and he wrote in quite ordinary language. Many years ago scholars noted that the Greek of the New Testament was different from that of the classical Greek writers. Some even proposed that the sacred books were written in a special "language of the Holy Spirit." Quite the opposite, we now know from hundreds of letters that have been found (such as that of Thonis) that Paul's language is the popular Greek of his day, the *koine* or common dialect.

There is no hint that Paul thought of himself as writing sacred scripture. To him the Old Testament was the inspired book. Since he was writing to the whole church at Thessalonica, he did urge that the letter be read publicly (1 Thess. 5:27). Christians for centuries have been sure that though Paul was not aware of it, he was miraculously inspired by the Holy Spirit as he wrote. But Paul writes simply as a pastor, quite unconscious that centuries later his words would be regarded as in some sense part of the "Word of God."

Finally, concerning Paul's letters, Wrede's comment about Galatians applies to some extent to almost all of Paul's writings. Wrede called Galatians "a fighting epsitle." Paul writes to particular situations in particular churches. He writes to meet challenges. He usually writes in the midst of controversies, if not to defend himself personally, at least to defend the gospel to which he has dedicated his life. For example, in 1 Thessalonians 2:1–12 Paul is defending himself against many kinds of slander. He writes with high emotion, and his letters are not really grasped if the emotions behind them are not felt. Often his letters follow no more carefully planned outline than do the letters of most readers of this book. Paul may break off a sentence in the middle in his excitement, may call his enemies ugly names, may flatter, apologize, preach, coax, or even quote poetry. He is a real man, writing to real people, often in some real crisis.

To understand a letter of Paul, therefore, it is highly important to look for clues as to what situation or occasion has caused him to write it. Paradoxically, readers often tend most clearly to find Paul speaking eternal truths when they are most conscious that he is speaking a particular message to a historic situation.

The letters to the church at Thessalonica illustrate all of these ideas.

First Thessalonians

Timothy brought Paul good news and bad news and a set of questions. Moved by what he had heard, Paul began to dictate a letter. It was a memorable moment in the history of literature. "Paul, Silvanus, and Timothy, to the church of the Thessalonians . . ." With those words, according to the most widely accepted chronology, the writing of the New Testament began.

The Occasion of First Thessalonians

We have noted that every letter of Paul grows out of a particular situation, often a crisis. To understand a letter, the student must look for hints as to the events which caused the author to write it. Reading through First Thessalonians, one comes upon a clear indication of the immediate occasion for this epistle.

> But now that Timothy has come to us from you, and has brought us the good news of your faith and love and reported that you always remember us kindly and long to see us, as we long to see you . . .
>
> (1 Thessolonians 3:6)

The verses leading up to this announcement give further background for understanding the letter. Forced out of Philippi, Paul had preached in Thessalonica, in spite of great opposition, he reminds his readers (1 Thess. 2:2). He had had particular success with the Gentiles but violent opposition from some Jews (2:14–16). All this had happened quite recently (2:17). He had been prevented by "Satan" from returning to them (2:17–18). Therefore, having gotten as far down the road as Athens, he had sent Timothy back to check on the progress of the new church. Now, presumably a bit further down the road at Corinth, he has heard Timothy's report and hastens to write them this letter.

All of this fits perfectly with the account Acts gives us of Paul's second missionary journey. Even commentators who brand Acts' stories as "legendary" do not hesitate to use Acts 17 to reconstruct the occasion of the writing of this letter. A quick review of that chapter will remind the reader that after a brush with the law at Philippi, Paul did indeed found the church at Thessalonica. He was assisted by Silas (the "Silvanus" mentioned in 1 Thess. 1:1) and Timothy (also mentioned in the letter). He did have his best success with Gentiles—and, by the way, with women—as is noted in Acts 17:4. But certain Jews stirred up such opposition that Paul escaped only by being smuggled out at night, just ahead of a lynch mob (Acts 17:5–10). Opponents from Thessalonica had even driven Paul out of the next town, Beroea (Acts 17:13). Paul had indeed gone on alone through Athens, instructing Silas and Timothy to join him later with a report. Soon he settled down a little farther west in Greece for an eighteen-month stay in Corinth. The account in Acts harmonizes so perfectly with what seems implied in First Thessalonians that Acts' additional details must be thought of as shedding trustworthy light on the letter.

We can even date it. The archaeologists have discovered an inscription which shows that Gallio was proconsul of Achaia only briefly, so that Paul's stay at Corinth during Gallio's period of office (Acts 18:12) must have been in about A.C. 51 or 52. If, as is implied, the letter was written soon after Paul's arrival in Corinth, then First Thessalonians gives us a picture of Christianity only some twenty years after the earthly life of Jesus!

The Purpose of First Thessalonians

First Thessalonians, then, is written as a substitute for a visit which is probably too dangerous for Paul to make, and in response to the report of the visit Timothy did make. Paul writes out of joy to congratulate the chruch at Thessalonica for all the good things he has heard about them. He writes to defend himself against false charges those opponents are still spreading about him. He writes to assure them of his continuing concern. He writes, as in all his letters, to exhort them to Christian living. And he writes to answer certain questions which, it appears, have been brought to him from the church by Timothy, perhaps in a letter of their own.

About Outlines of the Epistles Proposed

Except perhaps for Romans, all of Paul's letters are informal. None fits neatly into a systematic outline. All do fit into the general framework of letters we noted earlier in this chapter. Any outline is helpful only as it simplifies a letter, but to simplify is in some sense to distort. Though there are dangers, an outline is included in this GUIDE for each epistle, except the short, one-chapter letters. These outlines are intended to show how each letter may be seen as unified by certain principal themes. For one useful way of outlining First Thessalonians, see page 117.

Some Comments on the Content of First Thessalonians

The first chapter of the letter is all joy. Acts implies that it was only for three weeks that the Thessalonians had had Paul to teach them. He has been worried about the church, so soon left without its leader. But now Paul has heard good reports through Timothy. These simply confirm other good reports which, he tells them with pardonable exaggeration, have spread everywhere. As a matter of fact, the main street of Thessalonica was the *Via Egnatia*, the great highway linking Rome with Asia. News of what happened there would spread, which is doubtless one reason Paul was concerned that there be a strong church in that city. Macedonia was the country of Alexander the Great, who, as a missionary for Greek culture, had conquered the world. Thessalonica was named for his sister, as Philippi was named for his father. The news of the church at Thessalonica could have an impact in many places (1:8). Paul no doubt had been worried about the infant church which he had had to leave so suddenly. But these Christians had proved examples of the faith, just as Paul, Timothy, and Silas had tried to be examples to them.

Some commentators suggest that 1 Thessalonians 1:9–10 echoes a kind of early creed, one learned by Paul and taught to these Christians before a word of the New Testament was written. If so, perhaps one might summarize the faith heroically spread by these first Gentile converts somewhat like this:

> We turn to God from idols,
> to serve a living and true God,
> and to wait for his Son from heaven,
> whom he raised from the dead,
> Jesus who delivers us from the wrath to come.

Their loyalty to such beliefs has not been easy. Paul's enemies, having run him off, have continued to attack him by slander. Reading between the lines in chapter 2, one can find that the Thessalonians had heard such attacks on their former teacher as the following:

—"He is sexually immoral." 1 Thessalonians 2:3 speaks of what the translators discreetly call "uncleanness." Acts 17:4 specifically mentions the prominent place of women in the church Paul founded. Perhaps this gave a chance to the scandal-mongers. At the beginning of this chapter it was noted that centuries later this kind of lie was still being spread about Paul.

—"He is tricky, a liar" (2:3).

—"He is in it for money and what he can get out of it" (2:5–6). Paul was not the last traveling evangelist to face that charge. There were in the ancient world many traveling preachers of various religions who professed to work miracles (Acts 13:6; 19:13). Many deserved their bad reputations. In Paul's absence the charges against him may have sounded reasonable.

In reply, Paul reminds the Thessalonians of the life he and his associates had lived among them when he was their pastor. He had earned his own living, working with his hands (2:9–12). Acts 18:3 tells us Paul paid his own way by working as a tentmaker. He assures them of his continued concern. He negatively implies that the activity of his enemies is really that of "Satan" (2:18). He gloats over his assurance that God is cursing those sinners (2:16)! ("At times he looked like a man," we noted a later description of Paul as describing him; and Paul can be quite human in his attitudes toward those who oppose what he regards as God's work. See page 98.) To remind them of his continued concern, he reviews his sending Timothy to them and his receiving Timothy's report (2:17—3:10). The first half of the letter ends with a prayer for God's continued blessing on them.

First Thessalonians

Their Exiled Pastor Writes to a Very Young Church

"We beseech and exhort you . . . that as you learned from us how to live, . . . just as you are doing . . . do so more and more" (4:1).

1:1	2:1	4:1	4:13	5:12
Thanksgiving and Rejoicing Because of Good News from the Church	**Paul's Continued Concern for Their Church in the Midst of Opposition**	**An Exhortation to Keep Up the Good Work, Living in a Way Pleasing to God**	**Answers to Two Questions They Have Asked**	**Final Exhortation and Closing Greetings**
Paul's prayer of thanks 1:1-3	A reminder of how he ministered among them, in spite of opposition 2:1-12	Live moral lives. 4:1-8	What about those who have died before Christ's return? 4:13-18	
The good news he has heard which has made him thankful 1:4-10	Their good response, even though he had been driven out 2:13-16	Live lives of love and industriousness. 4:9-12	When will that return be? 5:1-11	
	His continuing concern, though separated from them 2:17—3:5			
	The good news Timothy has brought 3:6-13			

Author: Paul

Recipients: The church at Thessalonica, which Paul had founded but had been forced to leave quickly

Date: A.D. 50–51

Occasion: Timothy had brought Paul a report and some questions from the church.

Purpose: To rejoice with them in their faithfulness, to encourage them in spite of difficulties and attacks on Paul, and to answer their questions

Some editions of the New Testament leave a blank space between chapters 3 and 4 to show that the letter now moves to a different subject. It is typical of Paul's letters that the second half deals with more practical matters. Thus 1 Thessalonians 4:1–12 gives ethical instruction to new Christians, to whom the Christian ways may still have seemed strange. For example, New Testament standards concerning sex were quite different from those popular in the ancient pagan world, just as they are quite different from those which surveys indicate guide the practice of most Americans today. Paul flatly prohibits adultery and seeks to confine sexual intercourse to marriage (4:1–8).

His exhortation to love is typically loving. He assures them that they do not need to be reminded to love each other (4:9). He then proceeds to remind them to love each other, more and more!

The two questions which form the subject of the next two paragraphs reflect the eschatological expectation which was still strong in the church of A.D. 50–51. Jesus had come preaching that the kingdom was at hand. We have seen that many interpreters of Paul emphasize that his letters can be understood only in the light of his eschatology. The little "creed" quoted above (1:9–10) pictures the church as waiting for the "Son from heaven, . . . Jesus who delivers us from the wrath to come." In the light of this expectation, the Thessalonians, new in the faith, have become concerned about some of their number who have died. Have they missed out on the great day?

Paul's answer is to assure them that both the living and the dead will share equally in the coming of the Lord (4:13–18). In fact, the dead will be the first to join him in his return. "Therefore comfort one another with these words." This passage is the best loved in First Thessalonians, having been read at the funerals of many, many Christians.

In recent years it has also been the subject of curious distortion. Bumper stickers have proclaimed: "In case of the Rapture, this car will be driverless." "The Rapture," often pictured in sensational detail by certain preachers, is supposedly described in 1 Thessalonians 4:17, understood to mean that at some time Christ will gather "up" all believers off the earth, leaving unbelievers to assorted trials. Actually, however, Paul is simply affirming the good news that the dead in Christ will have a full share in the great day. The paragraph says nothing about unbelievers, on or off the earth. The very next paragraph, rather, seems to be a warning against trying to establish some kind of timetable or schedule of events of this sort. Paul's concern is not to map out details about the future, but to comfort the bereaved.

Therefore, to the second question, which was apparently "When will the end be?" Paul replies that nobody knows or needs to speculate about that. The Thessalonians need not try to guess about God's timetable. They are already "sons of light and sons of the day." They know that they are destined to obtain salvation (5:1–10). Nothing else about the end need concern the Christian.

Rather, Paul says in his closing exhortation, they are to do now the work given them. Note how 1 Thessalonians 5:15 sounds almost like a quotation from the Sermon on the Mount! And they are to respect their leaders, to be patient, to be loving.

Before his benediction Paul returns briefly to one theme which has been touched on previously in the letter; the importance of doing one's daily work. He had reminded them earlier how he himself had worked for a living even when he was their pastor (2:9). He had hinted that this was part of his example to them. Again in 4:11 he had urged them to work with their hands. Now a third time he is concerned to "admonish the idle" (5:14).

Evidently, however, these hints were too gentle. Within a few weeks, most scholars believe, Paul was writing again on this subject, this time harshly. "If any one will not work, let him not eat" (2 Thess. 3:10).

But that is a theme of the next letter.

Second Thessalonians

So excited were these new Christians about the end of the world, which they understood to be at hand, that they had actually quit their jobs. Why save money for an old age which will never come? Horrified by their idleness, apparently reported to him soon after his first letter was delivered to the church at Thessalonica, Paul wrote the second letter.

So, at least, tradition has understood Second Thessalonians. We must note that this interpretation has been challenged.

Problems Concerning the Authorship and Date of Second Thessalonians

At least four difficulties have been noted concerning the usual interpretation of this book.

1) Parts of Second Thessalonians are so similar to First Thessalonians that some have regarded it as a paraphrase of the first letter, with additions by a later author.

2) The tone of Second Thessalonians is much more severe than that of the warmly affectionate first letter.

3) The Christology (the doctrine of who Christ is) is said to be more advanced in Second Thessalonians.

4) Most important, it is said that the eschatology is quite different. In First Thessalonians Paul says that there is no way to predict when the end will be. It will come entirely without warning, "like a thief in the night" (5:2). But Second Thessalonians describes various things which must happen before the end can come (2 Thess. 2:1–12).

Some scholars, therefore, have proposed that Second Thessalonians comes from a later time and is by a later author.[13] Others have suggested that the two letters fit together better if Second Thessalonians is thought of as having been written first.

Most, however, hold to the traditional view, believing that the alleged differences either have been exaggerated or can be explained on the basis of the growing problem in the Thessalonian church.[14] That situation, as usually understood, will now be described.

The Occasion of Second Thessalonians

The kingdom of heaven must indeed be at hand. Paul had preached it; now his letter had reaffirmed it. So, at least, the Thessalonians understood it. Indeed, there is a hint that in a "dirty tricks" campaign, Paul's enemies had circulated yet another letter, forged by them, designed to whip up even more unfounded enthusiasm. Some members of the church at Thessalonica had actually quit their jobs to wait for the imminent return of the Lord. New in the faith, the infant church was confused.

Paul received a report of this situation, perhaps from whoever carried his first letter to Thessalonica. Therefore, within a few weeks after the first letter, he wrote a second one.

The Purpose of Second Thessalonians

As in First Thessalonians, Paul writes to encourage the new church in a time of confusion and opposition. But especially he seeks to stop the members of the congregation from supposing that the end of the world is necessarily within the next few days. Various trials must be endured first, he tells them. Therefore, the members of the church should go back to work and to godly living in the world.

Some Comments on the Content of Second Thessalonians

Since Second Thessalonians is one of the briefest of Paul's letters, only brief comment will be given here.

The most puzzling passage is the one concerning "the man of lawlessness" (2:1–12). Most scholars believe that Paul's words would have made more sense to his Thessalonian readers if he had referred to someone or something threatening or expected to threaten in his own day. But none of the various explanations suggested seems to fit perfectly. Here are three possibilities:

—The Roman emperor (or some soon-to-come emperor), with the forces of the empire. A few years earlier, Caligula had attempted to set up his image in the Temple at Jerusalem. Perhaps Paul is thinking of another Caligula who will take "his seat in the temple of God, proclaiming himself to be God"(2:4), as Caligula did.

—The Jewish high priest, with Paul's Jewish opponents. The reference to the Temple hints at this.

Second Thessalonians
On Working Until the End

"Now concerning the coming of our Lord, . . . we beg you . . . not to be . . . shaken in mind" (2:1–2).

1:1	2:1	2:13	3:6 3:18
Thanksgiving and Encouragement for Their Faithfulness in the Midst of Trials	**A Correction: Only After Further Trials Will the End Come**	**Paul's Prayer That They Will Stand Firm, and a Request That They Pray for Him, Too**	**A Strong Closing Appeal That Everyone Work for a Living Until the End**
Thanksgiving 1:1–4	The end is not yet. 2:1–2	His prayer 2:13–17	
Encouragement 1:5–12	The "man of lawlessness" must come before the end. 2:3–12	His request 3:1–5	

Author: Paul (some question this)
Recipients: The young church at Thessalonica
Date: A.D. 50–51 (some put it much later)
Occasion: Paul has received further news from Thessalonica telling of persecution from without and misunderstandings within that church.
Purpose: To encourage their faithfulness and work, and to correct misunderstandings about the end of the world

—Some completely supernatural force of evil. First John 2:18 speaks of the expectation of a coming "antichrist" and indicates in fact that several "antichrists" have already come. The standard Jewish eschatological expectation, brought over into Christian apocalyptic literature, pictured the "woes of the Messiah," a time of great trouble just before the end. (See above, pages 21–22 for the characteristics of apocalyptic literature.) Perhaps we can say no more than that Paul is reflecting this convention.[15]

It is equally unclear what Paul means by "what is restraining" the man of lawlessness (2:6). Perhaps Paul refers to the restraints placed by Roman law upon Paul's opponents. Perhaps Paul means his own activity. The whole passage obviously refers to some idea which Paul had already taught the Thessalonians and therefore does not need to explain again here (2:5).

Disappointed in predictions of dates made repeatedly in history, most Christians have come to recognize that the Bible over and over refuses to announce any clear timetable for the end of the world. Rather, the Christian is expected to live and do his work each day with that earnestness of purpose which might come with the conviction that any day could be the last before the judgment. Indeed, God's judgments do not always wait until the end of the world.

Fortunately, the main point is clear enough. Paul is saying that the Thessalonians are not to suppose that the world and all its troubles necessarily are at an end. They must be prepared to carry on through difficulties ahead.

The most quoted verse, one which was made law in the first permanent English settlement in America, Jamestown, is 2 Thessalonians 3:10: "If any one will not work, let him not eat." Or, as Bruce Metzger has paraphrased it: "No loaf for the loafer!"

VIII *Paul's Correspondence with Corinth*

The city was a major intersection in the transportation system of the ancient world. All north-south land traffic in Greece had to pass through Corinth, since it commanded the narrow isthmus that linked the two halves of the Greek peninsula. More important, seagoing vessels docked at its harbor, and their cargoes, or even the boats themselves, were pulled on rollers across the short stretch of land to the port on the other shore, a procedure quicker and cheaper than sailing around half the country to get there.

A sailors' town, famous for its sacred prostitute-priestesses of Aphrodite, Corinth attracted a polyglot population.

Into it, about A.D. 51, there had come the itinerant tentmaker-turned-preacher, Paul. Archaeologists have unearthed portions of a synagogue which may be the one in which he began to preach. Paul became a partner, both in tentmaking and in teaching, with two refugees from Rome, Aquila and Priscilla (1 Cor. 16:19; Acts 18:2). Though he was later to confess that he had begun his work at Corinth with "fear and trembling" (1 Cor. 2:3), the three, together with Silas and Timothy, were so successful that Paul stayed more than a year and a half. Apparently even leaders of the synagogue, Crispus and Sosthenes, were converted (Acts 18:8,17; 1 Cor. 1:1, 14). After Paul left, a convert named Apollos had carried on as pastor of the new church (1 Cor. 1:12; 3:5; cf. Acts 19:1). (Incidentally, Acts 18:1–18 and the Corinthian letters fit so well together, including the mention in both Acts and the letters of precisely these same people, that even those otherwise inclined to dismiss much of Acts as "legendary" admit that this part of Acts reflects accurate historical memory and do not hesitate to use it to interpret these epistles.)[1]

How many letters Paul wrote back to the church he had founded in Corinth we will never know. At least one appears to be lost (1 Cor. 5:9). Bornkamm claims to find fragments of at least six in what we call Second Corinthians.[2] Together, what has been preserved for us forms the largest body of correspondence in our Bible. A number of passages are among the best loved in the New Testament.

First Corinthians

—First Corinthians 11:23–26 is still read regularly in millions of celebrations of the Lord's Supper.

—Parts of 1 Corinthians 15 are likely to be read at the funeral of any Christian reader of this GUIDE.

—The prose-poem on love in 1 Corinthians 13 is the best-loved chapter in all the writings of Paul.

But it is also true that First Corinthians has been used as a battleground for sexists (1 Cor. 7 and 11:2–16); for believers in church union (ch. 1—3); for Roman Catholics vs. Protestants (11:24); for tongues-speakers (ch. 12—14); and even for vegetarians (ch. 8)!

Manifestly, the letter both merits and needs study.

The Occasion of First Corinthians

"I will stay in Ephesus until Pentecost," Paul writes in 1 Corinthians 16:8, so we can be pretty sure where he was as he wrote this letter. Obviously he had already been to Corinth at least once. So we may assume that First Corinthians was written sometime during his more than two-year stay in Ephesus on his third missionary journey, probably about A.D. 55 or 56 (Acts 19:10).

It was news from Corinth which prompted Paul to write. He had received a disturbing report of dissension in the church, brought him by "Chloe's people" (1:11), perhaps slaves or business associates of some woman of the church at either Corinth or Ephesus. Paul had also gotten from the church at Corinth a letter full of questions he now attempts to answer (7:1). And perhaps others had brought additional word from the church Paul had founded some three years earlier (16:17).

The news had not been all good. Somehow the church was being split into factions, each adopting the name of one leader: Paul, or Apollos, or Cephas (Peter), or even Christ (1:12). Paul was horrified. He now wrote to plead for unity.

Precisely what these different groups believed is not clear. Some relate them to the "Judaizers," the conservative faction advocating circumcision and obedience to all the Old Testament Law, centered, perhaps, back in Jerusalem. Apparently it is with them that the letter to the Galatians does battle. In the Corinthians letters, however, there is no mention of the ceremony of circumcision, the focus of the controversy with the Judaizers in Galatians. Indeed, more of Paul's opponents at Corinth seem to have been the opposite of legalists, advocating rather a very "liberated" kind of life-style. A curious variety of ideas is attacked by Paul, either directly or by implication:

—a claim to superior wisdom (1:18–31; 2:6–7; 8:1; etc.)

—a tendency to condone sexual immorality (ch. 7)

—a claim to be above restrictions against practices related to idol worship (chs. 8 and 10)

—attacks on Paul's authority (ch. 9)

—drunken disturbances at the Lord's Supper (11:17–34)

—a schismatic boasting about special gifts of the Spirit such as "speaking with tongues" (chs. 12–14)

—misunderstandings about the resurrection (ch. 15).

It may be that all these diverse errors can be grouped together around one idea, the claim of one or more of the factions at Corinth to have special, superior, spiritual wisdom. Perhaps some member of one group might have defended his position in this way:

"We 'Apollos' Christians are not beginners in the faith any longer, as were those whom Paul first baptized. We are now filled with the Spirit. Our spiritual gifts, such as speaking in tongues, show our superiority. We now have a knowledge of higher, more spiritual things. We know that Christians are not under the Law. Our motto is 'All things are lawful' [1 Cor. 6:12; 10:23]. Hang-ups about food offered to idols and the old taboos about sex and drinking concern material things. We spiritual Christians know that material things don't matter one way or the other. We have already, in the Spirit, begun to live the resurrection life. As for Paul and those other factions, they are just beginners."

Different parties may have made similar claims. But since there were apparently several rival cliques, it is not necessary to suppose that all Paul's opponents in Corinth fell into all the errors he attacks. His opponents may have represented a wide spectrum, from very conservative Judaizers to libertine Hellenists, even semi-pagans close to the later "Gnostics," who in the next century boasted that they had a superior *gnosis,* or knowledge (see below, pages 162–167).

The Purpose of First Corinthians

Paul writes to respond to the reports from "Chloe's people" and to answer the letter sent him by the young church at Corinth. His replies deal with a great variety of both theological and practical questions. His first great concern, however, is to reunite the church around the *kerygma* he had preached, the basic gospel centered on the death and resurrection of Jesus. Secondarily, Paul earnestly urges that these new Christians live in this world, as long as it lasts, the kind of lives appropriate for Christians.

Some Comments on the Content of First Corinthians

"I appeal to you, brethren, by the name of our Lord Jesus Christ, that all of you agree and that there be no dissensions among you, but that you be united in the same mind and the same judgment" (1:10). So begins the body of the letter, and with it the major theme is introduced.

To modern readers used to the fact that the Christian church in the United States alone is split into more than three hundred groups, each with a different name, a different denomination, Paul's concern seems strange. To him, however, only one name matters, "the name of our Lord Jesus Christ," and schism is sin. It is not, of course, the use of different names which is in itself the sin. He condemns all the groups, including the faction which boasts simply, "I belong to Christ" (1:12). It is the factions' separation from each other and the claims on which their schism is based which upset the Apostle.

If one counts the times the words "wise," "wisdom," and "foolishness" occur in 1 Corinthians 1:17–2:13, it will become evident that at least one faction has been claiming superior *knowledge*. Counting the occurrences of such related words as "power" and "weakness" will disclose a secondary theme, *power,* in which that party or some other was greatly interested.

Paul bluntly reminds the Corinthians that few in that church had any real claim either to wisdom or to power. Most of these first Christians were relatively poor and uneducated people, many even slaves. Even Paul himself had made no claim to power or wisdom (2:1–5). Power and wisdom for the Christian could come from only one source, the cross. By all worldly standards that cross represented defeat and absurdity. Nothing could seem more foolish to a Jewish Zealot, dreaming of butchering the Romans, than the story of the promised Messiah dying on a Roman cross. Greeks schooled in the rational philosophies of Plato and Aristotle were likely to dismiss accounts of God's self-sacrificing love for man as absurd. Now, within the church, factions claiming new spiritual gifts of higher insight or miraculous abilities were repeating the blindness of their non-Christian neighbors. Paul had claimed to "know" nothing "except Jesus Christ and him crucified" (2:2). It was around that original, basic *kerygma,* gospel, that the Corinthian church must reunite.

Not only did some members of the church at Corinth claim to have such spiritual knowledge that they were "above" Paul's theology; they also claimed to be above Paul's morality. "All things are lawful for me" (6:12) is placed in quotation marks in many modern translations (cf. 10:23) on the assumption that these "liberated" Christians were repeating this as a kind of slogan. They were so "liberated" that they had even tolerated the continued church membership of a man living in adultery with his own stepmother (5:1). They were willing for members to sue each other in courts of law (6:1–8). And they permitted church members to patronize the fabled prostitute-priestesses of Corinth (6:9–20).

"Do you not know that your body is a temple of the Holy Spirit?" Paul demands. Repeatedly using the word "body,"Paul tries to bring these advocates of a purely "spiritual" morality back down to earth (6:9–20). To a morality of physical license for "Spirit-filled" people, First Corinthians says a flat "No!"

Paul's views on marriage and on women, presented in 1 Corinthians 7 and in 11:2–16, have caused some advocates of women's liberation to brand the Apostle a kind of "male chauvinist pig." He recommends that a man should not even touch a woman, much less marry one! Marriage is permitted, but here the only basis mentioned is its being better than to "burn" with desire or to engage in fornication. No woman, he says here, should ever go to church without a veil. And

First Corinthians

Response to a Divided, "Spiritual-Minded" Church

"Now concerning the matters about which you wrote ... (7:1) ... the greatest ... is love" (13:13).

1:1 **Comments on Some Reports Paul Has Received About the Church at Corinth**	7:1 **Replies to Questions Asked in a Letter They Have Sent**	16:1 **Brief Miscellaneous Concluding Notes**
They are splitting up; Paul pleads for unity around the cross. 1—4	What about marriage for the Christian? It isn't sin, but Paul doesn't recommend it. 7:1–40	A solicitation for funds for the Jerusalem poor 16:1–4
A case of incest has been reported; Paul pleads for strict sexual morality. 5:1–13	May a Christian eat meat which has been sacrificed to a pagan god? Yes, but not if it gives the wrong impression to someone else. 8—10	Personal comments and greetings 16:5–24
Some are involved in a lawsuit; Paul pleads for settling issues among themselves. 6:1–8	What is the place of women? It is subordination "in the Lord." 11:1–16	16:24
Some claim to be above rules about the body; Paul renews his plea for morality. 6:9–20	Response to reported disorder in worship, and an account of the Lord's Supper 11:17–34	
	What is the relative importance of spiritual gifts? Different Christians have different gifts, but all should seek love. 12—14	
	What about the resurrection? It is the central truth. 15:1–58	

Author: Paul
Recipients: The church at Corinth, which Paul had founded
Date: A.D. 55–56
Occasion: Paul has received a report of dissension in the church and a letter full of questions.
Purpose: To plead for unity, to comment on reports he has received about them, and to answer their questions

"the head of a woman is her husband" (11:3). (It must be admitted about Paul that "at times he looked like a man"!)

However, Christian advocates of women's liberation (and others) have defended Paul's views here on several grounds. It is noted that the old bachelor does allow marriage, even if not on the highest grounds. Indeed, he even commands a concern for *mutual* sexual satisfaction (7:3). (Perhaps his very "spiritual" opponents especially needed this earthy advice.) He speaks of the woman as ruling over the man's body in the same verse in which he speaks of the man ruling over the woman's (7:4). If he puts severe dress standards upon women at Corinth, it is in part because Corinth is a special case, a city with an international reputation for prostitutes. He forbids a man's divorcing a faithful wife. And he bases his recommendation against marriage on his expectation of the imminent end of the world (7:29). Subsequently, as we shall see, a more carefully worked out eschatology was to make that approach somewhat obsolete. Paul admits that he is not in these matters always giving commands from the Lord (7:25).

Temples supplied the butcher shops of the ancient world. First Corinthians 8—10 deals with a question which must have confronted every first-century Christian housewife. Should a Christian eat meat which has first been offered to an idol? Suppose a church member is having lunch with a pagan and the entree is from the altar of Aphrodite? Should he or she refuse and offend the host, or eat and appear to condone idolatry? The issue in its first-century form is now irrelevant in countries where sacrifices to idols are completely out of fashion, but the principles upon which Paul's answer rests are applicable to many ethical questions of the present day. Here Paul sides with the "spiritually enlightened" party, agreeing that in itself there is no harm in eating meat offered to idols. But with the more conservative faction, he argues that the effect one's action may have on another person is all-important. "Eat whatever is sold in the meat market without raising any question on the ground of conscience" (10:25). But if your example may cause someone to think you are condoning idol worship, be a vegetarian (8:9–13). You need not be concerned about meat. You *must* be concerned about other people.

Reports of disorder in the church services at Corinth lead Paul to write some of the most familiar—and some of the most controversial—parts of this letter. He seems concerned, at least here, to "keep women in their place" in worship (11:2–16). Of much more permanent influence, Paul then gives the oldest account we have of the Lord's Supper, read in almost every service of Holy Communion through subsequent centuries (11:23–26). The words with which he introduces it—"received" and "delivered"—are technical terms to show that he is passing down a tradition which he himself was taught when he first became a Christian, perhaps only about three years after the event he describes. Thus the passage gives clear witness to the antiquity of the ceremony. The idea of the "new covenant" which Paul says Jesus announced at the Last Supper is so basic to the faith that the two parts of the Christian Bible are named the Old Covenant (or Testament) and the New Covenant. How literally one is to take Jesus' words "This is my body," whether the bread in the Mass is "substantially" Christ's flesh, has been a point of major controversy between Catholics and Protestants.

Evidently worship at Corinth was rather different from the formal ceremonies of most twentieth-century churches. "Each goes ahead with his own meal, and one is hungry and another is drunk" (11:21). Determined that "all things should be done decently and in order," Paul urges the men to take turns in speaking, rather than several speaking at once, and the women to do their questioning only at home (14:26–34).

Among the elements which apparently produced a kind of chaos in Corinthian worship was the practice of some of the "spiritually gifted" people to "speak in tongues." The spread of the "charismatic movement" in recent years has caused 1 Corinthians 12—14 to be one of the most discussed parts of the Bible. Are certain Christians given a "second blessing," a "baptism with (or in) the Holy Spirit," which ordinary Christians lack? Apparently there were those in the church at Corinth who felt that their gifts of tongues showed that they were superior, Spirit-filled Christians.

Paul answers in at least three ways. First (ch. 12) he proposes that the church is like a body. In an extended metaphor he asserts that each Christian (each part of that body) has his or her own gift from the one Spirit. Each part of the church and each gift is necessary for the welfare of the whole "body," the whole church. None can look down upon another. For a church member with one gift to think of himself as superior to another with a quite different gift would be as stupid as for a foot to feel superior to a hand!

Second, some gifts are better than others. "Earnestly desire the higher gifts" (12:31). But the highest is neither tongues nor knowledge, the two boasts of the "spiritual" people. The highest, which all should seek, is *love*. First Corinthians 13, the chapter in which that gift of Christian love is described, is the best-loved passage in all the writings of Paul. On pages 130–131, 1 Corinthians 13 is printed in such a way as to suggest its poetic structure. Note how, even here, the last stanza reflects Paul's eschatological orientation. In the *end,* only love matters.

Third (ch. 14), in public worship one should try to "prophesy," to say things which will make sense and will edify other people. Paul does not forbid speaking in tongues. He professes to do it himself, privately. But "in church I would rather speak five words with my mind, in order to instruct others, than ten thousand words in a tongue" (14:19).

First Corinthians 13 is best loved, but for the historian of Christian doctrine, 1 Corinthians 15 is the most revealing. Perhaps the "spiritual" party in the church claimed to be living so completely in the Spirit that for them no future bodily resurrection was necessary. In any event, somehow the resurrection had been brought into question. Paul again begins his answer with the words "delivered" and "received," apparently reminding them of a kind of creed he had been taught at his own conversion. Here, then, is the gospel of the very first Christians:

> . . . Christ died for our sins
>   in accordance with the scriptures, . . .
> he was buried, . . .
> he was raised on the third day
>   in accordance with the scriptures, . . .
> he appeared to Cephas,
>   then to the twelve.   (1 Corinthians 15:3–5)

Paul offers neither description nor proof of the resurrection, but he does cite witnesses, including many who were still alive as he wrote (15:6). His own encounter with the risen Christ is for him the final "proof." The fact of the resurrection is essential to the Christian faith. Without it nothing else in the gospel matters (15:14). With it there is hope for all people.

The resurrection is no present and purely "spiritual" experience, as apparently some of his "Spirit-filled" opponents had claimed. It is a "bodily" resurrection (15:38). And it is something to be hoped for beyond the ecstasy of the "spiritual" faction at Corinth. But that hope does add a new quality to life now. For the Christian lives in the confidence that because Christ rose, the dead will rise, too. In an ecstasy of his own, Paul breaks into song (15:54–55). And he closes the chapter with a shout of "Thanks be to God, who gives us the victory!" (15:57).

Practical preacher that he was, Paul adds a few words about taking up the offering. Several references in Paul's letters speak of his solicitation of funds for the poor of Jerusalem (Rom. 15:25, for example).

The letter ends with personal greetings, including those from Aquila and Priscilla (Prisca), with whom he had worked in Corinth (16:19). Finally (still at times looking like a man in spite of the angelic thirteenth chapter), Paul roundly damns those who have no "love for the Lord" (16:22)!

PAUL'S PROSE POEM ON LOVE

> If I speak in the tongues of men and of angels,
>   but have not love,
> I am a noisy gong or a clanging cymbal.
> And if I have prophetic powers, and understand all mysteries and all
>   knowledge,
> And if I have all faith, so as to remove mountains,
>   but have not love,
> I am nothing.
> If I give away all I have,

And if I deliver my body to be burned,
    but have not love,
I gain nothing.

Love is patient and kind;
Love is not jealous or boastful;
It is not arrogant or rude.
Love does not insist on its own way;
It is not irritable or resentful;
It does not rejoice at wrong,
But rejoices in the right.
Love bears all things,
    believes all things,
        hopes all things,
            endures all things.

Love never ends;
As for prophecies,
        they will pass away;
As for tongues,
        they will cease;
As for knowledge,
        it will pass away.
For our knowledge is imperfect and our prophecy is imperfect;
But when the perfect comes,
        the imperfect will pass away.
When I was a child,
    I spoke like a child,
        I thought like a child,
            I reasoned like a child;
When I became a man,
    I gave up childish ways.
For now we see in a mirror dimly,
    But then face to face.
Now I know in part;
    Then I shall understand fully, even as I have been fully
      understood.

So faith,
    hope,
        love abide,
These three;
But the greatest of these is LOVE.   (1 Corinthians 13)

Second Corinthians

A dramatic story of defeats and triumph—so many scholars reconstruct Second Corinthians as they read between its lines.

One must hasten to say that not all scholars agree on the reconstruction. Günther Bornkamm chops up Second Corinthians into perhaps six different fragments from the pen of Paul, plus one (6:14—7:1) by another author, included here by mistake.[4] W. G. Kümmel is equally sure that Second Corinthians is just one complete, unified letter, needing no reconstruction.[5]

A large number of scholars, however, find hints which suggest a view between these extremes. Second Corinthians 2:3–4 speaks of a painful letter, written "out of much affliction and anguish of heart." Can that be First Corinthians? There is nothing very painful in First Corinthians, and there are no signs that Paul was in anguish as he wrote it. Of course the "painful" letter may be lost. But perhaps—many scholars would say probably—at least part of that letter has been preserved as our 2 Corinthians 10—13. The first nine chapters of Second Corinthians, according to this view, contain another letter—or perhaps parts of more than one letter—written after the severe letter of chapters 10—13.

Surely the mood and content of these last four chapters are different from those of the first nine. If, with many scholars, we swap their order,[6] the following story emerges.

The Occasion of Second Corinthians 10—14

First Corinthians seemed to be a failure. Factions still divided the immature church. And now outsiders had come, stirring up more trouble. Precisely what doctrines these intruders taught is not clear, but Paul can speak of them as preaching "another Jesus" (2 Cor. 11:4–5). One thing is clear enough: in every way they could, they attempted to undermine the authority of the Apostle Paul.

Here are some of the charges they seem to have made against him:

—His letters sound big, but in person he is a weakling, nothing. What a poor preacher Paul is (10:10)! (Perhaps they contrasted Paul with Apollos, famed for his eloquence [Acts 18:24].)

—Paul is dirt poor (11:7–11). But look, we are raising lots of money!

—Paul was "crafty." He put on an act of being poor and humble to get control over you (12:16).

—But look at us! We are at the same time true Jews (11:22)—not like that half-way Gentile-Paul—and really true apostles (11:5), preaching the genuine gospel of Jesus (11:4). What proof has Paul that he speaks for God (13:3)?

Horrified, Paul had made a quick trip from Ephesus across the bay to Corinth. He had publicly warned these rivals that he would "not spare them" if they did not stop (13:1–3).

They had not stopped. Paul had been publicly humiliated (12:21). He recalls that earlier he had been so "utterly, unbearably crushed" that he had thought he would die (1:8).

Torn between a resolve to visit them a third time (13:1) and a fear of another debacle (1:23; 2:1), Paul wrote this letter "out of much affliction and anguish of heart and with many tears" (2:4).

The Purpose of 2 Corinthians 10—13

Though Paul later protested that he wrote "not to cause you pain but to let you know the abundant love that I have for you" (2:4; cf. 11:11), obviously he is also writing in a desperate effort to defend his own authority in order to defend the gospel he had preached at Corinth. He writes to "undermine the claim" of those who boast that they are "superlative apostles" and who are preaching "another Jesus than the one" Paul had preached. But though he writes about himself, he does so for the sake of the church he has founded (12:19–21; 13:9). Finally, he writes in the hope that a letter will cause them to repent so that he will not need to have another stern confrontation with them when he comes in person (13:10).

Some Comments on 2 Corinthians 10—13

Paul's defense centers on an incomparable autobiography!

> Five times I have received at the hands of the Jews the forty lashes less one. Three times I have been beaten with rods; once I was stoned. Three times I have been shipwrecked; a night and a day I have been adrift at sea; on frequent journeys, in danger from rivers, danger from robbers, danger from my own people, danger from Gentiles, danger in the city, danger in the wilderness, danger at sea, danger from false brethren; in toil and hardship, through many a sleepless night, in hunger and thirst, often without food, in cold and exposure. And, apart from other things, there is the daily pressure upon me of my anxiety for all the churches.
>
> (2 Corinthians 11:24–28)

Paul also reveals a good many other things about himself in these chapters. He shows a fine flair for sarcasm as he calls his rivals "superlative apostles" (11:5; 12:11) and as he pleads for "forgiveness" for the "sin" of not having gotten the Corinthians to support him financially (11:7; 12:13). He shows, too, his pastoral love for the people in his churches. He does write to assert his authority. "And why? Because I do not love you? God knows I do!" (11:11). Paul can even compare himself to a jealous lover desperately trying to prevent his girl from being seduced (11:2)! He also reveals himself to be a mystic, given to ecstatic experiences he could not attempt to put into words (12:1–10). Finally, he speaks of a "thorn in the flesh," presumably some kind of illness, which even his own prayers could not cure (12:7–8). Some have argued that the sickness might have been some kind of epilepsy related to his frequent visions. Others have proposed that Paul, who went blind at the time of his conversion, continued to suffer from bad eyesight. No one really knows.

Against his every instinct as a Christian, Paul is forced to "boast," feeling like a "fool" as he does so. Counting the times such words as "boast" and "foolishness" occur between 2 Corinthians 10:7 and 12:13 will help one realize how embarrassed Paul feels in having to try to match credentials with his critics. These chapters have been compared to Plato's *Apology*, in which Socrates, on trial, with an appealing mixture of humility and pride, also reluctantly defends his life.

In summary, Paul's defense rests on such arguments as the following: It was he who had first brought the Corinthians the gospel (10:14). His refusal to take money from them showed the purity of his motives (11:7–11). His credentials as a good Jew were equal to those of any of his critics (11:22). He had undergone for the gospel all the dangers and difficulties listed above (11:23–33). He had even been granted mystic experiences of the highest kind (12:1–10). And, finally, the Corinthians themselves could remember seeing in him "the signs of a true apostle . . . signs and wonders, and mighty works" (12:12).

But his only boast, really, is not himself, but Jesus Christ. "Let him who boasts, boast of the Lord" (10:17).

The letter ends with an appeal that before he comes they should examine themselves (13:5) and mend their ways (13:11), lest his next visit be as wretched as his last (12:20–21).

The Occasion of 2 Corinthians 1—9

"Comfort"!

Ten times in the first paragraph Paul uses that word in one form or another. Paul had been "utterly, unbearably crushed," as though he "had received the sentence of death" (1:8–9). But now he has been delivered from a "deadly peril" (1:10). The crisis has passed.

Clearly the mood of 2 Corinthians 1—9 is different from that of chapters 10—13, the chapters we have just been studying. The two parts fit together beautifully if we assume that when Paul's letters were collected, perhaps forty or fifty years later, two letters which now make up our "2 Corinthians" were put together in reverse order.

By following this assumption we can reconstruct Paul's activities between the letters. He had sent Titus to Corinth, perhaps carrying the letter which we have as chapters 10—13. He was so anxious for a reply that he could not wait for Titus' return, but went as far as Troas to meet him. Even though he had great success there in his preaching, Paul was so disturbed that when he did not find Titus at Troas, he pushed on to Macedonia (2:12–13). There at last he had found Titus and had received the good news. Titus had reported that the Corinthian Christians

Second Corinthians
Paul's Ministry—and Their Partnership in It
"We share abundantly in comfort" (1:5).
"Are they servants of Christ? I am a better one . . ." (11:23).

1:1	**10:1**
A Joyful Letter in Response to Titus' Report: Paul and the Corinthians Are Reconciled, Partners Again in Ministry	**A Severe Letter Defending Paul's Ministerial Authority as an Apostle Against Attacks Being Spread in Corinth**
A review of how Paul had been distressed over the apparent rejection of him, and his joy at the news of reconciliation Titus had brought — 1—2	Paul's apology for defending ("boasting of") his authority — 10:1—11:21a
Paul's ministry, in which confidence is renewed, and in which the Corinthians are partners again — 3:1—4:12	
The encouragement in that ministry which comes from the eschatological hope — 4:13—5:21	The signs that Paul really has apostolic authority:
	his credentials as a good Jew — 11:21b—22
A plea for continued partnership in ministry, in spite of difficulties — 6:1—7:4	his sacrifices for Christ — 11:23—33
	his religious experiences — 12:1—10
(6:14—7:1 is a parenthesis on some who are excluded from that partnership.)	his miracles and mighty works — 12:11—13
Picking up from chapter 2, Paul's joy in the good news of reconciliation Titus has brought — 7:5—16	A plea that they repent and accept his authority before his coming visit — 12:14—13:14
A plea for financial partnership in ministry to the poor of the Jerusalem church — 8—9	**13:14**

Author: Paul
Recipients: The church he had founded in Corinth
Date: About A.D. 53–54
Occasion: Chapters 1—9 grow out of a report from Titus that the Corinthian church is ready again to work with Paul in ministry. All is well again.
Chapters 10—13 reflect serious attacks on Paul that have spread in Corinth.
Purpose: 1—9: to rejoice and to encourage the church in mutual ministry with Paul
10—13: desperately to seek to reestablish Paul's authority before he visits them

longed to see Paul and had been grieved by his letter, and that he had every reason to be proud of his church again (7:5–16). "I rejoice," Paul writes, "because I [again] have perfect confidence in you" (7:16). The letter ends: "Thanks be to God for his inexpressible gift!" (9:15).

The Purpose of 2 Corinthians 1—9

Many themes are woven together in this very personal and emotional letter, but the most frequently recurring one is Paul's expression of restored comfort, joy, and pride, both in his own apostleship and in the share the Corinthians have with him in ministry. He writes to encourage them to continue to share in the ministers' work.

His newly restored joy in the midst of affliction, and the contrast between the glorious ministry and the limitations of human ministers leads Paul to write to encourage the Corinthians with the thought of the hoped for *eschaton*, the heavenly things to come at the end of earthly life (4:13—5:21).

Chapters 8—9, on the other hand, are clearly pointed toward one very practical purpose—raising money. That money is not for Paul, however, but for the gift Paul plans to take back to the poor in Jerusalem.

Some Comments on 2 Corinthians 1—9

"Any one whom you forgive, I also forgive," Paul now writes happily (2:10). All was forgiven. The conflict was over. In chapters 1—2 he reviews the agony of the past, climaxed by his failure to find Titus, from whom he had hoped to get some reassuring news.

"But thanks be to God" (2:14)! Paul breaks off the story, aware that his readers already know its happy ending. Paul does not pick up the narrative again until 2 Corinthians 7:5. Rather, his cry of thanksgiving over the renewal of their acceptance of and partnership in his ministry moves Paul into a discussion of what it means to be a Christian minister. Here Paul seems to use the word in a very different way from that which is familiar to modern church members. As Paul uses it, "minister" does not refer simply to himself or to any religious professional. It is applied also to ordinary members of the church at Corinth (3:6). Not only professional clergy, but also lay people are "ministers of a new covenant."

Paul uses at least three figures to describe the work of "ministers":

1) "You are a letter from Christ," he writes these Christians (3:3). They are "written not with ink but with the Spirit." Paul's "letters"—Spirit-filled lives—are contrasted with Moses' letters inscribed in dead stone. These lay ministers are Paul's message, and Christ's message, to Corinth.

2) These ministers are only clay pots ("earthen vessels"). But in them people may find the treasure of the gospel of Christ (4:7). "Ministers" may wear out their earthly bodies in service to others. Christ gave his life. But they are sustained by the hope of heavenly bodies to come (4:16—5:10). Read at many funer-

als, Paul's description of the resurrection body makes these verses especially valuable.

It is to spread this good news and the reconciliation which accompanies it that Christians are called to be "ambassadors" of heaven on this earth (5:20). Christ gave his life to reconcile us to God. Christians spread the good news of this reconciliation.

To this task Paul now summons his readers (6:1–13).

Anyone reading 6:11–13 and skipping directly to 7:2 will see how perfectly these two fit together and why most scholars regard 6:14—7:1 as misplaced. Paul's letters were not collected until the end of the century. The wonder is that so much of Paul's writings have been preserved, not that one fragment should be out of place. Perhaps this passage is part of the letter referred to in 1 Corinthians 5:9–11. It fits nicely the description of the letter given there. Finally, Paul picks up again on the story broken off in 2 Corinthians 2:14, the account of the good news Titus had brought Paul from Corinth (7:5–16). The story ends with Paul rejoicing in the restoration of his "perfect confidence" in the church.

Paul flatters the church members at Corinth by assuring them that they are so generous that there is no need for him to write about the offering he is collecting for the poor of Jerusalem (9:1). Nevertheless, he writes them two whole chapters on precisely that subject (8—9)!

Noting the abrupt shift from the heights of theology in chapters 1—7 to the mundane subject of money in chapers 8—9, some scholars have proposed that these two chapters must be part of yet another letter. However, the cause of the poor was dear to Paul's heart, and it does not appear to have seemed out of place to Paul to move from the sublime to this down-to-earth subject (cf. Gal. 2:10; 1 Cor. 16:1–4; Rom. 15:25–27). Paul had refused to take any money from the church at Corinth for his own personal support (2 Cor. 11:7–10), but he was willing to use every argument he could think of, psychological as well as theological, to raise money for the poor.

He begins with the example set the Corinthians by their neighbors to the north, the Macedonians (8:1–7). You already excel in faith, in utterance, in knowledge, etc., he praises them. Of course you will not want to let the Macedonian churches get ahead of you in giving.!

He is only asking them, he insists, to do their fair share (8:13–14).

The funds will be carefully guarded and audited, not by Paul alone, but by Titus and another "brother," unnamed, but apparently known and trusted by the Corinthians (8:16–24).

They have a reputation for generosity, Paul says. He just knows that they will want to live up to it (9:1–5)!

They will be rewarded by God to the extent that they give—or fail to give (9:6–14).

Perhaps in some of these arguments "he looked like a man." But his pleas are all set in the framework of his deeper, theological argument. Early in chapter 8 he had written, "For you know the grace of our Lord Jesus Christ, that though he was rich, yet for your sake he became poor, so that by his poverty you might become rich" (8:9). It is really in response to Jesus Christ that Paul expects the Corinthians to give. And in the same vein, he ends with a shout concerning the real motivation he proposes for giving: "Thanks be to God for his inexpressible gift!" (9:15).

IX   *Of Faith and Freedom*

Building especially on these two letters, Augustine penned the best-known Christian works written in the thousand years following the New Testament itself.

The Protestant Reformation was born out of Martin Luther's militant interpretation of these two epistles.

Twentieth-century pastors still preach them, and scholars still debate the implications of every major idea in them.

Together, Galatians and Romans have proved to be the most influential and perhaps the most controversial pair of letters ever written.

Most scholars date them as coming from approximately the same time (somewhere between A.D. 52 and 57), interpret them as dealing with many of the same basic themes, and think of them together as representing the most mature and distinctive thought of the New Testament's most prolific writer. Exactly how close they are in date and subject may be debated, but Galatians and Romans obviously do have so much in common that we will consider them as two parts of this one chapter.

Galatians

"I confess I have sinned."
"Then God will punish you."
"No, He will not do that."
"Why not? Does not the Law say so?"
"I have nothing to do with the Law."
"How so?"
"I have another law, the law of liberty."
"What do you mean—'liberty'?"
"The liberty of Christ, for Christ has made me free from the Law that
    held me down. That law is now in prison itself, held captive by
    grace and liberty."

So Theodore Graebner translated part of Luther's commentary on Galatians. Most commentators today, Catholic and Protestant, would agree that here Luther was correctly dramatizing a major theme of the epistle.

Commentators do not agree, however, concerning to whom Paul was writing this message of freedom from the Law. As early as John Calvin, scholars identified the term "Galatians" as referring to inhabitants of the region which is now northern Turkey. Paul traveled through this area on both his second and third missionary journeys (Acts 16:1; 18:23). The term "Galatians" had been applied to its inhabitants ever since it had been invaded by "Gauls" centuries earlier.

Others believe the letter was written to churches in the south of what is now Turkey. They argue that Luke says nothing of Paul's preaching in the North but describes in detail his founding and revisiting several churches in the South (Antioch, Iconium, Lystra, Derbe, etc. [Acts 13—14; 15:36—16:5]). These cities were within the Roman province called Galatia, and, it is argued, Paul usually used such Roman legal names. Barnabas had helped found these churches and is mentioned in Galatians 2:13.

In itself it makes little difference in the understanding of the meaning of the letter as to whether what is called the "North Galatian theory" or the "South Galatian theory" is correct. However, if the letter was written to the southern churches, founded on the first journey, then a much earlier date than is usually assigned is possible for Galatian. It may have been the first of the canonical letters of Paul, the earliest book in the New Testament. And if this is the case, the problem of Galatians' seeming conflict with Acts concerning the Jerusalem Council is solved. Comments on this highly uncertain hypothesis are reserved, however, until page 142.

The Occasion of Galatians

Martin Luther, in his classic *Commentary on St. Paul's Epistle to the Galatians*, described the situation Paul faced in these words:

> These Jewish-Christian fanatics who pushed themselves into the Galatian churches after Paul's departure, boasted that they were the descendants of Abraham, true ministers of Christ, having been trained by the apostles themselves, that they were able to perform miracles.
>
> In every way they sought to undermine the authority of St. Paul. They said to the Galatians: "You have no right to think highly of Paul. He was the last to turn to Christ. But we have seen Christ. We heard Him preach. Paul came later and is beneath us. Is it possible for us to be in error—we who have received the Holy Ghost? Paul stands alone. He has not seen Christ, nor has he had much contact with the other apostles. Indeed, he persecuted the Church of Christ for a long time."[2]

These troublemakers were attacking not just Paul, of course, but the gospel he had preached. The churches in Galatia were "quickly deserting" the understanding of Christianity Paul had taught (1:6). To their initial faith in Christ, they began to add an emphasis on law and ceremony, especially circumcision.

No one is quite sure who these intruders were. Traditionally commentators have called them "Judaizers" and have thought of them as very conservative Jewish Christians, perhaps having their headquarters in Jerusalem. These Jews apparently argued that in order for a man to be a good Christian, he should go through the ceremony of circumcision and live by the Jewish Law. Some recent interpreters have noted that the Galatians seem also to have been tempted to return to the worship of "elemental spirits" and to an emphasis on the observance of special "days, and months, and seasons, and years" (4:9–10). Perhaps, it has been argued, Paul's opponents were Gentiles who sought some kind of syncretism, a merger of Christianity, Jewish legalism, and some elements of paganism. More recently, scholars have answered that there are hints of such an emphasis on spirits and special days in certain Jewish sects. It is not necessary, perhaps, to suppose that Paul's enemies had their roots outside Palestine.

Whatever else these teachers may have advocated, they preached a kind of Jewish legalism which Paul believed could not be combined with the Christian faith. Angered by their attacks on his apostleship, but even more by there subversion of the gospel he had preached, Paul wrote this highly emotional letter.

The Purpose of Galatians

Luther misunderstood Galatians. So, at least, it can be argued. Galatians is *not* about "*justification* by faith ," as Luther and his followers through the centuries have believed. It is about *sanctification* by faith. It is not about how one gets sins forgiven. It is about how one is to live when that beginning forgiveness has been received.

Now of course Luther was right that Galatians does affirm that we are justified—forgiven, made right with God—by God's grace, received by faith. Yet Paul's emphasis in Galatians is on the subsequent, continuing life of freedom. The Galatians had, they knew, already received the Spirit of faith, not law (3:2). Now they were to continue to live not by law, but by the Spirit. "If we live by the Spirit, let us also walk by the Spirit," Paul pleads (5:25). To revert to legalism, symbolized by circumcision, would be to revert to slavery. Paul writes to encourage the Galatians to live the Spirit-filled lives of persons set free from the Law.

Some Comments on Galatians

Nicaea the slave was now free! The inscription gives no hint concerning where the money came from by which her freedom was purchased. In a religious formality, the price had been given to the god Apollo, though then it had gone to her master Sosibis. The inscription the archaeologists have found at Delphi reads in part as follows: "Apollo the Pythian *bought* from Sosibis of Amphissa, *for freedom*, a female slave, whose name is Nicaea . . . *with a price* of three minae of silver and a half mina . . . The *price* he has received.''[3] Henceforth Nicaea was a slave to her god, "bought" by the god for a price. But with respect to all human slavery, she could live free.

It is something like this that Paul argues in Galatians, often called "the Magna Carta of Christian liberty." Christ had "redeemed" us (4:5), bought us back, "for freedom" (5:1). "You are no longer a slave" (4:7) to anything human, Paul says. The Christian knows himself to have been bought and paid for by his God. Therefore, the Galatians must live as free men and women, lives energized by the Spirit, guided not by law but by love (5:14).

Galatians, as Wrede said, is a "fighting letter." How concerned Paul is to defend the Galatians' freedom is shown by two peculiarities of the letter's structure. In every other letter Paul begins with a prayer of thanksgiving, but in this letter he omits all that, plunging right into his angry defense. And at the end he adds in his own hand a long postscript in unusually large letters (6:11–18). Perhaps the letters were big because Paul had poor eyesight. But perhaps he wrote large to shout his message in ink. "For neither circumcision counts for anything, nor uncircumcision, but a new creation" (6:15).

The focus of the conflict was circumcision. To be perfect, thereby spiritual rather than carnal, it had been argued, what better symbol could be imagined than the actual cutting away of a piece of flesh! And the flesh sacrificed from the part of the body associated with lust! Paul, his opponents apparently charged, had not demanded that step toward perfection simply to make things easy for his converts, to please men (1:10).

Paul begins to defend his gospel by defending his own apostleship. In this defense Paul gives us a kind of two-chapter autobiography, his testimony to his Christian experience and authority as an Apostle. In this autobiography Paul is concerned to affirm two points. First, his authority is independent, "not from men nor through man, but through Jesus Christ" (1:1). He had not simply been a pupil of the Twelve at Jerusalem (1:16–24). He had such authority that he had even stood up against Peter ("opposed him to his face" [2:11]), "Cephas," who was later to be called "the first Pope."

But Paul is also concerned to show that his gospel of freedom from the Law, though not derived from the leaders of the Jerusalem church, had the full approval of the Jerusalem Apostles. He had "laid before them" what he had been teaching, ready to change if wrong (2:2). Yet Jesus' own brother James, plus Peter and John, the great Apostles, had shaken his hand and told him to carry on (2:9).

Galatians' story of this meeting is often said to be a more accurate account of the Jerusalem Council of Acts 15 (see pages 102–103). Luke, it is said, expanded into a large ecclesiastical assembly, climaxed by formal decrees, what was really a much smaller, private, and informal discussion. John Calvin and many twentieth-century scholars have held, however, that Galatians is describing an earlier meeting which took place during Paul's second visit to Jerusalem following his

Galatians
Living by Faith

"For in Christ Jesus neither circumcision or uncircumcision is of any avail, but faith, working through love" (5:6).

1:1	2	3:1	4	5:1	6	6:18

A Personal Defense by Paul of His Authority as an Apostle

Salutation
1:1-5

Paul's distress at the attacks on his gospel
1:6-10

A brief autobiography to show that Paul does have authority
1:11—2:14

The relation of that gospel to life: "the life I now live ... I live by faith ..."
2:15-21

A Defense of His Gospel of Freedom from the Law

The Galatians' own experience proves it. They, too, have begun to live by the Spirit through faith, not law.
3:1-5

The Jewish scriptures themselves also teach that we live by faith, not law.
3:6—4:31

A Plea to Continue to Live by Faith the Free, Spirit-Filled Life of Love

Since Christ has set us free, let us live free from the law, not slip back into legalism.
5:1-12

The free, Spirit-filled life is the life guided by love.
5:13—6:10

An emotional postscript written in Paul's own hand
6:11-18

Author: Paul
Recipients: Christians in some churches founded by Paul in what is now Turkey
Date: A.D. 55 (A.D. 49?)
Occasion: "Judaizers" have attacked Paul and urged these new Christians to live by the Jewish Law, of which circumcision is an important symbol.
Purpose: Paul writes to defend his teaching that we are to live by the Spirit, by faith, not by law

conversion (Acts 11:30). Galatians implies that the meeting it describes was during the second visit Paul made to Jerusalem as a Christian.

If Galatians is describing a meeting which took place prior to Paul's missionary journeys, then it may be that this letter was written as early as A.D. 49, even before First and Second Thessalonians. Against this view it is argued that Galatians 4:13 implies that Paul has been to the Galatian churches twice. That verse, however, can be understood in other ways. The "North Galatian theory" (page 140) would prohibit an early date for Galatians, but that theory also is uncertain. Those who tend, as does the present writer, to set a relatively high value on the historicity of Acts are likely to hold to the view that Galatians is an early letter and that it describes a meeting several years prior to the Jerusalem Council of Acts 15. The issue can probably never be settled to the satisfaction of all.

What is clear is that in the first two chapters Paul presents the case for both his independence of and his endorsement by the mother church at Jerusalem. He also introduces the theme of the letter. We already know, he says, "that a man is not justified by works of the law but through faith in Jesus Christ" (2:16). Now we must not slip back into legalism, "build up again those things which I tore down" (2:18). The Galatians, in their legalism, have gone to the opposite extreme from the "Spirit-filled" people of First Corinthians. The Corinthians simply lived as they pleased. In this letter Paul must urge the Galatian legalists to forget their hang-ups and to live the truly Spirit-filled life. He can describe it in these words: "It is no longer I who live, but Christ who lives in me; and the life I now live in the flesh I live by faith in the Son of God" (2:20).

Belief in a life received by faith from the Spirit, not the rules and regulations of the Jewish Torah, is defended in a two-chapter argument (3–4). The Galatians' initial experience of receiving salvation by faith, not by obedience to circumcision or any other law, shows that the Jewish Law is no longer relevant for Christians (3:1–5). And in a long, involved, and at times dubious exposition, Paul sets out to prove that the Jewish scriptures themselves taught the priority of faith over law. He uses such arguments as the following: "He who through faith is righteous shall live," he quotes from Habakkuk 2:4 (cf. Rom. 1:17, and see pages 151 ff.) Abraham had lived by faith long before the Law was given (3:6).

Paul now uses a bit of Roman law to illustrate how the promises to Abraham have now spread outside Judaism. As interpreted by G. M. Taylor,[4] the pattern is this: Roman inheritance laws were originally enacted to protect Roman citizens. Eventually, however, if a Roman wished to leave part of his estate to some non-Romans, he could do this. Technically he left all to one Roman heir. That heir, however, knowing that he was actually supposed to act for others as the executor of the estate, would, by another legal convention, "adopt" the others to whom the estate would go. He could then divide the inheritance with them. Christ, as Abraham's true heir, now "adopts" us, Paul says, and we also become heirs of the promises of Abraham (3:15–18).

Changing the figure, Paul says that the Old Testament Law was a temporary necessity until the eschatological deliverance brought by Christ. It was a "custodian" (3:24, cf. 4:2), a kind of stern "baby-sitter." Entertainments of the time poked fun at such sour-faced "custodians" who shouted "No!" to freedom-loving children as they protected them. A child under such restraint was little better than a slave. But now, Paul says, the Galatians have been set free and are not slaves, but are bought for freedom and adopted as grown-ups sons and daughters, heirs of the promises.

Galatians 3:28 summarizes what must have been among the most shocking implications of Paul's argument. In familiar liturgy a man might pray, "I thank thee, Lord, King of the universe, that I have not been born a Gentile, a slave, or a woman"! Paul announces that precisely these three barriers have been blasted away by the coming of Christ. "There is neither Jew nor Greek, there is neither slave nor free, there is neither male nor female; for you are all one in Christ Jesus." In civil rights struggles and in the battle for women's liberation, this verse was to become a rallying cry in the twentieth century.

Paul concludes the theological argument by using a dubious device popular among first-century biblical scholars—allegory (see above, page 3). Paul compares those who live by the Law to the children of Abraham's slave, Hagar, and those who live by faith and the Spirit to Abraham's free sons (4:21–31).

The final two chapters of Galatians are an appeal to live out the implications of this theology. You are free, Paul says. Therefore—at least as Augustine interpreted him—Paul says, "Love God—and do as you please!" In the twentieth century Joseph Fletcher was to argue, in part on the basis of Galatians, that the Christian is bound by no laws, not even the Ten Commandments.[5] The Christian is simply to do whatever love demands in a given situation. Even adultery may be the right thing for a Christian, Fletcher suggests, if in some situation it is required by love! The Judaizers must have been scandalized!

But there does remain the law of love (5:14). There does remain the guidance of the Holy Spirit (5:25). The one who loves God may do as he pleases. But he will please freely to choose to do as God's Holy Spirit guides, Paul is saying. And that will be to "bear one another's burdens, and so fulfil the law of Christ" (6:2). Thus the Christian will live not by license, but by the liberty of unconstrained love.

Martin Luther summarized Galatians' paradox of Christian freedom and servanthood in these famous words:

> A Christian man is the most free lord of all, and subject to none;
> a Christian man is the most dutiful servant of all, and subject to everyone.[6]

Romans

To Martin Luther, at least, Romans represented the high point of the whole Bible.

> This epistle is in truth the principal part of the New Testament and the

very purest Gospel. It fully deserves that every Christian should know it by heart, word for word, and should feed upon it every day, as daily bread for his soul. It cannot be read too often nor too deeply pondered, and the more it is studied the more precious and sweet to the taste does it become.[7]

Augustine, Calvin, Karl Barth, and many other giants of Christian theology have also built their thought upon Romans. It is generally recognized as the fullest, clearest, most systematic statement of Paul's most distinctive doctrines, especially his belief in "justification by faith."

It may seem odd, however, to speak of Romans as "the very purest Gospel." Matthew, Mark, Luke, and John are the books the church has called the "Gospels." Romans gives us hardly any information at all about the earthly life of Jesus. This is one reason why critics of Paul, including Harnack, have charged that a book such as Romans actually "ruins" the gospel (see above, page 111). It substitutes religion *about* Jesus, they argue, for the religion *of* Jesus.

In answer, Paul would probably reply that concern about the Jesus of the past is valid, of course. The next generation of Christian writers would explore that subject well enough, as we saw in chapters IV and V. But Paul was interested in the present, in the risen Christ now, and in the new age the risen Christ was now bringing. Paul's concern in Romans is "existential." He writes about his understanding of what Christ means to the believer now and in the future. That meaning is, for Paul, "gospel" (good news).

The Occasion of Romans

Surprisingly, Paul seems to have written his longest letter to to a church he had never visited. Though Roman Catholic tradition speaks of Peter as founding the church at Rome, the New Testament itself gives no hint as to its origin. Hero though Paul was to Luke, Acts accurately admits that the church was established in Rome before Paul got there (Acts 28:14–15).

He had not been there yet, but Paul did want to visit Rome! Acts 19:21 quotes Paul on his way to his last tragic visit to Jerusalem as exclaiming, "After I have been there, I must also see Rome." Paul begins his letter by swearing before God how eager he is to visit that church: "I long to see you" (1:9–11). "I have longed for many years to come to you," he repeats as he closes his epistle (15:23).

"At present," he writes, "I am going to Jerusalem with aid for the saints" (15:25). He had now collected for poor Christians in Jerusalem the money he had been seeking as he wrote to Corinth (15:26; cf, 1 Cor. 16:1–4). His ambition is to go to Jerusalem with this gift, then to travel to Rome, and at last to take the gospel all the way to Spain 15:28). Probably he writes from Cornith during his three-months stay in Greece on his last missionary journey, about A.D. 57 (Acts 20:1–3). Paul writes to prepare the church for his visit and to explain to them his particular approach to the Christian faith.

Since Paul has had little contact with the Roman church, this epistle, unlike his other letters, is not written to deal with some special problem in a particular congregation. Some things, however, can be inferred about this church at Rome:

1) It was a church of great importance, at least symbolically, because it was located in the capital of the world. Johannes Munck has called attention to Paul's belief that a mission among the Gentiles would make the Jews "jealous," causing them to want to become Christians too (11:11).[8] No greater symbol of the spread of God's promises to the nations could be given than the spread of Christianity at the heart of the empire.

2) "Tribulation," "distress," "persecution," "the sword"—there are strong hints in such words in Romans 8:31–39 that the chruch had already experienced some persecution. The Roman historian Suetonius tells us that about A.D. 52, "Since the Jews were continually making disturbances at the instigation of Chrestus, he [Claudius] expelled them from Rome"[9] (cf. Acts 18:2). Perhaps, "Chrestus" is a misspelling of "Christus"—an error common among non-Christians a century later, Chrestus being a familiar name and sounding almost like the title given Jesus. If so, then the disturbances may have been caused by dissension in the Jewish community in Rome over the first Christian preachers. In any event, those Christians who were Jews had experienced Claudius' persecution by the time Paul wrote Romans.

3) The church at Rome was a mixed congregation, containing both Jews and Gentiles. Scholars differ as to which group predominated. Most think of the church at Rome as largely Gentile. This view seems to be supported by Romans 1:5–6; 1:14; 11:13; and 15:16. But other verses seem addressed much more to Jews. Paul speaks to his readers about "Abraham, our forefather according to the flesh" (4:1) and "our forefather Isaac" (9:10). "I am speaking to those who know the law," (the Jewish Law), he writes in 7:1. "You call yourself a Jew," he challenges his imaginary reader (2:17). Three whole chapters (9—11) trace God's relationship to the Jews. And indeed, almost the whole book is to describe God's righteousness set in relationship to the Jewish Law. It seems to the present writer, therefore, that the letter can be more easily understood if it is thought of as being addressed to a largely Jewish congregation, though one in which uncircumcised Gentiles were participating more and more.

Paul is writing, therefore, to Jewish Christians and to Gentile converts who have been taught the Jewish Law. He is writing to a church which is growing, however, in the midst of Gentiles, in the very capital of the Gentiles, persecuted by Gentiles, and yet itself gradually coming to be dominated by members who are themselves uncircumcised Gentiles. It is to the theological tensions growing out of the relationship of the Jewish Christians to Gentile Christians, of those schooled in the Jewish Law to those who had previously scarcely heard of the Jewish Law, that Paul, Apostle to the Gentiles, writes this letter.

The Purpose of Romans

Paul writes to prepare the Roman Christians for his coming by describing for them his own understanding of the good news, the gospel. That seems clear enough. The whole letter is a systematically outlined, carefully reasoned exposition of that gospel—in contrast to his highly personal, belligerent, and sometimes disjointed defense in Galatians.

What was that gospel? At first the answer again seems clear. The whole message is summarized at the beginning in just two verses:

> For I am not ashamed of the gospel: it is the power of God for salvation to every one who has faith, to the Jew first and also to the Greek. For in it the righteousness of God is revealed through faith for faith; as it is written, "He who through faith is righteous shall live."
>
> (Romans 1:16–17; cf. Habakkuk 2:4)

Paul writes to present good news about "the righteousness of God" that is revealed "through faith." But readers of Romans are divided as to what these words mean.

The classical Reformation understanding is that Paul writes to describe a "righteousness," a getting right with God, which the believer receives through faith, not by any legalistic good deeds. God's kind of righteousness for man is set over against all human righteousness, which one might claim on the basis of one's own goodness, by obedience to the Law (10:3). The book is written, according to this view, to answer the question, "How can I get right with God?"

Luther, for example, defines "the righteousness of God" in these words: "how a person becomes righteous before God, namely, alone by faith." It is the believer's "justification." Similarly, Calvin comments, "I take the righteousness of God to mean, that which is approved before his tribunal." The extreme of this approach is that of Rudolf Bultmann, who can speak of the book as a presentation of Christian "anthropology," a book about humankind.[10]

While the believer's justification by faith is surely a great theme of the letter, the present writer finds the book as a whole making more sense when the basis of that message is understood as being first good news not about humankind, but about God. The believer's hope of salvation rests upon the goodness, the righteousness, the love of God. Paul writes to celebrate the goodness of God in his dealings with humankind.

The German scholar Bornkamm seeks to combine these two views:

> Astonishing as it may seem, in Romans 1:17 Paul speaks, *in one and the same sentence,* of the righteousness of God and that of the believer: nor are these two things, but one, God's righteousness. . . . God attributes his righteousness to man who is a sinner and not righteous in himself. God is righteous and proves his righteousness by justifying [forgiving,

pardoning, declaring acquitted] the person who has faith (Rom. 3:26).[11]

Romans is good news about God. It does answer the question "How can I be saved?" But is is also written to answer such questions as these: Does the faithlessness of some Jews nullify the faithfulness of God (3:3)? Is God unjust to inflict wrath upon us (3:5)? Is God the God of Jews only? Is he not the God of Gentiles also (3:29)? Is God's law sin, since we are justified apart from it (7:7,13)? Is there injustice on God's part (9:14)? Has God rejected his people (11:1)?

However, the righteousness, the goodness, which Paul ascribes to God is not a static attribute such as the goodness of the god described by such Greek philosophers as Aristotle. Aristotle wrote of "the Unmoved Mover." For Paul, by contrast, God's righteousness is in his activity—Christ's death and resurrection—in behalf of humankind. God is "for us" (8:31). The good news about God's active, loving concern for sinful man is now revealed, made clear, in the eschatological event of the coming of Christ.

This good news is revealed, Paul says, "through faith for faith" (1:17). The ancient scholar Jerome thought of that phrase as meaning "from the Old Testament faith into the New Testament faith." Calvin took it to imply the believer's growing, deepening trust. But Karl Barth is probably closer to Paul's theology when he understands it as "where the faithfulness of God encounters the fidelity of men."[12]

"Faith," as Paul uses the term, is never an end in itself. Paul never praises "faith" as such. It is always faith *in* something, or more accurately, in Someone. Nor is "faith" simply belief that certain statements are true. Faith, to Paul, is trust. It is commitment. It is a personal relationship to the God whose faithfulness to us is revealed in Christ.

That kind of faith leads both to forgiveness and to a special kind of life, now and in the *eschaton*, Paul is sure. "The just shall live by his faithfulness"—God's faithfulness to the believer and the believer's faithfulness to God.

To describe the righteousness of God and the forgiveness, the "justification," the righteousness God freely gives to those who have such faith, as well as the kind of life which results from it—this is the purpose of Romans.

Some Comments on Romans

In Romans, Paul presents his most original contributions to Christian theology, what he can call "my gospel" (2:16; 16:25). It is surprising, therefore, that he begins with what many scholars believe is a quotation from a very, very early Christian creed. Romans 1:3–4 summarizes a faith common to all the church, probably in a liturgical formula Paul could expect some of his readers to know by heart. "His" gospel, he believed, was implied in the earliest *kerygma* preached everywhere.

Romans
The Good News of the Righteousness of God

*"In it [the gospel] the righteousness of God is revealed through faith for faith. ...
'He who through faith is righteous shall live.'" (1:17).*

1:1 Introduction	1:18 The Righteousness of God Revealed in Judgment	3:21 The Righteousness of God Revealed in God's Free Justification of Those Who Have Faith	5:1 The Righteousness of God in the Experience of the Individual	9:1 The Righteousness of God in History: God's Dealings with the Jews	12:1 The Believer's Response to God's Righteousness: Righteous Living in the World	15:14 16:27 Concluding Doxology, Personal Comments, and Postscripts
Salutation 1:1-7	On pagans 1:18—2:16	The good news that righteousness announced 3:21-31	The experience of tension between law and grace 5:1—7:24	Paul's concern over the apparent rejection of the Jews 9:1-33	The response of love 12—13	
Paul's desire to visit them 1:8-15	On Jews 2:17—3:8	That righteousness illustrated in Abraham 4:1-25	The experience and hope of victory 7:25—8:39	The responsibility of Christians to spread the gospel to them and others 10:1-21	Concern especially for weaker brothers 14:1—15:13	
The theme of the letter stated: the gospel of the righteousness of God 1:16-17	On all people 3:9-20			Paul's continuing hope for the Jews 11:1-36		

Author: Paul
Recipients: The church at Rome
Date: A.D. 56
Occasion: Paul hopes to visit the church soon.
Purpose: To prepare for his visit by explaining to them his understanding of the gospel as good news about the righteousness of God

Paul could at times be blunt. With these strangers, however, he moves tactfully from this common faith, that Christ the Lord has come, to the apocalyptic implications Paul sees in that eschatological event. We have already examined the key verses in which he announces his understanding of the revelation of God's righteousness (1:16–17). The rest of the letter develops this theme so systematically that some commentators have speculated that Romans is an expansion of a lecture Paul may have given many times.

First he deals with the negative side of God's righteousness, what Karl Barth calls the "No" of God. God's righteous judgment upon sin is already being revealed in this Messianic age. That judgment on sin turns out to be sin itself. It reaches its climax in a double perversion, the opposite of God's good creation. (1) In idolatry humankind worships its own creations, not its Creator (1:23). (2) In homosexuality Paul sees a symbol of the reversal of the Creator's intention in human relationships (1:26–27).

If one asks, "What about people who don't know any better?" Paul replies that all should know better. Nature's Creator is revealed in creation (1:19), and moral standards are recognized even in untrained consciences (2:12–15). Yet neither Jew nor Gentile lives up to the good each knows.

Paul climaxes this section by pulling together passages from many parts of the Old Testament to show that every human being deserves condemnation by the righteous judgment of God. "None is righteous, no, not one" (3:10–18). Even those who have tried hard to obey God's Law are lost. In fact, what the Law has done for them is to make them more aware of their sin (3:20).

One can cite ancient Jewish rabbis who would agree with almost everything Paul has said up to this point. They had read these same verses concerning how all humankind deserve condemnation, but their prescription for this malady was usually repentance, fasting, prayer, and a new resolve to obey the Commandments.

Paul's is the announcement of the new age. *But now,* he says emphatically, an apocalyptic event has occurred. The righteous God has revealed his saving grace apart from the Law (3:21–26). The Jewish commentator Schoeps says that some rabbis of the time taught that the Law would end with the Messiah.[13] For Paul, that Messianic age had begun. Humankind now lives in the new era, not of law, but of faith.

To Jewish Christians, children of Abraham shocked by the announcement that the Law is no longer needed, Paul replies in chapter 4 that Abraham himself had never heard of the Law. Abraham received God's righteousnes by faith long before God's Law was given.

In Christ, Paul has said, God in heaven has declared sinful people righteous, forgiven. In chapters 5—8 Paul turns to the consequences of God's action in the lives of individuals here on earth. When in Romans 1:16 Paul spoke of the gospel as the "power" of God for salvation, the Greek word he used for "power" was the word from which our words "dynamite" and "dynamics" are dervied. Paul now describes the "dynamics" of God's salvation. For the person of faith there are joyful consequences of God's action: "peace," "character," "hope," "love" (5:1–11). Reconciled to God through Christ's death, the Christian also is saved by his life, a life the believer is now enabled to begin to share, at least in hope.

But there is a continuing, "dynamic" conflict, a cosmic struggle within and for the souls of men and women. Let the reader scan Romans 5:12—6:23 and make two lists. Over and over he will find such words as the following set in opposition to each other:

sin	free gift
death	life
law	grace
Adam (one man)	Christ (one man)

Paul attempts to illustrate in a series of figures how, in this conflict, the believer is freed from the righteousness of the Law and enabled to live by the righteousness of God.

1) We were all children of Adam, the fallen sinner, he says. But now, through Christ, humankind has a kind of second start (5:12–21).

2) We have "died" with Christ to the Law. Schoeps quotes an ancient rabbi as saying, "As soon as a man is dead, he is free from the obligation of the commands."[14] In baptism the believer has "died" with Christ and begins a new life of resurrection freedom (6:5–14). The Law has not died, but we have died in relation to it.

3) We were "slaves" of sin. But Christ has freed us to be "slaves" of God (6:15–23).

4) We were once "married" to the Law. But now our former "husband" is dead, and we are free (7:1–6).

In all of these figures, Paul argues not only for the reality of Christian freedom, but also for the importance of living daily the righteous lives of those set free by the righteousness of God. The basis of the appeal, however, is no longer legal obligation, but new opportunity, new power for living.

The description of the dynamic, personal struggle of these conflicting forces within the soul builds to a climax in Romans 7. In 7:7 Paul switches to the first person, using *I* to dramatize the personal intensity of the warfare. He gives his own spiritual autobiography, but only as typical of all believers. At the climax of the tension Paul cries, "Wretched man that I am! Who will deliver me from this body of death?" Some commentators have argued that here Paul is simply recalling, from his Christian perspective, how his life before his conversion now appears to him. Yet he is writing to people who are already Christians, and this language seems too dramatic to be simply a theological analysis of a memory. Luther and Calvin are right that this dynamic tension still exists in the souls of "born again" Christians, the best of whom, in Luther's phrase, is "at the same time justified and yet a sinner." Like a prisoner whose partner on a chain gang has died, the tormented sinner drags a corpse, a "body of death," his old nature, with him.

But the believer also knows deliverance! "Thanks be to God!" (7:25).

Romans 8 is Paul's almost lyrical celebration of Christ's victory for the believer in the struggle described in the preceding chapters. Now Paul uses yet another figure, the courtroom. The believer is pardoned, "set free," and "lives" in spite of deserving the death penalty. The Holy Spirit takes over in the soul of the one who has faith. "We are children of God," the Christian can exult, not prisoners condemned by the heavenly Judge (8:16). All history has longed for this eschatological era, which Christians have and will share with Christ (8:18–25).

True, these Roman Christians still face persecution. But "in all these things we are more than conquerors through him who loved us" (8:37). Romans 8 is the believer's shout of triumph.

What about those Jews who have not believed? Paul is so concerned for them that he could wish himself damned if that would convert his brother Jews (9:3). Romans 9–11 expresses his agonizing meditations on what was to this Christian Jew a distressing question. Paul's reasoning about it sometimes seems tortured, and his answers do not always seem quite consistent. But here are answers he proposes:

1) However it may seem, God is working out his righteous plan in history, his plan of election. Romans 9:1–29 presents one of Paul's most controversial doctrines, the idea of God's "election" or "predestination" of men and women, not becuase of their merit, but purely by God's grace.

2) If some Jews are lost, it is not because God is unrighteous, but because they are, Paul argues. It is their own fault (9:30–33).

3) Christians must take the responsibility. Christians must be missionaries, must spread the good news of salvation to all people (10:1–21).

4) As a matter of fact, some Jews *are* Christians (11:5).

5) Whatever the situation, Christians must never look down upon Jews. Rather, Gentile Christians' highest hope is that through Christ they have been allowed to be grafted onto the tree that is Israel. The Christian has become in a sense a kind of adopted Jew (11:17–24).

6) In the end "all Israel will be saved" (11:25–32).

7) For now, the whole matter is a mystery beyond even Paul's understanding (11:33–36).

Chapters 12—15, the last major section of Romans, form our best statement of Christian ethics according to Paul. Even so, these chapters do not give a complete statement of ethical principles, but rather deal with certain specific issues relevant to the Roman church. Several points are worth particular notice.

First, it is essential to understand the motivation of Christian living according to Paul. It is *not* that the Christian is to be a loving person in order to earn God's favor. To say that would be to get everything exactly backwards. Rather, the Christian ethic is an ethic of response, a "therefore" ethic. Since all that has been said in the first eleven chapters of Romans is true, Paul begins chapter 12, with *therefore:* "I appeal to you therefore . . . by the mercies of God." In gratitude to God for his righteous action of giving justification to us sinners, Paul says, we are to give ourselves to God.

That response is to be shown in humble service to others within the body, the church (12:1–8). Paul also writes of Christian love in action toward those persecuting the church. His words sound very much like those of Jesus in the Sermon on the Mount (12:14; cf. Matt. 5:43–44). The Christian is to carry out faithfully his civic responsibilities, even in Nero's Rome (13:1–7)! The guide and summary of Christian living can be put in one word: love (12:9–13; 13:8–10). In this eschatological hour, there is no longer time for drunkenness and quarreling, opposites of living out that love (13:11–14).

A long discussion concerns the particular problem of care for Christians who are "weaker" in the faith. The subject of those timid converts who refuse to eat meat lest they seem to participate in sacrifices to pagan gods is discussed again (14:1—15:6; cf. 1 Cor. 8—10; see p. 128). Paul counsels tolerance and concern. "We who are strong ought to bear with the failings of the weak" (15:1).

The letter concludes with some personal comments (see p. 146). Chapter 16 consists largely of personal greetings to friends.

Some ancient manuscripts omit all or most of chapter 16. It is suggested by many scholars that Paul would probably not have known as many people in the church at Rome as are listed in chapter 16, since he had never been there. Perhaps, it is proposed, this list belonged originally with another letter of Paul's. Or perhaps Paul sent another copy of this letter to some church such as the one at Ephesus, in which he did know many people, attaching these greetings to that copy. Romans may originally have been a sermon or a kind of circular letter to which the salutation and conclusion were added when it was sent as a letter. There is no way to be sure.

At any rate, the list is interesting. Priscilla (Prisca) and Aquila, whose home had indeed been at Rome, are mentioned first (16:3; cf. Acts 18:2; 1 Cor. 16:19). Several members of Paul's otherwise almost unknown family are included (16:7, 11, 21; cf. Acts 23:16). Even the secretary adds a greeting (16:22).

Romans is a profound theological treatise. But its closing list of common names reminds the student today that Paul expected ordinary church members to read it, to understand it, and to live by it.

X   *The Prison Epistles*

"I am an ambassador in chains" (Eph. 6:20).

Paul did make the journey to Rome he had so long and so eagerly anticipated, but he made it as a prisoner of the Romans. Acts gives us an account of Paul's arrest in Jerusalem, his defenses in various courts, and his appeal to Caesar. His dangerous voyage to Rome is described in vivid detail. We are told that he was welcomed in Rome by Christians, but received a very mixed response from the leaders of Rome's large Jewish community. Acts ends with Paul a prisoner under a kind of "house arrest," living in a private home under home guard. Here believers and inquirers might visit, and here, presumably, he could still write letters (Acts 28:30–31; see page 107).

Ancient Christian tradition says that in Rome, under Nero, Paul was martyred. The most likely date is about A.D. 64. Since he was a Roman citizen, he was not crucified. Crucifixion was the proper execution for an outsider, especially a slave. Paul was (traditionally) killed more "humanely"; they beheaded him!

From as early as the middle of the second century until the twentieth, at least four letters—Philippians, Colossians, Philemon, and Ephesians—were thought of as written by Paul during this time of Roman imprisonment. They have been regarded as in a sense Paul's last will and testament. "Remember my fetters," Colossians 4:18 had exhorted the reader. And picturing Paul "a prisoner . . . for Jesus Christ" (Philem. 9) awaiting his martyrdom in Rome, readers have fulfilled the hope expressed in Philippians 1:14, "Brethren have been made confident in the Lord because of my imprisonment."

Recently, however, many scholars have found reasons to believe that Paul may have written one or more of these letters during an earlier imprisonment, perhaps at Ephesus or while awaiting trial at Caesarea (Acts 23:33; 24:27).[1] Indeed, serious question has been raised as to whether it was Paul who wrote Colossians, and a large number of scholars *now* doubt that Paul wrote Ephesians.[2]

The case for dating these letters during some earlier imprisonment—for example, at Ephesus—rests on such grounds as the following:

1) It is eight hundred miles from Rome to Philippi. Some estimate that in the first century that journey might take as long as seven weeks. Yet Paul appears to have had repeated communication with the Philippian church. Similarly, Rome is a long way from Colossae. Is it not much more likely that the runaway slave

Onesimus would have sought refuge in Ephesus, a port only a hundred miles from his home?

2) Paul expresses high hope for visiting "soon" both in Philippi and in Colossae (Phil. 2:23–24; Philem. 22). Paul could have had much better reason for such hope during some short imprisonment in relatively nearby Ephesus.

3) Paul has with him Timothy, Mark, Aristarchus, Demas, Tychichus, and Luke (Philem. 24; Phil. 1:1; Col. 4:7–14; Eph. 6:21). Of these, Acts mentions only Luke as being with Paul at Rome.

4) In Philippians Paul is faced with Jewish opposition, a situation suggesting to some commentators that the letter belongs to the same period as Galatians.

5) Finally, the references to the "praetorian guard" (Phil. 1:13) and "those of Caesar's household" (4:22) were once thought to make clear that the letter was written in Rome. It has now been discovered, however, that these terms were used for certain Roman garrisons and civil servants throughout the empire.

Nevertheless, probably most scholars still think of these four letters as written—or purporting to be written—by Paul from Rome.[3] Placing them in the Caesarean imprisonment helps little with the problem of geography. As for relating them to an imprisonment in Ephesus, the big problem is that we have no clear record that Paul ever was in prison there. The problems of travel time are not insoluble, given the length of Paul's imprisonment in Rome and the fact that "all roads led to Rome," the center and focal point of the ancient world.

Fortunately, whichever way one decides, the meaning of the letters is not greatly changed. Without strong conviction about the matter one way or the other, the present writer is inclined for four reasons to believe that they were written from Rome. (1) The tradition that they came from Rome is ancient and consistent. (2) We know that Paul was a longtime prisoner in Rome. (3) Paul seems to be facing seriously and with a certain resignation the prospect of death. (4) The thought of some of these letters, if all of them are by Paul, seems to reflect a later stage in his theological development.

Philippians

"If there were a competition to decide which is the most beautiful of Paul's letters, the odds would be strongly on Philippians," writes A. M. Hunter.[4] "In no other letter does he share his inner spiritual life so freely with his readers," adds Kenneth Grayston. Philippians is so personal, so cordial, and so affectionate that Grayston gives it a subtitle, "The Apostle and His Friends."[5]

Christ's prisoner here writes such a courageous letter of good cheer that its theme might well be summarized as "Joy in a Jail."

The Occasion of Philippians

In which city Paul is confined can be debated, but it is clear that he is in prison (1:7, 13, 14, 17). Yet the letter is not a complaint, but a thank-you note. "I have . . . received from Epaphroditus the gifts you sent" Paul writes (4:18). "It was kind of you to share my trouble" (4:14). Long before, Paul had founded the church in Philippi (Acts 16). He had been in jail there, too. Since then, that church had supported him repeatedly, and now again they had come to his aid (4:15–18).

A friend from the church, Epaphroditus, had brought the gift, probably money. While with Paul, he had fallen ill and had nearly died. Paul sends the letter with Epaphroditus, rejoicing with the Philippians that they will see that he is well again (2:25–30).

As Paul writes, he does not know whether he will be released or be executed (1:20). Yet he reassures his friends that even while he is in prison, the gospel is being spread. And he cheerfully predicts that he will be set free to visit them "soon."

Two facts, however, do distress Paul. (1) Some kind of false teaching is being spread. "Some indeed preach Christ from envy and rivalry" (1:15). "Look out for the dogs," he warns the Philippians (3:2). Perhaps these verses refer to two different groups of false teachers, the first simply capitalizing on Paul's imprisonment to grab places of leadership in the church. More likely, the partisan preachers mentioned in chapter 1 are the same teachers attacked more fully in the second half of the letter. (2) There is some kind of dissension in the church at Philippi. Two women of the church have had a quarrel (4:2). Others evidently have taken sides. Concern about a threatened church split moves Paul to a plea for unity.

The Purpose of Philippians

Paul writes this letter for several purposes:

1) He writes to thank the church for their gift. "It was kind of you to share my trouble" (4:14).

2) He writes to reassure and encourage his friends at Philippi, even though he is in prison and facing possible execution. "I want you to know, brethren, that what has happened to me has really served to advance the gospel" (1:12). "Rejoice in the Lord always; again I will say, Rejoice" (4:4).

3) He wants to reassure them about their friend Epaphroditus, "that you may rejoice at seeing him again" (2:28).

4) He writes to plead with the church for Christ-like humility and love in the quarrel which threatens the congregation. "Complete my joy by being of the same mind, having the same love, being in full accord and of one mind" (2:2).

5) He writes to warn against some kind of false teaching which has reached, or he fears may soon reach, Philippi. "Look out for the dogs, look out for the evil-workers, look out for those who mutilate the flesh" (3:2).

Some Comments on Philippians

"Rejoice . . . again I will say rejoice" (4:4). Written though it is by a man facing death, Philippians is perhaps the most joyful letter in the New Testament. If he or she looks for the words "joy" and "rejoice," the reader will find them in almost every paragraph. In jail Paul is praying, but he is "making my prayer with joy" (1:4). Even when Christ is preached out of partisanship, Paul can still exult that "Christ is proclaimed; and in that I rejoice. Yes, and I shall rejoice" (1:18–19). Paul expects to visit Philippi if and when he is released, "for your progress and joy" (1:25). "Complete my joy," he pleads with those who are disputing, "by being of the same mind" (2:2). (Let the reader trace the theme on through 2:28–29; 3:1; 4:1, 4, 10.)

Paul's is joy in the face of difficulties. Some, Paul feels, are preaching Christ in the wrong way and from the wrong motives (1:15–18). Too little is said in chapter 1 about these preachers for us to know who they were or even if they were the same people whom he denounces as "dogs" in Philippians 3:2. It is clear that their false preaching disturbs Paul almost as much as his own imprisonment!

He is in prison—probably has been for some while—and is facing possible death. This seems to fit Paul's experience in Rome better than any imprisonment we know of earlier in his life. He has reached the point in life in which he would really welcome death, again a hint that this letter is written toward the end. He is confident that he will "be with the Lord" if he does die. Yet he cheerfully reassures the Philippians that he probably will be released and visit them again soon (1:19–26).

Paul is courageously sacrificing himself in Christ's service. He uses his report on his own situation and attitude to launch his plea for the Philippians to forget their personal differences and, surrendering their own pride, join in "striving side by side for the faith" (1:27–30). Paul's real example of self-sacrifice, however, is not himself, but his Lord.

Many scholars have recognized that Philippians 2:6–11 is an early Christian hymn. In this best-loved passage in Philippians, Paul is quoting a song probably familiar to those on both sides of the Philippian discord. The song voices a plea for harmony based on Christ,

> Who, though he was in the form of God,
> Did not count equality with God a thing to be grasped,
> But emptied himself,
> Taking the form of a servant,
> Being born in the likeness of men.
>
> And being found in human form
> He humbled himself
> And became obedient unto death,
> Even death on a cross.
>
> Therefore God has highly exalted him
> And bestowed on him the name which is above every name,

Philippians
Joy and Love in a Jail

"I rejoice ... greatly that ... you have ... concern for me" (4:10).

1:1	1:27	2:19	3:1	4:1 4:23
Paul's Own Situation: Joy in Spite of Prison and Dissension	**A Plea: Increase My Joy by Christ-like Humility and Cooperation**	**Good News About Two Friends**	**A Warning Against Certain False Teachers**	**Miscellaneous Concluding Notes**
A prayer rejoicing in their partnership 1:1–11	The plea for unity 1:27–2:4	Timothy will visit them. 2:19–24	Paul's own authority and example 3:1–16	A plea to two women leaders to end their quarrel 4:1–3
Joy at the spread of the gospel, in spite of prison and partisanship 1:12–18	The example: Christ's sacrifice 2:5–11	Epaphroditus has recovered and is returning to them. 2:25–30	Follow Paul, not false teachers. 3:17–21	A concluding benediction 4:4–7
Joy in Paul's hope for the future 1:19–26	Now they must be humble and sacrificial, too. 2:12–18			A thank-you note and some personal greetings 4:8–23

Author: Paul
Recipients: The church which Paul had founded at Philippi
Date: A.D. 64 (A.D. 57?)
Occasion: Paul, in prison, has received a gift and news from the church at Philippi.
Purpose: To thank them, and to encourage them to mutual cooperation and self-sacrifice

That at the name of Jesus every knee should bow,
In heaven and on earth and under the earth,
And every tongue confess
That Jesus Christ is Lord,
To the glory of God the Father.

Printing it thus, as three stanzas, emphasizes the three stages of the drama of salvation the hymn celebrated: Christ's preincarnate life in heaven, his servanthood and death on earth, and his exaltation now in heaven. Theologians have found profound meaning in the concept of Christ's "emptying" himself (*kenosis*) of his divine prerogatives of omniscience and omnipotence for his human, earthly service. The pattern of the "servant" is clearly that of Isaiah 53. (Let the reader compare Phil. 2:7 with Isa. 53:12; Phil. 2:8 with Isa. 53:7, 12, and Phil. 2:9 with Isa. 53:12a.) You disputing Philippians, Paul is pleading, follow Christ by laying aside the rights each side claims, as Christ laid aside his rights in order to serve us. The song ends with all creation uniting in that oldest of Christian creeds, "Jesus Christ is Lord."

"Look out for the dogs" (3:2)! Paul's abrupt calling of these heretics by such an ugly name has so startled many scholars that they have suggested that the passage it introduces cannot originally have been part of this lovely letter. Perhaps Philippians 3—4 was once not the second half of this epistle, but a separate note, or perhaps Philippians 3:2–20 is a fragment of another letter inserted here by mistake. Some scholars profess to find parts of three different letters in Philippians.[6] In support of this position, it is noted that Polycarp, in his own epistle to the Philippians a century later, reminded them that Paul had written them *letters*, implying that he knew of more than one. Yet themes from the first half of the letter recur in the second. Those who divide Philippians do not agree on precisely where the different parts end. We know that within one letter Paul could move from one kind of emotion to another. While the possibility of Philippians' being composed of parts of more than one epistle is widely recognized, it is probably true that most scholars still treat it as a unity.[7]

Who are these "dogs" who arouse such shocking wrath? The particular ways in which Paul defends his gospel and attacks theirs give us some clues. Apparently they advocated circumcision (3:2–3). They boasted of their credentials as model keepers of the Jewish Law (3:4–6). They claimed a special maturity, quite possibly that they had achieved perfection (3:12–16). And yet they tolerated such sensuous living that Paul could laugh at them, deriding them that "their god is the belly" (3:19)! Walter Schmithals has argued that these heretics must have championed an early form of what was later called "Gnosticism."[8] Of this odd blend of Judaism, Christianity, and Greek paganism, more will be said in relation to Colossians (see pages 162–168).

Paul's reply is to stress that true circumcision is spiritual, not physical (3:3).

His own credentials as a Jew are as good as anyone's (3:4–6). But, in language echoing that of Galatians and Romans, Paul rejoices now as a Christian in a "righteousness" given from God through faith, not the Old Testament Law (3:7–11). Humbly, Paul makes no claim to the perfection of which the Gnostics boasted. Using a figure from a track meet, Paul writes modestly and simply, "I press on toward the goal" (4:14). His salvation will come not from his own achievements, but from Christ (3:20–21).

Tactfully Paul praises the women who are quarreling at Philippi. Here there is no hint of commanding these women to "keep silence in the churches" (contrast 1 Cor. 14:34). Rather, these two are his equal partners with whom he once labored "side by side" (4:3).

Tactfully, too, Paul accepts the Philippians' gift with thanks, at the same time carefully asserting his independence. Paul wants to take no chances of being accused of being in the ministry simply for the money (4:10–20)!

With personal greetings, he ends this quite personal letter.

Philemon

Reading between the lines, one finds the little letter to Philemon suggesting one of the most appealing stories in the New Testament.

Onesimus the slave, having stolen from his master Philemon, had escaped to the city. (Whether it was in Rome or in Ephesus that he was hiding does not change the story.) Somehow he had come in contact with the Apostle Paul. Perhaps he had heard Philemon speak of the preacher who had won him to Christ. Where Paul, who had never been to Philemon's home in Colossae (Col. 2:1), had come to know Onesimus' master is never said. Paul could remind Philemon, the master, however, of "your owing me even your own self" (v. 19). Surely this must mean that it was through Paul that Philemon had become a Christian.

Now, through Paul, Onesimus had been converted too. He is "my child," Paul writes, "whose father I have become in my imprisonment" (v. 10). Paul has resolved to send the runaway thief back to his master.

The best Onesimus could hope for would seem to be a return to slavery. The law would fully support Philemon's punishing this fugitive by beating him and branding an "F" on his forehead; and it was within Philemon's rights under Roman law to crucify this thief and runaway!

Cautiously, tactfully, Paul pleads for his "child." Paul speaks of his own imprisonment. To that touch of pathos he adds the light touch of a pun. The name Onesimus means "useful." "Formerly he was useless to you, but now he is indeed useful to you and to me" (v. 11). But the basic appeal is to love. In sending Onesimus, " I am . . . sending my very heart" (v. 12).

It need not seem strange that Paul does not denounce the institution of slavery. Sixty million slaves were such an accepted part of the social system of the Roman Empire that it does not seem to have occurred to the tiny infant church to attempt to overthrow the whole institution. But Paul could lay down the principles which would some day bring about slavery's end (Gal. 3:28; Col. 3:11). He pleads with Philemon to take back Onesimus, "no longer as a slave but more than a slave, as a beloved brother" (v. 16). Both are now men "in Christ."

He pleads also on the basis of personal affection. Paul even offers his own "I.O.U." for anything Onesimus may have stolen (v. 18–19). "Refresh my heart in Christ," he ends his appeal (v. 20).

Competent scholars have proposed that Philemon and Onesimus may have lived not in Colossae, but in nearby Laodicea, and that Philemon may be the letter to the Laodiceans mentioned in Colossians 4:16. In view of the mention of Onesimus in Colossians 4:9 as "one of yourselves," most have rejected this idea.

Of much more interest is the question "How did the story end?" The answer is that nobody knows.

If, however, one looks for a hint of a happy ending beyond the letter itself, there is at least one possibility. Some fifty years later Ignatius wrote a letter to the church at Ephesus. Early in the letter he wrote praise of their great bishop. He even made exactly the same pun as had Paul, for that bishop's name was Onesimus.

And if one wants to carry even further such romantic speculation, this may be added. Some time, perhaps in the nineties, a disciple of Paul collected Paul's letters, beginning to gather those we have now. All the letters he collected were epistles dealing with great theological and ethical issues and addressed to whole churches—except for one single, private letter, the little epistle to Philemon. Is Goodspeed's conjecture purely wishful thinking that that one private letter was included because the collector was the former slave Onesimus, now bishop of Ephesus?[9] But perhaps such speculation goes beyond the proper scope of this New Testament GUIDE.

Colossians

Most people have understood Genesis 3 to be saying that it was Satan in the form of a snake who tempted Adam and Eve to eat the fruit of the tree of knowledge. Eating that fruit is regarded as the original sin. Some of the "Gnostics," however, said that the one who persuaded Adam was not Satan; it was Christ! The evil Creator-God of Judaism, they said, gave Adam a material body to hold him down to Eve. But Christ sought, by the tree of "knowledge" (*gnosis* in Greek), to lift Adam's soul up through the heavens toward the true, spiritual God.

Most scholars believe that the Epistle to the Colossians was written to attack a "philosophy" (2:8) which was a kind of early form of such "Gnosticism." That attack included what is widely considered to be the highest statement of the nature of Christ which Paul ever wrote—if, indeed, Paul wrote it.

The scholars are not nearly so well agreed, however, that Paul really was the author of Colossians.[10] At least four arguments are used by those who believe the letter is from a later hand:

1) Through brief, Colossians contains many words and phrases found rarely or never in the other letters of Paul. Several are found nowhere else in the New Testament

2) We know from attacks written against it that Gnosticism existed in the second century. It is argued that it is by no means certain, however, that the odd mixture of Greek, Hebrew, Christian, and Eastern thought attacked in Colossians existed as early as Paul's day.

3) Colossians contains ideas, especially ideas concerning Christology (the doctrine of the nature of Christ), which are quite different from any found in the known letters of Paul.

4) There are telltale hints of copying from earlier letters of Paul, it is alleged. For example, the list of names in Colossians 4 is suspiciously like that in Philemon.

Those who believe that Paul wrote Colossians reply as follows:[11]

1) There are many unusual words and phrases in Colossians, but these may be explained in part, at least, by the fact that Paul uses the vocabulary of the Gnostics as he seeks to show how Christ is superior to what Gnosticism offers.

2) Similarly, Paul is stimulated to use new ideas, ideas directly related to Gnosticism, in dealing with the heresy at Colossae. It would be foolish to suppose that Paul never had a new idea after he wrote Romans.

3) The similarities to Paul's other letters need not imply copying. They may instead suggest that Colossians is by the same author. Especially, it is argued, Colossians is so similar to and fits so well with Philemon, that it is surely by the same author, generally admitted to be Paul. It must even have been written at the same time.

4) Gnosticism, or something very similar to it, may well have existed in the first century. It is true that our copies of Gnostic writings come largely from the third century or even later. But there are hints of Gnostic-like ideas in what is attacked in such certainly Pauline books as First Corinthians and Galatians. The Dead Sea Scrolls include ideas which, though not a part of Gnosticism, are not unlike some of the ideas the Gnostics later developed. And writings by or about the Gnostics claim first-century roots for their doctrines.

5) Ancient and consistent tradition ascribes the letter to Paul, as, of course, does the epistle itself.

Two things are probably true: (1) Most commentaries and introductions still ascribe the book to the Apostle, but (2) but the number of those who believe that it is the work of a later disciple of Paul is growing.

For the reasons listed above, this GUIDE will go cautiously with the tradition of Pauline authorship.

The Occasion of Colossians

"I am in prison," Paul writes, presumably in Rome (see pages 155–156).

"We have heard of your faith," he begins in Colossians 1:4, though the Colossians "have not seen my face" (2:1). Apparently Paul has received a report brought by the founder of the congregation, Epaphras (1:7; 4:12).

The report has contained good news and bad news. Paul has been told of the Colossians' faith and love. But he also has been warned that there is spreading among them something which he calls "philosophy and empty deceit" (2:8). Knowing about this heresy helps us understand the letter.

According to the second-century theologian Irenaeus, there were many types of heresies with somewhat similar views. ("Gnosticism" is a name later given to several of them.) The oldest, however, he traces to Simon the Magician, who, according to Acts 8:9–24, tried to buy the gift of the spirit from Peter. Irenaeus reports several legends about Simon.

His traveling companion was a former prostitute named Helen, who was said to be a reincarnation of Helen of Troy! Simon, however,"said she was the first conception of his mind, the Mother of all, through whom in the beginning he had the idea of making angels and archangels. This Thought, leaping fourth from him . . . descended to the lower regions and generated angels and powers, by whom the world was made." When Helen was ensnared in a material body, Simon the savior came to earth to rescue her and "to offer man salvation through his 'knowledge.' "[12] Since we are saved by grace, not works, Simon taught, it does not matter how we live! Knowledge of heavenly matters is the only thing that counts.

For reasons which will be suggested in the comments on Colossians, most scholars believe that it was some similar heresy which threatened the church at Colossae. Warned about its spread, Paul wrote this letter.

The epistle is sent by Tychicus and Onesimus, the runaway slave (4:7–9; cf. Philemon).

The Purpose of Colossians

Paul writes, he says, so "that no one may delude you with beguiling speech" (2:4). He wants his readers instead to "be filled with the knowledge of his will in all spiritual wisdom and understanding" (1:9). The words sound like the claims of the Gnostics.

The knowledge Paul offers, however, will not be based on Gnostic speculations about angels and "elemental spirits of the universe" (2:20). It will be based on Christ, the image of God himself.

And it will have very practical ethical results. Each Colossian is to be guided to "lead a life worthy of the Lord" (1:10). This life, Paul insists, must be demonstrated in down-to-earth human relationships.

In summary, Paul is writing to set the cosmic Christ over against the cosmic speculations of the Gnostics, and to set loving duties toward other people over against Gnostic taboos, rituals, or license.

Some Comments on Colossians

Paul and the Intellectuals—so the late A. T. Robertson entitled a commentary on Colossians.[13] Clearly the great theme of the book is the relationship of Christ to certain intellectual and religious speculations about the cosmos.

Paul is not, of course, opposed to knowledge. Rather, Paul feels that Christ is the key which opens the door to the real knowledge of the highest kind. "Be filled with the knowledge . . . wisdom and understanding," Paul prays, "increasing in knowledge" (1:9–10). Christ, he says, has revealed "the mystery hidden for ages . . . but now manifest to his saints" (1:26). We are, he says, "teaching every man in all wisdom" (1:28). He "strives" that they may "have all the riches of assured understanding and the knowledge of God's mystery, of Christ, in whom are hid all the treasures of wisdom and knowledge" (2:2–3).

Christian wisdom, however, is set in contrast to false "philosophy and empty deceit" (2:8), and "human precepts and doctrines" (2:22). Rather, those who are in Christ are "renewed in knowledge." Movingly Paul asks the Colossians to pray that in spite of his being in chains, he may still make clear "the mystery" revealed in Christ (4:2–4; cf. 4:18).

When Paul describes this mystery which is revealed in Christ, he does so in such lofty terms that some scholars have doubted that it could be Paul using this kind of language within only thirty-five years of Jesus' death. The writer takes the highest terms of Gnostic speculation and sets Christ above them all.

For example, the Gnostics developed elaborate theories concerning angels and cosmic realms separating God from the earth. Early speculation imagined seven such gradations, one for each day of the week; later, thirty were described, one for each day of the month, with one female for the extra half-day! And finally, the followers of Basilides spoke of the "principalities, angels and powers of the three-hundred-sixty-five . . . heavens," one for every day of the year!

Colossians, however, pictures Christ as involved in the very creation of all "thrones or dominions or principalities or authorities" (1:16). If any of these are opposed to Christ, he has "disarmed the principalities and powers" by his death and resurrection (2:15).

The Gnostics spoke of the divine "fullness" *(pleroma)*. Having been used in various ways of the highest powers about which the Gnostics speculated, the word is now applied by Paul to Christ himself. "For in him all the fulness of God was pleased to dwell" (1:19; cf. 2:9). What fills God also fills Christ.

Colossians, however, pictures Christ not simply as the fulfillment of the Gnostics' speculations, but as in certain very significant ways their contradiction and reversal. On one point the varieties of Gnosticism agreed: God is spirit or mind; matter, this material world, eons away from God, is evil. The true God was

Colossians

The Genuine Wisdom Incarnate in Christ vs. "Gnostic" Speculation

"See to it that no one makes a prey of you by philosophy ... not according to Christ. For in him the whole fulness of deity dwells bodily" (2:8–9).

1:1	1:15	2:16	3:12	4:7	4:18
Paul's Prayers	**The Superiority of Christ and His Salvation to the "Knowledge" False Speculation Offers**	**A Practical Consequence: Rejection of the Ethics of the False Teachers**	**Instead, a Plea for the Morality of the Truly "Wise"**	**Concluding Personal Notes and Greetings**	
A prayer of thanksgiving for their church 1:1–8	The superiority of Christ 1:15–20	Legalistic rules, rituals, and ascetic practices are useless. 2:16–23	Its spirit, especially love 3:12–17		
He is praying that they may have the true, saving kind of knowledge which is in the gospel of Christ. 1:9–14	What Christ has done for them 1:21–23	The opposite, giving in to lust, anger, etc., must also be avoided. 3:1–11	Its concrete applications in human relationships in this world, to: wives—3:18 husbands—3:19 children—3:20 slaves—3:22–25 masters—4:1 all—4:2–6		
	Paul's concern to spread true knowledge 1:24—2:7				
	The true spiritual power that is in Christ 2:8–15				

Author: Paul (Some scholars believe it is by a later disciple of Paul.)
Recipients: The church at Colossae, which Paul has never visited
Date: A.D. 64 (Some put it about A.D. 57; others as late as the nineties.)
Occasion: In prison, Paul has received news of the spread of false, Gnostic-like, speculative preaching.
Purpose: To present the superiority of Christ and of the Christian life to such teaching

so far removed from the material earth as to be unknowable, and the creator of this world was by no means the highest god. Therefore, they believed that salvation could be attained by rising above this material world through spiritual knowledge of heavenly mysteries. (See page 164 for a brief account of how Simon the Magician is said to have presented these ideas.)

In language which must have shocked the Gnostics, Paul says that in Christ the whole *pleroma* dwelt "bodily" (2:9). He is the head of the *body* (the church) (1:8). In him all things are held together not simply by his "Thought" (as in the case of Simon the Magician) but by his "blood" (1:20) and "his body of flesh," an odd phrase designed to emphasize the flatly material nature of the incarnate Christ. This material world was created "in him" (1:16).

Salvation, the letter announces, comes not through "philosophy," but through the actual death and resurrection of Christ here on earth (2:11–15). The early Gnostic Basilides proposed that Jesus, as pure mind, could not have been crucified. Instead, he magically took the form of Simon of Cyrene, who had helped Jesus bear the cross. Jesus stood by and laughed while Simon was crucified! After all, you can't nail pure mind to a cross. Paul affirms the literal, physical death and resurrection of Jesus, to which the believer is united by baptism.

The second half of the letter relates this down-to-earth theology to a practical, down-to-earth ethic.

The Gnostics, believing God to be far removed from material things, divided in their ethics. Some became ascetics, abstaining as far as possible from material things. They developed regulations about "food and drink" (2:16). With regard to material things, the best rules seemed to them to be "Do not handle, Do not taste, Do not touch" (2:21). Or, by contrast, like Simon the Magician with his Helen, they announced that moral rules were only conventions. It did not matter to the spiritual god what you did with your body. "Worship of angels" (2:18) might be more important than whether or not one was sexually chaste.

Paul pleads for a different kind of spirituality. Those who truly set their "minds on things that are above" (3:2) have "died" to "anger, wrath, malice, slander, and foul talk" (3:5–8). They have put on love (3:12–17).

That love will manifest itself not in speculation, nor in taboos about food, but in the day-to-day relationships between people. The traditional barriers have all been transcended. "Here there cannot be Greek and Jew, circumcised and uncircumcised, barbarian, Scythian, slave, free man, but Christ is all, and in all" (3:11).

The writer goes through specific applications of this principle in the mundane areas of family life: to wives, husbands, children, fathers, slaves, and masters (3:18–4:1). Even conduct toward outsiders and such trivial, earthy matters as daily speech must reflect Christian love (4:5–6). A modern Christian saying is "Bread for myself is a material matter. Bread for my brother is a spiritual matter." Paul would have approved of that kind of spirituality.

A long list of personal greetings ending the letter reflects the warmth of Paul's own love for people.

Ephesians

"Paul, an apostle of Christ Jesus by the will of God, to the saints who are _____ . . . faithful in Christ Jesus" (Eph. 1:1).

Many regard Ephesians as one of the high points of the New Testament. But the very first verse plunges the reader into two problems: (1) Was the letter really written by Paul? and (2) Was it really written to the Ephesians?

The oldest Greek manuscripts of Ephesians leave a blank in verse 1, as we have done above. Only later did scribes fill in the blank with the words "in Ephesus." In the second century, Marcion wrote of the letter as being to the Laodiceans. (We know from Colossians 4:16 that Paul did write an important letter to Laodicea; the letter is now lost unless "Ephesians" is it.)

To add to the mystery, the letter seems to assume that Paul and its readers are not personally acquainted. "I have heard of your faith," the author writes (1:15). He assumes that they "have heard" of his ideas (3:2; cf. 4:21). Yet Paul had spent more than two years as pastor of the church in Ephesus (Acts 19:10). The letter contains no references to individuals or to particular problems in the Ephesian church—or in any other congregation, for that matter. In most of his letters Paul is engaged in a struggle over some problem affecting people whom he knows and loves. This epistle, however, sounds more like a circular letter or a relatively impersonal essay designed to be read in many congregations. Perhaps, then, "Ephesians" was originally sent to many churchs and got its name because it was at Ephesus that some early collector of epistles first found a copy.

More controversial is the question of authorship. The letter contains the name of Paul as its author (1:1; cf. 4:1), and from early in the second century until the nineteenth it was regarded as Paul's work. It must be said, however, that today most—though by no means all—scholars believe it to be the work of a later disciple of the Apostle.[14] The following reasons are given:

1) The style and vocabulary are different from those of the letters which all scholars agree are by Paul. Indeed, one enterprising critic fed Ephesians into a computer and received a print-out to the effect that Paul would never have used those words and phrases! In fact, some eighty-two words found in Ephesians are not found elsewhere in Paul's letters, and thirty-eight are found nowhere else in the New Testament. The sentences are longer and more involved then are most of Paul's. Most of the first three chapters are filled with prayers or liturgies, perhaps largely poetry. One commentator writes of Ephesians as "Paul set to music."

2) Ideas in Ephesians sometimes seem to conflict with those Paul expresses elsewhere. For example, in 1 Corinthians 7 Paul grudgingly admits that "it is better to marry than to be aflame with passion" (7:9). But Ephesians 5:21–33 movingly praises marriage as the earthly relationship most comparable to that of

Christ and his church! Could Paul have changed that much? Or again, "You have been saved," the author writes in Ephesians 2:8; but Paul elsewhere speaks of salvation as a continuing process or a future hope. In other letters Paul speaks of Christ as the coming eschatological Messiah whose imminent advent is eagerly awaited (1 Cor. 7:26, 31; 1 Thess. 1:10; 4:16–17). But in Ephesians the apocalyptic revelation is the church, not some coming catastrophic judgment.

3) Ephesians seems to have an attitude both toward Paul and toward the other Apostles which suggests that they are venerated as figures from the past. The Apostles are themselves now called the "foundation" of the church (2:20). (For Paul in 1 Cor. 3:11, the only possible foundation is Christ himself.) Paul's own great insight into divine mysteries is praised in Ephesians 3:2–5. (Paul himself wrote of such boasting as "foolishness" in 2 Cor. 10—11.) Such attitudes seem more appropriate for a later generation looking admiringly back on Paul and the Apostles.

4) Much of Ephesians is so nearly word-for-word like Colossians that many suspect copying. (For example, compare Eph. 6:21–22 with Col. 4:7–8.)

5) Finally, Ephesians seems to presuppose the emergence of a largely Gentile church in which the conflicts of Paul's day concerning Jewish Law are forgotten (2:11–13; contrast Galatians and Romans).

Nevertheless, at least one major recent comentary, the "Anchor Bible" volume on Ephesians, by Markus Barth, has argued strongly that Paul may be the author.[15] Differences in style and in thought may simply reflect the fact that Paul, when he wrote Ephesians, was fourteen years older and was writing for a different purpose than was the case when he wrote First Thessalonians. The similarities to Colossians are explained by asuming that both letters were writen at the same time, to be carried to different churches by Tychicus. Many ideas of Ephesians are so typical of Paul that it is difficult to believe that one who was only an imitator could have written the letter. Finally, it is universally agreed that Ephesians is a profound statement of the faith. If not Paul, conservative critics ask, then who could have produced this original masterpiece?

The present writer finds the case against Paul as the author so strong that he cannot with assurance interpret the letter as by the Apostle. At the same time, it is not quite strong enough to compel his assent.

Fortunately, there is the possibility of a kind of escape from the dilemma posed by the uncertainty of authorship. Perhaps in the case of Ephesians, the author, even if he is later then Paul, is so close in thought to the Apostle that no great difference in interpretation is required, whichever way one decides.

Francis W. Beare, in his commentary in "The Interpreters Bible," denies that Ephesians is by Paul. Nevertheless, Beare writes:

> Certainly no other writer of the early centuries shows anything remotely comparable to this man's grasp of the fundamental Pauline ideas, or a like

ability to bring out their universal implications. There is a kinship of thought here that is not to be explained on less intimate grounds then those of close personal discipleship. . . . Ephesians stands in extraordinarily close relationship to the Pauline epistles.[16]

Perhaps, then, we may think of the letter as a genuine reflection of the mind of Paul, even if doubts remain that all its words actually came from his pen. With this understanding,we will refer to the author as Paul.

The Occasion of Ephesians

"Paul, a prisoner for Jesus Christ," is pictured as writing as "an ambassador in chains" (3:1; 6:20; cf. 4:1). The letter is apparently sent by Tychicus, as was Colossians. The setting of the letter, therefore, as traditionally understood, is Paul's imprisonment in Rome—the same time as the writing of Colossians and Philemon, about A.D. 63–64 (cf. Col. 4:7–8). The Christians addressed are evidently Gentiles (2:11; 3:1). If the letter was written to the church at Ephesus, it must have been for the newer, Gentile members who had not known Paul when he was pastor in that city.

While the use of such words as "fulness" (1:23) and "mystery" (3:3) hint at some form of Gnostic heresy, there is not enough evidence of this kind to indicate that the letter is really the result of any particular conflict in any particular congregation.

E. J. Goodspeed proposed that an early publisher of Paul's letters composed Ephesians as an introduction to his collection around A.D. 90.

What appear to be quotations from Ephesians occur in other works as early as A.D. 115.

No commentator has successfully related the letter to a particular conflict or situation. There is a kind of timeless quality about Ephesians which perhaps is responsible in part for its popularity in many different eras, including our own. The proposal that it was originally a circular letter sent to several churches seems reasonable.

The Purpose of Ephesians

Ephesians is a celebration! It is written to express the author's joyful, prayerful realization that in Christ, God is achieving the climax of his purpose in history, the uniting of all peoples in Christ's church. The letter itself is written to promote that unity. And it is written to encourage Gentile converts to live as loving members of that church in a pagan world.

This purpose is clear, no matter who the author is or when the letter was written. If the letter is the work of a later hand, it may have had the additional purpose of reaffirming the authority of Paul and his gospel against the spread of early Gnostic heresies discrediting his memory.

Ephesians

God's Plan to Unite All in Christ's Church

"He has made known to us ... the mystery of his will ... in Christ ... to unite all things in him" (1:9—10).

1:1	2:1	3:1	4:1 ... 6:24
A Lyrical Celebration of God's Plan to Unite All Peoples in Christ's Church	**The Working Out of God's Plan in the Actual Experience of the Gentile Readers, Now Equally Included in the Church**	**Paul's Prayerful Concern That They Share His Vision of God's Plan and Be Strengthened by It**	**Four Resulting Charges to Gentile Converts**
Praise to God for choosing to include us in his plan 1:1-10	They have been saved by God's grace. 2:1-10	Paul's concern to share his insight into this plan of God 3:1-13	Promote the church's unity. 4:1-16
Early (Jewish) Christians and later (Gentile) converts share in the Spirit. 1:11-14	Now they are united with Jewish Christians in the church. 2:11-22	Paul's prayer for his readers: understanding and strength 3:14-21	Break with pagan ways 4:17—5:20
A prayer that they will understand this plan of God 1:15-23			Manifest Christian unity through Christian family life. 5:21—6:9
			Be good soldiers in God's army, the church. 6:10-20
			Concluding personal note and benediction 6:21-24

Author: Paul? (Most modern critical scholars believe it is by a later disciple of Paul.)
Recipients: Gentile converts (in Ephesus? Ephesus is not named in the earliest manuscripts.)
Date: A.D. 64? (Most put it a few years later, after Paul's death.)
Occasion: Paul is in prison (actually, or in the memory of a later writer).
Purpose: To celebrate the unity of the church, and to guide new converts in understanding that church and living as good church members

Some Comments on Ephesians

Calvin said that Ephesians was his favorite epistle. "It is the crown of St. Paul's writings," Markus Barth quotes Robinson as writing. And Barth himself adds that in Ephesians "Paul writes more openly and sublimely than in any one of his previous letters."[17]

The understanding of the plan of history which Paul had begun to work out in Romans 9—11 is now developed fully. Instead of the early church's expectation of the immediate end of history with the coming of Christ, Ephesians presents the uniting of all things in Christ as the now-manifest plan God has been working out all along.

Surely this theme of God's plan and purpose—the King James translation called it "predestination"—is a repeated one, especially in the first chapter. God "chose us in him before the foundation of the world" (1:4), and (pre) "destined" us (1:5, 12) simply according to the "purpose of his will" (1:5, 9, 11). All is part of God's "plan" (1:10).

For those disturbed by the logical problem involved in reconciling Paul's doctrine of "predestination" or "election" with the equally emphasized fact of individual responsibility, there may be some comfort in noting two things. (1) Much of chapter 1 seems to be poetry, or almost poetry. Poets often can express paradoxical truths that defy the logic of prose. And (2) the author readily admits that he is describing a "mystery," something that theological reasoning cannot explain (1:9; 3:1–4, 9).

That mystery involves the emerging unity of all peoples in the church. Christ "has broken down the dividing wall of hostility" separating Jews and Gentiles (2:14). Perhaps the only inscription still in existence which Jesus of Nazareth actually read is one that archaeologists have found which marked the limits in the Temple at Jerusalem beyond which no Gentile might pass: "No foreigner may enter within the balustrade and enclosure around the Sanctuary. Whoever is caught will render himself liable to the death penalty which wll inevitably follow."[18] There were barriers not simply of stone, but of hostility. The Roman historian Tacitus, typical of the anti-Semitic prejudice of his time, wrote: "The Jews regard as profane all that we hold sacred; on the other hand, they permit all that we abhor . . . The ways of the Jews are preposterous and mean."[19] In reaction, Jewish rabbis sometimes hated back. At least one is quoted as saying: "To the best of the Gentiles, death; to the best of snakes, a broken back."[20]

But now, Paul says, in Christ, Jew and Gentile are united! "All things" (1:10, 22), including all races, Jews and Greeks, have become "one new man" (2:15) in one "body" (1:23; 2:16), sharing one "access in one Spirit" to one "Father" (2:18; 3:14) as "fellow citizens" and "members of the household of God" (2:19), and are now built together as one structure, God's new "temple" (2:20–22). Gentiles and Jews are now "fellow heirs," "members of the same body'' (3:6), maintaining "the unity of the Spirit in the bond of peace," around "one hope . . . one Lord, one faith, one baptism" (4:3–5), under "one God" (4:6). Through the unity of the faith all church members form one "body" (2:16), in which, under Christ as the head, they are "members one of another" (4:25). The best earthly figure for such union is that of the perfect family, beautifully described in Ephesians 5:21—6:9.

Ephesians abounds in poetic metaphors for the church. When Ephesians 2:10 says that "we are his workmanship," the word in Greek is *poema*. The Jerusalem Bible translates that verse, "We are God's work of art." The writer's own artistic figures for the church include the following: "The body of Christ" (1:23; 1:22–23; 4:12; 5:23) "the bride of Christ" (5:21–23), "the commonwealth of Israel" (2:12–19), and "a holy temple" (2:11–22). Each figure expresses a different facet of the meaning the writer sees in the emerging church. He glories in this new manifestation of God's ancient plan.

Typical of letters of Paul, Ephesians falls into two halves. The first half glories in the good news of reconciliation. The second half urges the readers to live out this new unity in their relationships with others. "I therefore . . . beg you to lead a life worthy of the calling to which you have been called" (4:1), this second half begins.

All church members are to use their gifts in service to each other. All are to do the work of "ministry" (4:1–16). These Gentile converts are to renounce their old pagan ways (4:17—5:20). They are to live out in their families the kind of love Christ showers on his "bride" the church (5:21—6:9).

Finally, the letter closes with an elaborate metaphor in which Christians are urged to "put on the whole armor of God" to fight against the forces of evil about them. And as part of that fight, they are to pray, including prayer for Paul, "an ambassador in chains" (6:18–20).

These may have been the last words Paul ever wrote.

XI   *The Pastoral Epistles*

Ephesians celebrates joyfully, sometimes lyrically, the emergence of a great new apocalyptic fact, the church. The pastoral epistles lay down day-to-day guidelines for the faith and order of that developing organization.

Rules are not as exciting as celebrations. Often regarded as late (perhaps early second-century), not really by Paul, and moralistic, the pastorals (First and Second Timothy and Titus) are far from the best-loved books of the New Testament. Yet at least three things make them a valuable, if sometimes neglected, part of the canon.

1) They give us insight into the life of the church in a period later than most New Testament books and let us know what it was like to be a church member or leader in the days between the sudden bursting of the gospel upon the world at the time of the Apostles and the establishment of the formal pattern of church organization which soon developed.

A little past the middle of the the second century, Justin Martyr described a typical Sunday worship service:

> And on the day called Sunday there is a meeting in one place of those who live in cities or the country, and the memoirs of the apostles or the writings of the prophets are read as long as time permits. When the reader has finished, the president in a discourse urges and invites [us] to the imitation of these noble things. Then we all stand up together and offer prayers.[1]

For anyone who would like in imagination to worship with such a congregation and to see with them their leader and to hear both his words and those of the prayers and songs of the congregation, these letters, though written before the time of Justin, give a helpful picture. In them we hear echoes of the liturgy, hymns, creeds, and discipline of the post-apostolic congregations.

2) Many of the guidelines laid down in these letters are still regarded as applying to the church today. Scarcely a minister, elder, deacon, vestryman, or steward is installed in a modern congregation without the reading of a passage such as 1 Timothy 3 or Titus 1.

3) The pastorals represent one of the earliest efforts to do what Christian thinkers have sought to do in every age: to apply to new situations the teachings of the Apostles.

These proposals, however, presuppose a highly debatable view of the authorship and date of these little books. These problems must now be examined in detail.

The Problem of the Pastorals

Authorship and Date

First and Second Timothy and Titus have been grouped together at least since the Muratorian Canon in the latter part of the second century. That document spoke of them as revered for their help "in the arrangement of ecclesiastical discipline." In 1726 Paul Anton used of them the name "The Pastoral Epistles," recognizing that each is in the form of a letter of guidance from an older pastor, Paul, to a younger pastor. These three booklets are generally agreed to be on the same subjects and by the same author.

But was the author Paul?

There are certainly scholars who do believe that they are the work of that Apostle.[2] Arguments for this view include the following:

1) The letters themselves say clearly that they are by Paul (see the first word in each).

2) The Muratorian Canon attributes them to Paul, and other early documents quote from them as Paul's.

3) They are filled with personal references for which it is hard to imagine any purpose if they were created at a later date. For example, Paul requests that the cloak he had left at Troas be brought to him, and he warns against one "Alexander the coppersmith," unknown to us from any second-century literature (2 Tim. 4:12–15). Why would anyone in the second century invent these details?

4) Certain ideas seem typical of Paul. For example, in 2 Timothy 1:9 we read that God "saved us . . . not in virtue of our works but . . . the grace which he gave us in Christ Jesus." These words could come right out of Romans.

Some Christians, of course, feel required by their theology to hold that these letters are by Paul simply because they say they are. The majority who decide such matters on purely historical grounds, however, do not believe that these three letters, at least as we have them now, are by the Apostle.[3] They give the following reasons:

1) The style and vocabulary are quite different from those of other letters ascribed to the Apostle. Approximately one-third of the words in these books occur nowhere else in all of the other letters attributed to Paul, and some one hundred seventy words are found nowhere else in the New Testament.

2) They are not included among Paul's writings in such early lists as that of Marcion, nor are they in the Chester Beatty Papyri.

3) Certain ideas and the ways certain words are used in the pastorals seem to reflect a stage in the life of the church later than the life of Paul. For example,

"faith" to Paul means a dynamic, personal relationship, commitment, trust; and it is faith in a person, Jesus Christ. But in the Pastorals we read about *the* faith, referring rather to a set body of teachings, a creed, to be held against all false teachings. For example, 1 Timothy 4:1 warns "that in later times some will depart from *the* faith;" 1 Timothy 4:6 speaks of the "words of *the* faith and of . . good doctrine"; 2 Timothy 3:8 speaks of heretics as "worthless as regards to *tne* faith" (author's translation), and the first verse of Titus couples "*the* faith" with "knowledge of the truth" (italics added).

A new emphasis on creed is indicated by much more than the use of the article before "faith." The pastor writes of "sound teaching" or "sound doctrine" or "sound speech" (1 Tim. 1:10; 2 Tim. 4:3; Titus 1:9; 2:1,8), "sound words" (1 Tim. 6:3; 2 Tim. 4:3), and being "sound in the faith" (Titus 1:13; 2:2). "Sound" here seems to mean "correct" or "orthodox."

Moreover, the pastorals repeatedly give some "pattern of sound words" (creed) to be followed with care (2 Tim. 1:13). "The word stands firm" would be a valid translation of a phrase the pastor repeatedly uses in relation to some creedal formula (1 Tim. 1:15; 3:1; 4:9; 2 Tim. 2:11; Titus 3:8).

To most scholars this emphasis on formal creeds to be remembered and preserved seems to reflect a stage in the life of the church a generation removed from that of Paul.

4) The pastorals presuppose a church organization with a more elaborate, set structure than seems to have existed in Paul's day. There are bishops and/or elders (1 Tim. 3:1–7; 5:17–22; Titus 1:5–16), deacons (1 Tim. 3:8–13), and widows who are officially "enrolled" if they meet specified qualifications (1 Tim. 5:3–16). Neither the other letters of Paul nor Acts reflects such a well-defined structure.

5) While the differences should not be exaggerated, the ethical stance of the pastorals seems somewhat different from that previously found in Paul. The attitude toward the Law expressed in 1 Timothy 1:8 is rather different from that in Romans or Galatians. The ethic proposed is not one lived by the Spirit as one awaits the imminent end of the world. Instead, it is one quite similar to that of the best secular moralists of the time. "Prudent" or one of its cognates occurs nine times in the pastorals, only six times in all the rest of the New Testament.

6) The personal references cannot be fit into the life of Paul as we know it from Acts. In Titus, for example, Paul has spent some time in Crete, and he expects to spend the winter in Nicopolis (1:5; 3:12). Acts says nothing of either sojourn.

7) That the letters contain the name of Paul and personal references does not prove that he wrote them, it is alleged. We know that devout Christians in the early centuries did compose books not found in our New Testament and attributed them to Thomas, John, Paul, Peter, and other Apostles. To us this may seem dishonest; to them it obviously did not. Rather, it may have seemed a kind of mod-

esty to attribute ideas to one's teacher rather than proudly to claim them for oneself. Perhaps these letters should be thought of as dedicated to the memory of Paul rather than as actually from his pen.

Those who believe that Paul wrote these letters readily admit that they cannot be fit into Paul's life as we know it from Acts. They note hints in early tradition, however, that Paul was released after two years in prison in Rome (Acts 28:30–31). His trial, then, was his "first defense" mentioned in 2 Timothy 4:16. Paul then went to Spain (Rom. 15:24), they argue, and he also then did the traveling implied in the pastorals. The imprisonment mentioned in 2 Timothy 1:8, 16–17 and 2:9 followed a second and final arrest, according to this view. The differences in style, vocabulary, and thought are explained as reflecting the fact that Paul is now some ten years older than when he wrote Romans, that he is dealing with a different set of problems, and that he is making use of a different secretary.

Real as the differences are, there are certain areas of agreement. Those who believe that the letters were written during the lifetime of Paul still place them as late as possible within that limit, A.D. 67–68, and recognize that as an old man, Paul is dealing with situations from a time later than that of his other letters. On the other hand, many who believe that the letters come from a later time—around A.D. 110 is frequently suggested—admit that they may well contain valuable tradition from the thought and life of Paul. There is no need to deny the historical accuracy of the situation described in many of the personal references, and indeed a number of scholars suggest that they may be based on fragments of letters actually written by Paul or may even be later revisions of Pauline letters.

While the present writer believes the evidence against Pauline authorship must be accepted, he would recognize the truth in the comment of William Barclay:

> In the Pastoral Epistles we are still hearing the voice of Paul, and often hearing it speak with a unique personal intimacy; but we think that the form of the letters is due to a Christian teacher who summoned the help of Paul when the Church of the day needed the guidance which only he could give.[4]

The Purpose of the Pastorals

"O Timothy, guard what has been entrusted to you," the pastor writes, speaking of the orthodox faith expressed in the "sound" teaching or doctrine he is defending. "Avoid the godless chatter and contradictions of what is falsely called knowledge [*gnosis*]" (1 Tim. 6:20). It was to combat that *gnosis* by a disciplined church witnessing to a disciplined faith that the pastor wrote.

The heresy attacked seems to be very much like that early Jewish form of

Gnosticism we have already examined in relation to Colossians, and we will not repeat the description of it here (see pages 162–167). Those whom the pastorals attack seem to have taught a kind of asceticism with regard to food and drink (1 Tim. 5:23; Titus 1:15), and even discouraged marriage (1 Tim. 4:3)!

On the other hand, the pastor can accuse these heretics of gross immorality, perhaps because some of them regarded bodily matters such as adultery as of no importance once one had obtained truly spiritual knowledge (2 Tim. 3:6). The enigmatic reference to their denial of a future resurrection probably reflects their view that the body, being mere matter, is valueless (2 Tim. 2:18).

Their heresy involved elements of Judaism (Titus 1:10, 14).

They loved "endless genealogies" (1 Tim. 1:4) and "silly myths" (1 Tim. 4:7; cf. 2 Tim. 4:4).

Above all, they evidently loved to argue (1 Tim. 1:6; 6:4, 20; 2 Tim. 2:16, 23; Titus 3:9)!

In all this they sound like the Gnostics.

Against these heretics the pastor proposes a double weapon: (1) There is the church, which must be led by godly and heroic leaders. (2) There is the faith, which must be preserved with the help of formalized, traditional, heresy-free sayings.

His model for both sound doctrine and for heroic leadership is the Apostle Paul. In his name and in his tradition the pastor writes.

First Timothy

"I have no one like him." So Paul had written of Timothy, his young companion and assistant. "As a son with a father he has served with me in the gospel" (Phil. 2:20–22). Repeatedly Paul groups Timothy with himself as a "brother" and co-author of letters (2 Cor. 1:1; Phil. 1:1; Col. 1:1; 1 Thess. 1:1; 2 Thess. 1:1). Acts 16:1 pictures Timothy as joining Paul at Lystra early in Paul's second missionary journey, and he appears to have been closely associated with the Apostle from that time on. Whether in fact or in symbol, it is appropriate that Paul's message to the next generation should come in the form of a letter from the old Apostle to his younger "brother" and "son."

The Occasion of First Timothy

There are fewer references to Paul's situation in First Timothy than in the other pastorals. "As I urged you when I was going to Macedonia, remain at Ephesus," Paul begins (1:3). Paul hopes to rejoin Timothy soon, 3:14 and 4:13 imply. In the meantime, Timothy is pictured as a young pastor at work (4:12; cf. 5:1), to whom Paul gives fatherly advice (1:2).

"Certain persons . . . have wandered away into vain discussion, desiring to be teachers of the law." we are told (1:6). It is the need to respond to the spread of their heresy, "what is falsely called knowledge [*gnosis*]" (6:20), which, whether in Paul's day or a generation later, is the real occasion of the writing of this booklet.

The Purpose of First Timothy

"O Timothy, guard what has been entrusted to you," cries the writer at the conclusion of the epistle (6:20). The very reason the young pastor has been placed there is to "charge certain persons not to teach any different doctrine, nor to occupy themselves with myths and endless genealogies which promote speculations rather than the divine training that is in faith." (1:3–4). To this end the letter repeatedly reminds the reader of brief statements of sound doctrine, in the tradition handed down from Paul, which will stand firm against the false Gnostic teachings. Its purpose is to exhort the young pastor to teach the true faith.

It is known that certain Gnostic sects in the second and third centuries were fond of quoting Paul and claiming his authority for their ideas. It may be that the author of First Timothy chooses to write in the form of a letter by Paul in order to dramatize his certainty that Paul would have opposed all Gnostic fanaticism.

The letter is concerned, however, to guide not only the teaching, but also the practice of the church. "I am writing these instructions to you so that . . . you may know how one ought to behave in the household of God, which is the church" (3:14–15). The writer wants to make sure that only godly men guide the congregation, that worship is properly conducted, and that all members live exemplary lives. Indeed, though his words are ostensibly addressed only to one reader, the author really wants the whole church to hear his message. To this end, specific instructions are given concerning church officers, women, widows, and even slaves. A strict, but not ascetic, morality is commanded for all.

Some Comments on First Timothy

Those who hold that First Timothy is the work not of Paul, but of one of his admirers a generation later, believe they find signs of this in the first chapter. Paul would not need, they say, to remind Timothy that he is an Apostle (1:1), nor would he need to review for Timothy the story of his conversion (1:12–17). The chapter is appropriate, however, they say, for beginning a solemn warning against un-Pauline fanaticism to a later generation.

First Timothy 2—3 has been called the oldest extant guidebook on church order. The modern reader wishes that the pastor had described the duties of the bishop and the deacons. Apparently by the time this letter was written those duties were already well known. Here only the high moral requirements for these offices are listed. Though "bishop" is used in the singular, it is widely held that the word refers to the same office as does "elder," the two terms apparently being used synonymously in Titus 1:5–7. If so, there were apparently several bishops or

First Timothy
Instructions to a Young Pastor

"If you put these instructions before the brethren, you will be a good minister of Christ Jesus, nourished on the words of the faith and of ... good doctrine" (4:6).

1:1	2:1	3:1	3:14	5:1	6:2b 6:21
Opening Charge: Suppress Heresy, Teach Only What Is Proper	**Proper Worship**	**Proper Church Officers**	**Proper Doctrine**	**Proper Conduct Pertaining to Particular Groups**	**Proper Life vs. Worldly Life**
A warning against improper teaching 1:1-7	Prayer for and by all men 2:1-8	The bishop 3:1-7	A summary of proper doctrine 3:14-16	Older and younger church members 5:1-2	Heresy is accompanied by selfishness and greed. 6:2b-10
A warning against improper ethics 1:8-11	But with women kept subordinate 2:9-15	The deacons 3:8-13	A warning aginst heretics 4:1-5	Widows 5:3-16	By contrast, you must live righteously. 6:11-16
A reminder of Paul's own experience 1:12-17			The minister's duty to teach proper doctrine 4:6-16	Elders 5:17-22	Be rich, but in good deeds only. 6:17-19
The charge now delivered to the young pastor 1:18-20				(Miscellaneous instructions) 5:23-25	A closing charge 6:20-21
				Slaves 6:1-2a	

Author: Paul? (Most say a later disciple of Paul writing in his honor and memory.)
Recipient: "Timothy" (a young pastor)
Date: A.D. 68? (Most say early second century.)
Occasion: False teaching, accompanied by unrighteous living, threatens the church.
Purpose: To remind the young pastor of the tradition of sound doctrine and righteous living handed down from Paul

elders and several deacons in each congregation. The word for "bishop" could be translated "overseer" or "supervisor," and it soon came to be used of one church official who had oversight over several churches.

The description of the prayers (2:1–8) sheds light on early Christian worship. Even in times of persecution, Christians prayed for the emperor. There is relatively little evidence of persecution, however, in the pastoral epistles. The expected Christian life seems here to be one of respectable citizenship.

This letter's strict limits on women's participation in the life of the church (2:9–15) contrasts sharply with Paul's own more permissive attitude shown in other letters. Paul had hailed Priscilla (Rom. 16:1), Euodia, and Syntyche (Phil. 4:2) as fellow workers, and Phoebe he commended as a "deaconess" (Rom. 16:1). In spite of his restrictions on women at Corinth, he could write that in Christ all barriers enslaving women had been eliminated (Gal. 3:28). Perhaps the writer of First Timothy was driven to his extreme position in part as a reaction to practices of some Gnostics. (See page 164 for the place of Helen in the sect associated with Simon the Magician.)

Actually, the writer probably thought of himself as occupying a reasonable and moderate position in the matter of women, as in other ethical questions. He strongly resists sexual license—so strongly as to make all women keep quiet in church. But at the same time he rejects the fanaticism of those who would prohibit marriage (4:3; cf. 5:14). He recognizes the service of enrolled "widows" (5:10) and would have all women treated as "mothers" and "sisters" (5:2). Writings from the third century show us that the "widows" continued to be a kind of special order in the church in that era. Eventually, of course, various orders of enrolled "sisters" developed in the Catholic church.

The writer's moral ideal, as has been noted, is one of prudence, a balance between license and asceticism. The godly man must avoid intemperate use of wine (3:3), but Timothy should not be such as ascetic as not to use wine for medicine (5:23). Lustful desires are to be shunned (1:10), but marriage and having children are repeatedly encouraged (2:15; 3:2–3, 11–12; 4:2–3; 5:14). Food and clothes are good (6:8). But riches present too much temptation, and from the *love* of money may come all kinds of evils (6:9–10, 17–18).

Indeed, "everything created by God is good, and nothing is to be rejected if it is received with thanksgiving" (4:4). (Contrast the Gnostic view that all created things are evil!) The pastor's ideal is that of the chaste Christian family contentedly doing its duties in a respectable way within the Roman world. His is a practical Christianity.

Finally, brief note must also be taken of the "sound doctrine" he urges his reader to guard. The pastor reminds Timothy of the saying that "Christ Jesus came into the world to save sinners" (1:15). "There is one God, and there is one mediator between God and men, the man Christ Jesus," he affirms against the multitude of Gnostic divine mediators (2:5). First Timothy 3:16 is probably quoted from a hymn familiar at the time this letter was written. First Timothy 6:12–16 may be a fragment of the liturgy used when the young pastor was ordained or when he was baptized.

The young Christian's confession of faith is related to that of Christ before Pilate. And though the eschatological hope which was so central to Paul seems now to have become less prominent, Timothy is still to fight on "until the appearing of our Lord Jesus Christ" (6:14).

Second Timothy

From one generation to another—in the form of a letter from the aging church leader Paul to one who was to be a leader of the next generation—the letters to Timothy are written to urge the preservation of the true Christian tradition. Integrity of doctrine in a church led by men of integrity—this has been the theme of First Timothy.

These themes of First Timothy are repeated in Second Timothy, but a new emphasis is developed. The tradition being passed from Paul to the ongoing church is not simply one of sound doctrine or correct church order; it is the tradition of Paul's own self-sacrificial example of courage. In a time when many were deserting him and his gospel, Paul had also faced loneliness, persecution, and death. The reader must now carry on Paul's legacy of faithful witness.

"I have fought the good fight, I have finished the race, I have kept the faith," Paul the prisoner is presented as writing (2 Tim. 4:7). So you, in your generation, the letter pleads, must with the same courage "guard the truth that has been entrusted to you" (1:14).

The Occasion of Second Timothy

Whether still in actual fact or—more likely—in the memory of the later writer, Paul is writing from prison. "I am suffering and wearing fetters like a criminal," he writes (2:9), apparently in Rome (1:17). "I am already on the point of being sacrificed; the time of my departure has come" (4:6). In Philippians Paul expected to be released. In Second Timothy he knows he is about to die.

The imprisonment indicated in Second Timothy does not seem to fit well into the story in Acts. Paul had left a cloak and some books in Troas, though Acts implies that Paul had not been in Troas for years (4:13; contrast Acts 24:27). Similarly, Paul had left Trophimus ill at Miletus (4:19). The journey to a Roman prison described in Acts scarcely allows for visits at Troas and Miletus. If the letter was written by Paul, it was probably during a second Roman imprisonment.

Not only is Paul pictured as in chains, imprisoned in a shameful way, and facing death, but repeated references are made to the fact that he is lonely, with many forsaking him (1:15–17; 4:10–11, 16).

It is not clear where we are to think of Timothy as living. In 1 Timothy 1:3 he has been left to be pastor at Ephesus. In 2 Timothy 4:12 he is informed that Paul has now sent Tychicus to that city. But the situation Timothy faces is still much the same as that described in First Timothy. And that situation is one which contain parallels to the difficulties Paul is pictured as facing at the end of his life. Timothy is beginning in his generation to meet something of the loneliness and discouragement which Paul had endured. "Indeed all who desire to live a godly life in Christ Jesus will be persecuted" (3:12). "Times of stress" are at hand (3:1), "when people will not endure sound teaching" (4:3) "and will turn way" (4:4). In his own generation, the first reader of this letter is to face something of what Paul so courageously endured.

The Purpose of Second Timothy

"Do not be ashamed . . . of testifying to our Lord, nor of me his prisoner," the letter is written to urge the young pastor (1:8). He, too, faces the discouragement of seeing members of his flock fall away into a heresy proving more popular among some than does the orthodox faith. "But take your share of suffering for the gospel in the power of God" (1:8). You know the courageous example of Paul, the letter is written to say. Now follow it in your own ministry in your own situation.

To carry on that tradition, the young pastor is to "follow the pattern of . . . sound words" handed down from Paul (1:13). He is to "guard the truth that has been entrusted" to him (1:14). In the name of the Apostle, the writer summarizes his exhortation: "I charge you in the presence of God and of Christ Jesus . . . : preach the word, be urgent in season and out of season, convince, rebuke, and exhort, be unfailing in patience and in teaching" (4:1–2). The picture—in the present or in memory—of Paul's own "testifying" (the word can even be translated "martyrdom") is summoned to inspire and encourage a pastor as he faces the troubles of "testifying" in his generation.

Some Comments on Second Timothy

The theme of the passing on of the faith from generation to generation is introduced at the very beginning of the letter. Timothy is said to be of the third generation of believers (1:5). Timothy's gift of ministry also has been passed down to him in the laying on of Paul's hands at his ordination (1:6; cf. 1 Tim. 4:14).

But in the generation in which the reader of this letter lives, there is the temptation to find testifying for the gospel a source of embarrassment, even shame. Over against such shame, the reader must be reminded that the gospel really brings "power and love and self-control" (1:7).

Paul himself had not given in to shame, that reader is reminded, in spite of his suffering and imprisonment (1:8). Rather, he had had confidence that God would continue to protect the gospel which had been entrusted to him (1:12). Onesiphorus had not been ashamed to visit Paul even in a Roman jail (1:16). And

Second Timothy

Paul's Example of Life and Teaching for the Next Generation

"Follow the pattern ... you have ... from me" (1:13).

1:1	2:1	3:1	4:1	4:6 4:22
Timothy's Heritage of True Faith	**The Charge: Be Faithful to That Heritage**	**Defenses Against Heresies**	**A Summary Charge to Faithful Ministry**	**Personal Appeals by Paul**
His heritage from two generations and from Paul 1:1–7	Pass on what you have received, in spite of difficulties. 2:1–7	A warning against the heretics to come 3:1–9		His own testimony in the face of death 4:6–8
Paul's example of faithfulness 1:8–14	Be loyal to the gospel, as Paul has been loyal. 2:8–13	Two sources of sound guidance: — Paul's example 3:10–13		Personal requests and greetings 4:9–22
Some others have been heroically faithful; some have not. 1:15–18	By contrast, do not be like the heretics. 2:14–19 Instead, be a good vessel of truth, not a disputer. 2:20–26	— the Scripture 3:14–17		

Author: "Paul" (Most say a later disciple of Paul writing in his honor.)

Recipient: "Timothy" (a third-generation pastor)

Date: A.D. 68? (Most say later than Paul's life, perhaps early in the second century.)

Occasion: Paul, in fact or in the memory of the writer, is in prison facing death. Heresy threatens the church.

Purpose: To strengthen a later pastor in ministry and in faithfulness to sound doctrine through a reminder of the witness of Paul now Timothy, preacher to a new generation, is to hand on that gospel in such a way that he need not be ashamed (2:15).

One reason for shame and discouragement in this third-generation Christian is that so many are now deserting the gospel. This, too, the letter reminds its reader, is nothing new. The book includes the names of several people, otherwise unknown to us in the twentieth century but apparently still familiar at the time this letter was first read, who forsook or opposed Paul, names set over against those of heroes who remained faithful. Phygelus and Hermogenes (1:15), Demas (4:10), and Alexander (4:14) are contrasted with Onesiphorus, who had been undaunted by Paul's chains (1:16), and Luke, who alone faithfully remains with Paul (4:11). Others are separated from Paul because of their duties (4:10–20). The note of wistfulness and loneliness in the personal references in 2 Timothy 4 seems so real that it has convinced many that at least these verses are actually from Paul's pen. Even if not, there is no reason to doubt that they rest on accurate memory of the suffering which, we know from other sources, Paul certainly did endure. Remember that Paul went through the same kind of thing you face in your time, the writer is saying, knowing people who "will accumulate for themselves teachers to suit their own likings, and will turn away from listening to the truth and wander into myths. As for you, always be steady, endure suffering, do the work of an evangelist, fulfil your ministry" (4:3–5), even as Paul did. "Take your share of suffering as a good soldier of Christ" (2:3).

There are hints that the reader may also face quite tangible suffering. (Hebrews 13:23 tells us that Timothy did go to prison.) Twice we are reminded that Paul was in chains (1:16; 2:9). Second Timothy 2:11–13 appears to be an early Christian hymn, perhaps sung at the time a convert gave his testimony at his baptism. But one can well imagine that it had also been sung by martyrs who had gone to their deaths in the persecutions which had already cost many Christians their lives, and which world soon bring the deaths of thousands more. They sang:

> If we have died with him, we shall also live with him;
> If we endure, we shall also reign with him.

Timothy is urged to pass correct tradition along to teachers who will deliver it to future generations (2:2). The concern continues for fixing the tradition, setting it in forms which cannot be twisted to please those "having itching ears" (4:3), ready for Gnostic heresies. At least three times there are Passages which seem to reflect early creeds, liturgies, or hymns (1:10; 2:8; 2:11–13). And Timothy is urged to make use of the Old Testament Scriptures (3:15–16, and probably 4:13). Can the writer have guessed that the next generation would begin taking this letter itself as an official written standard in its battle with heresy?

At this stage, however, the church does not look primarily to a set of writings. Rather, it is the example of a person who has suffered which is to inspire the reader of this letter with a "spirit of power." The example is the courage of Paul. "I have fought the good fight, I have finished the race, I have kept the faith. Henceforth . . . the crown" (4:7–8).

"You, then, . . . be strong" (2:1).

Titus

"My brother Titus," Paul had called him (2 Cor. 2:13). This "very earnest" man (2 Cor. 8:16–17) had been the go-between in the dispute between Paul and the church at Corinth, and it was he who at last had been able to bring Paul the good news that all was well again in that church (see pages 134–136). A Gentile who had been an early convert to Christianity, Titus had accompanied Paul on the visit to Jerusalem in which Paul had discussed with Peter, James, and John the status of Gentile Christians in the church (Gal. 2:1–10).

It was appropriate, therefore, that the third of the pastoral epistles should bear the name of this assistant to the great Apostle to the Gentiles.

The Occasion of Titus

According to the letter, Paul has been to Crete (Titus 1:5) and expects to spend the winter in Nicopolis (3:12)—probably the city of that name in northern Greece. The epistle is addressed to Titus, who has been left to be the missionary pastor in Crete (1:5). Acts gives no hint of Paul's doing mission work in Crete or Nicopolis. Again, therefore, we must assume that if Paul actually wrote this letter, he did it at a time later than that described in Acts. (On the authorship of the pastorals, see pages 176–178.)

The situation implied in Titus is really much the same as that of First and Second Timothy. The author addresses Titus as his "true child" (1:4) and gives him advice concerning his work as a pastor. As in the other pastorals, the need is for leadership which will teach sound doctrine (1:9; 2:1) and good deeds (2:7). Presumably the kind of unsound doctrine against which the younger pastor is to contend is that early form of Gnosticism we have already examined (see above, pages 162–167).

The Purpose of Titus

As with the other pastorals, the letter is to guide and encourage a pastor of a new generation by sharing the wisdom of the Apostle Paul.

Some Comments on Titus

As in 1 Timothy 3:1–13 and 2 Timothy 2:1–2, the author emphasizes the importance of having the right leaders in the church. These are to be men of the highest character, but they also must "be able to give instruction in sound doctrine" (1:9).

These leaders are called elders *(presbuteroi)*, the term in 1:5 apparently at this

Titus

More Guidance for a Young Pastor

"... as for you, teach what befits sound doctrine" (2:1).

1:1	2:1	3:1
Salutation and a Reminder to Select a Good Group of Elders	**Teach Each Group in the Church Its Proper Behavior.**	**Remind All to Live Lives Appropriate for Those Who Have Become Christians.**
Greetings from a preacher of the true gospel	Older people	A call to moral virtue befitting those truly converted
1:1-4	2:1-3	3:1-7
A reminder: choose elders sound in life and teaching, not typical Cretans	Younger people	Not speculative (Gnostic) disputes
	2:4-6	3:8-11
1:5-16	(Through example)	Closing personal note
	2:7-8	3:12-15
	Slaves	
	2:9-10	
	All	
	2:11-15	

Author: Paul? (Most scholars believe it to be by a later disciple of Paul writing in his memory and honor.)
Recipient: "Titus," a young pastor
Date: A.D. 67? (Most critics date it after Paul's life, early in the second century.)
Occasion: "Titus" has been left in charge of a church given to Gnostic disputes and unrighteous living.
Purpose: To remind the young pastor of the importance of sound doctrine, leadership, and life

stage in the life of the church being synonymous with the term "bishop" (1:7). In their commentary, Dibelius and Conzelmann print a long description in which the pagan Onosander prescribes for a Roman general many of the same qualities Titus here demands for a bishop![5] There are close parallels between Titus 1 and 1 Timothy 3 concerning the qualifications of church officers.

Titus	**First Timothy**
above reproach (blameless)	above reproach
the husband of one wife	the husband of one wife
hospitable	hospitable
devoted to what is good	respectable
self-controlled	sober
children who are believers	children who are obedient
prudent	prudent
concerned with preaching	able to teach
just	
pious	
not arrogant	gentle
not irascible	peaceable
not given to wine	not given to wine
not given to brawling	not given to brawling
not fond of dishonest gain	not greedy
children who are obedient	able to govern his own house well
	not newly converted

The belief that the typical Cretan is a liar (1:12–13) can be traced back as far as Epimenides in 490 B.C. Callimachus in the third century B.C. wrote that "Cretans were always liars," his example being that they even claimed to have on Crete the tomb of Zeus, who, as king of the gods, could scarcely be dead!

The exhortations to moral living by different groups again parallel those found in Colossians, Ephesians, and the other pastoral epistles (2:1–10). Obviously the writer of the letter had in mind guiding the conduct not simply of Titus, but of his whole congregation.

Chapter 3 may contain echoes of an early liturgy for baptism. Some question may be raised as to whether the Apostle Paul would ever really have used the words of Titus 3:3 to describe his life before his conversion.

One final note: Titus 2:13 apparently contains one of the few places in which the New Testament unqualifiedly calls Jesus Christ "God." Repeatedly Jesus is called Son of God or described in other ways which imply his equality with God the Father or his doing work previously regarded as exclusively that of God. But in this verse we read of "our great God and Savior Jesus Christ." Christian theology was moving toward the Nicene Creed.

XII *Five "Open Letters"*

James L. Price suggests that we call these "open letters to Christians."[1]

Since early in the fourth century, the church has given the name "Catholic Epistles" or "General Epistles" to seven letters: James, First and Second Peter, First, Second, and Third John, and Jude. That name has meant not that they were addressed to the Roman Catholic Church, but that they were *not* addressed, as were the letters of Paul, to particular congregations named in their opening salutations. Rather, they are for the whole church, the church universal. These letters have in common also the fact that they are the only ones in our New Testament not traditionally attributed to Paul.

Because the letters of John have so much in common with the Fourth Gospel, we will delay discussion of them until chapter 13. But we will here discuss Hebrews with four of the "Catholic Epistles." Most scholars believe that Hebrews, too, was not written by Paul; and it, too, contains the name of no particular congregation in its greetings. (As was proposed on page 4, the Christian reader always seeks to read any book of the Bible as in some sense a letter addressed to himself.)

Hebrews

Donald George Miller used to tell his classes that the critics agreed on only one thing concerning Hebrews: nobody really knows anything about it!

Consider, for example, the question "Who wrote it?" The list of suggested authors is bewilderingly varied:

—The letter itself bears *no name.*

—It was finally accepted into the canon in part because it was believed by some to be by *Paul.* Most early writers in the Western (Roman) wing of the church doubted this, however, and almost all scholars today regard Hebrews as quite different from Paul's letters in vocabulary, style, and theological approach.

—Tertullian in the second century had been taught that it was by *Barnabas.*

—Other ancient authorities attributed it to *Luke;* still others said it was by *Clement,* an early bishop of Rome.

—Martin Luther suggested that it was by *Apollos,* basing his proposal on the similarities between the thought of Hebrews and that characteristic of Philo and other teachers from Alexandria. (Apollos was from Alexandria. [Acts 18:24].)

—A modern suggestion has been that it was by *a woman*, perhaps *Priscilla*. The argument for this is that though the author was evidently a teacher of skill and authority, the name has been lost. Was this, perhaps, because some church members were embarrassed that a woman had had so prominent a place?

—The early church father Origen's famous summary is really the best one can say. *God only knows* who wrote Hebrews!

From the letter itself one can only infer that the author was a master of Greek style, was thoroughly familiar with the Septuagint (the Greek translation of the Old Testament), and was a highly competent Christian theologian in a pattern rather different from that of Paul.

Is Hebrews really a letter?

The writer calls the work not an epistle, but a "word of exhortation," and the opening address found in other biblical letters is missing. Hebrews is a carefully constructed essay, tightly reasoned, building to a planned climax. It is probably the closest thing to a Sunday-morning sermon to be found in our New Testament.

Some scholars, therefore, have argued that Hebrews is not really a letter at all, but a sermon. The last chapter, they have proposed, was tacked on later, perhaps to make it seem like one of Paul's letters and thus gain wider acceptance in the church. However, chapter 13 fits so well with the rest of the book, and such personal knowledge of the readers is shown in other parts (6:9–10; 10:32–34; 12:4), that most scholars reject the view that chapter 13 is a later addition.[2]

To whom was it written?

This question is most important for interpreting the letter, and yet it is equally disputed.

The traditional view is that the epistle is written to a group of Jews who have become Christians but who are now tempted to drift back into Judaism. To them the writer presents Christ as superior to all that their old religion might offer: angels, Moses, the priesthood, and the old covenant. The traditional title, "The Letter to the Hebrews," reflects this understanding of the book.

Most modern interpreters, however, have argued that the letter may be as easily understood as addressed to Gentile Christians. It does not say that it is to Jewish Christians. It never mentions any revival of circumcision or legalism. The conflicts between Judaism and Christianity which were so bitter when Galatians was being written now seem forgotten. The people addressed are now becoming weak-kneed (12:12) and are falling "away from the living God" (3:12). They are becoming indifferent; but they could as well be Gentiles as Jews. The extensive use of Old Testament ideas, it is argued, proves nothing, because the Septuagint was the Bible of Gentile Christians as well as of Jews.

The present writer's own teacher, the late William Manson, has made a strong case for a version of the traditional view. The letter, Professor Manson argued, was written to a house-church in Rome composed of Jewish converts to Christianity who still maintained ties with the Jewish community. They were teetering on the dividing line between the original way of life of the first Jewish Christians and the growing fellowship of the world mission to the Gentiles. They were Christians, but they were reluctant to break their ties to Judaism and its older forms of worship.

It is certainly possible that the writer presents the superiority of Christ to the Old Testament religion as a way of encouraging Gentile Christians to persevere in the faith. It does seem simpler, however, to understand the letter in the more straightforward way characteristic of tradition and defended by Dr. Manson: that it presents Christ as superior to the Old Testament because it was into Judaism that the readers were tempted to backslide.[3]

The Occasion of Hebrews

Some Christians—whether former Jews or pagans—"holy brethren, who share in a heavenly call" (3:1), are now being tempted to "fall away" (3:12). They are in danger of "apostasy" (6:6), of "wavering" (10:23), and are even neglecting to attend worship services (10:25).

These Christians have had an admirable record in the past. In "the former days" they had "endured a hard struggle . . ., sometimes being publicly exposed to abuse and affliction" (10:32–33). The persecution had not, apparently, gone as far as the execution of martyrs (12:4), but it had caused the plundering of some Christians' property (10:34). Now both apathy and new persecution threaten (12:7). The readers now need to be told, "Do not throw away your confidence" (10:35).

That minority who, like Dr. Manson, assign Hebrews to an early date suggest that the earlier persecution referred to was the one in A.D. 49, in which Claudius expelled the Jews from Rome because of riots said to have been instigated by one "Chrestus" (see page 147). The letter itself is written as the more severe persecution under Nero threatens the church at Rome. Most scholars relate the letter to later persecutions.

That it was written to Christians in Rome is itself uncertain. Rome is suggested, however, by the greetings from "those who come from Italy" (13:24) and by the fact that Bishop Clement of Rome quoted the letter in an epistle of his own about A.D. 96.

The Purpose of Hebrews

The letter is written for a double purpose. (1) Theologically, it is to present the superiority of Jesus Christ to any alternative, such as the things the Old Testament offered. (2) Practically, it is to encourage the readers to move forward, not backward, in their faith.

Over and over one finds the readers urged not to "drift away" (2:1), not to "fall away" (3:12), not to "become dull of hearing" (5:11), not to "commit apostasy" (6:6), and not to "throw away . . . confidence" (10:35). (Hebrews warns so solemnly against backsliding that a few years later *The Shepherd of Hermas* was written in part to say that God does sometimes give lapsed Christians a second chance, though there are strict limits to his patience!)[4] Rather, Hebrews encourages its readers to "hold . . . confidence" (3:14), to "strive to enter" (4:11), "with confidence draw near" (4:16), "go on to maturity" (6:1), "have strong encouragement to seize the hope set before" them (6:18), "hold fast" (10:23), and "run with perseverance the race . . ., looking to Jesus the pioneer and perfecter" of that faith (12:1–2).

That encouragement lies in the fact that Christ is "much superior to" and "more excellent than" anything the Old Testament offered (1:4). His priesthood and covenant are "more excellent . . ., enacted on better promises" (8:6). He offers entrance into a place of worship "greater and more perfect" (9:11). He has opened a "new and living way" of access to God (10:20).

The letter is an exhortation to carry on, to go forward, encouraged by the realization of the transcendent value of Christ.

Some Comments on Hebrews

How do we know God? Hebrews begins with an answer: through Christ. Other, earlier ways are not condemned. But Hebrews 1:1–4 affirms that the revelation in God's Son is superior to all others. As early as verse 3, however, the author introduces his (or her) particular emphasis. John writes of the revealed *Logos*, or wisdom of God. Paul stresses the *righteousness* of God and our *justification*. But Hebrews 1:3 speaks of *purification*. The atmosphere of the letter is not that of the philosophy class nor of the law court, but of the Temple, ceremony, worship. The writer finds new meaning in religious symbols and cultic practices now transformed by Christ.

As seen from this perspective, the human problem is that we are stained with sin and cannot enter into the presence of God.

One solution, in the thought of both Jews and pagans, was the concept of angels. These creatures were regarded as halfway between God and humankind and thus able to link the two. Angels were said to have assisted at creation and to have given the Law. They could go up and down a ladder between God and even sinful Jacob. And speculation about these heavenly beings exercised a fascination for the ancient world in some ways analogous to the modern preoccupation with space travel and UFO's. Hebrews argues that God's Son is above God's angels. Yet at the same time, angels can never quite get low enough to make contact with people. This is because they have never been tempted, nor have they suffered. God is not really concerned about angels, but with people (2:16). Christ has identified himself completely with humanity. "Because he himself has suffered and been tempted, he is able to help those who are tempted" (2:18). As mediator, he is higher than the angels and yet more completely down-to-earth.

Hebrews

Christ: The Better Priest of the Better Covenant

"Since we have a great priest … let us hold fast the confession of our hope without wavering" (10:21–23).

1:1	3:1	4:14	8:1	11:1	12:1 13:25
Christ Is Better Than Angels.	**Christ Is Better Than Moses.**	**Christ Is Better Than the Old Priesthood**	**Christ's New Covenant Is Better Than the Old.**	**Faith's Heroes of the Old Testament Sought to Go Forward to This Better Covenant We Have in Christ.**	**Therefore, Let Us Go Forward with Christ in Faith, Love, and Obedience.**
The Old Testament exalts not angels, but the Son. 1:1–14	Moses was God's servant; Jesus was God's Son. 3:1–6	Being truly human, he can better represent us to God. 4:14—5:11	The old covenant rested only on symbols. 8:1—9:10	Abel 11:1–7 The Patriarchs 11:8–22	Go forward in faith, in spite of opposition. 12:1–28
Therefore, be faithful. 2:1–4	Under Moses the Hebrews never got what was promised. 3:7—4:13	So do not be sluggish, but go forward on God's promises. 6:1–20	But Christ has entered the real sanctuary, heaven. 9:11—10:18	Moses 11:23–31	Go forward in love and obedience. 13:1–25
For in Christ, God has identified not with angels, but with us. 2:5–18		Christ is a special kind of high priest, like Melchizedek. 7:1–28	Therefore, do not waver. 10:19–39	Many more 11:32–40	

Author: Unknown

Recipients: Christians—"brethren who share a heavenly call" (former Jews? in Rome?)

Date: Unknown (A.D. 90? A.D. 60?)

Occasion: Some are tempted to "fall away" (3:12), into "apostasy" (6:6).

Purpose: Having shown the superiority of Christ to everything in the old Testament (Covenant), to encourage apathetic Christians to move forward in the New Covenant

Second, "Jesus has been counted worthy of . . . more glory than Moses" (3:3). To the Hebrews Moses was Lincoln and Washington in one, their "Great Emancipator" and the founder of their nation. It was through him that God gave the Law. It was he who led God's people to the Promised Land; he was a kind of "pioneer" (12:2). Yet the story of Moses is one of frustration, Hebrews says. The religion of Moses never delivered on its promises because it could not overcome the sinfulness of a stubborn people. Of all those who left Egypt with Moses, only two made it into the land of Canaan. Three times the author quotes God's final announcement to those backsliders, "They shall never enter my rest" (3:11; 4:3, 5; cf. 3:18). Let us, however, go forward, the writer pleads, into what is promised through our leader, Christ (4:11–13).

Third, in Hebrews 4:14 we are introduced to the most distinctive theme of Hebrews, the concept of Christ as the great High Priest. For most Protestants, at least, priests today are somewhat out of fashion. To grasp the writer's message, we need imaginatively to recover the sense of dependence Jews felt regarding the priesthood. The priest was a kind of middleman between God and his people. He represented God to them; he represented them to God. God was too holy to be approached by ordinary men and women. It was only through the priest that impure people had access. The high priest might enter the holy of holies, the inner part of the tabernacle, only after elaborate ceremony, and then only once a year. But Jesus has entered heaven itself. True, Jesus was not born into the priestly tribe of Levi. But neither was Melchizedek, called a priest in Genesis 14:17–20 and Psalm 110:4. It was in Melchizedek's pattern of special priesthood that Jesus exercised his priestly mediation between God and people. But Christ has "no need, like those high priests, to offer sacrifices daily, first for his own sins and then for those of the people; he did this once for all when he offered up himself" (7:27).

Hebrews sees the symbols and ceremonies of Leviticus as "types," in a sense pictures, of the reality of access to God which the Christian was to claim in Christ. The book does this by making use of an idea well known among such Hellenistic-Jewish teachers as Philo, an idea derived ultimately from Plato. It is surely one of Plato's oddest ideas, but that philosopher proposed that there are really three kinds of beds. There are pictures and shadows of beds; there are what you sleep on every night; and there is the "ideal form" bed, in the mind and in heaven. What you sleep on at night is only a temporary manifestation of the ideal, heavenly bed, which is what is really real. This is Plato's perhaps exaggerated way of saying that spiritual, heavenly things are what really matter, what are eternal. Material things, like shadows, pass away.

As Hebrews describes Christ's priesthood and the new covenant, it presents these as the heavenly realities. The Law, found in books such as Leviticus, with its ceremonies, "has but a shadow of the good things to come instead of the true form of these realities" (10:1). The tabernacle and the altar served only as "a copy and shadow of the heavenly sanctuary" (8:5). But in Christ we have the reality. Jeremiah's dream of a new covenant has come true (8:8–12; cf. Jer. 31:31–34). The risen Christ has actually entered the true sanctuary of God, heaven itself, on our behalf. The whole Bible gets its subtitles from the idea developed in these chapters: the Old Testament (or Covenant) and the New Testament.

"Therefore, brethren, since we have confidence to enter the sanctuary . . ., and since we have a great priest . . ., let us draw near . . . in full assurance of faith" (10:19–22). So the writer summarizes.

The most celebrated chapter in Hebrews is the "Roll Call of Heroes of the Faith" (Abel and Abraham and Moses, etc.) in Hebrews 11. The point of the chapter, however, is that all of these were looking forward to something which lay beyond themselves.

That goal, the author announces, is in Christ (12:1–2). Yet Christ himself is seen as the "pioneer" (12:2), the one who leads forward in faith. "Faith" to the writer of Hebrews is courage, the vision to keep going forward into what Christ has promised.

"Therefore let us go forth to him outside the camp" (of Judaism or of anything less than Christianity), he pleads, on toward heaven, "the city which is to come" (13:13–14).

James

There are many different men named James mentioned in the New Testament. Unfortunately, it seems unlikely that any one of them is the author of our Epistle of James.

—The brother of John, the first of the Twelve to be martyred, hardly had time to write the book (Acts 12:2).

—James the son of Alphaeus (Mark 3:18) was one of the Twelve, but neither the Bible nor tradition indicates that he was a man of distinction.

—James the younger (Mark 15:40), perhaps the same as James the son of Mary (Mark 16:1), is perhaps the same as James the son of Alphaeus. Again we know nothing, though of course we cannot absolutely exclude the possibility of authorship.

—James the father of Jude (Judas) (Luke 6:16; Acts 1:13) could possibly be the same as one of these other Jameses. We know nothing about him, either.

—James the brother of Jesus (Mark 6:3; 1 Cor. 15:7; Gal. 1:19; Acts 12:17; 15:13; 21:18; Jude 1) is the James to whom tradition finally attributed this letter. It was partly on the basis of the belief that he was the author that the book at last received acceptance into the canon.

Several reasons make it seem unlikely that that tradition is historically accurate.

1) As late as the fourth century, Eusebius lists the book "called the Epistle of

James'' as "among the disputed books,'' says it was still "considered spurious,'' and notes that very few of the church fathers ever made any use of it. If the letter really had been by such a prominent leader in the early church as Jesus' brother, it is highly unlikely that there would still have been debate about its being included in the canon three hundred years later.

2) Language scholars tell us that the letter is written in polished Greek, not the dialect one would expect of the son of a Galilean carpenter.

3) The content of the letter shows no signs of its being by James the brother of Jesus and "Bishop of Jerusalem.'' The author makes no claim to being Jesus' brother, gives few if any hints of personal memory of Jesus' earthly life, discusses none of the problems the rest of the New Testament indicates were so much debated in the early church, and gives no reflection of James' leadership in the Jerusalem congregation. (Acts, Galatians, and tradition agree that James really was the leader of that church.)

4) On the contrary, the discussion of faith and works in James 2:18–26 seems to reflect a relatively late time when the letters or at least some of the ideas of Paul, misunderstood, had been circulating throughout the church.

5) It seems likely that James 1:1 reflects 1 Peter 1:1, and that James 4:10 reflects a knowledge of 1 Peter 5:6, thus putting the letter later than First Peter.

While the letter is probably not by Jesus' brother James, it is clear that it was gradually accepted because it was often associated with that early church leader. It is proper, therefore, to interpret the letter in part against the background of that tradition.[5]

Writing in the fourth century, Eusebius tells us that James was the first "bishop of Jerusalem.'' While that church historian may be reading back into the first century the fixed forms of government developed by his own time, it is clear that James really was an important leader in the Jerusalem church.

Paul tells us that on his first trip to Jerusalem after his conversion, he consulted with only two Apostles, Peter and James (Gal. 1:18–19). He names James first, along with Peter and John, as the three "pillars'' of the church before whom he later laid out his version of the gospel for assurance that he had not "run in vain'' (Gal. 2:2, 9). Acts seems to picture James as presiding at the Jerusalem Council (Acts 15:13–21). When Paul arrived at Jerusalem after this third missionary journey, Luke tells us that it was to James that he made his formal report (Acts 21:18).

While both Galatians and Acts say that James was in agreement with Paul and his mission to the Gentiles, there are in both hints that James was himself associated with the more conservative Jewish faction in the church (see Acts 15:20; 21:20–24). It was when "certain men came from James'' to Antioch that Peter stopped eating with Gentiles (Gal. 2:12).

The first-century Jewish historian Josephus—no Christian—tells us a story which fits rather nicely with part of the biblical picture. He says that James was known as "the Just." Seizing a moment of power after the death of Festus (Acts 25:1) and before a new governor arrived, the high priest Ananias had James—and certain others, presumably Christians—executed by stoning. James was so respected for his piety that protests were sent to King Agrippa.[6]

Eusebius reports legends which elaborate the story. "James the Just" was so far removed from the lusts of the world that he ate no meat, never got a shave or a haircut, used no sweet-smelling oil, and—perhaps most obvious of all such signs of this type of piety—never took a bath! He spent so much time praying that his knees became calloused like a camel's! He bore witness to Christ at his trial, was thrown off the wall of the Temple, stoned, and finally clubbed to death. But he died as had his brother, praying, "Father, forgive them, for they know not what they do." According to Eusebius, even Josephus says that the fall of Jerusalem, just a few years later, came about as divine retribution for the murder of so holy a man.[7]

Whatever its actual origin, therefore, the letter eventually came to be included in the canon because it had come to be understood as part of the legacy of this model early Jewish-Christian martyr.

The Occasion of James

The book is addressed "to the twelve tribes in the Dispersion" (1:1). By the time of the New Testament, Hebrew tribal organization had long since vanished. Surely the greeting means "to the Christian church scattered over the world." Writing, then, to so broad a group, the author makes no clear reference to any particular local situation. It is impossible to determine the occasion of the letter.

Some, building on its association with the first "bishop of Jerusalem," have argued that the epistle reflects early Palestinian Jewish-Christian piety. Most, for reasons such as those given above for rejecting the tradition that Jesus' brother was the author, have regarded it as the work of an unknown Hellenistic Jewish-Christian of late in the first century. This seems to the present writer more likely.

The fact is, however, that the book itself gives no clear indication of a special time or place in which it originated nor of any unusual situation to which it was addressed.

The Purpose of James

Form critics like to use of certain passages in the Bible the Greek word *paranaesis*, meaning "exhortation" or "moral instruction." Though Paul's letters typically begin with discussion of the *kerygma* (the good news of the gospel), theology, they usually move on to *paranaesis* (see, for example, Rom. 12—14; Eph. 4—6; Col. 3—4).

James
The Wisdom Which Produces Good Works
"So faith by itself, if it has no works, is dead" (2:17).

1:1	2:1	3:1	4:1	4:13
The Wise Person Faces Temptation with Good Deeds.	**True Wisdom Results in Loving Actions, Not Just "Faith".**	**The Truly Wise Control the Tongue and Show Wisdom by Life, Not Words.**	**The Truly Wise Also Control the Passions.**	**Thus the Truly Wise Are Patient.**
In trouble, rejoice and seek wisdom from God. 1:1–18	Show no partiality. 2:1–7	The difficulty of controlling one's tongue 3:1–12	Be humbly content, not covetous and jealous. 4:1–10	Submit humbly to God's plans. 4:13–17
Face your difficulties not with angry words and wickedness. 1:19–20	But obey the law of love. 2:8–13	The marks of genuine, God-given wisdom 3:13–18	And keep God's law by not judging others. 4:11–12	Though the selfish prosper now, their judgment will come. 5:1–11
Instead, face difficulties with good deeds. 1:21–27	Because not "faith" but good work is what counts 2:14–26			Wait for it with patience, prayer, and concern for each other. 5:12–20

Author: "James" (according to tradition, Jesus' brother, but probably an unknown Christian Jew)
Recipients: Apparently all Christians
Date: A.D. 50–120 (Most critics put it around A.D. 90–100.)
Occasion: Again, we do not know.
Purpose: Practical moral instruction emphasizing life, not just words or "faith "

James is entirely a book of *paranaesis*. Bruce Metzger counts sixty verbs as imperatives in the 108 verses of the epistle!

Indeed, one may question whether the book really should be called a letter. Though it has a letterlike beginning—even that is of a broad, impersonal kind—the ending is not at all like that of a letter. This writing is more like a sermon.

James, then, is a book of practical, moral instruction urging every Christian to manifest his religion not in words, but in deeds of love.

Some Comments on James

Although an outline is given on page 200, perhaps the first thing which must be said about James is that it cannot really be outlined. Luther, who as we shall see had other reasons for disliking James, complained that the author "makes a jumble of things."[8]

He does. But there is a reason. James is not attempting to write in the introduction-three-points-and-a-conclusion style of a modern preacher. His model is much more nearly that of the ancient Hebrew "wisdom literature." Proverbs, for example, cannot be outlined either. Many of its passages are simply collections of the wise, even witty, sayings of the kind beloved by the writers and readers of "wisdom literature" (see, for example, any chapter in Proverbs 10—29).

James shares with Proverbs and other books of Hebrew "wisdom" much more, of course, than a tendency to the disconnected style of a collection of wise sayings. He, like Proverbs, writes in praise of Godly wisdom (3:13, 15, 17; cf. Prov. 8—9, etc.). He exhorts his readers to many of the same virtues: giving to those in need (2:14–16; cf. Prov. 11:25); controlling one's tongue (3:1–12; cf. Prov. 17:28); and controlling one's temper (4:1; cf. Prov. 16:32). And James employs something of Proverbs' tendency to a kind of Jewish humor.

It may seem blasphemous to the more pious readers of this volume to suggest that anything in the Bible is meant to be funny. But there are passages in Proverbs where many centuries and translations have not obscured the humor. Proverbs intends at least a smile when it notes:

> Like a gold ring in a swine's snout
> is a beautiful woman without discretion. (Proverbs 11:22)

No one is really quite as lazy as Proverbs' drone, who cannot find the energy even to eat!

> The sluggard buries his hand in the dish;
> it wears him out to bring it back to his mouth. (Proverbs 26:15)

It is in this same vein that James writes of some of the sins he denounces.

James can picture at the church a rich man with gold rings being attentively ushered to a seat, while a poor man is made to stand somewhere or even told to sit on the floor (2:1–7)!

He can laugh at the hypocrite who piously says to the beggar, "Go in peace, be warmed and filled," but then does nothing to help (2:14–17)!

He can compare people who are perhaps dirty and disheveled, see the mess in a mirror, and forget to do anything about it to Christians who read about their sins in the Bible and then forget to clean up their lives (1:22–25)!

And he can propose that it is easier to put out a forest fire or to tame all kinds of wild animals than for a Christian to control his or her tongue (3:1–12)! (One other biblical teacher was fond of such humorous exaggeration. See Matt. 7:3; 19:24.)

Almost all readers will see wisdom in the wit of these passages. But debate has raged about such sayings of James as that "faith apart from works is dead" (2:26).

The present writer has sometimes placed the following quotations side by side on the chalkboard and asked his classes to vote on which sounds more like the New Testament:

| For by grace you have been saved through faith . . . not because of works. | A man is justified by works and not by faith alone. |

Both are in the New Testament, of course, one being from Ephesians 2:8–9, the other being from James 2:24.

Martin Luther took his stand on Paul's preaching of salvation through faith, not works. James' emphasis on works so upset Luther that he denounced it as a "rather straw-like epistle," by "some Jew or other," and proposed to drop it from the canon.

It is difficult to avoid the feeling that James is deliberately attempting to correct a view which must have been associated with Paul. A partial reconciliation of the conflict, however, can be achieved when one recognizes that James and Paul are using the word "faith" in quite different ways. By "faith" Paul means a personal trust in Jesus Christ as Lord and Savior. James is using "faith" to mean intellectual acceptance of certain doctrines as true. Thus James can write that "Even the demons believe—and shudder" (2:19). But such demons, of course, do not have what Paul means by saving "faith." James is attacking a misunderstanding of Paul's ideas. Paul advocated faith, salvation by faith alone, but it was the kind of faith described as "faith working through love" (Gal. 5:6).

Finally, it should be noted that, for all its emphasis on works in the style of Hebrew wisdom, James is a Christian book. There seems at first glance so little that is specifically Christian in James that some have proposed that it really was a bit of pre-Christian Jewish wisdom, slightly edited for church use. The writer, however, describes himself as "a servant of God and of the Lord Jesus Christ" (1:1). His readers, he says, "hold the faith of our Lord Jesus Christ, the Lord of Glory" (2:1). He recalls that God "brought us forth by the word of truth that we should be a kind of first fruits of his creatures" (1:18). This sounds more like a formula for Christian baptism than a bit of Old Testament wisdom. "The implanted word, which is able to save your souls" (1:21) surely must be the gospel, not the Law. The "honorable name by which you are called" is evidently that of Christ (2:7). And 5:8 places us in the midst of the typical Christian expectation that "the coming of the Lord is at hand."

Indeed, it could be argued that James is in certain ways closer to the teachings of Jesus, in style and in content, than are many of the other books of the New Testament which say more about him. Kümmel lists parallels such as the following:

James 1:5,17	Matthew 7:7 ff.
1:22	7:24 ff.
4:12	7:1
1:6	Mark 11:23–24

James is probably not copying from the written Gospels. He knew the same tradition of teachings on which the Gospels rest.

He knows especially the commandment which Jesus says really matters: "If you really fulfil the royal law, according to the scripture, 'You shall love your neighbor as yourself,' you do well"(2:8).

Jesus would say, "Amen!"

First Peter

In the case of the Apostle Peter, it is impossible completely to separate history from the rich legend which quickly became a part of the tradition associated with his memory.

Persecution, says one story, had broken out in Rome. Peter made his escape down the Appian Way. Suddenly he encountered Jesus, who was walking toward the city.

"Where are you going, Lord?"

"Into the city, to be crucified again."

Shamed by the vision, Peter returned courageously to face prison and death. Arrested and thrown into a dungeon, Peter still witnessed to his captors. At length, won by the holiness of the Apostle, two of his guards were converted. How could he baptize them in his cell? Miraculously, a fountain sprang from the floor, and Peter was able to wash clean from sin these newborn Christians. Then he was led out to be crucified—upside down, at his request, since he felt unworthy to die in the same manner as his Lord.

Perhaps the best-loved part of the tradition which comes from the memory of Peter is the first of two letters which bear his name. It, like the legend, centers on courage, holiness, and baptism, in the midst of persecution.

Several factors make most scholars cautious about attributing First Peter to the pen of the Apostle. (1) It is written in polished Greek, though we are told that Peter was an "uneducated, common" man (Acts 4:13). (2) It is so much like letters of Paul that it appears to come from a time when Paul's epistles were known throughout the church. (3) Most important, it seems to fit perfectly into the situation of worldwide persecution of the nineties and later, in which even to be called a Christian was a crime. We know of no such persecution in Asia Minor, where churches to which the letter is addressed were located, during Peter's lifetime.

As a matter of fact, the letter itself hints of some mediation in its authorship. "By Silvanus, a faithful brother as I regard him, I have written briefly to you," we are told near the end (5:12). Is the author perhaps hinting that the spirit but not the actual words are Peter's?[9]

Nevertheless, there are twentieth-century critics who still attribute the letter more directly to the Apostle. The early church, they note, rejected the so-called Apocalypse of Peter and the Gospel of Peter, and many rejected Second Peter, but First Peter was early and widely accepted as an authoritative word from the leader of the Twelve. If we do not know of comparable persecution in what is now Turkey during Peter's lifetime, we do know of it in Rome itself, and Peter may have written from the midst of that persecution warning others of what he felt would soon spread. (Persecution was widespread a few years later.) And if the Silvanus (Silas) by whom the letter was actually penned was the companion of Paul and his secretary in the letters to the Thessalonians (Acts 15:40; 1 Thess. 1:1; 2 Thess. 1:1), this might explain both the use of polished Greek and the echoes of Pauline phrases and ideas. The presupposition of a relatively undeveloped system of church government—still by "elders" (1 Peter 5:1)—the hopeful attitude still taken toward the Roman government (2:13–17; Luke 3:13), and the still strong expectation of "the end of all things" (4:7), are cited as evidence for a date within Peter's lifetime.

Only two things can be said with certainty. (1) The letter does speak directly to the kind of persecution which swept the Roman Empire early in the second century. (2) First Peter was so integral a part of the tradition of the Apostle that the early church interpreted it as his authoritative word.

The Occasion of First Peter

Pliny the Younger was puzzled. He had been sent to Bithynia, one of the provinces to whose Christians First Peter is addressed, to straighten things out. One of his problems was what to do with those stubborn Christians who absolutely refused even token worship of the emperor. About A.D. 112, seeking official advice, he wrote to the Emperor Trajan:

> Meanwhile this is the course I have taken with those who were accused before me as Christians. I asked them whether they were Christians, and if

they confessed, I asked them a second and a third time with threats of punishment. If they kept to it, I ordered them for execution; for I held no question that whatever it was they admitted, in any case obstinacy and unbending perversity deserve to be punished. . . .

Before long . . . an unsigned paper was presented, which gave the names of many. As for those who said that they neither were nor had ever been Christians, I . . . let them go, since they recited a prayer to the gods at my direction, made supplication with incense and wine to your statue . . . and moreover cursed Christ—things which (so it is said) those who are really Christians cannot be made to do. . . .

The emperor wrote back his approval:

You have adopted the proper course. . . . They are not to be sought out; but if they are accused and convicted they must be punished—yet on this condition, that whoso denies himself to be a Christian, and makes the fact plain by his action, that is, by worshiping our gods, shall obtain pardon . . ., however suspicious his past conduct may be. . . .[10]

Several facts about the situation of Christians are clearly indicated by this correspondence. (1) They are experiencing persecution not only in Rome, but in other places throughout the empire. (2) Just bearing the name of Christian is itself a crime. (3) Though they are not actually sought out by the government, the Christians might be arrested if their pagan neighbors chose to report them. (4) They then faced a simple choice: they could renounce their faith and easily go free; or they could confess that they were Christians and die.

How similar is the situation to which First Peter is written! (1) "Suffering is required of your brotherhood throughout the world" (5:9). It is a "fiery ordeal" (4:12) in which Christians actually share in the very sufferings of Christ himself (4:13). (2) They are "reproached for the name of Christ" (4:14). One might be arrested simply "as a Christian" (4:16). (3) Peter—in fact or in tradition—warns concerning pagan neighbors that they may "speak against you as wrongdoers" (2:12), though he is hopeful that if they maintain friendly conduct among their non-Christian neighbors, they may not need to fear the government (2:13–17; 3:13). (4) But they must be prepared to confess their faith no matter what danger that may bring (3:15–18). In a time of "fiery ordeal," Peter writes to Christians that "the devil prowls around like a roaring lion, seeking some one to devour" (5:8).

The Purpose of First Peter

"I have written briefly to you," the author summarizes at the end, "exhorting and declaring that this [sharing in Christ's sufferings and the Christian hope] is the true grace of God; stand fast in it" (5:12). Clearly, the first purpose of the letter is to help its readers see God's plan and purpose in the persecutions they may experience so that they can face them with courage and hope. "We have been born anew to a living hope" (1:3). "In this you rejoice, though now for a little while you may have to suffer various trials" (1:6). "Set your hope fully upon the grace that is coming to you at the revelation of Jesus Christ" (1:13). "Christ . . . suffered for you, leaving you an example" (2:21). "Do not be surprised at the fiery ordeal which comes upon you to prove you, as though something strange were happening to you. But rejoice in so far as you share Christ's sufferings, that you may also rejoice and be glad when his glory is revealed" (4:12–13).

Secondly, the book is written, apparently to new converts (especially former pagans), as an exhortation to moral living. Christians are to be "holy" (different, separate). "Let the time that is past suffice for doing what the Gentiles like to do, living in licentiousness" (4:3), he pleads. "Do not be conformed to the passions of your former ignorance, but as he who called you is holy, be holy yourselves in all your conduct" (1:14–15). "You were ransomed from the futile ways inherited from your fathers" (1:18). Now these readers are to live as part of the church, "a holy nation" (2:9), following Christ "in his steps" (2:21). Over and over the writer urges his readers to witness to their neighbors by loving conduct.

Finally, though the extent to which one may base interpretations of the letter on this is debated, there are strong hints that the letter is written as a kind of sermon for a baptism, perhaps for use at the Passover-Easter season.[11] Once the church had sent Peter to meet with newly baptized converts in Samaria (Acts 8:14). No Apostle could have visited with every new group being baptized, but by means of this circular letter, something of the Apostle's authoritative voice can be heard by new converts as they are told that "baptism now saves you" (3:21). Some who deny that the whole letter was itself written for use in the actual ceremony of baptism agree that it may well contain fragments of baptismal hymns or liturgies.

Some Comments on First Peter

The word "baptism" occurs only once in First Peter. "The Anchor Bible" translates 1 Peter 3:20–21 in part, "Just this [is the] analogous baptism [that] now saves you. It does not involve putting away the filth of the flesh, but is a pledge of good will to God. [And it saves you] through the resurrection of Jesus Christ."[12] Ideas implied here, however, are repeated themes throughout the whole letter: water, purification, pledge of holy living, salvation, resurrection, and new beginning. It is easy to imagine the use of this letter at an early church baptism.

"Blessed be the God and Father of our Lord Jesus Christ!" the leader cries in his opening praise. His hearers include beginning converts, "born anew to a living hope" (1:3). Through faith they have now obtained salvation (1:9). The whole history of the world has looked forward to this moment (1:10–12).

First Peter
Hope and Holiness in Persecution

"We have been born anew to a living hope. … You are a … royal priesthood, a holy nation" (1:3; 2:9).

1:1 A Call to Hope and to Holiness	2:11 Specific Ethical Instructions for Living as Holy "Priests" in a Pagan World	3:13 Priestly Witness to These Pagans in a Time of Persecution	4:12 That Time of Persecution Has Now Arrived. Do Your Duty in It with Joy and Hope. 5:14
Salutation 1:1-2	Among pagan neighbors 2:11-12	Witness with a clear conscience. 3:13-22	There is joyful meaning in the persecution you face. 4:12-19
Even in persecution, rejoice that you have been born anew to a "living hope." 1:3-9	In relation to the government 2:13-17	Use what little time is left for holy living. 4:1-11	Let each elder and each younger person do his part. 5:1-5
All history has awaited this day. 1:10-12	For servants 2:18-25		Face the persecution with humility, patience, and hope. 5:6-11
So leave your old life behind. 1:13-21	For wives 3:1-6		A closing postscript 5:12-14
And become part of the church, the new, holy priesthood. 1:22—2:10	For husbands 3:7		
	For all 3:8-12		

Author: Peter (at least according to tradition)
Recipients: Christians in what is now Turkey
Date: A.D. 64 (A.D. 112?)
Occasion: Persecution by the Roman government
Purpose: To encourage new converts and to exhort them to holy living

Now, therefore, they are exhorted to live lives of hope and of holiness. They are to "gird up" their minds (1:13). The allusion is to the preparation of the old Israel for the Passover journey out of Egypt and across the sea (Exod. 12:11). It may reflect also the fact that, at least according to the baptismal rite described by Hippolytus of Rome early in the third century, those who were about to be baptized removed their outer clothes. (Men and women were separated for the sacrament.) Together they say the "Our Father," as the New English Bible translates it, the Lord's Prayer (1:17). Now they are purified by the blood, not of the Passover lamb, but of Christ (1:19).

A few commentators suggest that the baptism is to be thought of as actually occurring between verses 21 and 22. The word from the Apostle can therefore resume in a different tense: "Having purified your souls" in this act of baptism "you have been born anew" (1:22–23).

"So put away all malice and all guile" (2:1), the sermon continues, leaving such attitudes behind as the baptized did their old clothes in order to put on the new robes symbolizing their new natures (cf. 1 Cor. 10:2; Gal. 3:27). In the liturgy described by Hippolytus, new "baby" Christians were given a ceremonial bowl of milk to drink following baptism (cf. 1 Peter 2:2).

But now they are no longer called "babies." They are summoned, as it were, from the place of baptism to the communion table, to the altar of sacrifice. "Come to him, to that living stone . . . and like living stones be yourselves built into a spiritual house, to be a holy priesthood" (2:4–5). Once they were pagans, nobodies. Now they are called "priests." The church is built of these people, "a chosen race, a royal priesthood, a holy nation, God's own people" (2:9).

There is a rich, complex imagery in this passage. On the one hand, surely there is intended a reflection of the experience of Peter himself, who had been so changed that he had received a new name, "the Rock." Upon such living stones the church itself was to be built (Matt. 16:13–20). Now these new church members are "living stones" too. But there are also echoes of the experience of Israel, that first people of God. When they had passed through the water of the sea, they came to Mount Sinai and there entered into a convenant pledge in which they were told that they were to become "a kingdom of priests and a holy nation" (Exod. 19:6). These Gentile converts, having also passed through the water, have now joined a holy priesthood.

It was necessary, however, to spell out in more detail what holy, priestly living means. These "aliens and exiles" on their journey are no longer quite at home in the wilderness of the pagan world (2:11). The letter moves on to describe specific areas in which they must act out their holiness. In almost all of these areas the emphasis is on submission, peaceable subordination of their own selfish desires to the concerns of others.

First, they are to "be subject for the Lord's sake to every human institution, . . . the emperor . . ., governors," and so on (2:13–17).

Servants are to be obedient to their masters, as Christ, the Suffering Servant, was obedient and never vengeful. First Peter 1:18–25 clearly echoes the Suffering Servant passage of Isaiah 53. Does it not also reflect the actual memory of Jesus' life and death?

Wives are to show their holiness in their family role and in the inner beauty of their lives (3:1–6).

Husbands equally are to show concern for their wives (3:7).

Turning now to the whole group, the letter summarizes by exhorting them all to love. "Do not return evil for evil," they are told, in words reminiscent of those of Jesus himself (3:8–12; cf. Matt. 5:38–48).

Such passages of *paranaesis* (ethical instruction), addressed specifically to different members of the household, occur so often in the New Testament as to suggest that they may have been a standard part of the oral tradition at baptism (cf. Col. 3:18—4:1; Eph. 5:21—6:9; Titus 2:2–10).

The function of a holy priest is, of course, to be a link between man and God. Built now into the church, these new Christians are to live submissive, loving lives for a purpose; they are to give priestly witness to their neighbors.

They are to be "zealots," it is true, but not "zealots" like the Jews who led pathetic revolts against their Roman persecutors (3:13). Rather, by word and deed they are to manifest Christian love, even to enemies.

This concern for witness to others, even persecutors, leads the author into the most obscure passage in the letter, 1 Peter 3:19–22 (cf. 4:6). In his death, the passage seems to say, Christ entered the world of departed spirits and even there bore witness to the gospel. The pseudepigraphic First Enoch related the spirits who mated with human women and brought the evils of Noah's day (Gen. 6:1–8) to past rulers of this world. If Christ bore witness even to them, the author is saying, his readers ought to witness to those in places of power today, even if in their own deaths. The water of the flood of Noah's day is compared to the water of baptism the hearers have so recently experienced.[13]

The former companions of these new converts will be "surprised" that their old friends "do not now join them in the same wild profligacy" (4:4). But Christians must hold firm in their new way of life, not reverting to pagan immorality in spite of their neighbors' opposition.

The "sermon" closes with an assurance that the *eschaton*, the end, is at hand. Therefore, these church members are to make every act count for God in the few days which remain (4:7–11).

With 1 Peter 4:12 we encounter one of the unexplained puzzles of the book. The "sermon" had seemed to end with the doxology of 4:11. Now, however, it resumes, and the situation seems to be somewhat different. Up until this point, persecution has been presented as a real possibility, but only a possibility. The author has written that "you may have to suffer various trials" (1:6). There is hope that "by doing right you should put to silence the ignorance of foolish men"

(2:15). "Now who is there to harm you if you are zealous for what is right?" the author reassures his readers (3:13). They must be prepared to suffer "if that should be God's will" (3:17). But there is still hope, apparently, that that may not come to pass.

With 1 Peter 4:12, however, the "fiery ordeal" is now coming upon the church. "The same experience of suffering is required of your brotherhood throughout the world" (5:9). "The devil prowls around like a roaring lion" (5:8). There is no longer doubt about it.

Perhaps the first part of the letter was a sermon originally composed by the author earlier. Now he sends it out in writing, adding the last verses in the light of the new, worsened situation.

What can enable these Christians to endure such persecution? There is the sense of the plan of the sovereign God (1:10–12). This is coupled with the apocalyptic conviction that persecution is a necessary part of the expected last stage of history, sometimes called "the tribulations of the Messiah" (4:12–13). There is the example of Christ in suffering (2:21–25). There is the hope of resurrection, based on the memory of Christ's resurrection (1:3, 21; 3:21–22). There is the testing and purification which suffering brings (4:1, 12). There is the sense of sharing in the sufferings of Christ himself (4:13). And there is the eschatological hope: "After you have suffered a little while, the God of all grace, who has called you to his eternal glory in Christ, will himself restore, establish, and strengthen you. To him be the dominion for ever and ever. Amen" (5:10–11).

Second Peter

—Second Peter is "the least valuable of the New Testament writings," says noted biblical scholar E. F. Scott.

—It is surely among the least read, studied, and loved.

—As far back as we can trace, the church doubted that it was really by the Apostle Peter.

—It was among the very last books to be accepted into the canon, with its authority seriously questioned down into the fourth century.

Yet in spite of all the doubts about its authorship and its frightening picture of coming judgment, it did finally become part of the canon. Perhaps the church began to see values in it which need to be rediscovered today.

The doubts were ancient and well founded. As late as the fourth century, Eusebius still contrasted Second Peter with First Peter. The latter was everywhere accepted as by the Apostle. Second Peter, however, he classed as "disputed." It was not rejected in the way the so-called Apocalypse of Peter was (and the Gospel and the Acts attributed to him). But it was not included in the oldest list of canonical books, it is not found in some ancient versions of the New Testament, and until this day most scholars believe that it is the work of a much later writer who modestly and piously attributed his essay to the great leader of the early church.

Here are some of the reasons for doubting that Peter wrote Second Peter.

1) Most early Christian writers did not quote from it. We find no traces of the book before the middle of the second century.

2) It is so different in style, vocabulary, and approach that it is hard to believe that it could be by the same man who wrote First Peter.

3) Its content implies a late date. Paul's writings apparently have been collected and are known to the readers. They are even referred to now as "scripture" (2 Peter 3:1–16). Apparently some years have gone by since "the fathers fell asleep" (3:4); the first generation of Christians has passed away. One major concern of the letter is to deal with the problem that so many years have gone by and Jesus still has not come again. The great purpose of the letter is to remind the readers of the tradition which comes down through the years from the Apostles.

4) The author almost certainly quotes from Jude, itself a relatively late book, and he probably makes use of other New Testament books.

Yet the church did include it—genuinely apostolic or not—in the canon, perhaps because it needed its message.[14]

The Occasion of Second Peter

"There will be false teachers among you, who will secretly bring in destructive heresies" (2:1), Peter is pictured as warning shortly before his death (1:14). In 2:10 the future tense is dropped. Actually these teachers are now already at work. "Bold and wilful, they are not afraid to revile the glorious ones" (2:10). Immoral, "they count it pleasure to revel in the daytime" (2:13). "Forsaking the right way they have gone astray" (2:15).

Precisely what they were teaching is not clear. Some had begun to scoff at the hope of Christ's return (3:3–12). Some had twisted things in Paul's letters (3:16). They had practiced immorality and had attempted to make money by their heretical teaching (2:12, 14). Probably they were among the various Gnostic groups we have previously encountered (see pages 162–167).

Perhaps as late as well into the second century, an orthodox teacher in the tradition of Peter now attempts to warn against these heretics.

The Purpose of Second Peter

"I have written to you . . . that you should remember the predictions of the holy prophets and the commandment of the Lord and Savior through your apostles" (3:1–2). So the writer summarizes his purpose.

The author wishes to remind his readers that there is an orthodox tradition from Christ and the Apostles. Christians must hold to it over against all novel heresies brought in by greedy and immoral heretics. They are especially urged not to lose their faith in the prophecies of the coming again of Christ for judgment and salvation.

Some Comments on Second Peter

It is perhaps a hundred years after Jesus had promised that "The kingdom of

God is at hand" (Mark 1:15). For a century Christians have waited for Christ's return in judgment. "Where is the promise of his coming?" scoffing teachers now demand. "For ever since the fathers fell asleep, all things have continued as they were from the beginning of creation" (3:4). In the name of the authoritative tradition which comes from Peter, leader of the Apostles, Second Peter undertakes to refute these heretics and to encourage orthodox believers.

The letter is written as from a Jewish Christian to Gentile Christians. William Barclay notes that the only other place in which Peter's name appears in the form "Symeon" in the Greek is in Acts 15:14, when Simon Peter helps to open the door for Gentiles to be admitted into the church. After the salutation in verse 1, these Gentile Christians are praised as having "a faith of equal standing" with that of the first Jewish Christians.[15]

There are hints that the letter is intended to appeal to readers who are products of the Greco-Roman culture of their time, influenced by philosophy, especially Stoicism. Readers are instructed to seek knowledge, not "passion," and thereby "become partakers of the divine nature" (1:4), an idea more frequent in Stoic than in Christian literature. The resulting virtues are described in a list much like those advocated in Stoic ethics. The list begins, however, with "faith," and it ends with "love," so that however adapted to appeal to Stoic readers, it is distinctly Christian. The earth, we are told, was "formed out of water" (3:5), an idea which would appeal to readers familiar with the thought of Thales, "the first Greek philosopher." And that the world will be destroyed by fire was an idea as familiar to the Stoics as to Jews and Christians (3:7).

While designed to appeal to readers within a pagan culture, the letter reasserts strongly the authority of the Christian tradition handed down from Peter and the Apostles. Over against "cleverly devised myths" of the heretics (1:16) are set the facts about Jesus. All facts of which the author reminds his readers—such words as "remind" and "remember" are favorites of his—could be learned from the New Testament writings and need not require belief that the author was actually himself the eyewitness Peter, in whose name he writes. The transfiguration is seen as a foretaste of Christ's glory on the coming day of judgment (1:17–18; cf. Matt. 17:18). The basis of sound Christian doctrine, the author insists, must be such facts of Christ and the teachings of the prophets interpreted, not by the whim of any teacher, but according to the Holy Spirit and in the apostolic tradition.

Chapter 2 denounces the alternative to this tradition, the teachings of the immoral heretics. Much of this chapter seems to be an expansion of the book of Jude, which also denounces heretics (see pages 214–217). Here are a few of the many parallels:

Second Peter	Jude
. . . there will be false teachers	For admission has been secretly

Second Peter

The Apostolic Tradition and the Coming Judgment Day

"There will be false teachers among you . . ." (2:1).

"Remember the predictions of the holy prophets and the commandment of the Lord and Savior through your apostles" (3:2).

1:1	2:1	3:1 3:18
Seek the True, Apostolic Knowledge Which Results in Godly Living.	**Beware of the Teachers of Falsehoods.**	**Wait Patiently for the Judgment Day, Avoiding the False Teachers' Immorality and Error.**
True knowledge and the progress in godliness which it produces 1:1–11	A warning: false prophets must be expected. 2:1–3	Though delayed, the great day is surely coming. 3:1–10
Its basis: the divine authority of the apostolic tradition 1:12–21	God's judgment on such people in the past 2:4–10	Therefore wait patiently: living holy lives 3:11–13
	The immorality of such false teachers 2:11–16	And avoiding error 3:14–18
	The judgment upon them 2:17–22	

Author: "Peter" (Most scholars would say a later disciple of Peter writing in his memory and honor.)

Recipients: All Christians

Date: A.D.64? (probably much later, perhaps A.D. 125)

Occasion: False teachings are spreading, and hope of Christ's return is fading.

Purpose: To remind the readers of the authoritative apostolic teaching and to restore hope in the coming again of Christ among you, who will secretly bring in destructive heresies, even denying the Master : . . ., bringing upon themselves swift destruction. . . . And many will follow their licentiousness. (2:1–2)

gained by some who long ago were designated for this condemnation, ungodly persons who pervert the grace . . . into licentiousness and deny our only Master. (v. 4)

. . . God did not spare the angels when they sinned, . . . turning the cities of Sodom and Gomorrah to ashes . . . an example . . . (2:4–6)

And the angels . . . have been kept by him . . . in the nether gloom . . .; just as Sodom and Gomorrah . . . an example . . . (vv. 6–7)

[They] indulge in the lust of defiling passion and despise authority. . . . They are not afraid to revile the glorious ones, whereas angels . . . do not pronounce a reviling judgement upon them. . . . But these, like irrational animals . . . (2:10–12)

. . . these . . . men defile the flesh, reject authority, and revile the glorious ones. But . . . Michael . . . did not presume to pronounce a reviling judgment upon [even the devil] . . . But these men . . . as irrational animals . . . (vv. 8–10)

The heretics are said to respect neither prophets, Apostles, angels, nor even Christ. Bo Reicke, in "The Anchor Bible," speculates that their contempt for authority (2:10) even included political subversion.[16] Second Peter graphically warns of their condemnation at the coming judgment, using symbols derived from Jewish literature popular in that day, including some not found in our Bibles.

To those who have lost faith that that judgment day will ever come, the letter offers several answers: (1) God made the world in the beginning, and he can bring it to an end (3:5–7). (2) God's timetable is not ours. "With the Lord one day is as a thousand years, and a thousand years as one day" (3:8). (3) The reason for the delay is the patience of God, his hope that men will yet repent (3:9). But that day will surely come, unexpectedly, "like a thief" (3:10).

The true believer need not fear, however. The stories of destructive judgment recalled from the past (the flood and the burning of Sodom) also include the stories of rescue for the righteous (Noah and Lot, 2:5–7).

Therefore, though the letter vividly describes judgment, the readers need not lose hope. As true believers, "according to his promise we wait for new heavens and a new earth in which righteousness dwells" (3:13).

Jude

Apparently it was to Jesus' family that the Jerusalem church looked for leadership for nearly a century after his death.

Joseph never participates in the Gospel story after the account in Luke 2 of

Jesus' visit to the Temple at age twelve. Tradition has it that Joseph died while Jesus was still a youth.

Mary, so highly regarded in the Gospels, appears briefly with the disciples of Jesus in the Upper Room after the resurrection (Acts 1:14), then drops out of the story. Perhaps she died soon after Pentecost.

The brothers of Jesus, however, are placed side by side with the Apostles in Acts 1:14. We have seen that James, one of these brothers, became the leader of the Jerusalem church. Two centuries later, Eusebius spoke of him as having been "bishop of Jerusalem" (see pages 198–199). According to Eusibius, after the martyrdom of James, the surviving Apostles and disciples, "with those that were related to our Lord according to the flesh," came together to choose James' successor. They selected Simeon, a cousin of Jesus, who was "bishop" until well into the second century.[17]

Two grandsons of another of Jesus' brothers, Jude, were almost martyred under Domitian. Apparently fearing that as descendants of David they might be involved in some underground rebellion, the authorities interrogated them. They were able to convince their questioners, however, by displaying their calloused hands and describing their thirty-nine acre farm, that they were harmless. The only kingdom to which they laid claim, they assured the judge, was "not of this world." They were dismissed.[18]

The little book of Jude was finally accepted into the canon in part because it came to be regarded as the work of Jude, one of the four brothers of Jesus (Mark 6:3). Actually Jude (or Judas) was a very common name—there were five men of that name in the New Testament—and the author makes no claim to being a brother of the Lord. He does call himself a brother of James, however (v. 1), and it is argued that modesty prevents his boasting of being related to Christ.

Defenders of the tradition argue that no other person named Jude was prominent enough to have his work treasured by the church. (Judas Iscariot is out of the question, of course, and the other Jude among the Twelve was the son, not the brother, of someone named James [Luke 6:16].) Jude's claim to be "brother of James" clearly identifies him as Jesus' brother also, it is argued.

Most scholars, however, note hints that the book is from a time later than the first generation of Christians. Jude urges his readers to "contend for the faith which was once for all delivered to the saints" (v. 3), a concern, like that of the pastoral epistles, for the preservation of correct doctrine handed kown from the past. His readers are urged to "remember . . . the predictions of the apostles of our Lord" (v. 17), as though these were prophecies of leaders of the past now (at a later time) being fulfilled.

Moreover, if the book was indeed by a brother of Jesus and of the "bishop of Jerusalem," James, it seems unlikely that it would have been so little used by early Christian writers and that it would have been so slow in winning a place in the canon.

In any event, it gives us no hint of the kind of information about Jesus of Nazareth we might have hoped for from one who had grown up with Jesus as a brother.[19]

The Occasion and Purpose of Jude

The author had intended, he tells us, to write "of our common salvation," perhaps a sermon summarizing the gospel. But he has now received news that "admission has been secretly gained by . . . ungodly persons" (vv. 3–4), teachers who have perverted the faith. The letter is a ringing denunciation of these heretics in the name of apostolic orthodoxy.

Some Comments on Jude

Second Peter, especially chapter 2, appears to be a revision of Jude (see page 212).

Precisely who the heretics were is not clear. Jude's emphasis on "the only God" (v. 25) suggests the possibility that they taught the Gnostic doctrine that there were two gods, the true God and the evil creator of this world (see pages 162–169). They are said to "deny our only . . . Lord" (v. 4). This may imply that they regarded Christ as did some of the Gnostics, as only one link (though the highest) in the chain between humankind and the true God. These heretics apparently both practiced and encouraged immorality, perhaps arguing, as did Simon the Magician, that since we are under grace, not law, licentiousness will be forgiven (v. 4). (See page 164.) Clearly they rejected orthodoxy and authority (vv. 3, 4, 8, 18, for example).

The body of the book is a thunderous warning of the coming damnation of these heretics. Three examples of judgment are cited from the past. God "destroyed those who did not believe" among the Israelites whom he had liberated from Egypt (v. 5). The angels of Genesis 6 who lusted after human women were damned to hell (v. 6). And the cities of Sodom and Gomorrah were burned for their sins (v. 7; cf. Gen. 19). So, Jude warns, these heretics will be destroyed.

The obscure story in Genesis 6:1–4 concerning the "sons of God" who mated with human women and thus precipitated the flood was elaborated in a non-canonical ("pseudepigraphic") Jewish book called First Enoch, said to be a prophecy composed by the character mentioned in Genesis 5:21–24. The Old Testament itself does not tell us that they were put "in eternal chains in the nether gloom" (v. 6). But First Enoch vividly develops the story.

Verses 8–9 also contain an allusion to another book of popular legend. The non-canonical *Assumption of Moses* told how God had sent the archangel Michael to bury Moses, who died alone (Deut. 34). The devil had tried to claim Moses' body on the grounds that the body was matter and thus the devil's domain, and that Moses was a murderer (Exod. 2:12). Recognizing that the devil was an angel, even though a fallen one, Michael had respectfully refrained from abusing him (v. 8). But the heretics, Jude charges, have not hesitated to revile duly constituted authority. "Woe to them!" (v. 11). They are compared to Cain, the first murderer (Gen. 4:8), to Balaam (Num. 22—24), whom Jewish tradition had come to portray as a villain, and Korah (Num. 16), who led a rebellion against even Moses himself (v. 11).

Again Jude cites, even quotes, First Enoch to support his picture of the coming judgment (vv. 14–15). Many years later, Jerome, who produced the great translation of the Bible into Latin, speculated that the reason that Jude was rejected by many in the early church was because of his use of these non-canonical books.

With its angry denunciations of heretics long dead, whose doctrines we can now only guess at, and with its warnings based on allusions which, however forceful in their own day, are obscure now, Jude is not a favorite book in the twentieth century. But the doxology which forms its two closing verses has been used for centuries in the liturgies of many denominations. It forms a fitting close for this chapter on "Five 'Open Letters.'"

> Now to him who is able to keep you from falling and to present you without blemish before the presence of his glory with rejoicing, to the only God, our Savior through Jesus Christ our Lord, be glory, majesty, dominion, and authority, before all time and now and for ever. Amen.

XIII   *The Johannine Literature*

Now two days later there was the dedication-festival of the idol-temple [of
Artemis at Ephesus]. So while everyone was wearing white, John alone
put on black clothing and went up to the temple; and they seized him and
tried to kill him. . . . But John . . . went upon on a high platform, and said
to them, Men of Ephesus . . . You all say that you have Artemis as your
goddess; so pray in her name that I and I alone, may die; or if you cannot
do this, then I alone will call upon my own God and because of your unbelief I will put you all to death. . .   And while John was saying this, of a
sudden the altar of Artemis split into many pieces, and all the offerings
laid up in the temple suddenly fell to the floor, and its goodness was broken, and so were more than seven images; and half the temple fell down,
so that the priest was killed at one stroke as the roof came down. Then the
assembled Ephesians cried out, ' There is but one God, the God of
John!''[1]

There is a happy ending to this story. Through the faith of one of John's followers, the pagan priest who had been killed was raised from the dead. But, John told
him, he still was not really living. Believe in Christ, the Apostle urged, ''and you
shall live for all eternity.'' ''And then and there he believed on the Lord Jesus,
and from that time kept company with John.''

Actually, that tale is a bit of pious fiction, written probably no earlier than a
century after the death of John. It is found in a kind of holy novel about this ''Son
of Thunder'' called the Acts of John. One cannot really learn from it anything
about the destruction of the pagan temple at Ephesus, which certainly did not
occur during John's lifetime.

What it does tell us is something of the high place which the Apostle John had
in early Christian tradition. It probably does preserve some memory that the
Apostle taught in Ephesus and had followers and disciples. It is fact that in John's
name tradition was to group five books of our New Testament.

More New Testament books are attributed to John than to any other single
writer except Paul. This, of course, does not mean that John, the son of Zebedee,
and one of the twelve Apostles, actually penned them all. We have seen that

Timothy and Silas assisted Paul in writing some of his letters, that First Peter came to us "by Silvanus," and that Hebrews was admitted to the canon in part because it was attributed to Paul, even though he probably had nothing to do with its composition. It is widely held that more than one writer was involved in the production of such varied books as Revelation, the Gospel According to John, and the three Epistles of John. In all probability we are dealing with a school of disciples which grew up around the Apostle and with a tradition which grew up around his memory. As a matter of fact, none of the five claims to be by an Apostle. But it was to this great leader that the church later attributed the authority of some of its best-loved—and most puzzling—sacred books.

In this final chapter we now turn to them.

Revelation

If one had to describe certain passages from Revelation in one word, that word might well be "weird."

A great beast rises from the sea. It has ten horns and seven heads, each horn having a crown, and the beast is said to combine the characteristics of a leopard, a bear, and a lion! It is associated with a dragon and with another beast having two horns like a lamb and a voice like a dragon. A great prostitute is seated upon many waters and at the same time on a dragon and also on a beast which has seven heads, each of which is seven hills! From above, a Lamb looks down—or is it a warrior on a white horse?—and prepares to conquer. Holy martyrs cry from heaven for vengeance. What is the reader to make of all this?

One solution has been to ignore or even to reject Revelation. After all, its traditional attribution to the Apostle John is dubious. The book names its writer as John (Rev. 1:1, 4, 9; 22:8), but there were many men of that name. The writer nowhere calls himself an Apostle, but rather seems to speak of the twelve Apostles with the reverence of a later Christian (21:14). As early as about A.D. 200, Bishop Dionysius of Alexandria noted that Revelation was so completely different from the Gospel According to John in style, vocabulary, and thought, that the two could not possibly be by the same author. If Revelation was by the Apostle, it is strange that the church was so slow in accepting it into the canon. As late as the fourth century, Eusebius wrote that there was still much dispute about the authority of Revelation. He himself was not at all sure that it was by the Apostle.[2] It was one of the last books to be admitted to the canon. Luther loved the Bible, but he held Revelation in low esteem. Calvin wrote commentaries on almost every book but Revelation, admitting that he did not understand it. Swiss Reformation leader Zwingli announced, "Revelation is not a book of the Bible."

By contrast, many, including some fanatics, have found Revelation a kind of "happy hunting ground" for fanciful interpretations, professing to discover in its symbols predictions of events in their own times which showed that the end of the world was at hand. Tensions mounted all over Europe as the year A.D. 1000 approached. Surely this must be the end of "the millennium," the thousand years mentioned in Revelation 20:4! At the time of the Reformation, radical groups were sure that the prophesied end was at hand. Several denominations were born in the nineteenth century out of computations which indicated to their satisfaction that the predictions of Revelation were then taking place. Shortly before World War I, thousands were persuaded, in part on the basis of Revelation, to accept the slogan "Millions now living will never see death," convinced that Christ would return within their lifetime. The present writer remembers the evangelists of his youth who saw the approaching World War II as clearly foretold in Revelation. The number of the beast, 666 (Rev. 13:18), was "clearly" shown to be a cryptogram for the name of Mussolini, and later, as he became less important than his German disciple, for Hitler. Russia and Germany were Gog and Magog (20:8). Armageddon, the final battle, was at hand.

As late as 1970, Hal Lindsey's *The Late Great Planet Earth* carried on this tradition, its sales totaling more than a million copies.[3] It identified the ten horns of the beast (13:1) with the (then) ten nations of the European Common Market, which was in the news at that time. Lindsey found the People's Republic of China, which he called "The Yellow Menace," and the pan-Arab union, which the late president Nasser of Egypt was in the sixties attempting to form, predicted in Revelation's picture of the very last days. The "great harlot" was said by Lindsey to be the Methodist, Presbyterian, Baptist, Episcopalian, Lutheran, and other churches which form the National and World Councils of Churches! It seemed obvious to thousands of Lindsey's followers—and to followers of others of like mind—that those living in 1970 were all members of what the title of another of Lindsey's best-sellers was to call the "Terminal Generation."

How Lindsey's successors will reinterpret Revelation to show it predicting the news events of subsequent decades cannot yet be foreseen, of course. There is a sense, however, in which all these "millenarian" interpreters have been correct. If one asks the writer of Revelation about the time schedule for his predictions, his own answer is quite clear. The very first verse of the book says that it is about things which "must soon take place" (1:1). The book ends with the promise of Christ, "Surely I am coming soon." John's readers were to live then as those who might encounter Christ's judgment and deliverance at any moment. His readers then, and by implication his readers in every age who read him with faith, are expected to respond, "Amen. Come, Lord Jesus!" (22:20.)

To get at what John actually meant by his strange figures, however, it is essential to remember two things which we have noted earlier. In chapter 1 certain principles of interpretation were laid down, and we have tried consistently to follow them. One of these was that any book must be interpreted in the light of its historical context. Revelation, like any other New Testament book, was written in a certain historical situation, to readers in that situation; knowing that occasion will help us to understand the letter. Whatever its lessons for subsequent ages, we must try first to see what it must have meant to those seven churches to which it is addressed.

Second, Revelation is a book typical of what is called "apocalyptic literature." On pages 21–22 the characteristics of that literature were described, and the reader should review those pages now. Many, many such books have come down to us, from both Christian and Jewish sources. Almost all describe events happening at the time the book is written as having been prophesied by some great figure of the past. Written in times of persecution, almost all picture cosmic catastrophes and conflicts as now beginning. Almost all indicate that victory and judgment by God are at hand. Almost all describe these things in symbolic language and as seen from the perspective of heaven.

Revelation accepts this general framework and takes its figures from Daniel, Ezekiel, and other apocalyptic works. The reader, however, must look for the Christian meaning which the writer has poured into this ancient mold. It is the church which he sees persecuted, and it is Jesus Christ whom he expects to come and conquer in the end.

The writer tells us that his name was John (1:1, 4, 9; 22:8). He makes no claim, however, to being John the Apostle. Indeed, he seems to look back upon the Twelve with respect (21:14). His vocabulary, thought, and style are so different from those of the Gospel According to John that they can scarcely be by the same author. If Revelation were by the Apostle, it would probably not have been so long delayed in receiving acceptance into the canon.

But who the author was is of little importance in a book of this type. Had it been an account of the life of Jesus, it would matter a great deal whether it was by one of the Twelve. But it is an account of mystic visions. Such visions do not derive their authority from the one who receives them, but from the One who gives them.

The Occasion of Revelation

Consistent ancient tradition dated Revelation as having been written during the persecution of the church under the emperor Domitian, thus probably A.D. 90–96.

The Roman historian Tacitus tells how, earlier, Nero had blamed Christians for the burning of Rome, which Nero himself may have started.

> Wanton cruelty marked their execution. Covered with skins of wild beasts they were torn in pieces by dogs, and thus perished; many were crucified, or burned alive, and even set on fire to serve as an illumination by night, after daylight had expired. Nero had offered his own gardens for the spectacle . . . To glut the cruelty of one man . . . they were being destroyed.[4]

Now, thirty years later, it seemed that Nero had come to life again to persecute the church not only in Rome, but all over the world. The fourth-century

Christian historian Eusebius describes the persecution of the nineties in these words:

> Domitian, indeed, having exercised his cruelty against many, and unjustly slain no small number of noble and illustrious men at Rome, and having, without cause, punished vast numbers of honourable men with exile and the confiscation of their property, at length established himself as the successor of Nero, in his hatred and hostility to God. He was the second that raised a persecution against us. . . . In this persecution, it is handed down by tradition, that the apostle and evangelist John, who was yet living, in consequence of his testimony to the divine word, was condemned to dwell on the island of Patmos. . . . Tertullian also has mentioned Domitian thus: "Domitian . . . was, in fact, a limb of Nero for cruelty."[5]

For entertainment Domitian used to spend hours sticking sharp points through the bodies of flies! He murdered friends and even relatives. It did seem that Nero had come again, worse than ever.

John writes that "the devil is about to throw some of you into prison" (2:10). He writes of those "who have come out of the great tribulation" (7:14). The "great harlot," "Babylon" (seated on seven hills and hence surely standing for Rome, the city set on seven hills), is "drunk with the blood of the saints and the blood of the martyrs of Jesus" (17:6). He sees "the souls of those who had been beheaded for their testimony to Jesus and for the word of God, and who had not worshiped the beast or its image" (20:4). John is obviously writing in a time of terrible persecution.

The reason for this martyrdom is indicated in the verse just quoted. Beastly Rome had now demanded not only obedience, which Christians had always carefully given, but worship of the emperor. The cult of emperor-worship had been growing. But it reached its climax with Domitian, who attempted to enforce it throughout the empire. He decreed that all his official proclamations should begin, "Our lord and god orders this to be done." Shrines were set up, some of them in the cities to whose churches Revelation was addressed. The persecution was more active than some later attacks described on pages 204–205.

Among those arrested, apparently, was the author of Revelation himself. "I John, your brother, who share with you in Jesus the tribulation and the kingdom and the patient endurance, was on the island called Patmos on account of the word of God and the testimony of Jesus," he begins (1:9). Tourists are still shown the traditional site of this preacher's island prison.

The Purpose of Revelation

"Be faithful unto death, and I will give you the crown of life" (2:10). "He who conquers, I will grant him to sit with me on my throne" (3:21). Over and over, in the letters to the seven churches, the risen Christ makes some promise of this kind for persecuted Christians (cf. 2:7, 17, 26; 3:5, 12).

John writes to help his readers view the persecution they face from the perspective of heaven. He writes to help them see it from the perspective of the One who can say, "I am the Alpha and the Omega, the beginning and the end" (21:6; cf. 1:8; 22:13). He writes to help them see it from the perspective of followers of the One who was himself martyred, but who has now risen to glory.

He writes in this strange, figurative, apocalyptic style because it was familiar to his readers. But it may be that he uses it partly because it was a kind of code which would attract less attention from Roman police. To predict with joy the downfall of Rome would be treason. To speak of the destruction of a "beast" or "Babylon" might seem harmless enough to a confused Roman censor. There is a story of a letter sent to a former missionary from Christians in Communist China in the days of persecution soon after the revolution there. The letter consisted of a recital of the Marxist teachings against religion. But it ended with one word which slipped by the censors: "Emmanuel" (Matt. 1:23),which means "God is with us"! This is the spirit of Revelation. The book is written as a kind of secret, coded word of encouragement to Christians who may soon be going to die for their faith rather than worship the emperor.

Some Comments on Revelation

From the first chapter the author warns us that we are not to take his words literally, but as symbols. He reports a vision of the risen Christ in all his majesty, but this is not a portrait of the actual physical appearance of the human Jesus of Nazareth. Little children would hardly be attracted to this figure with a sword protruding from this mouth! (Contrast Mark 10:14.) It is carefully explained that the seven lampstands are symbols of the seven churches to whom the letter is addressed (1:20), and much of the other symbolism is clear. Christ's eyes are like flames, penetrating everything. The feet are like brass, in contrast to the image of this world's empires described in Daniel as having feet of clay (Dan. 2:33), a foundation sure to collapse. Most important, this cosmic Christ stands among the churches and holds their guardian angels in the hollow of his hand (1:12–20)!

There follow seven quite straightforward letters to the seven individual churches to which the book is addressed. Though they may be representative of the whole church of this day, these are real churches in real communities, and the letters deal with their real problems. The very popular *Scofield Reference Bible*, many of whose notes have been found helpful by thousands of users since its publication in 1917, proposes that these letters are to be interpreted in three ways. They are, as stated above, letters to these particular churches for their time. This is true. They are also of value to all churches in all ages. Christians have discovered this in their own experience. But Dr. Scofield also maintained that each of these letters referred to the church in a given period of history. Thyatira, for

Revelation

The Apocalypse: A Symbolic Vision of Catastrophic Conflicts and the Final Victory of Christ

"Come up hither, and I will show you what must take place after this" (4:1).

1:1 Opening Vision of Christ, and Letters to Seven Churches	4:1 A Vision of Heaven	6:1 The Seven Seals of the Scroll of Destiny	8:1 The Seven Trumpets Sounded by Angels	11:1 Christians Are Persecuted All Over the Earth	15:1 Seven Bowls of Troubles Are Poured on Earth.	21:1 22:21 The End: The New Heaven and the New Earth
Introduction 1:1-8	The scene around God's throne 4	Six seals of troubles opened 6	Six plagues fall on earth. 8—9	A "beast" battles God's witnesses. 11	Seven catastrophes, climaxed by the fall of "Babylon" 15—16	John's final vision of a transformed, perfected cosmos 21:1—22:5
A vision of the exalted Christ 1:9-20	The scroll of destiny being opened by the Lamb (Christ) 5	But God's people are protected 7	But a scroll of yet further prophecy is given. 10	A "dragon" pursues a "mother" (God's people). 12	The destruction of "Babylon" (Rome) 17—18	Closing blessings and words of assurance 22:6-21
Letters to seven churches about their particular needs 2—3				"Beasts" of political and religious power war on God's people. 13	The conquering Christ revealed 19	
				But the "saints" are saved. 14	The millennium and final victory over Satan accomplished 20	

Author: "John" (traditionally the Apostle, but this is not stated)
Recipients: Seven churches in what is now Turkey
Date: A.D. 96
Occasion: Widespread persecution of Christians by Rome
Purpose: To inspire Christians to endure to the end through a vision of Christ's final victory

example, is said to stand for the medieval church, dated from A .ɪ. 500 to A .ɪ. 1500. Sardis, according to Scofield, is the Reformation church. We are now in the Laodicean age, the age of apostasy.[6] There is not one shred of evidence in Scripture for this scheme, which is entirely imposed upon the Bible by the imagination of Dr. Scofield. This view, however, has been widely circulated as though it were scriptural. Rather, each letter in Revelation 2—3 is to a clearly identifiable church in what is now Turkey, encouraging it in a persecution going on at the time the letter was written.

In chapter 4 the writer is summoned to look at the world scene from the perspective of heaven. Again, there is no biblical evidence that the writer here has in mind a "rapture" in which all Christians are caught up into heaven, as Dr. Scofield proposed. It is the writer himself who, from his prison, is given a vision of heaven. He sees God seated on the heavenly throne, described in imagery derived in large part from the Jewish scriptures. Precious stones and symbolic animals indicate that all creation praises the Creator, and twenty-four elders, the representatives of the church, sing his praises. The rainbow (4:3) around the throne is the reminder of the covenant (Gen. 9:12–13).

Chapter 5 centers on one other symbolic animal, the Lamb, who is, of course, Jesus Christ (John 1:29). Only he can open the seals of the scroll on which is written the destiny of the world.

As the seals in turn are opened, the writer gazes down from heaven upon the catastrophes which now befall the earth. When the first astronauts landed on the moon, the most fascinating pictures that they took were not those of the barren moonscape; they were pictures of earth, seen from that transcendent perspective. So now Revelation describes in vivid imagery a succession of terrible times coming upon the earth. But it does so from the new vantage point of heaven.

These are described, as the outline on page 225 shows, in terms of seven seals, the seventh of which turns into seven trumpets, the last of which but introduces seven bowls. Each seems to present troubles worse than its predecessor. It would seem to be a mistake to try to take these literally. John is an artist who, with his series of sevens (a holy number to the Jews), paints a growing picture of spreading chaos.

For example, the Four Horsemen of the Apocalypse (6:1–8) seem to stand for conquest, war, famine, and death, a hellish sequence which has recurred in every age. Typically, however, the fifth seal shows the martyrs safe beneath the throne of God (6:9–11). Nature itself begins to fall apart with the sixth seal (6:12–17), but once again we are assured of the salvation of those whom God has "sealed" (ch. 7). "And God will wipe away every tear from their eyes" (7:17).

Again, it would be to miss the biblical symbolism if one were to take literally the number "a hundred and forty-four thousand"—twelve times twelve thousand (7:4). Twelve is the number of completion in Hebrew poetry, and as such it is used repeatedly in Revelation (12:1; 21:12; 22:2, for example).

Chapters 8—10 repeat the same kind of scene, with the seven trumpets heralding troubles even more intense than those of the seals. Yet these horrors at their worst last only "forty-two months" (11:2), only half of "seven" years, the period of perfection on God's timetable.

In chapters 12—15 the sequence of seals, trumpets, and bowls seems to be interrupted while we are introduced to strange creatures which appear to symbolize very real dangers John's readers were encountering. They harass "a woman clothed with the sun" (12:1) who gives birth to a child. Apparently she stands for the people of God, the Jews, from whom Christ was born, and the church, pursued through the "wilderness" of this world.

One pursuer is a red dragon, clearly identified as the Devil or Satan (12:3, 9). In league with him is "a beast rising out of the sea, with ten horns and seven heads" (13:1), who receives authority on earth from the beast (Satan). Apparently this is the Roman Empire, since in 17:10 we are told clearly that what is represented here is a series of kings. Domitian was, in fact, the seventh emperor ("head") of the Roman Empire to establish any permanent reign. The ten horns are also kings, the reason apparently being that following Nero there were three rulers whose reigns were so brief that they are here regarded as only "horns," not "heads." Note that all have crowns to show that they stand for kings (13:1). "One of its heads seemed to have a mortal wound, but its mortal wound was healed" (13:3). This apparently refers to the idea of the return of Nero, feared in popular thought, much as after World War II it was rumored that Hitler was not dead and would someday return. In a sense Domitian, as we have seen, could himself be regarded as a kind of reincarnation of Nero.

Yet a third beastly creature appears in 13:11, making all the earth worship the beast from the sea. This would appear to be a reference to the agency of the emperor-worship cult, now seeking to force every resident of the empire as a patriotic duty to worship Caesar as "lord and god." Marvelous ingenuity has been exercised through the centuries to identify this beast who has the cryptic number 666 (13:18). The most likely explanation is that the letters of the name Neron, given their value as numbers—Romans did not use arabic digits in those days—add up to 666. If one takes the other form of the name, Nero, the total is 616, a number found in some manuscripts instead of 666.

In spite of these threats, chapter 14 again gives assurance of the superior power of divine protection for God's people.

Seven bowls now shower seven plagues on this world (15–16). With the sixth we are prepared for the great final conflict between God and the forces of Satan. "Armageddon" (16:16) apparently refers to the area of Megiddo, where many of the great battles of Hebrew history were fought. That bloody plain was far more a symbol to the Jews than Gettysburg is to Americans or Waterloo to Europeans. The concept of a final conflict is standard in apocalyptic literature.

As the forces assemble, we meet the "great harlot" (17:1), cryptically but clearly identified by the fact that she sits on seven hills (17:9). Rome was known as the city on seven hills. Thus we find arrayed against the church the Roman Empire, the emperor-worship cult, and now the city of Rome itself.

Yet already (chapter 18) an angel sings a taunting song of victory over this "Babylon." Babylon was the imperial city which was the oppressor of God's people in the Old Testament; it is here a symbol for Rome in the New. "Fallen, fallen is Babylon the great!" (18:2).

A final horseman appears in 19:11–16, this one being Jesus Christ himself. Under his leadership Satan and all his hosts are thrown into hell (19:20). The victory is won!

Perhaps the most debated chapter in the Bible is Revelation 20. Early in church history some forms of "chilianism" or "millenarianism," taking this chapter literally, were branded as heresy. Throughout history, however, many devout and scholarly Christians have continued to take it quite literally. They have expected Christ to come to earth, help lead a big physical battle in which Satan is defeated, and then set up an actual kingdom on this material earth, with Jerusalem as its capital city, for a period of exactly one thousand years. "Millennium" means one thousand years, and those who expect the coming of Christ before such a thousand-year period on earth are often called "premillennialists." After the one thousand year period, Satan is to be released briefly. Then he will be defeated again, and there will be the final judgment and the new heaven and the new earth.

Since the days of Augustine, most Christians have understood this chapter figuratively. Satan was "bound" with the first coming of Christ, and the "thousand years" of Christ on this earth, according to this view, is the period of the church, his kingdom on earth here and now. In the end it will be replaced by the transcendent new heaven and new earth.

What was in John's mind may be more nearly the following: Hebrew eschatology sometimes pictured the reign of the Messiah as on this earth, sometimes as completely transcending this domain of space and time. John has combined these two views. First there is a special reward for the martyrs. Their outstanding devotion gives them a thousand years of reign on earth with Christ before believers who have not had to pay such a price receive their reward. It is to be noted that the thousand years of ruling with Christ is limited to "those who had been beheaded for their testimony to Jesus and for the word of God, and who had not worshiped the beast" (20:4). Probably all that is meant here is a beautiful way of saying to those who are suffering most that they will have their special reward. To take Revelation literally here, when its figurative character is so clear elsewhere, is to be inconsistent in one's interpretation.

One must also emphasize that the millennium is not mentioned anywhere else in Scripture and therefore should not be made central to one's doctrine, however it is interpreted.

The final scene in Revelation (chapters 21—22) is an artistic picture of the new heaven and the new earth. The church, the new Jerusalem, is pictured as the bride of Christ, as Israel was the Lord's "bride" in the Old Testament (Jer. 31:32) and as Paul had spoken of the church (Eph. 5:21–33). The twelves, the number of completion and perfection, abound in the description of the city. All now at last is peace and glory.

There is one final note concerning the style of Revelation which is of great importance for understanding the book: Revelation is full of songs. A glance through it in any modern translation will show many lines printed as poetry. The heavenly court around the throne is pictured as singing, "Holy, holy, holy" (4:8). From that point on, we find song after song.

Donald George Miller used to tell his classes of a student who complained, "I don't understand Revelation, but every time I read it I feel like singing." "That is understanding it!" was the reply.

Thus it is not surprising that the classic commentary on Revelation is not a book, but part of an oratorio. Handel set to music verses from Revelation to produce his "Hallelujah Chorus":

> Hallelujah! For the Lord God omnipotent reigneth.
> The kingdom of this world is become
> The kingdom of our Lord, and of his Christ,
> And he shall reign for ever and ever.
> King of kings, and Lord of lords,
> Hallelujah! (Cf. Rev. 19:6 and 11:15, 19:16.)

First John

According to tradition, James was so far removed from the pleasures of this world that he never took a bath. By contrast, we are told that John did bathe. Once, however, according to Eusebius, John jumped from the bath and ran shouting into the street. The heretic Cerinthus had entered the bathhouse, and John feared that at any moment the roof might fall in judgment upon that teacher of false doctrine![7]

It is not necessary to take that story as historic fact in order to recognize the truth it dramatized. First John is written to help its readers distinguish between true and false versions of the Christian faith. It is a warning against Gnostic heresy, of which Cerinthus was one teacher.

The letter is anonymous. Tradition ascribes it to John the Apostle and son of Zebedee. The letter is so similar in thought and language to the Fourth Gospel that it must be either by the same author or at least by someone of the same "Johannine school." There are hints, however, that the epistle, with its strong effort to combat Gnosticism, is in part endeavoring to correct misunderstandings which sprang from the Fourth Gospel's repeated use of Gnostic-like words and concepts.[8]

The Occasion of First John

"Now many antichrists have come," the author writes. "They went out from us, but they were not of us" (1 John 2:18–19). Evidently these "antichrists" who have split off from the church are false teachers. "Many false prophets have gone out into the world." (4:1).

Something of what these false teachers taught can be inferred from what seem to be quotations from them scattered through the letter. Apparently they claimed to "have fellowship" with God (1:6), to "have no sin" (1:8; cf. 1:10), to "know" God in some special way (2:4), to be "in the light" (2:9), and to "love God" (4:20). Evidently they claimed perfection, piety, and the enlightenment of divine knowledge. Yet they showed little concern for their brothers in the Christian fellowship (2:9; 3:14–15; 4:20–21; etc.) had now abandoned them (2:18–19). The writer regards them, in spite of their boasted "knowledge," as living sinful lives (2:4, 19; 3:8–10; for example).

Their Christology (their doctrine concerning who Jesus Christ is) was heretical, too. "Who is the liar but he who denies that Jesus is the Christ?" (2:22) our writer demands bluntly. Probably these teachers professed to believe in "Christ," but they did not want to identify "Christ" with the man "Jesus." According to the ancient scholar Irenaeus, Cerinthus

> represented Jesus as having not been born of a virgin, but as being the son of Joseph and Mary according to the ordinary course of human generation. . . . Morever, after his baptism, Christ descended upon him in the form of a dove from the Supreme Ruler, and that then he proclaimed the unknown Father, and performed miracles. But at last Christ departed from Jesus, and that then Jesus suffered and rose again, while Christ remained impassible, inasmuch as he was a spiritual being.[9]

Believing that the physical is evil, these "enlightened" and "spiritual-minded" Gnostics denied a genuine incarnation, the belief that in Jesus, the Christ had really died for us. Later the term "Docetists" (from the Greek word *dokein,* "to seem) was applied to heretics who proposed that Christ only *seemed* to be a real man. If it is not the heresy of Cerinthus specifically, it is at least this general kind of error which John is attacking.

The Purpose of First John

"I write this to you about those who would deceive you," the author tells his readers (2:26). His repeatedly expressed concern is to provide tests by which the Christian may distinguish true knowledge *(gnosis)* from its false imitation. "By this we know, . . ." he writes over and over, in one form or anorther (see 2:5; 3:10, 14, 16, 19; 4:2, 13; 5:2; for example). The Greek word *ginoskein* ("to know") occurs twenty-five times in First John, and the similar word *oida* occurs

First John
Love: The Test of True Christianity

"We know that we have passed out of death into life, because we love the brethren" (3:14).

1:1	2:18	3:1	4:1 5:21
A Brief Written Summary of the True Christian Message	**A Warning Against the Teachers of a False Message**	**The Life of Love for all Abiding in the True Fellowship of the Family of God**	**How to Tell the Truth from the False**
Prologue — the basis of that message: the incarnation in the real man Jesus 1:1-4	Heretics have split off from the fellowship 2:18-25	God accepts us as his children. 3:1-3	The doctrinal test: true Christians confess that Jesus Christ has come in the flesh 4:1-6
Our need for the message: we are all sinners. 1:5-10	A plea that the readers will remain in the fellowship and in true Christianity 2:26-29	Children of God are characterized by right living. 3:4-10	The test of love: those born into God's family as his children love their brothers 4:7-21
The good news of the message: Jesus Christ saves us from sin 2:1-2		The essence of right living is love. 3:11-18	The victory God gives his children through faith 5:1-5
The proper response to the message: obedience, love, and the rejection of worldliness 2:3-17		Living as God's children, we pray with confidence in our Father, seek to please him through love, and have his Spirit in us. 3:19-24	The guarantees of the true faith: the experience of the Spirit, the pledge of baptism, and the fact of Jesus' death 5:6-12
			Postscript repeating some themes 5:13-21

Author: Unnamed (according to tradition, John)
Recipients: Christians who may be tempted by these false teachings
Date: c. A.D. 100?
Occasion: False teachers have caused a split in the church (2:19)
Purpose: To guide the readers to continue in the true faith, which is manifested in love (2:26)

fifteen times. Seventeen times the letter says "we know", and twelve times the readers are assured that "you know."

John's concern, however, in contrast to that of the Gnostics, is not just intellectual. "My little children, I am writing this to you so that you may not sin" (2:1). He knows that the life of love ranks with sound doctrine among the tests of true Christianity. Over and over he points his readers to these two tests: a true belief in Jesus and a life of obedience to God through love for one's brothers.[10]

Some Comments on First John

Commentators agree on only one thing about outlining First John: the task is impossible. Over and over the author repeats his major themes, saying the same thing in new ways. The figure of a spiral has often been used to describe the structure of the letter. It goes around and around, yet it rises as it repeats. The outline given on page 231 may be useful, however, for pointing to some main ideas of the epistle.

It begins with a prologue much like that of the Gospel According to John 1:1–18. The basis of the true Christian message is the genuine incarnation, the material, physical fact of the real human Jesus. "That . . . which we have seen with our eyes . . .and touched with our hands . . . we . . . proclaim to you" (1:1–3). A later Gnostic work, by contrast, falsely pictured John as saying that sometimes when he touched Christ his hand could pass through Christ's body as though it were not really there. This author will have nothing to do with such Gnostic contempt for the material world. His down-to-earth gospel rests, he begins, on historic fact. William Temple, late archbishop of Canterbury, is said to have called Christianity "the most materialistic religion in the world."

The problem we face, as First John presents it, is not matter, and it is not ignorance. It is sin. In First John "light," a favorite word of the Gnostics, is not the "enlightenment" of knowledge of which they boasted. To "walk in the light" is not to know something, but to be something, to live in a certain way. Though the Gnostics may have boasted that they had achieved perfection, 1 John 1:5–10 realistically protests that we all walk in darkness because we all sin.

Jesus Christ saves us from sin. The proper response to that salvation is to seek to avoid further sinning (2:1–17). The readers of this letter have no need for some additional special "knowledge." Knowing the gospel message, they already know the truth (2:21).

Set over against that basic Christian "message" (1:5) is the teaching against which this letter is written (2:18–29). Throughout the letter tests are given for distinguishing true Christianity from false. "Test the spirits," the readers are urged (4:1).

One test is doctrinal. "By this you know the Spirit of God: every spirit which confesses that Jesus Christ has come in the flesh is of God." (4:2). Gnostics would be horrified at that use of the word "flesh" (cf. 2:23; 4:15; 5:1, 12).

A second tes: is righteous living. "And by this we may be sure that we know him" (have real ¿nosis), "if we keep his commandments" (2:3; cf. 3:10, 24; 5:3; etc.).

The most important commandment, of course, is the commandment to love. "We know that we have passed out of death into life, because we love the brethren" (3:14; cf. 2:10–11; 3:23; 4:7, 16, 20–21). That verse is probably the best summary of the message of this letter. Any claim to Christianity which does not manifest itself in active concern for others is a lie (4:20)!

That love has its roots in the nature of God himself. "God is light" (1:5), as the Gnostics knew. But "God is love" (4:8, 16). That is a distinctly Christian description of the character of God.

Indeed, the author of this little book, in showing the difference between true Christianity and its Gnostic perversion, has shown the basic difference between Christianity and all other religions. In many ways Christianity is much like Hinduism, Buddhism, and Islam, but there are at least two points at which Christianity is unique: (1) Christianity takes love as its ultimate concern. It announces that God himself is love, and it summarizes its ethical demand in response to that God in one word: love. (2) Christianity proclaims the real, historic person Jesus as the incarnation of that God of love and is centered around him.

Thus, First John can summarize much of Christianity in one very brief sentence: "We love, because he first loved us" (4:19).

Second John

John was a frail old man, says the legend told by Jerome, but he was still loved by his congregation at Ephesus. At length they had to carry him to the church services. Repeatedly they would ask him to preach, but he would only reply, "Little children, let us love one another."

"Tell us more," they would beg him. Would he not tell them other things about the Lord?

"Little children, let us love one another," he would simply repeat. "That is his commandment; it is enough."

"I beg you . . . not as though I were writing a new commandment, but the one we have had from the beginning, that we love one another" (v. 5). This is the heart of the little letter called Second John. The command is not new, indeed, being a repeated theme of First John and of the Fourth Gospel (cf. 1 John 3:23; 4:7, 21; John 15:12; etc.).

In fact, the second letter of John seems to be largely a brief summary of the first. (see above, pages 229–233). Again, there is encouragement for true belief (v. 4; cf. 2 John 2:21–23). There is again a warning against false teachers, "deceivers" who "have gone out into the world, men who will not acknowledge the coming of Jesus Christ in the flesh" (v. 7; cf. 1 John 4:2). Apparently these are the same "Docetics" heretics denounced in 1 John 2:18–27 (see above, p.

230). The writer's hope is that his readers will "abide" in the true faith (v. 9; cf. 1 John 2:27–28; 3:24; 4:15).

It may be pleasant to imagine that the letter is written by "the elder" (v. 1) to his wife. Almost certainly, however, "the elect lady" (v. 1) is a beautiful figure for some particular church beloved by "the elder." The last verse gives greetings from the "children" of the elect lady's "sister," almost certainly meaning the members of one congregation greeting another. The church is becoming a worldwide "family."

Who was this "elder?" Eusebius quotes from Papias' mention of one "John the Presbyter," a second, respected leader of the church at Ephesus, a younger contemporary of the Apostle John.[11] Third John is also attributed to "the elder." Perhaps this man is the author of all three epistles and even of the Gospel According to John. The letters themselves, however, do not name their writer, and we cannot with any assurance do so either (see below, pages 240–243).

Verses 10–11 touch on what became a problem in the church in the second century, hospitality for itinerant evangelists and teachers. For light on that problem we must turn to Third John.

Third John

Paul was not the last Christian teacher to go from city to city needing some place to stay in each town. By the middle of the second century, hospitality for such traveling evangelists had become a problem. Some were apparently a nuisance, overstaying their welcome. And how were true teachers, worthy of free room and board, to be recognized?

In *The Teaching of the Twelve Apostles*, often called the *Didache*, a manual on church order written in that period, we read:

> Everyone "who comes" to you "in the name of the Lord" must be welcomed. Afterward, when you have tested him, you will find out about him, for you have insight into right and wrong. If it is a traveler who arrives, help him all you can. But he must not stay with you more than two days, or if necessary, three. If he wants to settle with you and is an artisan, he must work for his living. If, however, he has no trade, use your judgment in taking steps for him to live with you as a Christian without being idle. If he refuses to do this, he is trading on Christ. You must be on your guard against such people.[12]

Third John deals with a related problem. In this little letter "the elder" writes to his friend, a respected leader in some church, Gaius, apparently asking him to provide hospitality for a traveling teacher, Demetrius. (Perhaps Demetrius carried this note as a letter of introduction.) Someone else in the church, by contrast, a man named Diotrephes, "who likes to put himself first" (v. 9), has refused to receive such teachers when they come from "the elder." He has even excommunicated those who have entertained these travelers and has refused to accept "the elder's" authority, and apparently may ignore a letter—First or Second John?—sent to the church (v. 9). "The elder" expects a confrontation with the rebellious Diotrephes soon (v. 10). (We know nothing of Diotrephes except from this letter.)

Since, like Second John, the letter is written by "the elder," and since its ending is so nearly identical to that of Second John (vv.13–15; cf. 2 John 12–13), it seems likely that Second and Third John are by the same author. Perhaps First or Second John is the letter mentioned in verse 9, and Demetrius carried it to the congregation along with Third John, his letter of recommendation to the loyal Gaius.

However, there is a contrast between Second and Third John. In Second John "the elder" warns against showing hospitality to false teachers. In Third John, Diotrephes has had the elder's own representative turned away as a false teacher. Bultmann has even raised the question as to whether the author of Third John may have been regarded as a Gnostic heretic and therefore excluded by the orthodox Diotrephes.[13] We wish we had Diotrephes' response!

First John seems to have been accepted into the canon without dispute. But Second and Third John were disputed down into the fourth century. Perhaps it was because they were written late, because they were so brief, because Second John seemed repetitious of First John, and because Third John dealt mostly with individuals unknown outside one particular congregation. Perhaps it was because there was uncertainty as to whether they really were—as was later believed—by John the Apostle. We turn now to the most important of the Johannine books, the Fourth Gospel, and the complex question of its authorship.

The Gospel According to John

Dr. James Sprunt once wrote, "the Gospel according to John has been translated into more languages, read by more people, beloved by more readers, carried by more Christians, and used of God for more good than any other piece of literature in the history of the world."[14]

Probably it has also been more debated.

Some Contrasts Between John and the Synoptics

The biggest cause of debate about John is that it is so different from the Synoptics, the other three Gospels.[15]

True, the story as John tells it is essentially the same as that found in Mark. In both, that story begins with John the Baptist. It tells how Jesus called the disciples, healed, fed the five thousand, even walked on water, taught in such a way as to win the intense love of some and the undying hatred of others, rode at last into Jerusalem on a donkey at the Passover season, ate the Last Supper with his disciples, was arrested, was condemned by both Jewish and Roman authorities, and died on a Roman cross. It describes his triumphant resurrection. And this story of Jesus is interpreted as the story of the Son of God.

Mark and John are so similar, even in wording and details, that most—though by no means all—scholars believe that the author of John had read Mark before he wrote his Gospel.

There are, however, striking differences between the account of Jesus' life found in John and the accounts found in the other Gospels. Some of these differences can be explained, perhaps, by John's desire to tell what the others have left out. Some can be partially explained, we will see, by his special purpose and method in writing. Some of these differences we may never understand. Here are a few of the contrasts.

1) There is a difference in the location of the events reported. Almost all of Jesus' ministry appears in the other three Gospels to have taken place in Galilee. John concentrates on Jesus' teachings in Jerusalem at the time of the great feasts as they are celebrated there. (It is not unlikely, by the way, that John is here helpfully giving us new, factual information, since as a devout Jew, Jesus surely must have participated in such festivals. Indeed, the Synoptics hint that he did so frequently, but give us no details. [See Matt. 23:37.])

2) In John the form in which Jesus' teachings are reported is quite different. In Matthew 13:34 we are told that "he said nothing . . . without a parable." Over and over the Synoptics report stories such as the Prodigal Son, the Good Samaritan, or the parable of the Soils. In John, Jesus does use figures of speech, but there are no parables at all, no stories, at least none comparable to those of the synoptics. Jesus' sayings are preserved in the Synoptics typically in brief, often rather witty couplets. "Those who are are well have no need of a physician, but those who are sick" (Mark 2:17). "The sabbath was made for man, not man for the sabbath" (Mark 2:27). In John, Jesus seems often to speak in long monologues or to engage in debates with his enemies.

3) In the three Synoptic Gospels, the heart of Jesus' message is "The kingdom of God is at hand" (Mark 1:15; see above pages 44–46). Almost every parable is about the kingdom. The Sermon on the Mount describes its citizens. The disciples are sent out to proclaim it. In John the phrase "the kingdom of God" appears only once (John 3:3, 5).

4) The first three Gospels each conclude the account of Jesus' teachings with the record of a discourse by Jesus on the coming of the Son of man at the end of the world for the last judgment (Matt. 24—25; Mark 13; Luke 21). The last teachings of Jesus reported in John also look forward to a coming, but it is the coming of the Holy Spirit to be continually present with the disciples (John 14:26; 15:26; 16:7; etc.). The more conventional eschatological hope is not abandoned in John, though a few scholars propose that references to it are insertions by later, more "orthodox" editors (see John 5:27–29; 6:39–40, 44, 54; 12:48; 14:3). But the emphasis in John is on what C. H. Dodd has called "realized eschatology"

(see page 45). We saw that Second Peter must deal with scoffers disillusioned because the promised coming of the glorious end of time still had not occurred years and years after Jesus' death and resurrection (see above, page 212). John's answer, in effect, is to say, "Look! What is there that you have hoped for and have not already received in the coming of Christ and the Holy Spirit? We now already have resurrection (John 11:24–25), judgment (12:31), and eternal life" (5:24; 17:3). And he pictures Jesus himself as preaching this kind of eschatology.

5) In the Fourth Gospel Jesus seems to have been recognized as the Son of God right from the beginning of his ministry (John 1:49), at least by his disciples. In the other Gospels, while the devils know who Jesus is (Mark 1:24), others seem only gradually to come to an understanding of his nature. Peter's Great Confession that Jesus is the Christ produces a crisis and turning point in the story (see above, pages 50–52).

6) The greatest contrast of all, however, and the one which is by far the most difficult to explain, is this: In John, Jesus appears from the very first quite openly and publicly to proclaim that he is the Christ, the Son of God, and to teach at length concerning his own nature and his relationship to the Father (John 1:51; 4:26; 5:19). Quite openly he announces himself to be the Son of God (5:19–46), who existed before the birth of Abraham (8:58), and to announce to everyone such sayings as "I am the bread of life" (6:48), "I am the good shepherd" (10:11), and "I am the light of the world" (8:12). How one explains "the Messianic secret" of the Synoptics (above, page 51) may be debated, but all explanations seem to agree emphatically that Jesus of Nazareth did not go around publicly preaching about himself in this way. Rather, he is said in the Synoptics to have forbidden people to spread the news that he was the Messiah, and to have concentrated his message on the kingdom. In John, however, Jesus publicly and repeatedly demands belief that he is the Son of God, and does his miracles in order to win that kind of faith. His words are not about the kingdom, but about himself.

"John or the Synoptics—you can believe one or the other, but you can't possibly believe both!" So, on the basis of the contrasts listed above (and a number of others, some of which will be noted subsequently), certain critics have been arguing for a century. There simply is no easy answer to this challenge. Some partial solution to the problems raised by these contrasts can be found, however, by noting the special purposes for which John wrote.

The Purpose of John in Relation to the Synoptics

Way back soon after the year A.D. 200, a Christian professor in Alexandria, Clement, noting the contrast between John and the Synoptics, undertook to explain it in this way:

John, last of all, perceiving that what had reference to the body in the gospel of our Savior, was sufficiently detailed, and being encouraged by his familiar friends, and urged by the spirit, he wrote a spiritual gospel.[16]

Apparently the relationship this ancient professor recognized was this: John believed that the other Gospels had adequately recorded the "bodily," observable facts. He now wrote to give us the "spiritual" meaning of those facts.

To illustrate: What happened on July 4, 1776, and the days immediately following? A chemist might reply that ink of a certain chemical composition adhered to a piece of paper of a certain material structure. He would be right, of course. A historian would say that the Declaration of Independence was adopted, and might debate about the day on which it was signed. He, too, would be correct. But Abraham Lincoln would reply to our question in this way: "Fourscore and seven years ago our fathers brought forth on this continent a new nation, conceived in liberty, and dedicated to the proposition that all men are created equal." It would not matter to Lincoln that on July 4 there was not literally a "conception" or a "birth" or a "dedication." He would not be interested, for the purposes of his Gettysburg Address, in whether or not the Declaration was adopted and signed on the same day. He was describing the "spiritual" meaning, the abiding significance, of the great events of the past. He was telling us the truth, the profound truth, of that bit of history as we had come to know it in our lives over the decades.

John, like Lincoln, seeks to tell us the abiding "spiritual" significance of the events of the past, to show in the ancient stories meanings which he believes the risen Christ has now made clear through his Spirit.

For example, the other three Gospels had told the story of how Jesus fed the five thousand. John tells it too. But it is John who now, perhaps seventy years later, hears in that story what Christ is saying through it: "I am the bread of life" (John 6:48).

Again, Luke retold the parable of the Lost Sheep, setting it in what seems a most natural context as Jesus' defense to the Pharisees of his associating with outcasts (Luke 15:1–7). Matthew retold the same story, but he included with it sayings which helped make it applicable to the later problem of how to deal with a straying church member (Matt. 18:10–18). John can assume that his readers already know the parable; he does not tell it again. But seventy years later he hears, with the help of the Spirit, what Christ is eternally saying in that parable: "I am the good shepherd" (John 10:11).

It is important, of course, not to exaggerate the difference in purpose between John and the Synoptics. The Synoptics, too, are theological interpretations of the meaning of Jesus for us. Mark, first to be written and perhaps closest to the memory of the "bodily" facts of Jesus' life, was written to present his Lord as "Jesus

Christ, the Son of God'' (Mark 1:1). (Pages 64–72 described some of the theological points Mark was making as he wrote his Gospel.) And John, on the other
hand, is also interested in "bodily" facts.

Nevertheless, there is a difference in emphasis. John makes much better sense
in relation to the Synoptics when one keeps in mind the difference in purpose.
Compare Luke 1:1–4 (see above, page 24) with John's statement of purpose in
John 20:30–31, and both similarity and difference of aim will appear.

To John's statement of purpose we must turn now.

The Stated Purpose of the Gospel According to John

> Now Jesus did many other signs in the presence of the disciples, which are
> not written in this book; but these are written that you may believe that
> Jesus is the Christ, the Son of God, and that believing you may have life in
> his name.   (John 20:30–31)

So John himself summarizes his purpose. Several words and phrases are of special importance in this statement.

First, John tells us that he has carefully selected what he will tell. No doubt he
knows many, many more stories, those of Jesus' ministry in Galilee, for example,
which, perhaps because they have been told by others, he does not repeat. Indeed,
with Oriental hyperbole, we are told in the last verse of the book: "But there are
also many other things which Jesus did; were every one of them to be written, I
suppose that the world itself could not contain the books that would be written"
(21:25). From a great body of material, John has selected only what best suits his
particular aim.

Second, what he has chosen to tell us are what he calls "signs." A sign is
something which points beyond itself to what it signifies. John 2—11 is often
called "The Book of Signs." Of Jesus' many miracles, John has chosen to
describe only seven (see the outline on page 245). But each miracle is interpreted
as a "sign," its significance being presented in a long meditation related to it.
Thus, for example, in John 9, Jesus gives sight to a blind man. This is related to
the truth that Jesus is "the light of the world" (John 8:12; 9:5). And in John 11
Jesus raises Lazarus from the dead. The meaning seen in this "sign" is that Jesus
is the "resurrection and the life" (11:25).

These signs are reported so that we may "believe." The word "believe"
occurs nearly a hundred times in John, and such related words as "belief" and
"unbelief" are frequently repeated. Noting the use of the Greek philosophical
concept of the *Logos*, the "Word" or "Reason," in John 1, some scholars have
proposed that John is writing to win Gentiles to faith. Others have noted the long
arguments with "the Jews" in such passages as John 5, 6, and 9, and have proposed that John wrote to persuade his fellow Jews to join in becoming Christians.
The Upper Room discourses, however, seem obviously to be meditations

designed for developing the faith of those who are already Christians. Repeatedly in John one reads of some person who has a little faith but needs to have his belief deepened. John writes primarily to deepen and strengthen the faith of Christians. The climax of the book is when "doubting Thomas" comes to full faith as he meets the risen Christ and cries his confession, "My Lord and my God!" (20:28).

"Jesus is the Christ, the Son of God." John writes to help the reader understand who Jesus is. John presents the most highly developed Christology (doctrine of the nature of Christ) in all the New Testament. His most distinctive contribution of this kind is a series of sayings, usually with accompanying meditations, using an emphatic form of the Greek almost as though the words "I am" were in capitals. These "I AM sayings" are:

"I am the bread of life" (John 6:48).
"I am the light of the world" (8:12).
"I am the door of the sheep" (10:7).
"I am the good shepherd" (10:11).
"I am the resurrection and the life" (11:25).
"I am the way, and the truth, and the life" (14:6).
"I am the vine" (15:5).
"Before Abraham was, I am" (8:58).

Thus repeatedly the book explains the meaning of Jesus by using what are in a sense the most familiar and simple and universally understandable of symbols: light, bread, a vine, and so forth. Into these he pours profound meaning.

Finally, John says that he writes so that his readers may have "life." This word occurs more than forty times in John. In a sense John is a very practical book. The author is not greatly interested in speculation about the future, and his primary concern is not a report of interesting events of the past. He wants to help the reader to a new kind of life right now. "This is eternal life," he writes of a present reality, not something to come after death, "that they know thee the only true God, and Jesus Christ whom thou hast sent" (John 17:3).

Secondary purposes may be noted, most being clearly related to special situations the church faced near the end of the first century. The writer wants to describe Christ in relation to the continuing movement begun by John the Baptist, the growing Gnostic heresy, and the bitter controversies developing between church and synagogue. These will be discussed below. But noting these more particular concerns of the writer leads us to the questions of authorship and date of the Gospel.

The Authorship of John

The Fourth Gospel is given to us as an anonymous work. It is true that all editors now print as its heading "The Gospel According to John," but this is the editor's title, not part of the text itself. As to the identity of the writer, the Bible itself simply leaves us to guess.

People have been guessing for centuries. Curiously, one early group of very orthodox Christians believed that John was too "spiritual" and branded it the work of the heretic Cerinthus. But the overwhelming majority of early Christian writers, from at least as early as the Muratorian Canon of about A.D. 170, have ascribed it to someone named "John," and that John has usually been understood to be the son of Zebedee and one of the twelve Apostles. That John was an important early Christian leader is attested by the Synoptics, Acts, and later legend, and Paul refers to him as one of the "pillars" of the Jerusalem church (Gal. 2:9).

While the Gospel itself does not name its author, it does indicate its source as being "the disciple whom Jesus loved." Several times this unnamed person is mentioned (13:23; 19:26; 20:2; 21:7). At the end of the book this disciple appears once more (21:20), and now we are told, "This is the disciple who is bearing witness to these things, and who has written these things; and we know that his testimony is true" (21:24). Somewhat similarly, the story of Jesus' death is interrupted with the comment, "He who saw it has borne witness—his testimony is true, and he knows that he tells the truth—that you also may believe" (19:35).

Who is this disciple who leans upon Jesus' breast as the Twelve recline around the table at the Last Supper, to whom the dying Jesus commits the care of his mother, and who is said to be the source of the Gospel? A few have proposed that he is simply an ideal figure, standing for all who believe.[17] Ideal figures do not write gospels, however. Dr. Floyd Filson, in *"The Layman's Bible Commentary"* volume on John, argues that it is Lazarus.[18] Four times, Filson notes, it is stated specifically that Jesus loved Lazarus (11:3, 5, 11, 36). Then in chapter 13 we begin to read simply of "the disciple whom Jesus loved." Few scholars, however, have followed Filson in this identification. To most it seems incredible that Jesus' "beloved disciple" could be one who is never mentioned in the New Testament outside of this Gospel and around whom no church tradition ever gathered.

Generally it has been argued that this especially beloved disciple must be one of the most prominent of the Twelve. Peter, Andrew, and several others are referred to by name in the Fourth Gospel. John, however, so frequently mentioned elsewhere in the New Testament, is never named in this book. It is proposed, therefore, that John refers to himself this way, modestly concealing his own name.

Supporters of the traditional view that John the Apostle wrote this Gospel have offered such arguments as the following: The earliest Christian writers who discuss these matters affirm it. The book has always borne John's name in its title. The writer must, it is said, have been a Palestinian Jew, as was John. This is shown by the fact that he knows Jewish law and customs and opinions (1:21;

4:25; 7:40f.; 12:34; 18:31; etc.), the language of Palestine (19:17), details of Palestinian geography (1:28, 2:1; 3:23; 11:54; for example), and the ceremonies of the Jewish feasts (7:2, 37; 10:22; etc.). There is such vividness of detail that even some who doubt that the book comes to us in its present form from an Apostle believe that it must go back for its ultimate source to someone who was an eyewitness at many of the events described.

Some twentieth-century discoveries have been used to support the traditional view. At one time it was argued that the Fourth Gospel may have been written as late as A.D. 175, obviously beyond the lifetime even of a man famed in part for his longevity (21:22). The discovery in Egypt of a papyrus containing part of John and written no later than A.D. 125 or 130 has forced acceptance of an earlier date. Most scholars now place John between A.D. 90 and 100. Similarly, the discovery of the Dead Sea Scrolls has indicated that certain ideas such as the warfare of light with darkness, characteristic of John, were current in first-century Palestine and need not have been derived from later Gentile thought. Finally, some linguists find hints of oral or written sources in John which were originally in Aramaic, the language of John's native Palestine, not of the later mission to the Gentiles.[19]

It must be repeated, however, that the Gospel comes to us an anonymous book. Only very conservative scholars today are likely to ascribe it actually to the pen of the Apostle. There are several reasons.

Most important, the differences between John and the Synoptics, noted above, are so great that it is difficult to believe that the Fourth Gospel, in the form in which we now have it, is the work of one who actually remembered Jesus of Nazareth from long personal experience. If we assume that the historic facts are roughly as Mark presents them, it seems unlikely that one who was present at them could, for example, picture Jesus as publicly debating his own divine nature with his enemies early in his ministry. Such debates belong to a later stage in Christian history.

Actually, a careful reading of the ascription to the beloved disciple suggests that the work has more than one author. "We know that his testimony is true" (John 21:24). Who are "we"? The most natural understanding of the verse is that "we" refers to the writers of the volume in the form in which we now have it. They are claiming, however, that its ultimate source is the testimony, including the written testimony, of the beloved disciple.

The phrase "the disciple whom Jesus loved" is scarcely a modest way for one to describe oneself. It would be highly appropriate, however, for students of John to describe their revered teacher in this way. Even if it be suggested that, as may indeed be the case, John 21 is an appendix added to the book after his death, we have almost the same phrase in the body of the book in 19:35: "his testimony is true." Taken as they stand, these verses seem to indicate that while the book rests on the authority of the beloved disciple, it comes to us through the work of later writers also.

As a matter of fact, there are hints in ancient tradition that John was not alone in the production of this Gospel. Clement of Alexandria, as we have seen, speaks of John as writing after "being urged by his friends." The Muratorian Canon says that John wrote "aided by the revision of all" his bishops and fellow disciples. To the present writer, as to many others, it seems likely that that "revision" was more extensive than has traditionally been recognized.

Actually, though there is no consensus as to the content of these sources, many scholars feel that they detect signs that the Gospel has brought together a number of earlier sources, written and oral. Most often suggested among these is a "Book of Signs" reporting seven miracles of Jesus.[20] In view of the consistent tradition which relates the Gospel to John, it would seem to the present writer likely that excerpts from sermons of that Apostle were among these sources. Moreover, it would seem likely that the Gospel was produced in a church of which John had been the leader. He was the "author" in the sense of being the "authority" on which the Gospel rested. But those who actually wrote what we now have probably completed their work after John's death. They applied the Apostle's message to issues of their own day. And in so doing, they gave us what most Christian scholars would consider among the most mature, advanced, and profound theological treatises ever written.[21]

We cannot identify these pupils of John, perhaps in Ephesus, who penned what we now have. It is true that the second-century Christian scholar Papias speaks of two men in Ephesus named John: the Apostle John and the Elder ("presbyter") John. Apparently the Elder was a younger contemporary of the Apostle. In view of the fact that Second and Third John are said to be by "the elder" (see the first verse of each) and are traditionally ascribed to "John," many have suggested that the Elder John was also the final writer of the Gospel. This helped attach the name "John" to the book. This, however, is only attractive speculation.

For convenience, and out of respect for a helpful tradition, we will refer to the anonymous author as John in the section-by-section comments on the Gospel.

The Prologue and the Witness of John the Baptist—John 1

> O God most glorious . . .
> Nature's great King, through endless years the same;
>
> . . . .
> Vehicle of the universal Word, that flows
> Through all, and the light celestial glows
>
> . . . .
> One Word through all things everlastingly.
> One Word—whose voice alas! the wicked spurn. . . .[22]

By the time the Gospel According to John was written, men and women for three centuries had been singing Cleanthes' "Hymn to Zeus." In it they had sung of God's "Word," the *Logos*.

Bridging the gap between pagan and Christian thought, John begins with another hymn about the *Logos*, the Word of God. Stoics and Christians knew that there was really only one God and that in the beginning it was through that "Word," that manifestation of the Divine Mind, that the world was created. "In the beginning was the Explanation," one could translate John's first words. There was that through which God sought to show how everything makes sense. Both Stoics and Christians knew that humankind had often rejected that expression of divine reason.

Three centuries after John, the great Augustine was to write that before he became a Christian he had learned from Greek philosophy everything in the prologue of John until he came to verse 14. "And the Word became flesh and dwelt among us." That was the good news unknown to any pagan! In Jesus the *Logos* had become flesh, had become completely human.

The rabbi-philosopher Philo had already proposed relationships between biblical religion and Greek philosophy. Indeed it must be enphasized that John is written not by a Greek philosopher, but by a Jewish Christian. For an introduction he uses the *Logos* concept. But his roots are in the Jewish scriptures. The concept of the divine wisdom in Proverbs 8 is surely part of the background of John's hymn. John begins by expressing the meaning of Christ in terms derived from the Jewish scriptures, as do the first sermons, but also in terms familiar to former pagans.

These were Gnostic terms, too. But the strong word used about the incarnation, that in Jesus the Word had become *flesh,* clearly separated John from the heretics. John uses so many Gnostic figures and concepts that, as has been noted earlier, some Christians later claimed that the book was written by the Gnostic heretic Cerinthus. Yet from time to time he reminds the reader of the genuine humanity of Jesus. It is John who tells us that Jesus wept (11:35). It is John who records Jesus' cry from the cross, "I thirst" (19:28). Here in the prologue he insists on the fact that in Jesus the *Logos* became *"flesh."*[23]

John begins by setting Jesus in relation to philosophical and Gnostic speculation. But he also relates Jesus to the movement of John the Baptist. In Mark, Jesus' ministry begins when John the Baptizer's ends. But in the Fourth Gospel, for a brief period at least, the two are working at the same time. Here there may be some reflection of the fact that a John the Baptist cult survived for many years after the prophet's death. Acts 19:1–7 implies the existence of this group in Ephesus, the traditional center of the Apostle John's ministry. The Fourth Gospel, therefore, though it follows the convention of beginning its story of Jesus with the ministry of John the Baptizer, says nothing of Jesus' having been baptized by John. That might imply to some followers of the Baptist that their prophet had been somehow superior to Jesus. Instead, the whole emphasis in this

The Gospel According to John
The Spiritual Gospel

'I a.. the way, and the truth, and the life." (14:6).

1:1 Introduction	2:1 Seven Signs	And Their Meanings	12:1 Last Entry, Last Supper	18:1 21:25 The Cross and the Ressurection
Prologue 1:1-18	1) Water changed to wine 2:1-11	Christ transforms, changing the temple (2:12–25), giving new birth (3:1–21); he is transforming "water" (3:22—4:54).	Entry into Jerusalem and coming of the Greeks to Christ 12	Arrest and trials 18
The witness of John the Baptizer and his disciples 1:19-51	2) A son healed, 3) and a lame man healed on the day of rest 4:46—5:9	Christ is the Son of God, carrying on his Father's work. 5:10-47	Jesus washes his disciples' feet. 13	Crucifixion 19
	4) Five thousand fed bread, and 5) Christ walks on water 6:1-21	Christ is the bread of life. 6:22-71	He promises to return, but also to send the Spirit. 14	Resurrection 20
	6) Christ heals a blind man. 9:1-41	Christ is the light of the world. 7—10	The vine and the branches 15	Epilogue 21
	7) Christ raises Lazarus. 11	Christ is the resurrection and the life. 11	The Spirit will guide. 16	
			Christ's high-priestly prayer 17	

Author: Unnamed (traditionally the Apostle John, more likely disciples of John)
Recipients: Unnamed, apparently all seeking greater faith
Date: Probably A.D. 90-100
Occasion: No special occasion is stated. Probably some conflicts between church and synagogue are reflected.
Purpose: "That you may believe that Jesus is the Christ, the Son of God, and ... have life ..." (20:31)

Gospel's account of John is on his witness to the superiority of Jesus. "Behold, the Lamb of God," John cries as he sees Christ (1:29). The figure is from the Passover celebration, which will be the season of Jesus' death. Followers of John now transfer their allegiance to Jesus, as the Gospel writer wants the contemporary disciples of John the Baptist to do. And John appears once again briefly—in a passage which some think may originally have been part of the first chapter—to say of Jesus, "He must increase, but I must decrease" (3:30).

The Book of Signs—John 2—11

John 2—11 contains the story of seven miracles, selected from many and interpreted as "signs." Around each of five of these the book gives us a meditation in the form of a monologue by Jesus, usually introduced by a dialogue with an individual or—more often—a group. The outline on page 245 shows how this part of the book can be understood as being built around these signs and their interpretations. As stated above, several scholars have suggested that the "Book of Signs" originally recounted the miracles independently, the discourses being added later. If this is so, it is not possible now to separate out the original source with certainty.

Surprisingly, John places the story of the cleansing of the Temple at the beginning of Jesus' ministry, right after the "sign" of changing the water into wine. We have seen that the Synoptics themselves are more interested in the theological points a story illustrates than in its historic sequence. They do not agree on the order of all events. Nevertheless, it does seem important to place historically the cleansing of the Temple within the last week of Jesus' ministry, because—in Mark at least—it is this act which so infuriates the authorities in Jerusalem that it brings about the final plot to destroy Jesus. In John, however, the raising of Lazarus from the dead is given as the climax of Jesus' "signs" and the final blow to the old order which eventuates in the crucifixion.

Apparently John places the cleansing of the Temple here because his opening theme is the transformation which the coming of Christ produces. At a wedding Christ changes water into wine. Now, at the Passover, Christ changes the Temple. In chapter 3 he informs a representative of official Judaism, Nicodemus, "You must be born anew." His success with this "ruler of the Jews" is questionable, but, symbolically, with a sinful woman—a Samaritan, not a Jew (chapter 4)—Jesus has great success. She is changed, and old barriers between races and old patterns of worship are broken down. Christianity is seen breaking out of the Jewish Temple, officialdom, race, and cult. The old lifeless water is being changed into wine.

The second sign is that of the healing of a father's son (4:46–54). It introduces in chapter 5 a long discussion of the Father-Son relationship existing between God and Jesus.

The immediate occasion of the controversy which produces this discussion is that Jesus heals a man on the Sabbath (5:2–9). This act, his enemies charge, constituted forbidden "work" on the Sabbath. Jesus' reply is to say, "My Father is working still, and I am working" (5:17). Like the healing on the Sabbath described in Mark 3:1–6, this incident so infuriates the authorities that already they begin to plot to kill him.

What infuriates them here, however, is not simply the violation of the Sabbath law, but the claim implied in Jesus' answer that he is the Son of God. The rest of the chapter analyzes for the reader what it means that Jesus is the Son of the Father. "Who is the man?" (5:12). John never mentions Jesus' being conceived by the Holy Spirit and born of a virgin. Rather, he interprets what Christians mean when they call Jesus "Son of God" in ways such as these: He is the one through whom the Father continues his work (5:17). He has authority from God (5:19); he is especially beloved by God (5:20); through him God gives life to men (5:21); he is the agent of God's judgment (5:22, 27); he is like God in that he has "life" within himself (5:26); and through him God speaks (5:28).

How do Christians know that this is true? Some answers here are that John the Baptist bore witness to Christ (5:36); Jesus' great deeds show who he is (5:36); God the Father speaks directly to the heart of the believer about Jesus (5:37–38); and the Scripture itself tells us who he is (5:39).

The story of the feeding of the five thousand is one of the relatively few, other than the crucifixion and the resurrection, that are found in all four Gospels. No doubt it was frequently retold among Christians because it seemed especially appropriate at the Communion service. It is in the light of the Communion that John interprets it in chapter 6. The other three Gospels have told the story; it is John who tells its meaning. In it Jesus is saying, "I am the bread of life" (6:48). Though John has the longest account of the Last Supper, five whole chapters (13—17), nowhere in them does he mention the actual institution of the Lord's Supper. His readers already know how the Lord's Supper began. Rather, he gives us a Communion meditation here. "He who eats my flesh and drinks my blood has eternal life" (6:54).

The whole story is set in the context of the Passover (6:4). That ancient festival celebrated how the Jews, having first eaten a meal of special bread, crossed the sea to freedom and entered into a covenant with God. Wandering in the wilderness, they again ate a special bread, the manna God miraculously sent down to them daily from heaven. The disciples, too, cross a sea (6:16–21), with Jesus walking on the water. Jewish expectation of the *eschaton*, the end of the world, included the hope of a great Messianic banquet with the Messiah. All of these ideas are now used to explain the meaning of the Communion service. "Your fathers ate the manna in the wilderness, and they died. This is the bread which comes down from heaven, that a man may eat of it and not die" (6:49–50).

Chapters 7—10 have as their background the Feast of Tabernacles. The outline on page 245 takes the seven "signs" as the basic structure of the first half of

John, but it is equally valid to outline the book around Jewish festivals. Chapters 2—4 are set in the context of the Passover, chapter 5 involves the Sabbath, and chapter 6 returns to the Passover. In the ceremonies related to the Feast of Tabernacles, each day for a week a golden pitcher of water was carried in a procession to the Temple to remind the people how God had provided water for them when, centuries earlier, they had wandered in the desert as they escaped from Egypt. It is against this background that we are to understand Jesus' invitation, "If any one thirst, let him come to me and drink" (7:37).

Similarly, during this festival great fires were lit high on the Temple each night, a reminder of the pillar of fire which guided the Hebrews through the wilderness (Exod. 13:21). This, too, is used to explain the meaning of Jesus: "I am the light of the world" (8:12; 9:5). The "sign" related to this saying is, appropriately, the restoring of sight to a man born blind (ch. 9).

Much of this section, like chapters 5 and 6, centers on long disputes between Jesus and "the Jews." Such passages have sometimes been misused as proof-texts for anti-Semitic bigotry. This, however, is a gross misunderstanding. Jesus himself was a Jew. The holy family were Jews, the twelve Apostles were Jews, and all the first Christians were Jews. John uses the term not to refer to a race or an ethnic group, but to those who reject Christ. These passages must be read in the light of the controversy between church and synagogue which raged at the time this book was being written. "The Jews had already agreed that if any one should confess him to be Christ, he was to be put out of the synagogue" (9:22). The use of the word "already" implies that the writer knows how, later on, Christians were everywhere put out of the synagogues. Some time after the fall of Jerusalem in A.D. 70, a council of rabbis convened at Jamnia to take steps to preserve Judaism in the crisis entailed by no longer having a Temple or a homeland. They inserted the following bit of liturgy into synagogue worship:

> For the apostates let there be no hope
> . . . .
> Let the Nazarenes [Christians] and
> the Minim [heretics] be destroyed in a moment.
> And let them be blotted out of the Book of life and not be inscribed together with the righteous.[24]

Between the lines of John, one can read the equally bitter reply of the church to the synagogue. To perpetuate today late first-century controversies between the synagogue and the emerging church would be to pervert what is best in both Judaism and Christianity.

Actually these chapters present three parties: Jesus, boldly defying his enemies (7:26); Jewish leaders, seen not so much as individuals, but as symbols of unbelief, seeking to discredit Jesus (7:47–48); and the crowd, confused and vacillating (7:40–44).

Jesus' enemies try to have him arrested (7:32), but the police return empty-handed. "Nobody else ever talked like that," is all that they can say to explain their hesitation (7:46). The Jewish leaders hate Jesus because he is a threat to their high position. Jesus has no official sanction (7:48) they argue; he does not come from their ranks in Jerusalem (7:52). He is a nobody, and they are somebodies, yet he is challenging their hold on the people (7:26).

The people are confused and divided. Some believe in Jesus (8:30). Some think him a devil (8:48). All the way through this section they are asking questions: "Where is he?" (7:11). "Can it be that . . . this is the Christ?" (7:26). "Where is he going?" (7:35). "What does he mean?" (7:36). "Where is your Father?" (8:19). "Who are you?" (8:25). "Who do you claim to be?" (8:53).

Jesus claims no earthly authority. Over and over he tries to explain that he has come from God (8:16, 23, 42). It is not the town he comes from (7:27), nor his ancestry (8:33, 37), nor the approval of the authorities (7:48), but his life which shows who he is (8:46–47).

All this controversy reaches a climax in chapter 9 with the story of Christ's giving sight to a man born blind. The man stands as a symbol of those in the confused crowd who do come to believe in Jesus. Over and over the crowd and the authorities question him after he has been healed: "Where is he?" (9:12). "How did he heal you?" (9:15). "What do you say about him?" (9:17). The simple fellow can only answer, "Whether he is a sinner, I do not know; one thing I know, that though I was blind, now I see" (9:25). It is the Pharisees (the unbelievers) who are really blind (9:40–41). They have rejected "the light of the world."

The section ends with a meditation which is this Gospel's developed version of the parable of the Lost Sheep. The Jews, of course, are the people of God, his "sheep" (Psalm 100:3). But the discourse looks forward to the inclusion now of Gentiles, too. "And I have other sheep, that are not of this fold; I must bring them also" (10:16). For Jews and Gentiles the Good Shepherd lays down his life (10:11).

The end of the dispute is set against the background of the Feast of the Dedication, which commemorated the restoration of the Temple in 164 B.C. after the Syrians who defiled it had been expelled. Efforts to kill Jesus are now repeated (10:31, 39). Jesus is forced to retreat beyond Jordan, and the public disputes cease.

The seventh and the climactic sign is the raising of Lazarus, the sign that Jesus is "the resurrection and the life." The conventionally expressed eschatology of Martha is not contradicted. "I know that he will rise again in the resurrection at the last day" (11:24). But there is added to it the "realized eschatology" of John. Already the resurrection has begun. With Christ the new life is already here.

But "from that day on they took counsel how to put him to death" (11:53).

The Entry into Jerusalem and the Last Supper—John 12—17

John's description of how they put Jesus to death is in many ways quite like the accounts in the Synoptics. For example, the "triumphal entry" in John is much as it is in Mark.

John 12 does add one characteristic story. Some Greeks come to one of the disciples saying, "Sir, we wish to see Jesus" (12:21). This is taken as a sign that "the hour has come for the Son of man to be glorified" (12:23). The coming of these Greeks apparently is seen as a symbol of the turning of the Gentile world to Christ. Jesus is now ready to die. "Now"—not just at the end, but now with Jesus' death—"is the judgment of this world" (12:31).

Five whole chapters (13—17), probably the best-loved part of the book, are devoted to the Last Supper, largely to a meditation on the coming of the Holy Spirit and on the continuing relationship of Christ to those who love him.

The scene is introduced by an acted parable. Jesus, said at this point to be fully aware that he has come from God, takes the role ordinarily assigned to the lowest servant: he washes the disciples' feet. His gesture is a symbolic preparatory acting out of the sacrifice which is to occur on the next day. Later in chapter 13, Judas goes out to betray Jesus, and Jesus announces that his death is at hand.

In chapter 14 Jesus is pictured as promising his return, "that where I am you may be also" (14:3). Perhaps the best-known of the "I am" sayings is given: "I am the way, the truth, and the life" (14:6). But the coming which is especially promised is not simply the return of Jesus at the end, but the imminent coming of the Holy Spirit. Though the promised return of Christ has been delayed, John seems to be saying, the experience of the coming of the Spirit is one in which his readers have already shared or can share. Christ will send the "Counselor" (14:16), who is the Spirit (14:17), who is actually Jesus' own presence with them (14:18)—a special gift to those with faith (14:19).

Through this Spirit, chapter 15 adds, Christ and his church will be linked as a vine and its branches. Thus joined, believers will share in his power to do great things, to "bear much fruit" (15:8). The vine (Christ with his church) is to be bound together by love (15:12–17). The commandment to love is not new, but love is given a new standard. "A new commandment I give to you, that you love one another; even as I have loved you" (13:34). That is new!

That Spirit also will continue, even after Jesus is no longer with them, to teach Christians new things, chapter 16 adds. "I have yet many things to say to you, but you cannot bear them now. When the Spirit of truth comes, he will guide you into all the truth" (16:12–13). Indeed, many of the sayings of Christ in John may be thought of as among these new things being said by the risen Christ through his Spirit.

The picture of Jesus' last words with his disciples before his crucifixion is closed with what is sometimes called Christ's "high-priestly prayer" (John 17). He glorifies the God who has given him all power, even power to give eternal life to all. "And this is eternal life," we are told, "that they know thee the only true God, and Jesus Christ whom thou hast sent" (17:3). What had been the focus of the eschatological hope for centuries is now present for believers: eternal life itself. Christ's great prayer is for the unity of the church, not just a spiritual unity, but a unity so visible that the world will be won by it. He prays "that they may all be one . . . so that the world may believe" (17:21).

That prayer has not yet been answered fully.

The Crucifixion and the Resurrection—John 18—21

We have already seen that in the Synoptics the account of Jesus' arrest, trial, and crucifixion is given with far more attention to detail than that of any other part of Jesus' life. There is every reason to believe that it is historically of high accuracy. Not surprisingly, therefore, John's account is quite similar.

One thing which this Gospel adds is a conversation said to have taken place between Jesus and Pilate. In it the sense in which Jesus is a "king" is discussed. "My kingship is not of this world. . . . I have come into the world, to bear witness to the truth" (18:36–37). Moreover, John pictures Jesus as acting throughout with the calm authority of a king. Not only is he entirely innocent, as his judges admit, but he has more power than the Jewish police (18:6) or even the Roman governor (19:11). He talks to Pilate not as a prisoner, but as a king (18:33–38). Indeed, Pilate recognizes that Jesus really is a king (19:14). And as a king, Jesus calmly disposes of his affairs from the cross (19:25–27). In John he dies, not with a cry of dereliction ("My God, my God, why hast thou forsaken me?"), but with a triumphant announcement, "It is finished" (19:30). In John it is in the cross itself, not just the resurrection, that Jesus is "glorified."

And yet John pauses from time to time to emphasize that Jesus really did suffer. John has presented the heavenly Christ in Jesus, the one who has come from heaven and returns to heaven, the one who is "not of this world," and whose kingdom is light against this world's darkness. He does this so much that Rudolf Bultmann proposes that the writer must have been a converted Gnostic, repeatedly using Gnostic ideas to describe the meaning of Christ. The Gnostics, too, believed that the Spirit would reveal new truths and had, in fact, done so for them. There is so much language in John similar to that of the Gnostics that they subsequently liked to quote from this Gospel, even claiming that John had been a kind of Gnostic. In reaction, as noted previously, some very orthodox Christians later proposed that the Gnostic heretic Cerinthus had written the book. (Contrast the legend that John ran from the bathhouse Cerinthus entered, recounted on page 229!)

Yet John's account of the crucifixion is in sharp contrast to that found in the Acts of John, a kind of holy novel composed by the Gnostics a century later. In it, at the moment of the crucifixion, Christ is said to come to John, who is hiding in a cave on the Mount of Olives, to explain to him that the man dying on the cross is not really the eternal Christ.

> And I saw the Lord himself above the Cross, having no shape but only a kind of voice . . . which said to me. . . . This Cross of Light is sometimes

called Logos by me for your sakes, sometimes mind, sometimes Jesus, sometimes Christ, sometimes a door. . . . But this is not that wooden Cross which you shall see when you go down from here; nor am I the (man) who is on the Cross. . . . So then I have suffered none of those things which they will say of me.[25]

The Son of God, to the Gnostics, was too "spiritual" to suffer.

By contrast, John pictures for us Jesus Christ scourged, dressed in a royal purple robe, with a crown of thorns on his head, and ridiculed. "Behold the man!" Pilate cries. And from the cross this very human Christ gives a cry of very human need, "I thirst" (19:28). "And he bowed his head and gave up his spirit" (19:30).

While the other Gospels indicate that Jesus was crucified after eating the Passover meal the night before, John seems to say that Jesus was crucified on the day the Passover lamb was being slain (19:31). Thus Jesus' earthly ministry ended in fulfillment of the words with which John introduced it: "Behold, the Lamb of God, who takes away the sin of the world!" (1:29).

We have already seen that our accounts of the resurrection differ in details but agree on essentials. In John the risen Christ appears to Mary Magdalene at the tomb, then, as in Luke, to the disciples on Sunday evening.

John's special contribution to the resurrection story, however, is his account of "doubting Thomas" (20:24–29). Representative of all who come later than Easter and who have difficulty with faith, Thomas, not in the fellowship at first, now is privileged to see the risen Christ for himself. This Gospel has been filled with titles for Jesus: *Logos*, Son of God, light, the way, and many others. But Thomas is allowed to voice the confession which is the climax of New Testament Christology. He encounters the risen Christ, the print of the nails still visible on his real body, and Thomas cries, "My Lord and my God!" (20:28).

Most scholars regard John 21 as an appendix added later by the same writer or by others of the "Johannine school." It adds the story of an appearance of the risen Christ in Galilee, thus helping to bring the account more into line with Matthew's report. It also describes an encounter between the risen Christ and Peter, possibly giving details of an appearance mentioned by Paul (1 Cor. 15:5) and perhaps included in the last ending of Mark (Mark 16:7).

There are also words to the "disciple whom Jesus loved" (21:20–23). Apparently John had lived to be a very old man, and the church had believed that Jesus would return before his death. The paragraph makes clear that this was not literally Jesus' promise.

It is probably with the statement of purpose in John 20:30–31 that the book originally ended. We have seen that John had purposes which in certain ways were quite different from those of all other writers in the New Testament. And yet what John says of his own aim would apply in many ways to the aim of every New Testament book.

It was stated in chapter 1 of this volume that from start to finish the New Testament is a call to decision. One has not really been introduced to the New Testament when he or she has simply memorized dates and outlines of its twenty-seven books. The introduction is complete only as the reader meets the Figure who is central in these pages and senses the challenge that Person represents.

Therefore, it is appropriate to close the present volume itself as John closed his, by quoting again his words:

> Now Jesus did many other signs in the presence of the disciples, which are not written in this book; but these are written that you may believe that Jesus is the Christ, the Son of God, and that believing you may have life in his name. (John 20:30–31)

Notes

I—Some Principles of Biblical Interpretation

1. Clement of Alexandria, *The Instructor* II, viii, as found in Alexander Roberts and James·Donaldson, eds., *The Ante-Nicene Fathers*, vol. 2 (Grand Rapids: Eerdmans, 1956), pp. 253–254.
2. Rudolf Bultmann, *Jesus Christ and Mythology* (New York: Charles Scribner's Sons, 1958), p. 20.
3. *Ibid.*, pp. 35–36. It is important to understand that when Bultmann and his followers use the word "myth" in reference to some New Testament story, they do not mean "lie." They mean an inner, spiritual truth expressed in the form of a story.
4. See James M. Robinson, *A New Quest of the Historical Jesus* (Naperville, Ill.: Alec R. Allenson, 1959). See also below, chapter 3, note 4.
5. This recent approach to biblical interpretation, called "the new hermeneutic" and growing in part out of the emphases of Karl Barth and Rudolf Bultmann, has reminded us that the Bible comes to us as powerful "Word" from God, a language which makes things happen in people's lives if it is properly grasped—or, more accurately, if one is properly grasped by it. Writing of "the new hermeneutic," William G. Doty summarizes that in interpretation thus understood, "We do not have a situation in which we have mastery over something, but in which something masters us." He quotes James Robinson: "In dealings with the text, *its* being interpreted by us turns into *our* being interpreted by the text." (*Contemporary New Testament Interpretation* [Englewood Cliffs, N.J.: Prentice-Hall, 1972], pp. 31–32.)

II—The Historical Setting of the Gospels

1. Adapted from A. C. Bouquet, *Everyday Life in New Testament Times* (New York: Charles Scribner's Sons, 1954).
2. *The Assumption of Moses* 10:5, as translated in R. H. Charles, ed., *The Apocrypha and Pseudepigrapha of the Old Testament*, vol. 2 (Oxford: The Clarendon Press, 1913), p. 422.
3. From *The Book of Hymns*, Psalm III in Theodor H. Gaster, trans., *The Dead Sea Scriptures* (Garden City, N.Y.: Doubleday, 1957), pp. 136–137.
4. *Enoch* 55:4, as found in R. H. Charles, *The Book of Enoch* (London: SPCK, 1925), p. 73.

III—The Writing of the Gospels

1. C. H. Dodd, *The Apostolic Preaching and Its Developments* (London: Hodder & Stoughton, 1944), p. 20.
2. For a classic introduction to form criticism, see Rudolf Bultmann, "The Study of the Synoptic Gospels," in Frederick Clifton Grant, ed. and trans., *Form Criticism: A New Method of New Testament Research* (New York: Willett, Clark & Co., 1934), pp. 11–75. For a fuller discussion see E. Basil Redlich, *Form Criticism: Its*

Values and Limitations (New York: Scribner's, 1939) and Edgar V. McKnight, *What Is Form Criticism?* (Philadelphia: Fortress Press, 1969). For briefer descriptions of some of the methods, values, and limitations of this approach, see William Manson, *Jesus the Messiah* (London: Hodder & Stoughton, 1943), pp. 20—32 and *passim;* William Barclay, *Introduction to the First Three Gospels* (Philadelphia: The Westminster Press, 1975), pp. 24–28; I. Howard Marshall, ed., *New Testament Interpretation* (Grand Rapids: Eerdmans, 1977), pp. 153–164; and most of the New Testament introductions and general reference works cited in notes and "For Further Reading," below.

3. For a collection of such apocryphal stories, see Hugh J. Schonfield, *Readings in the Apocryphal Gospels* (London: Thomas Nelson & Sons, 1940).

4. For a much more skeptical view of the Gospels as history, see Rudolf Bultmann, *The Historical Jesus and the Kerygma* (Nashville: Abingdon Press, 1964) and "The Study of the Synoptic Gospels," noted above. Bultmann finds only about three pages of sayings of Jesus to be authentic (pp. 61–63). The view the present writer prefers is closer to that of Vincent Taylor, *The Life and Ministry of Jesus* (Nashville: Abingdon Press, 1955), pp. 35–44, and of William Manson, *op. cit.,* above, note 2. For a scholarly and persuasive defense of a very conservative position, see I. Howard Marshall, *I Believe in the Historical Jesus* (Grand Rapids: Eerdmans, 1977). A recent reaffirmation of a more skeptical approach is that of Norman Perrin, who questions any story or saying in the Gospels which can be explained on the basis of the later needs of the church or paralleled in Rabbinic Judaism. This seems to the present writer to take too lightly the facts that the church grew out of the coming of Jesus and that Jesus, whatever else he was, was a Jew.

5. For examples of those denying the priority of Mark and the dependence of Matthew upon it, see W. F. Albright and C. S. Mann, *Matthew*, in "The Anchor Bible," (Garden City, N.Y.: Doubleday, 1971), especially pp. xxvii–clxxvii, and William R. Farmer, *The Synoptic Problem* (New York: Macmillan, 1964). The vast majority of scholars, however, at least among Protestants, argue for the priority of Mark. There are so many verbal agreements that one must be copying from another, and it seems incredible that Mark, in abbreviating Matthew, would add details to some stories but leave out the Sermon on the Mount, for example.

6. Eusebius, *Ecclesiastical History* V 8, in Henry Bettenson, ed., *Documents of the Christian Church* New York: Oxford University Press, 1947), p. 40.

7. *Ibid.* V iii 39, p. 39.

8. The traditional view presented here has recently been attacked by many. See, for example, Frederick C. Grant, *Mark*, in "The Interpreter's Bible," vol. 7, (Nashville: Abingdon Press, 1951), pp. 629–647, and Eduard Schweizer, *Jesus*, trans. David E. Green (Richmond: John Knox Press, 1971). Among their arguments are these: The Gospel is said to reflect too much the influence of developing oral and perhaps written tradition to rest on the memory of an Apostle (Peter). Its theology is too highly developed. And it betrays a lack of knowledge of Galilean geography. In reply, scholars have argued that the tradition ascribing the Gospel to Mark is very ancient and widespread and is inexplicable if not based on fact, since Mark was not especially prominent otherwise in church history. Peter's sermons were themselves a good source for "oral tradition." Peter's prominence in the Gospel indicates that it is by one of his disciples. As a native of Jerusalem, Mark need not have been an expert on Galilean geography. And the Gospel itself shows signs of having been written for Romans at a time of persecution and at a date about the time of Nero's persecution. Ancient tradition from several sources places Peter in Rome at that

time. See also pages 63–64 and chapter 5, note 2. Scholars who are hesitant about giving the traditional name "Mark" to the author are still likely to place the writing of the Gospel in Rome at a time shortly after Peter's death.

9. Among those who reject the "Q" hypothesis are the German scholar J. Jeremias, who believes that oral tradition was strong enough to provide the common source; William Farmer (see note 5 above), and John Drury, *Tradition and Design in Luke's Gospel* (Atlanta: John Knox Press, 1976), who holds that Luke used Matthew itself. The great majority of scholars, however, still support the view that there was a written document, "Q."

10. Eusebius, *op. cit.*, V iii 39, p. 39.

11. For the classic presentation of the arguments for and against this traditional view, see F. J. Foakes Jackson and Kirsopp Lake, eds., *The Beginnings of Christianity*, vol. 2 (London: Macmillan, 1922), pp. 209–359. Most of what has subsequently been written on the subject on either side is anticipated there. See also pp. 83–86, below.

12. Eusebius, *Ecclesiastical History* VI 14, as quoted in James L. Price, *Interpreting the New Testament*, 2nd ed. (New York: Holt, Rinehart & Winston, 1961), p. 539.

13. B. H. Streeter, *The Four Gospels* (London: Macmillan, 1924). For a contrasting approach, see J. A. T. Robinson, *Redating the New Testament* (Philadelphia: The Westminster Press, 1976). Robinson puts the writing of all four Gospels within the decade of the fifties. At this writing, however, Robinson's views have not been followed by many.

IV—The Gospel According to Matthew

1. Edgar J. Goodspeed, *Matthew, Apostle and Evangelist* (Philadelphia: The John C. Winston Co., 1949), p. 20.

2. The classic development of this approach is in Albert Schweitzer, *The Quest of the Historical Jesus* (New York: Macmillan, 1948 [originally published in 1906]).

3. See, for example, Walter Rauschenbusch, *A Theology for the Social Gospel* (New York: Macmillan, 1918), pp. 131–145.

4. C. H. Dodd in *A Companion to the Bible*, ed. T. W. Manson (New York: Charles Scribner's Sons, 1939), pp. 373–389.

5. Augustine, *The City of God*, book XX, chapter IX.

6. William Barclay, *The Gospel of Matthew*, vol. 1, 2nd ed. (Philadelphia: The Westminster Press, 1958), p. 90.

7. For example, this explanation of the "Messianic secret" is that of C. H. Dodd, in the work named in note 4, above.

8. I have borrowed this phrase from James L. Price, *Interpreting the New Testament*. Earlier, C. H. Dodd, in the work cited in note 4, above, had called them "acts of prophetic symbolism."

V—Mark and Luke

1. A pioneer work in redaction criticism is Willi Marxsen, *Mark the Evangelist* (Nashville: Abingdon Press, 1969). For a brief critical review of its values and limitations, see the article by Stephen S. Smalley in I. Howard Marshall, ed., *New Testament Interpretation*, pp. 181–195.

2. See above, pp. 30–31 and chapter 3, note 8. The view here defended is well stated in A. E. J. Rawlinson, *St. Mark*, 7th ed. (London: Methuen, 1949), pp. xl ff. It is that of A. M. Hunter, *The Gospel According to Saint Mark* (London: SCM Press, 1948), pp. 13–18; Vincent Taylor, *The Gospel According to Saint Mark* (London:

Macmillan, 1952), pp. 26–32; and C. E. B. Cranfield, *The Gospel According to Saint Mark* (Cambridge: At the University Press, 1966), pp. 3–6; and it is defended in various works by William Barclay, E. F. Scott, Bruce Metzger, and C. F. D. Moule. Reginald Fuller rejects the view that Mark is by an actual companion of Peter, yet suggests that the Gospel may go back *ultimately* to Peter's preaching *(A Critical Introduction to the New Testament* [London: Duckworth, 1966], pp. 104–106). Those who, like Fuller, reject the identification of the author with the John Mark mentioned frequently in the New Testament (Acts 12:12; 15:39; 2 Tim. 4:11; 1 Peter 5:13) still usually regard Mark as the earliest Gospel, coming from the church at Rome, and from within a few years after Nero's persecution of the church. A minority place it as late as A.D. 71, believing that they see in it signs that Jerusalem has been destroyed and that the writer wishes to distinguish Christians from the ill-fated Zealots.

3. Tacitus, *Annals*, as quoted in James L. Price, *Interpreting the New Testament*, p. 196.
4. Norman Perrin, *The New Testament: An Introduction* (New York: Harcourt Brace Jovanovich, 1974), p. 144.
5. On the subject of the devil and demonology, see such books as R. H. Robbins, *The Encyclopedia of Witchcraft and Demonology* (New York: Crown Publishers, 1959) and S. Vernon McCasland and David Cole Wilson, *By the Finger of God* (New York: Macmillan, 1951).
6. So W. F. Albright and C. S. Mann, *op. cit.*, pp. lxxxviii–xciv.
7. On the title "Son of man," see the preceding note and the article on this subject by S. E. Johnson in *The Interpreter's Dictionary of the Bible*, vol. 4 (Nashville: Abingdon Press, 1962), pp. 413–420.
8. On "the Jesus of history," see chapter 3, note 4.
9. For example, see Norman Perrin, *The Resurrection According to Matthew, Mark, and Luke* (Philadelphia: Fortress Press, 1977). Perrin does not propose, however, that Mark did not believe in the resurrection. Mark's picture of the risen Christ is given in his story of the transfiguration (Mark 9:2–8), according to Perrin. Mark assumes that his readers already know stories of appearances. Mark wants, instead, to leave his readers looking forward to the coming great appearance of Christ at the end of the world.
10. One form of the concept of Jesus as liberator is that of Christ as the "Black Messiah," presented by black theologians such as Albert Cleage and James H. Cone. See Cone's *Black Theology of Liberation* (Philadelphia: J. B. Lippincott, 1970), p. 204.
11. The concept of Christ as liberator related to economic and political oppression had been especially developed by Gustavo Gutiérrez, *A Theology of Liberation* (Maryknoll, N.Y.: Orbis Books, 1973).
12. See Letty M. Russell, *Human Liberation in a Feminist Perspective* (Philadelphia: The Westminster Press, 1974).
13. David Hume, *An Enquiry Concerning Human Understanding*, section x, as found, for example, in L. A. Selby-Bigge, ed., *Enquiries Concerning the Human Understanding and Concerning the Principles of Morals*, 2nd ed. (Oxford: The Clarendon Press, 1957), pp. 109–131.
14. See above, pp. 4–5.
15. C. S. Lewis, in *Miracles* (New York: Macmillan, 1947), gives a popular and, to the present writer, persuasive case for the traditional Christian belief in miracles. For a discussion from the point of view of form cirticism, affirming the antiquity of the

tradition that Jesus did miracles, see Reginald H. Fuller, *Interpreting the Miracles* (Philadelphia: The Westminster Press, 1963).

16. The most thorough study of the subject of Jesus' birth, one which examines all these problems in scholarly fashion, is that of Raymond E. Brown, *The Birth of the Messiah* (Garden City, N.Y. : Doubleday, 1977). Brown makes helpful defense of belief in the virgin birth, pages 517–533.

17. For a careful effort to try to harmonize the apparent differences in the accounts of the resurrection, written from a very conservative point of view, see George Eldon Ladd, *I Believe in the Resurrection of Jesus* (London: Hodder & Stoughton, 1975), pp. 79–103. Though helpful, even Ladd perhaps does not succeed in solving all the problems. Vincent Taylor, in *The Formation of the Gospel Tradition* (London: Macmillan, 1935), pp. 59–62, is helpful in suggesting reasons why the early church retold various stories about the resurrection in many different places and thus soon had varying accounts. Rudolf Bultmann, whose views are quite different from those of Ladd, writes, "In the word of preaching and there alone we meet the risen Lord." *(Kerygma and Myth* [London: SPCK, 1960], p. 43.) More traditionally-minded Christians, including the present writer, would hold that Bultmann's view is helpful though incomplete. Bultmann is correct that it is the claim of Christian faith that in "the word of preaching"—one might add teaching and Christian fellowship—the believer does meet the risen Lord. Thus belief in the resurrection rests not simply on historical research, but also on inner experience, "existential encounter."

VI—The Acts of the Apostles

1. See above, pages 32–33 for the ascription of the book to Luke. It is usually argued that Luke must have been written after the fall of Jerusalem because certain details in Luke's account of the predicted fall (Luke 21), added to his source in Mark 13, suggest knowledge of the actual event itself. It is often alleged also that Acts relies on a knowledge of the works of Josephus, which would mean that it could not have been written before some time in the nineties. The evidence for this, however, is quite uncertain. The present writer would date Acts about A.D. 85.

2. J. W. Hunkin in Jackson and Lake, eds., *The Beginnings of Christianity, op. cit.*, p. 433.

3. For example, Gunther Bornkamm indicates early in his biography entitled *Paul*, trans. D. M. G. Stalker (New York: Harper & Row, 1971), p. xxi, that he will not regard Acts as a reliable source. Somewhat inconsistently, however, he finds Acts so helpful that he uses it repeatedly in his book. For example, in dealing with Paul at Corinth in Acts 18, he writes, "The account in Acts furnishes reliable, detailed information about which there is no dispute" (p. 68).

4. Can the following be only coincidences? In Acts believers are called "disciples," "saints," or "brethren," but though Luke knows the title "Christians," he, like Paul, avoids it. The Twelve, with Peter and John particularly named, are pictured as heading the church, and certain others share in its leadership, such as James and the other brothers of Jesus, and Barnabas. Assuming the South Galatian theory, we find in Galatians coincidences with Acts such as the mention of Barnabas as prominent, miracles having taken place, persecution as a problem, and the reception of Paul as a god. The Thessalonian Epistles agree with Acts 17 as to the presence of a large Gentile element in the church there, the hostility of the Jews, the close association of Silas and Timothy, and perhaps certain elements in Paul's teaching. Both

Acts and the Letters to the Corinthians indicate that at Corinth, Paul worked at a trade. Crispus is named as a prominent convert, and Aquila and Priscilla and Apollos are related to Corinth in both. Paul's escape from Damascus by being smuggled over the wall in a basket appears in both Acts 9:25 and in 2 Corinthians 11:32–33. Romans agrees with Acts in implying that Paul planned to visit Rome after traveling to Jerusalem first. Minor characters in Acts appear also in Paul's letters: Silvanus (Silas), Sopater, Aristarchus, Tychicus, Trophimus, and Gaius. That the name of Luke himself never occurs in Acts—only references to "we"—is itself significant. Acts' picture of Paul's bringing alms on his last trip to Jerusalem fits with numerous references in the Epistles. In the chapters on the letters of Paul, we will see other points at which Acts helps us understand the Epistles. If Luke is accurate in so many details on which we can check, it may be argued that he is accurate in others which we cannot.

5   For example, Acts is correct concerning the proconsulship of Sergius Paulus (Acts 13:7) in name, date, and title, a fact remarkable in view of the constantly changing political situation in the Roman Empire. Acts is correct about such geographical details, according to Ramsay, as that Pisidian Antioch was the center of what was officially called a *region*, and that it technically was not in Pisidia. The proconsulship of Gallio, though only a brief one, has been confirmed. See such books as *St. Paul the Traveller and the Roman Citizen* by Sir William M. Ramsay (London: Hodder & Stoughton, 1895).

6   Assuming that the author of the "we passages" was the author of the rest of the book, he was personally acquainted with Paul, had visited with Philip, and had been to Jerusalem, where he had been welcomed by Jesus' brother (Acts 21:18). It is widely held that here and there, especially in the speeches in Acts, there are hints of sources in Aramaic, the dialect spoken in Palestine in the first century. Similarities of stories have caused some to propose that Luke had before him two accounts of the same event.

7   Joseph Klausner, *From Jesus to Paul*, trans. William F. Stinespring (New York: Macmillan, 1944), p. 218. For a good presentation of the present writer's view that Luke is both theologian *and* historian, see William Neil, *The Acts of the Apostles* (London: Oliphants, 1973), pp. 14–60.

8   Hans Conzelmann, *An Outline of the Theology of the New Testament* (London: SCM Press, 1969), pp. 149–152.

9.   J. A. Ross Mackenzie, *The Word in Action* (Richmond: John Knox Press, 1973).

10.   Hugh J. Schonfield, *The Passover Plot* (New York: B. Geis Associates, 1966).

11.   C. S. Mann, *The Acts of the Apostles*, in "The Anchor Bible" (Garden City, N.Y.: Doubleday, 1967), pp. 271–275, notes this idea and also suggests that perhaps the disciples amazed the crowd simply by their interpretation of passages used in the Pentecost liturgy.

12.   C. H. Dodd, *The Apostolic Preaching and Its Developments*, pp. 21–23.

13.   It is often objected that the speeches in Acts are in the style and vocabulary of Luke. Luke, however, put sayings of Jesus from Mark into his own style and vocabulary without greatly altering them, and many find echoes of Aramaic sources in the sermons in Acts. It is true that Thucydides speaks of composing speeches as he wrote history, but he also says that he tried, as nearly as he could, "to give the general purport of what was actually said." Luke would seem to have done the same. Compare William Neil, *op. cit.*, pp. 38–45. Neil holds that the speeches are a valid source of knowledge of early Christian thought.

14. What follows is developed in much more detail in the present writer's earlier book, *The Christ of the Earliest Christians* (Richmond: John Knox Press, 1959).
15. *The Assumption of Moses* 10:5, as found in R. H. Charles, *op. cit.*
16. Josephus, *Antiquities* XIV, as quoted in C. K. Barrett, ed., *The New Testament Background: Selected Documents* (New York: Harper & Row, 1961), p. 137.
17. W. M. Calder, "Lystra," in James Orr, gen. ed., *The International Standard Bible Encyclopaedia*, vol. 3 (Grand Rapids: Eerdmans, 1939), p. 1944.
18. *Ibid.*

VII—Introducing the Letters of Paul

1. These and several of the following quotations are selected from various ones found in Wayne A. Meeks, ed., *The Writings of St. Paul* (New York: W. W. Norton & Co., 1972).
2 From a lost Ebionite document as quoted by Epiphanius (A.D 315–403), found in Meeks, *op. cit.*, pp. 177–178
3. Marcion, *The Antitheses* 18, as quoted in Meeks, *op. cit.*, p. 190
4. From Luther's commentary on Galatians, as quoted in Meeks, *op. cit* , p 242
5. *Ibid.*, p. 248.
6 Albert Schweitzer, *Paul and His Interpreters* (London: Adam & Charles Black, 1948 [originally published in 1912]), p. 238.
7 *Ibid.*, p. 244.
8. From Albert Schweitzer, *The Mysticism of Paul the Apostle,* as quoted in Meeks, *op. cit.*, p. 389.
9. Adolf Harnack, *What Is Christianity?*, 3rd and rev. ed., trans. Thomas Bailey Saunders (New York: G. P. Putnam's Sons, 1904), pp. 186–188.
10. "Every assertion about God is simultaneously an assertion about man and vice versa. For this reason and in this sense Paul's theology is, at the same time, anthropology." (Rudolf Bultmann, *Theology of the New Testament,* vol. 1, trans. Kendrick Grobel [London: SCM Press, 1952], p. 191.)
11. Ernst Kasemann, *Perspectives on Paul* (Philadelphia: Fortress Press, 1971), p. 65, presenting his own view in contrast to that of Rudolf Bultmann in *History and Eschatology*. Compare also Kasemann's *New Testament Questions of Today* (London: SCM Press, 1969), p. 137.
12. As quoted in C. K. Barrett, *The New Testament Background*, pp. 38–39.
13. Among those rejecting the Pauline authorship of Second Thessalonians are: Norman Perrin, *The New Testament: An Introduction*, pp. 119–120, and Bornkamm, *op. cit.*
14. Among many defending the traditional view are John W. Bailey, "The Interpreter's Bible," vol. 11 (Nashville: Abingdon Press, 1955), pp. 249–251, and Werner Georg Kummel, *Introduction to the New Testament*, trans. A. J. Mattill, Jr. (Nashville: Abingdon Press, 1966), pp. 264–269.
15. Bailey, *op. cit.*, pp. 326–330, gives a fuller discussion of "The Man of Lawlessness." For a different approach, based on a different translation, which sees "what is restraining" (2:6) rather as "what is oppressing," and sees signs of persecution at the time of the letter, see Gerhard Kroedel, "Proclamation" commentary on Second Thessalonians (Philadelphia: Fortress Press, 1978), pp. 88–96. (Kroedel believes Second Thessalonians was written after Paul's lifetime.)

VIII—Paul's Correspondence with Corinth

1. For example, see Günther Bornkamm, *op. cit.*, pp. 68–77, and Werner Georg Kümmel, *op. cit.*, pp. 181–182.
2. Bornkamm, *op. cit.*, pp. 244–246.
3. The identification of Paul's chief opponents as "spiritual-minded" rather than as the same kind of Judaizing legalists who upset the Galatians' churches seems to be that of Bornkamm, Johannes Munck, and many others. While Hans Conzelmann does not want to call them "Gnostics," he speaks of them as "proto-Gnostics" in *1 Corinthians* (Philadelphia: Fortress Press, 1975 [German ed. 1969]), p. 15.
4. Bornkamm, *op. cit.*
5. Kümmel, *op. cit.*, pp. 211–215.
6. Among those who place 2 Cor. 10—13 as a letter earlier than 2 Cor. 1—9 are such scholars as Floyd Filson, T. W. Manson, C. H. Dodd, R. H. Strachan, Edgar J. Goodspeed, William Barclay, C. Milo Connick, and E. F. Scott. C. K. Barrett divides Second Corinthians at chapter 10, but believes that chapters 1—9 are earlier than 10—14. More recently, F. F. Bruce shares Barrett's view. See his *1 and 2 Corinthians*, "New Century Bible" series (London: Oliphants, 1971), pp. 166–172.

IX—Of Faith and Freedom

1. Martin Luther, *Commentary on Galatians*, 2:19, abridged translation by Theodore Graebner, 4th ed. (Grand Rapids: Zondervan, n.d.), p. 76.
2. *Ibid.*, 1:1, p. 9.
3. As quoted in A. Lukyn Williams, *The Epistle of Paul the Apostle to the Galatians* (Cambridge: At the University Press, 1936), pp. 67–68.
4. Greer M. Taylor, "The Function of PISTIS XRISTOU in Galatians," *Journal of Biblical Literature*, vol. LXXXV (1966), pp. 58–76.
5. Joseph Fletcher, *Situation Ethics* (Philadelphia: The Westminster Press, 1966), pp. 30, 49, and *passim*.
6. Martin Luther, "Concerning Christian Liberty," as found in Harry Emerson Fosdick, ed., *Great Voices of the Reformation* (New York: Random House, 1952), p. 81.
7. Luther, "Preface to St. Paul's Epistle to the Romans," *ibid.*, p. 118.
8 Johannes Munck, *Paul and the Salvation of Mankind* (Richmond: John Knox Press, 1959), pp. 42–49.
9. Suetonius, *Vita Claudii* xxv. 4, as found in Henry Bettenson, ed., *Documents of the Christian Church* (New York: Oxford University Press, 1947), p. 4.
10. See chapter 7, note 10.
11. Bornkamm, *op. cit.*, p. 137.
12. Karl Barth, *The Epistle to the Romans*, trans. from 6th German edition by E. C. Hoskyns (London: Oxford University Press, 1933), p. 42.
13. Hans Joachim Schoeps, from *Paul: The Theology of the Apostle in the Light of Jewish Religious History*, as found in Meeks, *op. cit.*, p. 349.
14. *Ibid.*

X—The Prison Epistles

1. Among those who prefer the Ephesian location for some or all of the prison epistles are Leander Keck, Norman Perrin, and Eduard Lohse.

2. See below, pp. 162–163 and 168–170, and notes 11 and 15, below.
3. For a full discussion and defense of the traditional location, Rome, see Ernest F. Scott, "The Epistle to the Philippians," in "The Interpreter's Bible," vol. 11 (Nashville: Abingdon Press, 1955), pp. 5–8, and Francis W. Beare on Colossians in the same volume, pp. 134–137. Compare James Price, *op. cit.*, pp. 419–422.
4. Archibald M. Hunter, *Philippians*, vol. 22 in "The Layman's Bible Commentary" series (Richmond: John Knox Press, 1959), p. 78.
5. Kenneth Grayston, *The Letters of Paul to the Philippians and to the Thessalonians* (Cambridge: At the University Press, 1967), p. 11.
6. Among those who divide Philippians are Norman Perrin, Francis W. Beare, and E. J. Goodspeed.
7. Philippians is regarded as a unity by E. F. Scott, *op. cit.*, pp. 8–9; compare various commentaries and introductions by A. M. Hunter, Bruce Metzger, Martin Dibelius, and C. Milo Connick.
8. Walter Schmithals, *Paul and the Gnostics*, trans. John E. Steely (Nashville: Abingdon, 1972), pp. 65–122.
9. See the case for this made by John Knox, *Philemon*, in "The Interpreter's Bible," vol. 11 (Nashville: Abingdon, 1955), pp. 557–560.
10. Among those who deny that Paul wrote Colossians are Joseph Burgess in *The Letter to the Colossians* in the "Proclamation" commentaries series (Philadelphia: Fortress Press, 1978), pp. 61–67. See also works cited by Norman Perrin and Gunther Bornkamm. Eduard Lohse, in his widely acclaimed *Colossians and Philemon* (Philadelphia: Fortress Press, 1971), agrees. For a full discussion of the issues, see Francis W. Beare, *op. cit.*, pp. 133–145. He, too, doubts that Colossians is by Paul.
11. Among those defending Pauline authorship of Colossians are Robert M. Grant, *A Historical Introduction to the New Testament* (New York: Harper & Row, 1963), pp. 190–192; James Price, *op. cit.*, pp. 431–432; and the more conservative scholars such as William Barclay, *The Letters to the Philippians, Colossians, and Thessalonians* (Philadelphia: The Westminster Press, 1959), pp. 121–122.
12. Irenaeus, "Against Heresies," as found in Robert M. Grant, ed., *Gnosticism: An Anthology* (London: Collins, 1961), pp. 24–25.
13. A. T. Robinson, *Paul and the Intellectuals* (Garden City, N.Y.: Doubleday, 1928).
14. See, for example, J. Paul Sampley, *Ephesians*, in the "Proclamation" commentaries series (Philadelphia: Fortress Press, 1978), pp. 9–12; compare the works cited by Bornkamm, Perrin, R. M. Grant, and others.
15. Markus Barth, *Ephesians*, vol. 1, in "The Anchor Bible" (Garden City, N.Y.: Doubleday, 1974), pp. 36–50. See also A. Van Roon, *The Authenticity of Ephesians* (Leiden: Brill, 1974).
16. Francis W. Beare, *Ephesians*, "The Interpreter's Bible," vol. 10 (Nashville: Abingdon, 1953), pp. 603–604.
17. Markus Barth, *op. cit.*, p. 50.
18. As quoted in Jack Finegan, *Light from the Ancient Past* (Princeton: Princeton University Press, 1946), p. 246.
19. From Tacitus' *Histories* V. 4–5, as quoted in Lamar Williamson, Jr., *God's Work of Art* (Richmond: CLC Press, 1971), pp. 34–35.
20. From *Mekilta* of Rabbi Ishmael, Exodus 14:7, as quoted in Williamson, *op. cit.*, p. 35.

XI—The Pastoral Epistles

1. Justin Martyr, *First Apology* 67, as found in Cyril C. Richardson, trans. and ed., *Early Christian Fathers* (New York: Macmillan, 1970), p. 287.
2. For a defense of Pauline authorship of the Pastorals, see J. N. D. Kelly, *A Commentary on the Pastoral Epistles* (New York: Harper & Row, 1963), pp. 1–34; also Donald Guthrie, *New Testament Introduction*, vol. 2 (Chicago: Inter-Varsity Press, 1962), pp. 198–237.
3. See, for example, the very scholarly commentary by Martin Dibelius and Hans Conzelmann, *The Pastoral Epistles* (Philadelphia: Fortress Press, 1972). Compare the works of more moderate critics such as E. F. Scott. William Barclay, *The Letters to Timothy, Titus and Philemon*, rev. ed. (Philadelphia: The Westminster Press, 1975), pp. 3–13, adopts the view that these letters as we have them contain fragments of letters actually from the pen of Paul but edited by a later hand.
4. Barclay, *The Letters to Timothy, Titus and Philemon*, p. 17.
5. Dibelius and Conzelmann, *op. cit.*, pp. 158–160.

XII—Five "Open Letters"

1. Price, *op. cit.*, p. 485.
2. For example, R. H. Fuller interprets chapter 13 as an addition by the author himself, as he sent off as a letter what had been oneof his sermons ("The Letter to the Hebrews," in *Hebrews, James, 1 and 2 Peter, Jude, Revelation*, "Proclamation" commentaries [Philadelphia: Fortress Press, 1977], pp. 21–23).
3. For the position here taken, see William Manson, *The Epistle to the Hebrews* (London: Hodder & Stoughton, 1951). For a recent presentation of the more popular view, see Fuller, *op. cit.*, pp. 1–5, 25–27; compare Kummel, *Introduction*, pp. 279–281.
4. ". . . he has opportunity to repent but once." (*Shepherd of Hermas*, book II, 4, iii, in Roberts and Donaldson, eds., *The Ante-Nicene Fathers*, vol. 2, p. 22 [cf. I, 3, v and vii]).
5. Among those rejecting the tradition that the epistle is by Jesus' brother are Kummel, Price, and Burton Scott Easton. See the latter's discussion of various views on the authorship and sources of the book in "James," "The Interpreter's Bible," vol. 12 (Nashville: Abingdon, 1957), pp. 3–15. For a defense of the view that the book is by Jesus' brother, see John Wick Bowman, "James," in "The Layman's Bible Commentary" series, vol. 24 (Richmond: John Knox Press, 1962), pp. 93–94.
6. Josephus, *Jewish Antiquities* XX ix 1.
7. Eusebius, *Ecclesiastical History* II xxiii, in C. F. Crusé, trans., *The Ecclesiastical History of Eusebius Pamphilus* (London: G. Bell, 1917), p. 66.
8. From Luther's "Preface to the Epistles of Saint James and Saint Jude," quoted in Kümmel, *Introduction to the New Testament*, p. 287.
9. For a relatively recent full discussion deciding against Peter as author, see Ernest Best, *I Peter*, "New Century Bible" series (London: Oliphants, 1971), pp. 49–63. For an older, classic defense of Peter's authorship, see Edward Gordon Selwyn, *The First Epistle of St. Peter* (London: Macmillan, 1949), pp. 7–38. Selwyn allows Silvanus a large share in the actual wording of the letter in Greek. Compare Bo Reicke, *The Epistles of James, Peter, and Jude*, "The Anchor Bible," vol. 37 (Garden City, N.Y.: Doubleday, 1964), pp. 71–72. Reicke believes the content is from Peter.

10. From Pliny's *Epistles* X 97, as quoted in Price, *op. cit.*, pp. 479–480.
11. So Bo Reicke, *op. cit.*, pp. 74–75. For a fuller discussion of this interpretation, see Ernest Best, *op. cit.*, pp. 21–27. Best, however, rejects this view but does believe that First Peter includes bits of baptismal liturgy.
12. Bo Reicke, *op. cit.*, p. 106.
13. This interpretation is proposed by Bo Reicke, *op. cit.*, pp. 106–113.
14. Virtually all the New Testament introductions and commentary series to which reference has been made previously reject the view that Second Peter is from the pen of the Apostle himself. Petrine authorship is defended, however, by the consistently conservative Donald Guthrie, *New Testament Introduction*, vol. 2, pp. 143–171.
15. William Barclay, *The Letters of James and Peter*, rev. ed., "Daily Study Bible" series (Philadelphia: The Westminster Press, 1976), p. 145.
16. Reicke, *op. cit.*, pp. 166–167.
17. Eusebius, *Ecclesiastical History* III xi, as translated by Cruse, p. 88.
18. *Ibid.* III xx, p. 92.
19. For a fuller discussion of the authorship of Jude, see Kummel, *Introduction to the New Testament*, pp. 300–301 and Albert E. Barnett, "Jude," in "The Interpreter's Bible," vol. 12 (Nashville: Abingdon, 1957), pp. 317–319. Both reject the view that it is by a brother of Jesus. Donald Guthrie defends the tradition in *New Testament Introduction*, vol. 2, pp. 227–229.

XIII—The Johannine Literature

1. *The Acts of John* 38–42, as found in Edgar Hennecke, *New Testament Apocrypha*, ed.Wilhelm Schneemelcher, English trans. ed. by R. McL. Wilson, vol. 2 (London: Lutterworth Press, 1965), pp. 236–237.
2. J. Massyngberde Ford, *Revelation*, in "The Anchor Bible" (Garden City, N.Y.: Doubleday, 1975), pp. 28–57, argues that much of Revelation is the work of a disciple of John the Baptist and is thus really pre-Christian. Others have believed they detected Jewish sources in the book. However, the similarities to Jewish apocalyptic writings may be explained in part on the basis of a general similarity among most works in this form. While the writer probably did use sources, as is indicated by the apparent repetitions and fresh starts from time to time, current emphasis among critics has been on the unity of the book. See Elisabeth Schussler Fiorenza, "The Revelation to John," in *Hebrews, James, 1 and 2 Peter, Jude, Revelation*, "Proclamation" commentaries (Philadelphia: Fortress Press, 1977), p. 100. Only the most consistently conservative commentators such as Guthrie, *op. cit.*, vol. 3, argue that the Apostle is the author.
3. Hal Lindsey, *The Late Great Planet Earth* (Grand Rapids: Zondervan, 1970).
4. See chapter 5, note 3.
5. Eusebius, *op. cit.* III xvii–xx, as translated by Cruse, pp. 101–103.
6. Rev. C. I. Scofield, ed., *The New Scofield Reference Bible* (New York: Oxford University Press, 1967), headings and notes on Revelation 2—3, pp. 1353–1355.
7. Eusebius, *op. cit.* III xxviii, trans. Cruse, p. 103. It is said that there were some fifty varieties of Gnosticism. It is not here proposed that First John necessarily is written specifically against the particular kind which Cerinthus represented, but simply against some form of that general approach.
8. Rudolf Bultmann writes that at least the source of certain discourses in the Fourth Gospel "is Gnostic in outlook." He recognizes that the Fourth Gospel is also anti-Gnostic, but one of its editors has used Gnostic language, he believes, in order to

convert Gnostics (*The Gospel of John: A Commentary* [Philadelphia: The West-minster Press, 1971]). It is certain that the Gnostics subsequently claimed John as one of their own. First John, therefore, may be written in part to correct this kind of misunderstanding of the Gospel.

9. Irenaeus, *Against Heresies* I xxvi, as found in Roberts and Donaldson, eds., *The Ante-Nicene Fathers*, vol. 1, p. 352.

10. For a very different interpretation of First John, see J. C. O'Neill, *The Puzzle of I John* (London: SPCK, 1966). O'Neill argues that the author was a member of a Jewish sect, many of whom had become Christians. His opponents are Jews who had not converted to Christianity. The book is outlined around a kind of liturgy. At this time O'Neill has not been widely followed in this view.

11. Eusebius, *op. cit.* III xxxix, trans. Cruse, p. 127.

12. The *Didache* 12:1–5, as found in Richardson, ed., *Early Christian Fathers*, p. 177.

13. Rudolf Bultmann, *The Johannine Epistles* (Philadelphia: Fortress Press, 1973 [German ed. 1967]), p. 101.

14. James Sprunt, *These Are Written* (Richmond: Presbyterian Board of Publication, 1949), p. 7.

15. In the next few pages there are a number of unacknowledged quotations from an earlier work by the present writer and his wife, DeVere M. Ramsay, *Written That You May Believe*, Teacher's Guide (Richmond: Board of Christian Education, Presbyterian Church in the United States, 1958).

16. Clement, quoted by Eusebius, *op. cit.* VI xiv.

17. So Perrin, *Introduction*, p. 245.

18. Floyd V. Filson, *The Gospel According to John*, "The Layman's Bible Commentary," vol. 19 (Richmond: John Knox Press, 1963), pp. 19–26.

19. For a defense of Johannine authorship, see Donald Guthrie, *New Testament Introduction*, vol. 1, pp. 216–246.

20. For example, Robert Tomson Fortner has actually attempted to reconstruct this signs source, which he believes to be the work of a Jewish-Christian convert (*The Gospel of Signs* [Cambridge: At the University Press, 1970]). Compare the commentaries on John by Bultmann and by C. H. Dodd.

21. The view that the Fourth Gospel was the product of more than one writer, perhaps of a kind of "Johannine school," is defended in various forms by such diverse scholars as the moderately conservative William Barclay, *The Gospel of John*, rev. ed., vol. 1 (Philadelphia: The Westminster Press, 1975), pp. 15–24; the somewhat radical Norman Perrin, *Introduction*, pp. 223, 249; and the Roman Catholic scholar Raymond E. Brown, *The Gospel According to John*, "The Anchor Bible" (Garden City, N.Y.: Doubleday, 1970), pp. lxxxvii–cii.

22. Cleanthes, "Hymn to Zeus," as quoted in Jason L. Saunders, ed., *Greek and Roman Philosophy After Aristotle* (New York: The Free Press, 1966), p. 149.

23. See note 9, above.

24. As quoted in Perrin, *Introduction*, p. 230.

25. *The Acts of John* 98–101, as found in Hennecke, *New Testament Apocrypha*, pp. 233–234.

For Further Reading

Any list such as the following must be highly selective and based on subjective evaluation. Many, many excellent books are not included. The reader is encouraged to note the approximately one hundred titles in the notes above.

Commentaries

Three sets of commentaries especially designed for lay people have seemed particularly useful to the present writer.

"The Layman's Bible Commentary" series, edited by Balmer H. Kelly, is remarkably compact, is scholarly, and yet is quite clearly written (Richmond: John Knox Press, 1959–64).

The commentary series called "The Daily Study Bible" is the delightfully written fruit of a lifetime of study by the late Scottish scholar William Barclay (Philadelphia: The Westminster Press, 1957–61).

"The Cambridge Bible Commentary" series, designed especially for British secondary schools, has a fresh approach which comes partly from its use of the New English Version of the Bible (Cambridge: At the University Press).

Four among many sets of commentaries designed to provide more critical detail are: "The Interpreter's Bible" (Nashville: Abingdon Press, 1952–57), for many years a standard reference work produced in America; "The New Century Bible" (London: Oliphants) the work of generally moderate to conservative British scholars; "The Anchor Bible" (Garden City, N.Y.: Doubleday), uniting the work of Protestant, Catholic, and Jewish scholars; and "Hermeneia" (Philadelphia: Fortress Press), a series including translations of works by German scholars often of a more liberal critical approach.

The Interpreter's One-Volume Commentary on the Bible, edited by Charles M. Laymon (Nashville: Abingdon, 1971) has the advantage of packing a remarkable amount of cirtical scholarship between just two covers.

Introductions

The present writer particularly likes *Interpreting the New Testament* by James L. Price (New York: Holt, Rinehart, & Winston, 2nd ed. 1971).

The "Proclamation" commentaries series is a set of introductions published in the middle seventies and generally reflecting a more liberal critical stance (Philadelphia: Fortress Press). For an approach representing the "conservative evangelical" orientation see Donald Guthrie, *New Testament Introduction* (Downers Grove, Ill.: Inter-Varsity Fellowship, rev. ed. 1971). Norman Perrin in *The New Testament: An Introduction* (New York: Harcourt Brace Jovanovich, 1974), reflects certain influences of the Bultmannian school on an American scholar. Werner Georg Kümmel, *Introduction to the New Testament* (Nashville: Abingdon, rev. English ed. 1975), brings German critical scholarship to readers of English through the translation by Howard Clark Kee.

Three other introductions, among many widely used in colleges and universities, are: Kee *et al.*, *Understanding the New Testament* (Englewood Cliffs, N.J.. Prentice-Hall 3rd ed. 1973); Spivey and Smith, *The Anatomy of the New Testament* (New York: Macmillan, 1974); and C. Milo Connick, *The New Testament: An Introduction to Its History, Literature, and Thought* (Encino, Calif.: Dickenson, 2nd ed. 1978).

Designed for use in secondary schools in America is *The New Testament: Its Background, Growth, and Content,* by Bruce Metzger (Nashville: Abingdon, 1965).

Among the most recent introductions are *An Introduction to New Testament Literature* (Nashville: Abingdon Press, 1978) in which Donald Juel analyzes the New Testament, particularly in relation to its varieties of literary style and structure, and *Reading the New Testament: An Introduction* (New York: Paulist Press, 1978) by Pheme Perkins, a Roman Catholic writer with an ecumenical approach.

General Reference Works

For discussion of methods of biblical interpretation, laymen will find useful the articles in "The Layman's Bible Commentary," vol. 1 (Richmond: John Knox Press, 1959).

New critical methods of biblical interpretation are described in such books as: Richard N. Soulen, *Handbook of Biblical Criticism* (Atlanta: John Knox Press, 1976); William G. Doty, *Contemporary New Testament Interpretation* (Englewood Cliffs, N.J.: Prentice-Hall, 1972); and I. Howard Marshall, ed., *New Testament Interpretation* (Grand Rapids: Eerdmans, 1977).

Helpful for ready reference for biblical subject matter is *The New Westminster Dictionary of the Bible*, edited by Henry Snyder Gehman (Philadelphia: The Westminster Press, 1970). Much more detailed is the four-volume *Interpreter's Dictionary of the Bible* (Nashville: Abingdon Press, 1962).

Study Bible

The present writer uses *The Oxford Annotated Bible* (New York: Oxford University Press, 1962), with its excellent notes by Herbert G. May and Bruce M. Metzger.

Index